1994

Research in Language Learning
Principles, Processes, and Prospects

Edited by Alice Omaggio Hadley

In Conjunction with the American Council
on the Teaching of
Foreign
Languages

National Textbook Company
a division of *NTC Publishing Group* • Lincolnwood, Illinois USA

Contents

149, 508

Foreword

This volume has been developed in part as a response to the challenge issued by the Research Committee of the 1989 ACTFL Professional Priorities Conference to make "a strong commitment to communication and collaboration among all those who place a high priority on [research] in our field."[1] Among the priorities listed by the committee was the need to (1) broaden the scope of research to include a variety of paradigms and procedures and (2) expand opportunities for researchers and practitioners to communicate with one another about issues of mutual concern and interest.

In order to address these issues, the 1993 series volume is devoted to the topic of research. To foster greater communication among researchers and practitioners, an advisory board was chosen to include experts in both foreign language learning and second-language acquisition, representing the commonly and less commonly taught languages as well as ESL. The board met for several days in February 1992 to conceptualize a plan for the volume; after much deliberation, it was determined that the book had to be written in a way that would be accessible to both researchers and practitioners, that the research topics needed to bridge the perceived gap between foreign languages and ESL, and that the primary focus needed to be placed on the types of questions being asked today as well as the principles of research used to answer them.

I am extremely grateful to have had the opportunity to work with the members of the Advisory Board, who not only devoted hours to the planning of the volume, but also gave of their time and efforts to read and respond to the chapter drafts. They are Diane W. Birckbichler, Cheryl Brown, Robert Bley-Vroman, John Clark, Patricia Dunkel, Sally Magnan, June Phillips, Lynn Sandstedt, Ray Clifford, and Gerard Ervin. Several other experts in the field graciously agreed to read and comment on the chapter drafts: Kathryn Corl, Fred Davidson, Linda Harlow, Donna Johnson, Stanley Shinall, Robert Terry, Bill VanPatten, and Galal Walker. Their careful reading and commentary was invaluable, and their generosity in time very much appreciated.

I am especially indebted to the chapter authors for their hard work on this project, and for their cooperation and patience during the long process of volume preparation. Thanks are also due to Ed Scebold, Executive Director of ACTFL, and to Keith Fry, Executive Editor at National Textbook, both of whom graciously provided expert assistance. I would also like to thank Gail Guntermann and June Phillips, who, as former editors of ACTFL volumes, provided valuable advice. Finally, I want to express my gratitude to my editorial assistant, Elizabeth Martin, who cheerfully dedicated long hours to the project and who assisted in every aspect of the volume preparation. This volume has resulted from the collaborative efforts of all of these individuals, whose dedication serves the profession well as we continue to address the challenges that lie ahead.

Note

1. Bailey, Kathleen M., Alice Omaggio Hadley, Sally S. Magnan, and Janet Swaffar. "Priority: Research in the 1990s: Focus on Theory Building, Instructional Innovation, and Collaboration," *Foreign Language Annals* 24,2 (1991): 98.

Introduction

Research in Language Learning:
Toward Communication and Synthesis

Alice Omaggio Hadley

University of Illinois at Urbana-Champaign

It has been ten years since an ACTFL Foreign Language Education Series volume has been devoted exclusively to the topic of research (see James 1983). Yet in that one brief decade, there has been a remarkable number of new studies in second-language acquisition and foreign language learning, accompanied by a substantial increase in professional publications and conferences devoted to research in all areas of the field.[1] This rapid expansion of knowledge brings with it the potential for significant change and improvement in our classrooms, as well as the development of new theoretical perspectives on how language learning takes place.

The recent proliferation of studies may also lead, however, to confusion if there is little integration of results, few attempts at synthesis, a lack of effective communication among researchers in foreign languages and English as a second language (ESL), and little or no linkage with practitioners. Clearly the profession at large would benefit not only from knowing more about substantive findings in our field in recent years, but also from understanding how research leading to these findings has been developed and interpreted.

The 1993 ACTFL Series volume attempts to clarify the various principles and processes involved in conducting research in language learning today, as well as discuss some significant new developments in the field and identify possible areas for further inquiry as we continue to expand our knowledge base in the 1990s. Each chapter might be thought of as an essay on a particular facet or area of research, reflecting the author's perspective of the field and documented with some of the major substantive research

Alice Omaggio Hadley (Ph.D., The Ohio State University) is Associate Professor of French at the University of Illinois in Urbana-Champaign, where she is Director of Basic Language Instruction, comprising first- and second-year language courses. She supervises graduate teaching assistants and is responsible for the curriculum development, testing, and administration of the elementary and intermediate course sequence. She is co-author of several college French texts and has written a book on language teaching methodology, *Teaching Language in Context* (Heinle & Heinle 1986, 1993). Her publications have appeared in various professional journals and she has given numerous workshops throughout the country.

findings in recent years. The volume focuses primarily on research that has a potential impact for the classroom, although studies dealing with uninstructed or "natural" language acquisition have been included as well.

The volume begins with an overview, written by Donna Johnson, of methodological issues in classroom-oriented second-language research. The author outlines the kinds of topics that researchers are investigating in the field today, reflects on the role of the teacher in the research process, and presents a clear exposition of six approaches to conducting research that have been most prominent in recent years. Her discussion of research methodology and practice provides an excellent introduction to the chapters that follow, and should be of considerable value to practitioners and experienced researchers alike.

In the second chapter, Lynn Eubank and Maria Beck explore issues in generative research on second- and foreign language acquisition. Beginning with a brief review of fundamental assumptions and insights that have been gained from native-language acquisition research, they discuss how knowledge of a second/foreign language is thought to be acquired from a generative point of view. Included in their discussion is the issue of the relevance of Universal Grammar) to L2 acquisition and the relationship between acquisition processes in L1 and L2. The authors describe studies on the nature and development of interlanguage and discuss methodological issues associated with this research, as well as research that examines the role of formal instruction in second-language acquisition.

Chapter 3 looks at the way language acquisition and use is affected by sociocultural factors and how insights from the field of sociolinguistics can contribute to communicative language teaching. Written by Elite Olshtain, this chapter explores various definitions of communicative competence and focuses more specifically on sociolinguistic competence and its development. An overview of current research on speech-act behavior is provided, including a discussion of methodological issues germane to this area of investigation. The chapter concludes with a discussion of the reading process as a communicative activity, a topic that is explored in greater depth in chapter 6.

In chapter 4, Evelyn Hatch and Asako Yoshitomi provide a clear and comprehensive overview of research into cognitive processes in language learning. They take the position that "language learning reflects the acquisition of social, cognitive, and linguistic knowledge in a gradually integrated system" and that any explanation of how language acquisition occurs must be "neurally plausible" (p. 66). The cognitive view of language learning contrasts strongly with the view of language acquisition discussed in chapter 2, in that cognitive researchers question whether separate and specialized processes other than those used for all learning are needed for language acquisition. The authors review various models of cognition and language that have been proposed within this research perspective, and provide a useful analysis of the strengths and weaknesses of methods used in conducting cognitive research.

Chapter 5, written by J. Michael O'Malley and Anna Uhl Chamot, explores the important issue of the role of learner characteristics in second-language acquisition. The contribution of individual differences—including factors such as age, gender, aptitude, personality characteristics, cognitive style, motivation, and strategy use—is examined in light of recent research in this area of the field. The authors take a cognitive-theoretical view of learning, which assumes that learning is a dynamic process that can and should be brought under the learner's active control. Research about ways in which learners can be strategically involved in their own learning is reviewed, and those characteristics that have been shown to be most amenable to instructional influence are highlighted, making this a chapter that should be of particular interest to classroom teachers.

Chapters 6 and 7 examine recent research into the ways in which second-language learners process and produce language. In chapter 6, Janet Swaffar and Susan Bacon provide various perspectives on listening and reading research and discuss innovations in research design arising from new theoretical viewpoints about comprehension processes. In chapter 7, Susan Gass and Sally Magnan look at second-language acquisition in speaking and writing, distinguishing the research traditions and issues in these two skill areas as well as their potential relationships and broader implications for the theory-building process. Again, both of these chapters should be of special interest to practitioners, as research in these skill areas is particularly relevant to language teaching and classroom practice.

In chapter 8, Michael Everson provides a comprehensive and much needed review of research being conducted in the "less commonly taught" languages, or LCTs. He organizes his review of this research by highlighting the questions that scholars in this area are asking, ranging from issues associated with the learning of new orthographies to broad methodological considerations. The chapter focuses on both research processes and results, and useful summaries of findings in each of the main areas of interest have been provided. This chapter will be of interest not only to scholars and practitioners in the LCTs, but also to the broader foreign language teaching community, as the profession considers common areas of inquiry that can be explored across language families and insights that can be derived from collaborative efforts among researchers in all of the world's languages.

In chapter 9, Grant Henning provides an overview of research in the important area of testing and assessment, highlighting measurement issues that have been the subject of research investigations in recent years. He discusses twelve language testing paradigms that have been of particular interest to the field, addressing important issues that are associated with these topics. Questions explored include issues associated with the nature of proficiency and the modeling of communicative competence; research into measurement theory, item formats, and test bias; computerized assessment; the identification of test constructs and the setting of performance standards; the measurement of functional abilities; aptitude testing; self-assessment; and the role of attitudes and test context on performance.

In the last chapter, John L. D. Clark and Fred Davidson provide a thought-provoking discussion of ways in which the language-teaching profession might consolidate its research efforts and communicate more effectively about the activities associated with language acquisition research. They propose a framework for collaboration, referred to as a Research Consolidation Project (RCP), which would be a highly networked, voluntary research initiative allowing for effective communication about such issues as topic selection, study design, instrumentation and data gathering, strategies and tools for data analysis, and sharing of results through the use of "intelligent" data bases. The chapter ends with a plan for implementing such a project, and a summary of the benefits that the authors believe could be derived from such a collaborative endeavor.

Because the topics in a volume such as this are complex and, for many readers, somewhat unfamiliar, the authors of the chapters have provided a set of definitions of important terms used in their discussions. These definitions have formed the basis of a glossary, which can be found on pages 279–94. Readers will also find indexes to persons cited and to topics and institutions at the end of the volume.

All those who have been involved in the preparation of this book hope that it will be useful to both researchers and practitioners in the field of language learning and that it will begin to help us bridge the gaps that currently exist among the related domains within our discipline. We have tried to include research of interest to those in both foreign languages and in English as a second language, and to include topics that are of special importance to scholars in the less commonly taught languages. It is our belief that the profession must continue to work collaboratively—to work toward greater communication and synthesis—if we are to make progress in the rest of this decade and into the twenty-first century. It is hoped that this volume will contribute to the achievement of these important goals.

Notes

1. See, for example, the introductions to texts on second-language research such as McLaughlin (1987) and Larsen-Freeman and Long (1991), as well as Johnson (chapter 1, this volume), for commentaries on this trend.

References

Introduction: Research in Language Learning:
Toward Communication and Synthesis

James, Charles J., ed. 1983. *Practical Applications of Research in Foreign Language Teaching*. The ACTFL Foreign Language Education Series. Lincolnwood, IL: National Textbook.

Larsen-Freeman, Diane, and Michael Long. 1991. *An Introduction to Second Language Acquisition Research*. London, Eng.: Longman.

McLaughlin, Barry. 1987. *Theories of Second Language Learning*. London, Eng.: Edward Arnold.

Classroom-Oriented Research in Second-Language Learning

Donna M. Johnson
University of Arizona

Introduction

The purpose of this chapter is to provide a discussion of some methodological issues in classroom-oriented L2 research. The term *classroom-oriented research* is defined very broadly here to include research conducted in classrooms, research that deals with learning and teaching in institutional contexts, and other research that is highly relevant to language teaching and learning. I have attempted to use examples and provide references to work that falls within all areas of the learning and teaching of additional languages including foreign language (FL) learning and teaching, the learning and teaching of English as a second language (ESL), and English as a foreign language (EFL). While most examples come from research conducted in the United States, because that is the work with which I am most familiar, I believe that we need to guard against ethnocentrism in our research, taking more multilingual, multicultural, and global perspectives (Kachru 1992).

In the last decade there has been much growth in research in the field of second- and foreign language learning and teaching. The increased professional activity is reflected in the growing number of books, journals, and specialized conferences devoted to issues in research. For example, in the past there were only a limited number of books on second-language research. A striking development is the quantity of new books on L2 research that have been written and published in recent years (e.g., Faerch and Kasper 1987; Allwright 1988; Brown 1988; Chaudron 1988; Seliger and Shohamy 1989; Cazden 1990 [review]; Cohen 1990; Hatch and Lazaraton 1990; Freed 1991; Larsen-Freeman

---

Donna M. Johnson (Ph.D., Stanford University), is Associate Professor in the English Department at the University of Arizona, where she directs the English Language/Linguistics Program and teaches in the Interdisciplinary Ph.D. Program in Second Language Acquisition and Teaching (SLAT). She has taught Spanish, French, English, and content-based courses in FL, EFL, BE, ESL, and VESL programs in the United States, Guatemala, and Brazil. She is author of *Approaches of Research in Second Language Learning* (1992, Longman), and coeditor (with Duane H. Roen) of *Richness in Writing* (1989, Longman). Her articles have appeared in *Language in Society, Written Communication, TESOL Quarterly, Journal of Second Language Writing, Applied Linguistics, Pragmatics and Language Learning, Journal of Intensive English Studies, Language Arts, C.A.L.L. Digest, NABE Journal, Hispania,* and *Educational and Psychological Measurement.*

and Long 1991; Hatch 1992; Johnson 1992). Another significant development is the appearance of books specifically addressed to teacher researchers. These books are aimed at guiding teachers in planning and conducting their own studies (Nunan 1989; (Allwright and Bailey 1991). In addition to the greater availability of books about research, the number of journals has increased, with field standards such as *Studies in Second Language Acquisition, Language Learning, Modern Language Journal, TESOL Quarterly,* and *Applied Linguistics* and reviews such as *ARAL* and *AILA Review* now supplemented by newer journals including *Journal of Second Language Writing, Applied Language Learning, Issues in Applied Linguistics, Pragmatics and Language Learning, CALICO,* and *Language Testing.* Increased professional activity is also evident in the growing number of specialized conferences that focus on second- and foreign language research. These include, for example, the conference of the American Association for Applied Linguistics, the Second Language Research Forum, the conference on Pragmatics and Language Learning at the University of Illinois, and the Research Perspectives on Adult Language Learning and Acquisition at Ohio State University.

Topics of Research

Increased research activity during the last decade has been accompanied by a focus on a broader range of topics that represents more serious attention to the many contexts of language learning, to its dynamic nature, and to broader views of language and language use. For example, language loss is a topic that has gained in prominence, in studies both of children and of adults (Weltens, de Bot, and van Els 1986). This emphasis represents a more dynamic view of language learning and forgetting processes. It also requires linking these processes to contextual factors such as the roles of languages in societies, communities, homes, and schooling. Studies of pragmatics across cultures and of interlanguage pragmatics have emerged as another important area of investigation (Kasper and Dahl 1991; Kasper in press) with implications for teaching and learning at all levels of proficiency (Valdman 1992). Even beginning language students can appreciate how variations in apologies, for example, can carry important social meaning and they can put such knowledge to use right away. In the realm of student characteristics, interest in learning strategies remains strong (Oxford and Lavine 1992), while research in affective factors has experienced a resurgence (Horwitz and Young 1991), now with multiple methods of studying these factors in a wider variety of activities, including writing. Research on the definition and measurement of language proficiency and on language testing remains prominent, with increased attention to the adequate assessment of writing ability, assessment of the ability of advanced learners to teach effectively in various languages, and analysis of the role of testing in schools (Bachman 1990; Kroll 1990; Huebner and Jensen 1992). Research on the roles of computer technology in second-language use and learning continues to grow (Dunkel 1991) and both research on CALL and research via CALL are expanding areas of investigation (Chapelle 1992). Content-based language learning continues to be a focus of study as language teachers increase links with content subjects. The growing prominence of discourse analysis in addressing issues of language learning, use, and teaching can be seen, for example, in research on writing in an additional language (McKay 1984; Edelsky 1986; Johnson and Roen 1989; Kroll 1990) and studies in comparative rhetoric (e.g., Connor and Kaplan 1987; Purves 1988; Leki 1991).

Teachers and Research

Another significant development in L2 research is the rise of the teacher-researcher or action research movement. Typically, teachers have been viewed as "consumers" of research who are expected to read research and then apply the findings to their classrooms (Borg 1981). This mechanical, consumer model of applying research has been replaced by different notions of what it means to "apply" research as well as by different conceptions of teachers' roles in conducting research. Teachers are now viewed as reflective practitioners who construct personal meanings from research they read. Teachers may also be active researchers who contribute to the research endeavor by conducting studies, often in their own classrooms, participating in collaborative projects, and/or changing practice based on findings (Allwright and Bailey 1991; Nunan 1989). The movement has become institutionalized in that some professional organizations offer research grants to teachers for research in their own classrooms and some U.S. school districts require classroom investigation for advancement. Dangers of this movement are that teachers can be abused and overworked or that research, which should be *disciplined inquiry,* can become trivial inquiry lacking in depth, scope, and validity. Potential benefits of the movement, on the other hand, can include the cooperative construction of investigative projects that are of interest to both teachers and researchers, more credible to more audiences, and useful for practice. As Chen and I (Johnson and Chen 1992) have discussed elsewhere, language teachers, because of their cultural experiences and linguistic knowledge, have a great deal to contribute to cooperative research projects. Whether teachers choose to participate in research or not, however, it is essential that classroom-oriented research or action research be both understandable and credible to teachers so that they can benefit from it. Working toward this goal requires attention both to improving methodology and to improving the writing of research reports. My view is that many of the methodological improvements that need to be made in L2 research will not only improve the rigor and quality of the research, but will make it more credible, and therefore more useful, to teachers.

Overview of Chapter

This chapter addresses methodological issues within the framework of six different approaches to L2 research: correlational approaches, case studies, survey research, ethnographic research, experiments, and discourse analysis. The six approaches are used simply as an organizing framework. Clearly, there are other important approaches that are not addressed here, such as multisite, multimethod, large-scale studies; program evaluation; historical studies; and so on, but these six are probably the most prominent.

The six approaches are not mutually exclusive. On the contrary, many studies combine a number of approaches very effectively (e.g., Kleinsasser and Savignon 1991; Kleinsasser 1992). For example, a survey may be primarily descriptive and quantitative, but may involve in-depth qualitative interviews with a small sample to develop questions for the survey or to seek explanations. A classroom experiment may be accompanied by rich descriptions of the different instructional interventions or by analysis of classroom discourse. An essentially qualitative ethnographic study may be supplemented by quantitative analyses of students' written texts. With the assumption that the complementary use of multiple methods not only is common, but can be highly effective, the six approaches represent general methodological orientations. The focus in this chapter is not on the purity or centrality of any one approach, but on how studies that are conducted primarily within that approach might be improved.

Some researchers suggest that being bimethodological or multimethodological is a mark of scholarly sophistication (Eisner and Peshkin 1990). This may be a reasonable goal for an individual to some degree. That is, researchers in training should have at least some expertise in a range of qualitative and quantitative methods, their philosophical bases, and the ways in which they might or might not be complementary. For the field of second/foreign language learning and teaching as a whole, I contend that a more multimethodological emphasis is essential.

The main points stressed in the chapter are these: We need to search out ways to strive for greater validity, more adequate interpretation and explanation, and greater credibility in our research. These goals can be pursued through a number of interrelated means. We can make greater use of qualitative methods, both for their own sake and through combining qualitative with quantitative techniques in the same study or research program. We need to pay much more attention to context in our research. That is, rather than simply describing and accounting for the interrelationships between task contexts or immediate discourse contexts and language use/learning, we need to address wider and richer notions of context more consistently in our classroom-oriented research. These can include intertextual, cultural, situational, home and community, and longitudinal contexts. We also need to incorporate richer descriptions of the students we study, including, for example, their cultural experiences, their dynamic multilingualism, their personal characteristics, and their approaches to learning. Too often we describe them simply as beginning, intermediate, or advanced, or simply as native speakers vs. nonnative speakers, lumping them into simple categories that can lead us to ignore interesting and important phenomena. Finally, we need a stronger fundamental commitment to a broad view of language that includes written as well as spoken communication and in which discourse—language beyond the sentence—is central. With greater attention to these goals, we may be able to produce research that not only is more valid and more credible, but is useful and helps bridge the perceived research–teaching gap.

We now turn to a discussion of the six basic approaches. Within each approach, some uses of the approach are addressed and some suggestions are made for improving methodology.

Correlational Approaches

The purpose of correlational studies, which are widely used in L2 research, is to understand relationships among characteristics of people, aspects of language use or language learning, classroom practices, and/or other entities. The term *correlational* refers not to how one collects data, but to the types of research questions that are asked, the ways data are represented, and the kinds of analyses that are undertaken. Correlational research is by nature quantitative. That is, either constructs are measured using techniques that yield quantitative results or data are gathered and then converted to a quantitative form through analysis, because numbers are required to conduct correlational analyses. Correlational studies generally provide information about groups of students or entities, but it is usually not the purpose of strictly correlational studies to provide detailed information about individuals.

Uses of Correlational Research

Correlational approaches have been used extensively to explore a host of topics such as language testing, language aptitude, language-learning strategies, language-use anxiety, and language variation. Complex correlational studies, such as those in Gardner's (1985 and 1991) research program, use statistical procedures that allow researchers to examine a large number of factors at once. While taking more variables into account has the potential of enhancing the validity of a study, the trend toward using more elaborate statistical programs is a direct result of the increasingly impressive capabilities of computer technology.

One interesting example of a study in this paradigm is Ely's (1986) examination of university students who were studying Spanish in a U.S. language class. He used causal modeling to study relationships among students' voluntary oral participation in the classroom, their affective characteristics, and learning outcomes. Among his results, he found that language class discomfort was a negative predictor of risk-taking (both measured by questionnaire), while risk-taking was a significant positive predictor of self-initiated classroom participation (i.e., volunteering). Participation was a significant positive predictor of oral correctness for first-quarter students but not of oral fluency or written correctness.

Methodological Issues

The major disadvantage of either simple or complex correlational research is its reductionist nature. Complex constructs such as attitudes, affective variables, language proficiency, cultural background, and teacher behaviors must be reduced to a set of numbers. Therefore, the value of a correlational study depends heavily on how well the theoretical constructs are defined and how well they are measured. Careful scrutiny of published studies often reveals that constructs were defined narrowly or that measures were not convincingly valid. For example, as an indicator of second-language writing proficiency, a measure of the grammatical accuracy of verbs would be too narrow. Rather, many other factors also contribute to overall writing proficiency, such as lexical choice, rhetorical structure, and appropriate audience-involvement strategies. Many correlational studies rely heavily on questionnaires that have questionable validity. For readers to take such work seriously, researchers need to explain why they consider the measures they use to be valid in the context in which they were used. Discussions of validity should also include an explanation of how the instruments were developed. For example, developing measures through qualitative procedures such as extensive observations and interviews, combined with careful pilot testing and revision, can enhance validity. In some cases, certain approaches to measurement prove invalid or unreliable and must be either abandoned or drastically modified (see, for example, the interesting reports of Degenhart and Takala 1988 on rating scales and of Ellis 1991 on grammaticality judgments).

To address validity, researchers should also discuss how cultural and contextual factors might have affected responses. For example, factors such as classroom climate, ethnicity of the researcher, and how respondents perceive audience and purpose can shape answers in important ways (Johnson and Saville-Troike 1992). These fundamental matters of validity need to be discussed in published reports. In beginning research methods courses it is a good idea to steer students or teacher-researchers away from using questionnaires early in their pilot studies. They gain few insights about the broad questions they have posed in this way. Rather, they can usually learn much more by conducting observations and interviews, especially during the first phases of their data collection.

Combining Approaches

While reductionism and lack of validity are dangers in correlational research, an important advantage is that relationships can be detected that might not be apparent otherwise. Correlational analyses, combined with other kinds of analysis within the same study or research program, can help researchers look at issues from different perspectives. I will provide one example from some of my own work in discourse analysis.

Working with colleagues, I have conducted a number of analyses of politeness strategies and complimenting in the written discourse of graduate students, both native speakers of English and advanced learners of English (Johnson and Roen 1992). For the NS writers, we found that women writing peer reviews used a discernible female-to-female complimenting style. This style involved using higher frequencies of positive evaluative terms (e.g., interesting, good), intensifiers (e.g., *really* good), and personal references (e.g., I, you, we). Examining the same phenomenon in the writing of advanced learners of English, I found that while L2 women writers used some aspects of the L1 writers' female-to-female complimenting style, they did not vary their language use according to gender of addressee to the degree or in the same ways that the L1 women writers did (Johnson 1992). Up to this point, these studies involved both qualitative and quantitative analyses of discourse.

A correlational approach, however, was most useful to address our next research question. We wanted to know whether the use of such strategies by the NSs was related to ratings of writing quality. To simplify a bit, results of our subsequent correlational analyses revealed that certain complimenting strategies that characterized the female-to-female style (specifically the use of compliment intensifiers and personal referencing) were correlated with lower ratings of writing quality (Roen and Johnson 1992). That is, there was some evidence of bias against the female-to-female style. One implication of this finding for advanced L2 learning is that there may be some negative consequences associated with displays of nativelike sociolinguistic competence. The use of correlational analysis in combination with discourse analysis allowed us to address a variety of questions and to view these phenomena from different perspectives. In conclusion, correlational research can provide valuable information about groups and can be improved through the complementary use of qualitative procedures and increased attention to valid measurement.

Case Studies

Too often, because of the nature of correlational, survey, and experimental research, and their privileged status in L2 research, very little is learned about individual language learners, teachers, or classes. Case studies stand in sharp contrast to these approaches by providing insights into the complexities of particular cases in their particular contexts. While case studies have been a prominent approach to research in child language acquisition, linguistic anthropology, and anthropology, they have not achieved much status in classroom-oriented second-language research until fairly recently. Rather, many writers have given them short shrift. Yet, in my opinion, case studies will become increasingly important in classroom-oriented research on language learning and teaching as researchers seek more adequate sociocultural and contextual explanation of learning and teaching processes and outcomes.

A case study, which is defined in terms of the unit of analysis, is an examination of a case in its context. The case may be a student, a teacher, a classroom, a school, an agency, an institution, or a community. A case might also be a communicative interaction, as Gumperz explains in his (1986) discussion of classroom-oriented interactional sociolinguistics.

Researchers may choose to study several cases and compare them, yet the number of cases is normally very small because the essence of the case-study approach is a holistic look at the particulars of the case in its natural context. Stake describes a case study as the study of a "bounded system" in which researchers focus on the unity and wholeness of a system, while confining their attention to issues that are relevant to the research questions posed (Stake 1988: 258). Case studies that are ethnographic in orientation generally involve extensive observation and offer cultural explanation for the phenomena observed.

Uses of Case Studies

A prominent use of case studies has been to trace the second or bilingual oral language development of children (e.g., Hakuta 1976, 1986; Wong Fillmore 1976; Hatch 1978). Case studies have been used to explore many other issues including child literacy development (Hudelson 1989; Peyton and Seyoum 1989), adult language learning (Schmidt 1983; Schmidt and Frota 1986), language and content learning (Hawkins 1988; Benson 1989; Adamson 1993), composing and reading processes and strategies (Zamel 1983; Hosenfeld 1984; Jones 1985; Raimes 1985; Cohen 1991), adult literacy (Rigg 1985), teaching strategies (Enright 1986; Cumming 1992), sociocultural bases of communicative interaction (Crago 1992), and program evaluation.

An interesting example of a case study is Schmidt and Frota's (1986) examination of Schmidt's learning of Portuguese during a five-month stay in Rio de Janeiro, Brazil. Schmidt kept a daily journal in which he recorded salient aspects of his own language experiences in and out of class. In addition, he and Frota taped unstructured conversations in Portuguese, transcribed them, and analyzed his interaction patterns and use of Portuguese nouns and verb phrases. Among the various findings, they described ways that the language class provided resources that he could put to immediate use outside of class to enhance his comprehension.

Another example of case-study research is the work of Wong Fillmore (1992). She describes a Chinese-born teacher, "Mrs. F," who, opposed to bilingual education, used only English with her students. Because the students were interacting primarily with this teacher, who was not highly proficient in English, and with other language learners like themselves, they were losing their Chinese but were not developing high levels of proficiency in English. That is, they were "learning from learners," as Wong Fillmore puts it. Another consequence of this situation was that the students were becoming less able to communicate fully in Chinese with their non-English-speaking parents. Wong Fillmore offers useful suggestions for teachers working in such situations.

A very different kind of case study is Cumming's (1992) analysis of the instructional routines of ESL composition instructors. He observed and took notes in the classes of three experienced instructors weekly for the duration of their courses. He found that teachers viewed their classes as workshops, in that they emphasized student task performance over teacher presentation of content. His analysis revealed that they followed a fairly consistent set of six routines: attracting students' attention; introducing tasks; providing guidance/feedback; establishing criteria; collectively constructing an outline, interpretation, or paradigm; and engaging in individual work with teacher guidance. Cumming also found that routines varied along a dimension of *proactive* ("presented to the whole class, planned in advance") to *responsive* ("occurring in unplanned exchanges negotiated with individual student," p. 22). The experienced composition instructors that he observed skillfully alternated among the six routines, embedding them within one another as needed, and alternating between proactive and responsive teaching. They established their routines early in the course and then used them fairly consistently throughout its duration. This study complements the many studies of teacher response to student writing by providing a naturalistic look at teacher responsiveness within the classroom, thus contributing to a more holistic view of L2 composition teaching.

Methodological Issues

From the perspective of quantitative and experimental paradigms, case studies are often viewed as nonrigorous. Certainly, there are fewer widely agreed-upon criteria for rigorous case-study methodology than for correlational, experimental, and survey approaches. Rather, case-study methodologies must be selected or developed in relation to the research questions posed and must be flexible enough to allow exploration of important issues that come to light as the study progresses. The rigor lies, in part, in how well this is done. In reports of research, methodological rigor can be addressed by describing (1) the development of a flexible, working research design that involves productive refocusing; (2) the use of multiple data-collection procedures; (3) the collection of adequate amounts of information over time about the case and about important aspects of the context; (4) the validity or credibility of the information; (5) the data analysis procedures; and (6) the typicality and the range of examples. A good analysis in a case study is one that identifies important issues regarding the case in its context, discovers how these issues pattern and interrelate, explains how these interrelationships influence the phenomena under study, and offers fresh insights.

Case-study research is a valuable approach to research that deserves to be much more widely used in studying language learning in a variety of situations. Case studies allow us to gain a more holistic view of teaching and learning in context and provide a way to take important personal, social, and cultural phenomena into account. An additional benefit of case studies is that they are often very accessible and interesting to teacher readers.

Survey Research

The purpose of a survey is to provide information about characteristics of an entire group of interest (a population) by studying a subset of that group (a sample).

Researchers select a sample that is similar in important ways to (representative of) the population as a whole, study the sample, and then make generalizations to the population.

Uses of Surveys

Surveys can provide valuable information about the status of the profession and about the political, demographic, and programmatic contexts in which teachers teach and students learn languages. For example, they can provide information about course offerings, teaching methods and materials, teachers' employment and work conditions, program administration, and professional development. All these issues are related to classroom practice.

A national survey of foreign languages taught in U.S. elementary and secondary schools provides an example (Rhodes and Oxford 1988). The national sample consisted of 5 percent of elementary and secondary schools, both public and private. While a response rate of only 52 percent was achieved, the authors did not generalize inappropriately to the population. Of those schools that responded, the most frequently taught languages in both secondary and elementary schools were Spanish, French, German, and Latin. Other important languages in the world, such as Chinese, Japanese, and Russian, were taught by fewer schools than was Latin. The authors also noted that only 3 percent of the respondents reported offering programs such as intensive FLES or immersion that were designed to develop high levels of competence.

More recently, the Modern Language Association surveyed 2,796 two- and four-year institutions of higher education (IHEs) to determine the number of students registered in foreign language courses (Brod and Huber 1992). The article implies that this was the entire population of IHEs because there is no mention of sampling. A 98.2 percent response rate was achieved using a "postcard questionnaire" mailed to registrars. Results indicated that Spanish was the most widely taught language, accounting for 45.1 percent of registrations, followed by (in decreasing order of registrations) French, German, Italian, Japanese, and Russian. Some significant trends were that Japanese moved into seventh position in 1986 and into fifth position in 1990, while Chinese moved from ninth place to eighth place in 1990. A most interesting preliminary report, it would benefit from explanation of the sample and more graphic displays of the data that effectively show trends over time.

Another interesting and useful survey was a study of the methods course in TESOL teacher-preparation programs conducted by Uber-Grosse (1991). She mailed a two-page questionnaire to 120 ESOL teacher-preparation programs and, after a follow-up mailing, achieved a response rate of 78 percent. The data that she reported included textbooks most used; course goals, content, emphasis, and sequence; and course requirements and assignments. Salient trends included providing choice in assignments to meet the varying needs of students; the use of journals, including teaching, tutoring, and reading journals; and a focus on encouraging reflective teaching. She noted that in teacher-preparation courses "excessive attention is devoted to coverage of individual methods that are rarely used, such as the Silent Way and Suggestopedia" (p. 43) and that there is "a striking lack of emphasis on either classroom-based research or the use of technology in the classroom" (p. 43). The author was also disappointed to learn that only about one-quarter of the programs made use of videotapes; she recommended increased use of video resources in teaching methods courses.

Methodological Issues

As these examples illustrate, the major advantage of surveys is their breadth. With good questions, an adequate sample, and good response rates, surveys can provide a broad picture of important topics and trends in our field.

An important limitation of surveys is that because they sacrifice depth and thoroughness for breadth and representativeness, they usually do not provide a rich picture of the complexities in any one situation. This limitation, though, reflects the very nature of surveys. I believe that the key problems with many surveys in our field are these: (1) questionable validity of instruments, (2) unexplained sampling procedures, (3) low response rates, (4) bias due to nonresponse, and (5) lack of use of complementary qualitative data collection procedures. Each of these areas can be improved through increased attention.

First, because the validity of a survey depends on the validity of the responses to questions, authors should describe the procedures they used to develop good questions that adequately get at the phenomena of interest. As with correlational research, the instrument-development phase of the study should involve some intensive qualitative work to explore the relevant issues in varied settings. Careful pilot testing, interviewing, and revision of the survey instruments is crucial for enhancing validity and should also be described in published reports. Authors should also describe the procedures they used to ensure that the respondents understood the language used in the instruments.

Second, the population of interest should be described and the rationale for and methods of sampling from that population clearly explained. This is important because any generalizations to the population must be related to the sampling design. Too often results are inappropriately generalized.

Perhaps the most persistent problem in surveys in our field, however, is low response rates. Response rates as low as 10 percent appear in the literature. When response rates are low, the writer can report only that, for example, "50 percent of those who responded reported X." The reader, then, is left wondering what those who did not respond might have reported. Some suggest that researchers should perform nonresponse-bias checks when response rates fall below 90 percent, a very rigorous standard for many studies

(Smith and Glass 1987: 235). Even when more realistic standards are set, it may be better to survey a smaller sample and put more effort into obtaining higher response rates. In published reports, authors should at least address potential bias due to nonresponse.

Finally, qualitative and quantitative procedures can be used in complementary ways, not only during instrument development, but also during data collection. For example, more intensive qualitative study of a few cases or respondents can provide insights that will enhance interpretation of the broad survey findings. Such multimethod approaches have long been used in multisite, multimethod, large-scale research and are becoming more widely used in studies that are smaller in scope as well. This is a very positive trend because such approaches should not only enhance validity and offer richer insights, but should make reports more interesting to read.

Ethnographic Research

Second-language scholars held out hope in the late 1970s that ethnographic approaches to research in language teaching and learning would become prominent. For example, Politzer (1981: 30), while warning against "blitzkrieg ethnographies" (a term used by Rist 1980), suggested that a substantial increase in ethnographic studies that offer a real understanding of what happens in classrooms should be among the attainable goals of the 1980s. While ethnographically oriented research in elementary-level classrooms has increased greatly, there is still a striking paucity of such work in foreign language classes and for adolescent and adult learners. For a field in which cultural issues are crucial, this remains a serious gap.

There is a great deal of discussion about what constitutes "real ethnography." As Watson-Gegeo (1988) has pointed out in her excellent discussion of ethnography in ESL, the term has been used very loosely. Here I will use the term *ethnography* as well as the term *ethnographically oriented research,* a somewhat broader term than ethnography, to refer to work that involves the holistic study of social and cultural phenomena— including communication—in context, and the cultural interpretation of behavior. Ethnographic and ethnographically oriented research on L2 learning and teaching re- quires extensive and usually long-term observation, not simply one or two visits to a classroom. It often involves the collection of discourse in context, rather than sentence- level language data or isolated speech-act data. For example, the collection of individual instances of speech acts, which Wolfson (1989) and others have termed ethnographic, is a naturalistic data collection technique, but it is not ethnographic because it does not involve long-term observation and interviewing ("watching and asking") in a particular cultural setting with attention to whole speech events in relation to cultural context.

Major qualitative and ethnographic research traditions from anthropology, educa- tion, and sociolinguistics that are relevant to the field of second-language learning and teaching include the ethnography of communication (Hymes 1972; Heath 1983; Saville- Troike 1989), educational ethnography and the ethnography of schooling (Spindler 1982), linguistic anthropology (e.g., Ochs 1988; Basso 1990), discourse analysis, and, in some cases, interactional sociolinguistics in cross-cultural communication (Gumperz 1982, 1986; Tannen 1984).

Uses of Ethnographic Research

Ethnographic studies have been used to address a variety of topics. There is a growing and very useful body of literature on the culture of Native American students in the United States and Canada and how school culture may conflict with home and community values and practices (Mohatt and Erickson 1981; Scollon and Scollon 1981; Philips 1983; Macias 1987; Crago 1992). The research of Ochs and Schieffelin (Ochs and Schieffelin 1984; Schieffelin and Ochs 1986; Ochs 1988), Heath (1983), Clancy (1986, on Japanese), Eisenberg (1986, on Spanish), and others has illustrated ways that language socialization differs across cultures and how socialization practices are linked to cultural values. This work is relevant to both L2 teachers and theorists because it illustrates that some theories of language acquisition are based on ethnocentric cultural assumptions about how parents, children, and peers communicate. Willett's (1987) study extended language socialization work into second-language acquisition in school by studying preschool children from Brazil and Korea and illustrating how their classroom interaction styles, their language use, and their second-language acquisition patterns are related to their cultural backgrounds. In bilingual education, ethnographic studies such as those by Guthrie (1985) and Edelsky (1986) in the United States and by Hornberger (1987) in Peru have added to our understanding of relationships between bilingual schooling and the wider cultural context. Studies by Wong Fillmore (1992), Delgado-Gaitan (1992), and Harry (1992) provide information about parents' attitudes toward and roles in their children's education. Microethnographic work such as that by Carrasco (1981) and Moll (1989) has provided useful information about the same children's variable behavior in different learning environments. Cultural information learned from ethnographic studies can have a powerful impact on teachers. For example, teachers who read work such as Basso's (1990) "To Give Up on Words" or "Stalking with Stories" or Scollon and Scollon's (1981) "Athabaskan-English Interethnic Communication," gain a deeper understanding of what it means to communicate within a different culture.

From this brief list of studies, it is clear that most ethnographic work has been conducted with young students. There is a great need for more ethnographically oriented studies of older learners. We need ethnographic studies of schooling in diverse countries, of life in language institutes, of culturally diverse foreign language classrooms. One reason for the paucity of such ethnographic studies is that data collection is extremely time-consuming. Another reason is that ethnographic research has strong historic ties to the disciplines of linguistics and psychology, with weaker, but growing ties to anthropology and sociolinguistics. Most L2/FL researchers were not trained in ethnographic or qualitative traditions nor are most of us skilled in the rich descriptive writing of ethnographic reporting or educational connoisseurship. A related problem is that there are no L2 or FL journals that are devoted primarily to qualitative research. Some journals that are central to our field have been slow to incorporate qualitative studies. As a result, relevant ethnographic and qualitative work is not as directly accessible to the L2/FL community as it might be.

Experimental Research

Unlike ethnographic studies, experimental studies are abundant in the field of second-language acquisition and teaching. In experimental research, the researcher's goal is to establish a cause-and-effect relationship between two phenomena, to establish that a specific set of actions or conditions (the independent variable) causes changes in some outcome (the dependent variable). The essential feature of the true classroom experiment—that subjects be randomly assigned to experimental and control groups—is often impractical, undesirable, or even illegal. Therefore, true experiments conducted in authentic classrooms are rare. Experiments are most often conducted in labs or in simulated classroom settings, while quasi-experiments are most feasible in natural classroom settings.

Even though experimental research has been the focus of a great deal of criticism and the basic assumptions of the paradigm challenged (see Guba and Lincoln 1989; Eisner and Peshkin 1990), the experimental paradigm has remained dominant in research in second/foreign language learning. Its privileged status is evident in most major journals and in several of the recent books on second-language research methods (Brown 1988; Seliger and Shohamy 1989; Hatch and Lazaraton 1990).

Uses of Experiments

Small-scale teaching experiments can be quite useful when they are well executed and well described. A good classroom-oriented experimental study is one by Doughty (1991) in which she examined the effects on learning of different methods of teaching relativization. The study is interesting because it explored a theoretically important question in SLA and also compared three realistic instructional techniques to one another. Thus, it has something to say to readers interested in teaching, theory, and/ or research. To simplify a bit, Doughty addressed two major research questions. First, she compared "meaning-oriented" and "rule-oriented" teaching techniques to an "exposure only" control group to determine which method promoted the most growth in the ability to relativize accurately. In her report, Doughty explained these instructional techniques briefly, but in enough detail that they are fairly clear to readers. Second, she asked whether SL instruction that targeted marked relative clauses facilitated the acquisition of less marked types of relative clauses.

The study suffers from some minor problems that are typical of studies with small numbers of subjects, such as unexplained initial differences among groups and some ceiling effects. Nevertheless, in general, the experiment was well conducted and the report well written. Doughty found that, while all three groups improved, both the meaning-oriented group and the rule-oriented group improved more than did the control group. Second, she found that, as predicted, instruction on marked forms appeared to generalize to less marked forms, but that it also appeared to generalize to other more marked forms. Further probing beyond her stated hypotheses revealed that the meaning-oriented group demonstrated superior comprehension of the content of lessons. To teachers, she suggested that providing comprehensible input along with making structures salient/noticeable in a meaningful context is an effective approach to teaching relativization. The study thus provides an example of valuable classroom-oriented experimentation.

Methodological Issues

The major advantages of experiments derive from their carefully planned design and procedures. As Porter (1988) puts it: "By concentrating on only a few variables, the difficult measurement problems of each can be given careful attention" (p. 410). A major problem is that experiments, like correlational studies, are essentially reductionist. Constructs may be measured with procedures or instruments that lack adequate levels of validity or reliability or that operationalize the construct in a very narrow way. The nature of this reduction is shaped by the theoretical orientations of the researchers. Notions of objectivity, then, are called into question when the theories and biases that the researcher brings to the study shape not only the original research question, but also the way constructs are narrowed and measured and, finally, the way results are interpreted.

It is interesting to note, however, that research questions in the experimental approach often match the kinds of questions that teachers often ask. They want to know if one particular task, one teaching method, one type of learning environment, or one type of program is more effective than another for their own students. While experiments can sometimes offer at least some limited answers to such questions for a particular group of students in a particular sociocultural setting, generalizability to other students, tasks, and settings may be severely limited. Moreover, experimental studies often fail to provide insights into *why* different instructional practices produce different results. That is, too often in reports of experiments the treatment conditions, which are not only of great interest to teachers but essential for interpreting findings, are described only in the briefest terms, so that the reader has difficulty picturing the teaching/learning activities. Too often readers are told very little about the students who participated and almost nothing about important contextual factors. Journal editors can improve this state of affairs by encouraging richer descriptions of treatments, students, and contexts. One way that researchers can provide more insightful descriptions is by incorporating the students' point of view. Authors can produce two related articles for publication, one with its major emphasis on the instructional activities investigated and the other with its major emphasis on the research methodology. Without a doubt, richer descriptions of the different experimental treatments, the students, and relevant aspects of the sociocultural context will provide a much more solid basis for explaining and interpreting the meaning of the findings. Moreover, such description will give readers more information on which they can make appropriate generalizations, making the research more interesting and useful.

Discourse Analysis

Discourse analysis, the study of language beyond the sentence, has become an increasingly important approach to research in the use, learning, and teaching of additional languages and cultures. The prominence of discourse analysis as a focus of research represents a broader view of language and language learning. As Tannen (1989: 6) points out, the term "discourse analysis" does not refer to a particular theoretical perspective or a single method of analysis. Rather, the field is interdisciplinary and multidisciplinary and researchers who analyze discourse do so for many purposes. Our central interest in this chapter is in analyses of spoken discourse or written texts that can inform language teaching and learning.

Readers may have noticed that discourse analysis has been addressed throughout the chapter. It is an approach to research that can be used in conjunction with experimental, correlational, ethnographic, case-study, or survey approaches. Moreover, researchers can combine qualitative analyses of discourse structures and strategies, for example, with quantitative analyses that relate the use of discourse strategies to student characteristics, aspects of task or context, or ratings of quality.

Uses of Discourse Analysis

Discourse analysis is carried out to address a wide variety of questions. It provides information about what language learners need to learn, such as rhetorical structure and style, teacher–student interaction, student–student interaction, the pragmatics of discourse, scripts for school, politeness strategies, coherence conventions, and cohesive devices. Discourse analysis provides insights into issues as diverse as how language teachers in Hong Kong adapt their classroom discourse to communicative methods (Willett 1982) and what makes the lectures of Korean teaching assistants difficult for U.S. English-speaking students to understand (Tyler, Jefferies, and Davies 1988).

Much SLA research has employed discourse analysis to examine how learners negotiate meaning in conversations with fluent speakers and how conversational processes can contribute to developing linguistic competence, especially syntactic structures (Gass and Varonis 1991; Larsen-Freeman and Long 1991; Pica 1992). Much of this work, because it has been carried out by eliciting language in experimental settings, provides a somewhat restricted notion of meaning negotiation. That is, context is confined to conversational context. Analysis of spoken discourse recorded in the full context of classroom activities has the advantage of providing examples of richer, more authentic language use and learning as it is intertwined with content engagement. For example, in her study of fourth-grade ESL students in their content and language classes, Hawkins (1988) presented evidence of scaffolding and concrete signs of language learning resulting from scaffolded interaction. Examining relationships between context and discourse, she found that scaffolding was more likely to be present in situations and activities that were both interactively and cognitively demanding—that is, in activities in which students were actively involved in the interaction and the emphasis was on interpretive and critical comprehension (p. 28). She also found that students achieved cognitive accomplishments that they are not normally thought capable of achieving because of their level of proficiency in the L2. In this study, context was viewed more broadly to include not only cognitive and interactive context, but activities across classes and across time. (For further discussion of scaffolding, see Cazden 1988.)

Work by Kleifgen and Saville-Troike (1992) also shows how analysis of discourse based on long-term classroom observation can provide a richer picture of classroom communication and negotiation. Their work illustrates how processes of interpretation and meaning negotiation involve interrelationships between linguistic, situational, and cultural background knowledge. They observed and videotaped 29 children, ages 3–10, interacting with teachers and peers in elementary and nursery-school classes. The use of wireless microphones allowed them to capture information about how children interpreted what was going on. They present segments of communicative events that illustrate how children draw very heavily on world and cultural background knowledge, as well as on situational knowledge, to interpret and negotiate meanings. This kind of naturalistic, richly contextualized data provides a strong argument for not only examining sociocultural and linguistic processes together rather than as isolated phenomena, but also for more integrated approaches to educating ESL children (see Genesee in press).

Discourse analytic work within foreign language classrooms has also increased (e.g., Kinginger and Savignon 1991). Kramsch's (1992) analyses of foreign-language-classroom discourse, which are also carried out from the analytical perspective of the ethnography of communication, show, for example, that students' and teachers' different and shifting footings can sometimes result in incoherent dialogue.

Discourse analytic work in cross-cultural communication, such as the studies collected in Gumperz (1982), is highly relevant to language learning and teaching. Similarly, Yamada's (1990) comparative work on Japanese-American differences in business meetings and Tsuda's (1984) comparative study of Japanese and American sales encounters provide authentic empirical information that not only can sensitize teachers and students to differences in communicative style, but can provide a basis for developing teaching materials. Similarly, work in contrastive rhetoric (Connor and Kaplan 1987; Smith 1987; Purves 1988; Grabe and Kaplan 1989; Leki 1991), is useful in helping teachers and students understand the values and expectations of audiences in different cultures and discourse communities.

Methodological Issues

There seem to be two fundamental approaches to discourse analysis—those using essentially a bottom-up approach and those incorporating a top-down perspective. The first approach begins with a linguistic feature of interest, such as a particular structure, and examines its forms and functioning in discourse (Hatch 1992). This bottom-up approach is more linguistic in orientation. Other approaches within the second basic type begin with a description of a communicative event in its situational context and analyze aspects of discourse as they relate to context (Hymes 1972; Tannen 1984 and 1989; Briggs 1988; Duranti and Goodwin 1992). These top-down approaches are ethnographic and sociolinguistic in orientation. They are often preferable for classroom research because they can account for broad contextual factors, leading to a more holistic view of phenomena, more valid interpretation, and more adequate answers to research questions that interest teachers. Moreover, analysis of discourse in its full, natural context can help illuminate ways that language use is tied to culture.

Several other methodological issues bear mention. One advantage of discourse analysis is that a video recording, audio recording, or written classroom texts can be studied repeatedly to investigate a number of phenomena. Issues often come to light through recursive study that the researcher could not have predicted beforehand, that were not apparent at the time of data collection, or that were not noticed upon first passes through the data. In addition, the use of playback sessions allows for interpretation of learners' language and behavior not only by researchers, but by teachers and by learners themselves. This practice can result in more enlightened interpretations of findings.

An important problem in discourse-analytic work is that researchers often present interesting examples of learner discourse to illustrate a phenomenon, but too often fail to give readers any indication of how frequent, how representative, and how variable such phenomena are. Another annoying problem is that, often, in presenting segments of discourse in a report, too little introductory contextual information is provided and it is difficult to make much sense of the discourse presented. Journal and book editors can improve these problems by asking authors to present adequate contextual information to accompany the presentation of segments of discourse. Regardless of such problems, discourse analysis, either on its own or in combination with other methods, contributes a great deal to our knowledge of language use and learning in various sociocultural contexts.

Conclusion

The major purpose of this chapter has been to provide a discussion of some methodological issues in classroom-oriented L2 research. Six approaches to research have been used to illustrate the types of studies that are conducted, to point out salient methodological problems, and to offer suggestions for improvement. The examples have come from a variety of language teaching settings and from learners of different ages in different life circumstances. I have argued that research techniques from quantitative and qualitative paradigms can often be used in complementary fashion to provide different perspectives on an issue and that qualitative techniques should be used more widely to help strive for validity in the collection and interpretation of information. With greater attention to the methodological issues addressed in this chapter, it is hoped that classroom-oriented research can be not only more rigorous, but that it can be of greater use to teachers and teacher educators.

References

Classroom-Oriented Research in Second-Language Learning

Adamson, H. D. 1993. *Academic Competence: Theory and Classroom Practice: Preparing ESL Students for Content Courses.* White Plains, NY: Longman.

Allwright, Dick. 1988. *Observation in the Language Classroom.* London, Eng.: Longman.

————, and Kathleen M. Bailey. 1991. *Focus on the Language Classroom: An Introduction to Classroom Research for Language Teachers.* Cambridge, Eng.: Cambridge Univ. Press.

Bachman, Lyle. 1990. *Fundamental Considerations in Language Testing.* Oxford, Eng.: Oxford Univ. Press.

Basso, Keith H. 1990. *Western Apache Language and Culture: Essays in Linguistic Anthropology.* Tucson: Univ. of Arizona Press.

Benson, Malcolm J. 1989. "The Academic Listening Task: A Case Study." *TESOL Quarterly* 23: 421–45.

Borg, Walter R. 1981. *Applying Educational Research: A Practical Guide for Teachers.* White Plains, NY: Longman.

Briggs, Charles. 1988. *Competence in Performance: The Creativity of Tradition in Mexicano Verbal Art.* Philadelphia: Univ. of Pennsylvania Press.

Brod, Richard, and Bettina J. Huber. 1992. "Foreign Language Enrollments in United States Institutions of Higher Education, Fall 1990." *ADFL Bulletin* 23: 6–10.

Brown, James D. 1988. *Understanding Research in Second Language Learning: A Teacher's Guide to Statistics and Research Design.* Cambridge, Eng.: Cambridge Univ. Press.

Carrasco, Robert L. 1981. "Expanded Awareness of Student Performance: A Case Study in Applied Ethnographic Monitoring in a Bilingual Classroom," pp. 153–77 in Henry T. Trueba, Grace Pung Guthrie, Kathryn Hu-Pei Au, eds., *Culture and the Bilingual Classroom: Studies in Classroom Ethnography.* Rowley, MA: Newbury House.

Cazden, Courtney B. 1988. *Classroom Discourse: The Language of Teaching and Learning.* Portsmouth, NH: Heinemann.

––––––. 1990. "Recent Publications on Classroom Research." *TESOL Quarterly* 24: 717–24.

Chapelle, Carol A. 1992. "Research on CALL and CALL Research." *Athelstan Newsletter* 5,1: 3, 6, 7.

Chaudron, Craig. 1988. *Second Language Classrooms: Research on Teaching and Learning.* Cambridge, Eng.: Cambridge Univ. Press.

Clancy, Patricia M. 1986. "The Acquisition of Communicative Style in Japanese," pp. 213–50 in Bambi B. Schieffelin and Elinor Ochs, eds., *Language Socialization across Cultures.* Cambridge, Eng.: Cambridge Univ. Press.

Cohen, Andrew D. 1990. *Language Learning: Insights for Learners, Teachers, and Researchers.* New York: Newbury House.

––––––. 1991. "Feedback on Writing: The Use of Verbal Report." *Studies in Second Language Acquisition* 13: 133–59.

Connor, Ulla, and Robert B. Kaplan, eds. 1987. *Writing across Languages: Analysis of L2 Text.* Reading, MA: Addison-Wesley.

Crago, Martha B. 1992. "Communicative Interaction and Second Language Acquisition: An Inuit Example." *TESOL Quarterly* 26: 487–505.

Cumming, Alister. 1992. "Instructional Routines in ESL Composition Teaching: A Case Study of Three Teachers." *Journal of Second Language Writing* 1,1: 17–35.

Degenhart, R. Elaine, and Sauli Takala. 1988. "Developing a Rating Method for Stylistic Preference: A Cross-Cultural Pilot Study," pp. 79–106 in Alan C. Purves, ed., *Writing across Languages and Cultures: Issues in Contrastive Rhetoric.* Newbury Park, CA: Sage.

Delgado-Gaitan, Concha. 1992. "School Matters in the Mexican-American Home: Socializing Children to Education." *American Educational Research Journal* 29: 495–513.

Doughty, Catherine. 1991. "Second Language Instruction Does Make a Difference: Evidence from an Empirical Study of SL Relativization." *Studies in Second Language Acquisition* 13: 431–69.

Dunkel, Patricia, ed. 1991. *Computer-Assisted Language Learning and Testing: Research Issues and Practice.* New York: Newbury House.

Duranti, Alessandro, and Charles Goodwin, eds. 1992. *Rethinking Context: Language as an Interactive Phenomenon.* Cambridge, Eng.: Cambridge Univ. Press.

Edelsky, Carole. 1986. *Writing in a Bilingual Program: Había una Vez.* Norwood, NJ: Ablex.

Eisenberg, Ann R. 1986. "Teasing: Verbal Play in Two Mexicano Homes," pp. 182–98 in Bambi B. Schieffelin and Elinor Ochs, eds., *Language Socialization across Cultures.* Cambridge, Eng.: Cambridge Univ. Press.

Eisner, Elliot W., and A. Peshkin. 1990. *Qualitative Inquiry in Education: The Continuing Debate.* New York: Teachers College Press.

Ellis, Rod. 1991. "Grammaticality Judgments and Second Language Acquisition." *Studies in Second Language Acquisition* 13: 161–86.

Ely, Christopher M. 1986. "An Analysis of Discomfort, Risktaking, Sociability, and Motivation in the L2 Classroom." *Language Learning* 36: 1–25.

Enright, D. Scott. 1986. "Use Everything You Have to Teach English: Providing Useful Input to Young Language Learners," pp. 115–62 in Pat Rigg and D. Scott Enright, eds., *Children and ESL: Integrating Perspectives.* Washington, DC: Teachers of English to Speakers of Other Languages.

Faerch, Claus, and Gabriele Kasper, eds. 1987. *Introspection in Second Language Research.* Clevedon, Eng.: Multilingual Matters.

Freed, Barbara F., ed. 1991. *Foreign Language Acquisition Research and the Classroom.* Lexington, MA: Heath.

Gardner, Robert C. 1985. *Social Psychology and Second Language Learning: The Role of Attitudes and Motivation.* London, Eng.: Edward Arnold.

———. 1991. "Second-Language Learning in Adults: Correlates of Proficiency." *Applied Language Learning* 2,1: 1–28.

Gass, Susan, and Evangeline M. Varonis. 1991. "Miscommunication in Nonnative Speaker Discourse," pp. 121–45 in Nikolas Coupland, Howard Giles, and John M. Wiemann, eds., *"Miscommunication" and Problematic Talk.* Newbury Park, CA: Sage.

Genesee, Fred, ed. In press. *An Integrative Approach to Educating Second Language Children.* Cambridge, Eng.: Cambridge Univ. Press.

Grabe, William, and Robert R. Kaplan. 1989. "Writing in a Second Language: Contrastive Rhetoric," pp. 263–83 in Donna M. Johnson and Duane H. Roen, eds., *Richness in Writing: Empowering ESL Students.* White Plains, NY: Longman.

Guba, Egon G., and Yvonna S. Lincoln. 1989. *Fourth Generation Evaluation.* Newbury Park, CA: Sage.

Gumperz, John J. 1982. *Language and Social Identity.* New York: Cambridge Univ. Press.

———. 1986. "Interactional Sociolinguistics in the Study of Schooling," pp. 45–68 in Jenny Cook-Gumperz, ed., *The Social Construction of Literacy.* Cambridge, Eng.: Cambridge Univ. Press.

Guthrie, Grace Pung. 1985. *A School Divided: An Ethnography of Bilingual Education in a Chinese Community.* Hillsdale, NJ: Erlbaum.

Hakuta, Kenji. 1976. "A Case Study of a Japanese Child Learning English." *Language Learning* 26: 321–51.

———. 1986. *Mirror of Language: The Debate on Bilingualism.* New York: Basic Books.

Harry, Beth. 1992. "An Ethnographic Study of Cross-Cultural Communication with Puerto Rican–American Families in the Special Education System." *American Educational Research Journal* 29: 471–94.

Hatch, Evelyn, ed. 1978. *Second Language Acquisition: A Book of Readings.* Rowley, MA: Newbury House.

———. 1992. *Discourse and Language Education.* Cambridge, Eng.: Cambridge Univ. Press.

——, and Anne Lazaraton. 1990. *The Research Manual: Design and Statistics for Applied Linguistics.* New York: Newbury House.

Hawkins, Barbara A. 1988. "Scaffolded Classroom Interaction and Its Relation to Second Language Acquisition for Language Minority Children." Unpublished Ph.D. diss., Univ. of California–Los Angeles.

Heath, Shirley Brice. 1983. *Ways with Words*. Cambridge, Eng.: Cambridge Univ. Press.

Hornberger, Nancy H. 1987. "Bilingual Education Success, but Policy Failure." *Language in Society* 16: 205–26.

Horwitz, Elaine K., and Dolly J. Young. 1991. *Language Anxiety: From Theory and Research to Classroom Implications*. Englewood Cliffs, NJ: Prentice-Hall.

Hosenfeld, Carol. 1984. "Case Studies of Ninth Grade Readers," pp. 231–49 in J. Charles Alderson and A. H. Urquhart, eds., *Teaching in a Foreign Language*. London, Eng.: Longman.

Hudelson, Sarah. 1989. "A Tale of Two Children: Individual Differences in ESL Children's Writing," pp. 84–99 in Donna M. Johnson and Duane H. Roen, eds., *Richness in Writing: Empowering ESL Students*. White Plains, NY: Longman.

Huebner, Thom, and Anne Jensen. 1992. "A Study of Foreign Language Proficiency-Based Testing in Secondary Schools." *Foreign Language Annals* 25,2: 105–15.

Hymes, Dell. 1972. "Models of the Interaction of Language and Social Life," in John J. Gumperz and Dell Hymes, eds., *Directions in Sociolinguistics: The Ethnography of Communication*. New York: Holt, Rinehart and Winston.

Johnson, Donna M. 1992. "Interpersonal Involvement in Discourse: Gender Variation in L2 Writers' Complimenting Strategies." *Journal of Second Language Writing* 1,3: 51–71.

———, and Lihe Chen. 1992. "Researchers, Teachers, and Inquiry," pp. 221–27 in Donna M. Johnson, ed., *Approaches to Research in Second Language Learning*. White Plains, NY: Longman.

——, and Duane H. Roen, eds. 1989. *Richness in Writing: Empowering ESL Students*. White Plains, NY: Longman.

——, and Duane H. Roen. 1992. "Complimenting and Involvement in Peer Review: Gender Variation." *Language in Society* 21,1: 27–57.

——, and Muriel Saville-Troike. 1992. "Validity and Reliability in Qualitative Research on Second Language Acquisition and Teaching." *TESOL Quarterly* 26,3: 602–5.

Jones, Stan. 1985. "Problems with Monitor Use in Second Language Composing," in Mike Rose, ed., *When a Writer Can't Write*. New York: Guilford.

Kachru, Braj. 1992. "Why Applied Linguistics Leaks." Plenary address at the annual meeting of the American Association for Applied Linguistics, Seattle, WA.

Kasper, Gabriele. In press. "Interlanguage Pragmatics," in Gabriele Kasper and Shoshana Blum-Kulka, eds., *Interlanguage Pragmatics*. New York: Oxford Univ. Press.

———, and Merete Dahl. 1991. "Research Methods in Interlanguage Pragmatics." *Studies in Second Language Acquisition* 13: 215–47.

Kinginger, Celeste S., and Sandra J. Savignon. 1991. "Four Conversations: Task Variation and Classroom Learner Discourse," pp. 85–106 in Mary E. McGroarty and Christian J. Faltis, eds., *Languages in School and Society: Policy and Pedagogy*. Berlin, Ger.: Mouton de Gruyter.

Kleifgen, Jo Anne, and Muriel Saville-Troike. 1992. "Achieving Coherence in Multilingual Interaction." *Discourse Processes* 15: 183–206.

Kleinsasser, Robert C. 1992. "A Tale of Two Technical Cultures: Foreign Language Teaching." Paper presented at a meeting of the American Educational Research Association, San Francisco, CA, April.

———, and Sandra J. Savignon. 1991. "Linguistics, Language Pedagogy, and Teachers' Technical Cultures," pp. 289–301 in James E. Alatis, ed. Georgetown University Round Table on Languages and Linguistics. Washington, DC: Georgetown Univ. Press.

Kramsch, Claire. 1992. "Different Words, Different Worlds: Can SLA Accommodate Culture?" Paper presented at the SLAT Colloquium Series, Univ. of Arizona, Tucson.
——, and Sally McConnell-Ginet, eds. 1992. *Text and Context: Cross-Disciplinary Perspectives on Language Study.* Lexington, MA: Heath.

Kroll, Barbara, ed. 1990. *Second Language Writing: Research Insights for the Classroom.* Cambridge, Eng.: Cambridge Univ. Press.

Larsen-Freeman, Diane, and Michael H. Long. 1991. *An Introduction to Second Language Acquisition Research.* London, Eng.: Longman.

Leki, Ilona. 1991. "Twenty-five Years of Contrastive Rhetoric: Text Analysis and Writing Pedagogies. *TESOL Quarterly* 25,1: 123–43.

Macias, Jose. 1987. "The Hidden Curriculum of Papago Teachers: American Indian Strategies for Mitigating Cultural Discontinuity in Early Schooling," pp. 363–80 in George Spindler and Louise Spindler, eds., *Interpretive Ethnography of Education: At Home and Abroad.* Hillsdale, NJ: Erlbaum.

McKay, Sandra Lee, ed. 1984. *Composing in a Second Language.* Rowley, MA: Newbury House.

Mohatt, Gerald, and Frederick Erickson. 1981. "Cultural Differences in Teaching Styles in an Odawa School: A Sociolinguistic Approach," pp. 105–19 in Henry T. Trueba, Grace Pung Guthrie, and Kathryn Hu-Pei Au, eds., *Culture and the Bilingual Classroom: Studies in Classroom Ethnography.* Rowley, MA: Newbury House.

Moll, Luis C. 1989. "Teaching Second Language Students: A Vygotskian Perspective," pp. 55–69 in Donna M. Johnson and Duane H. Roen, eds., *Richness in Writing.* White Plains, NY: Longman.

Nunan, David. 1989. *Understanding Language Classrooms: A Guide for Teacher-Initiated Action.* New York: Prentice-Hall.

Ochs, Elinor. 1988. *Culture and Language Development: Language Acquisition and Language Socialization in a Samoan Village.* Cambridge, Eng.: Cambridge Univ. Press.

——, and Bambi B. Schieffelin. 1984. "Language Acquisition and Socialization: Three Developmental Stories and Their Implications," pp. 276–320 in Richard A. Shweder and Robert A. LeVine, eds., *Culture Theory: Essays on Mind, Self, and Emotion.* Cambridge, Eng.: Cambridge Univ. Press.

Oxford, Rebecca L., and Roberta Z. Lavine. 1992. "Teacher-Student Style Wars in the Language Classroom: Research Insights and Suggestions." *ADFL Bulletin* 23,2: 38–45.

Peyton, Joy Kreeft, and Mulugetta Seyoum. 1989. "The Effect of Teacher Strategies on Students' Interactive Writing: The Case of Dialogue Journals." *Research in the Teaching of English* 23,2: 310–34.

Philips, Susan U. 1983. *The Invisible Culture: Communication in Classroom and Community in the Warm Springs Indian Reservation.* White Plains, NY: Longman.

Pica, Teresa. 1992. "The Textual Outcomes of Native Speaker–Non-Native Speaker Negotiation: What Do They Reveal about Second Language Learning?" pp. 198–237 in Claire Kramsch and Sally McConnell-Ginet, eds., *Text and Context: Cross-Disciplinary Perspectives on Language Study.* Lexington, MA: Heath.

Politzer, Robert L. 1981. "Effective Language Teaching: Insights from Research," pp. 23–35 in James E. Alatis, Howard B. Altman, and Penelope M. Alatis, eds., *The Second Language Classroom: Directions for the 1980s.* New York: Oxford Univ. Press.

Porter, Andrew C. 1988. "Comparative Experiments in Educational Research," pp. 391–411 in Richard M. Jaeger, ed., *Complementary Methods for Research in Education.* Washington, DC: American Educational Research Assn.

Purves, Alan, ed. 1988. *Writing across Languages and Cultures.* Newbury Park, CA: Sage.

Raimes, Ann. 1985. "What Unskilled ESL Students Do as They Write: A Classroom Study of Composing." *TESOL Quarterly* 19: 229–58.

Rhodes, Nancy C., and Rebecca L. Oxford. 1988. "Foreign Languages in Elementary and Secondary Schools: Results of a National Survey." *Foreign Language Annals* 21: 51–69.

Rigg, Pat. 1985. "Petra: Learning to Read at 45." *Journal of Education* 167: 129–39.

Rist, Ray C. 1980. "Blitzkrieg Ethnography: On the Transformation of Method into a Movement." *Educational Researcher* 9,2: 8–10.

Roen, Duane H., and Donna M. Johnson. 1992. "Perceiving the Effectiveness of Written Discourse through Gender Lenses: The Contribution of Complimenting." *Written Communication* 9,4: 435–64.

Saville-Troike, Muriel. 1989. *The Ethnography of Communication: An Introduction.* 2nd ed. Oxford, Eng.: Basil Blackwell.

Schieffelin, Bambi B., and Elinor Ochs. 1986. *Language Socialization across Cultures.* Cambridge, Eng.: Cambridge Univ. Press.

Schmidt, Richard W. 1983. "Interaction, Acculturation, and the Acquisition of Communicative Competence: A Case Study of an Adult," pp. 137–74 in Nessa Wolfson and Elliot Judd, eds., *Sociolinguistics and Language Acquisition.* Rowley, MA: Newbury House.

————, and Sylvia Nagem Frota. 1986. "Developing Basic Conversational Ability in a Second Language: A Case Study of an Adult Learner of Portuguese," pp. 237–326 in Richard R. Day, ed., *Talking to Learn: Conversation in Second Language Acquisition.* Rowley, MA: Newbury House.

Scollon, Ron, and Suzanne B. K. Scollon. 1981. *Narrative, Literacy and Face in Interethnic Communication.* Norwood, NJ: Ablex. [Chapter 2 is reprinted in Donal Carbaugh, ed., *Cultural Communication and Intercultural Contact.* Hillsdale, NJ: Erlbaum, 1990.]

Seliger, Herbert W., and Elana Shohamy. 1989. *Second Language Research Methods.* Oxford, Eng.: Oxford Univ. Press.

Smith, Larry E., ed. 1987. *Discourse across Cultures: Strategies in World Englishes.* Englewood Cliffs, NJ: Prentice-Hall.

Smith, Mary L., and Gene V. Glass. 1987. *Research and Evaluation in Education and the Social Sciences.* Englewood Cliffs, NJ: Prentice-Hall.

Spindler, George. 1982. *Doing the Ethnography of Schooling.* New York: CBS College Publishing.

Stake, Robert E. 1988. "Case Study Methods in Educational Research: Seeking Sweet Water," pp. 253–78 in Richard M. Jaeger, ed., *Complementary Methods for Research in Education.* Washington, DC: American Education Research Assn.

Tannen, Deborah. 1984. *Conversational Style: Analyzing Talk among Friends.* Norwood, NJ: Ablex.

————. 1989. *Talking Voices: Repetition, Dialogue, and Imagery in Conversational Discourse.* Cambridge, Eng.: Cambridge Univ. Press.

Tsuda, Aoi S. N. D. 1984. *Sales Talk in Japan and the United States.* Washington, DC: Georgetown Univ. Press.

Tyler, Andrea E., Ann A. Jefferies, and Catherine E. Davies. 1988. "The Effect of Discourse Structuring Devices on Listener Perceptions of Coherence in Non-Native University Teachers' Spoken Discourse." *World Englishes* 7,2: 101–10.

Uber-Grosse, Christine. 1991. "The TESOL Methods Course." *TESOL Quarterly* 25,1: 29–49.

Valdman, Albert. 1992. "Authenticity, Variation, and Communication in the Foreign Language Classroom," pp. 79–97 in Claire Kramsch and Sally McConnell-Ginet, eds., *Text and Context: Cross-Disciplinary Perspectives on Language Study.* Lexington, MA: Heath.

Watson-Gegeo, Karen. 1988. "Ethnography in ESL: Defining the Essentials." *TESOL Quarterly* 22: 575–92.

Weltens, B., Kees de Bot, and Theo van Els. 1986. *Language Attrition in Progress.* Dordrecht, Neth.: Foris.

Willett, Jerri. 1982. "New Methods within an Old Tradition." *Journal of Intercultural Studies* 3: 19–38.

————. 1987. "Contrasting Acculturation Patterns of Two Non-English-Speaking Preschoolers," pp. 79–84 in Henry T. Trueba, ed., *Success or Failure: Learning and the Language Minority Student.* New York: Newbury House.

Wolfson, Nessa. 1989. *Perspectives: Sociolinguistics and TESOL.* New York: Newbury House.

Wong Fillmore, Lily. 1976. "The Second Time Around: Cognitive and Social Strategies in Second Language Acquisition." Unpublished Ph.D. diss., Stanford Univ.

————. 1992. "Learning a Language from Learners," pp. 46–66 in Claire Kramsch and Sally McConnell-Ginet, eds., *Text and Context: Cross-Disciplinary Perspectives on Language Study.* Lexington, MA: Heath.

Yamada, Haru. 1990. "Topic Management and Turn Distribution in Business Meetings: American versus Japanese Strategies." *Text* 10,3: 271–95.

Zamel, Vivian. 1983. "The Composing Processes of Advanced ESL Students: Six Case Studies." *TESOL Quarterly* 17: 165–87.

2

Generative Research on Second-Language Acquisition[1]

Lynn Eubank
Maria Beck
University of North Texas

These are exciting times in generative research on second/foreign language (L2) acquisition, and the reason is clear: Compared to our understanding of learner language of just ten years ago, our present understanding has become far more precise, and the perspectives being explored are now much more refined, with research designed to yield fundamental insights into L2 acquisition and L2 knowledge. We are, nonetheless, far from understanding as much as we would like to: L2 knowledge and L2 acquisition, while perhaps less elusive than before, are still mysterious, and from that alone, one would be wise to be cautious about pedagogical advice offered on the basis of current generative work on L2 acquisition.

Several fundamental assumptions and insights about native-language knowledge form the starting point for generative research on L2; we therefore begin by reviewing these assumptions and developing a sketch of the current understanding in generative circles of what it means to "know" a language. In the second section we turn to generative research on L2 knowledge and acquisition. We will not, however, attempt to provide a comprehensive review of this research. Our intention instead is primarily to profile some of the specifically L2 questions that have been pursued as well as some of the research means that have been employed to answer these questions.

Lynn Eubank (Ph.D., University of Texas at Austin) is a faculty member in the linguistics division of the Department of English at the University of North Texas. Most of his publications have dealt with the role of Universal Grammar in L2 acquisition; his current interests include dysphasia and neurobiology.

Maria Beck (Ph.D., University of Texas at Austin) is a faculty member in the German division of the Department of Foreign Languages at the University of North Texas. Beck's interests include L2 teacher education and training as well as the conceptual underpinnings of L2 structural knowledge in generative theory.

Native-Language Knowledge and Acquisition

The first-order assumption of generative research is this: We draw a distinction between knowledge of linguistic structure and its use. By knowledge, we mean not the kind of structural knowledge that the native speaker gains as a result of formal classroom instruction, but rather a far more fundamental and completely implicit kind of knowledge, a kind shared not just by educated native speakers, but by *all* native speakers, regardless of educational preparation. We can observe the manifestations of this implicit structural knowledge in sentences like those in 1 through 3 below, where native speakers uniformly regard the *a* sentences as structurally more well-formed than their *b* counterparts. (Following standard practice in linguistics, we mark the structurally ill-formed sentences with an asterisk.)

1. a. Where did you say who went?
    b. *Who did you say where went?
2. a. Where did you say that Mary went?
    b. *Where did you note the fact that Mary went?
3. a. John said that Jane hurt herself.
    b. *Jane said that John hurt herself.

The object of inquiry in generative research on acquisition is the implicit structural knowledge of native speakers and how they come to possess it.

It is worthwhile to reflect on just how special the acquisition of such implicit structural knowledge is. The basic assumption is that *all* children *inevitably* acquire this sort of implicit knowledge. This feat is thus of an entirely different order from learning in domains where parental or institutional instruction is involved (history, reading, math, etc.) and calls for an explanation of a different order as well. Indeed, as Hornstein and Lightfoot (1981) as well as Wexler and Culicover (1980) pointed out some time ago, in spite of the diversity of environmental conditions in which children find themselves, and in spite of the diverse communicative needs or motivations of children themselves, the acquisition of adultlike implicit structural knowledge proceeds without disruption. As Steve Pinker of MIT once quipped, the only sure-fire way to stop the acquisition of this kind of knowledge is to grow the child in a barrel.

Before turning to an explanation for this special kind of acquisition, it is important to approach one other facet of it, namely, the interplay between the child's inherent learning capacity and the child's linguistic environment, that is, between nature and nurture. In this regard, the crucial insight of modern generative theory is this: That which requires explanation is not only that children inevitably come to possess implicit structural knowledge; but also that they come to know more implicit structural knowledge than was provided in their acquisitional environment in the first place. The common ethological term employed to describe this condition is *underdetermination*.

It would be unwise to let this idea pass without further explanation. What needs to be explained here is in just what way learners know more than they were exposed to. To do this, we require a more careful examination of linguistic nature and nurture: what children's exposure to linguistic information includes during the course of acquisition, and precisely what implicit structural knowledge they come to possess.

Linguistic Nurture: What Children Are Exposed To

Serious examination of children's nurturing experience began in the late 1960s and early 1970s (see, e.g., Brown and Hanlon 1970; Slobin 1972). In such discussions, it is commonplace to speak of different types of linguistic data that the child's nurturing exposure to language might be said to include. Several types of data can be distinguished, among them, negative data, indirect data, and direct data.

Negative Data.

Negative data provide straightforward information that shows the learner the ill-formedness of a linguistic structure. An example of this type would be a correction to the child's utterance by some adult caretaker, usually a parent. The question is, are negative data required for the acquisition of implicit structural knowledge? As Pinker (e.g., 1989) has argued, the inevitability of acquisition across children offers some important clues: Since all children come to possess the relevant kind of implicit knowledge, negative data, if they were required for the acquisition of such knowledge, would have to be not only equally and unambiguously available to all children, but also utilized by all children. If it can be shown, however, that such negative data are not uniformly available and employed, then one would have reason to believe that negative data are not essential to language acquisition.

As one might expect, these considerations have been researched extensively. Some have argued that negative data do indeed play a role in acquisition. (See, e.g., Bohannon and Stanowicz 1988; Bohannon, MacWhinney, and Snow 1990.) As Pinker (1989) and Marcus (1993) show, however, none of these studies has been able to demonstrate that negative data meet the requirements mentioned above. In other words, negative data are neither equally nor unambiguously available to all children; and even when such information is available, children are notorious for ignoring it. For this reason, the premise in generative research on acquisition is that negative data play no necessary role in the acquisition of implicit structural knowledge.

Indirect Data.

The idea behind indirect data is that children would notice what adult speakers do *not* do. That is, children notice that exemplars of the particular structures they themselves produce do not occur in their linguistic environment. For instance, children at an early stage of acquisition often omit the third-person singular agreement marker, saying "daddy go" instead of "daddy goes." The question is, how do children come to know that this agreement marker is obligatory in English? One way that children might learn the obligatory nature of the agreement marker would be simply to notice that adult speakers do not omit it in their speech; that is, that their linguistic environment (nurture) includes no instances of "daddy go." From this realization, children might conclude that their own more inconsistent use is incorrect.

This possibility is workable in principle, but it also requires some very strong assumptions about children's memory capacities. Thus, for children to notice the presence/absence of particular structural arrangements, they would have to keep a running record of these arrangements over a fairly long period of time, noting the rate of use or nonuse in the adult model. In other words, children would require memory for particular structures. This possibility is, however, difficult to maintain because even adults, with their superior cognitive capacity, are not particularly good at remembering the structure of particular sentences they have seen or heard. (Consider, for example, the difficulty one might have in trying to recall the exact wording of the six example sentences shown in 1–3 above.) In other words, indirect data are, in principle, possible as a source of linguistic knowledge, but they also presuppose an extraordinary ability on the part of children. Rather than assuming such an ability, acquisition researchers working within the generative framework exclude indirect data as well from their considerations (see, e.g., Pinker 1989).

Positive Data.

So we turn to positive data, which amount to nothing more than simple exposure to linguistic utterances (i.e., phrases and clauses) in context. All children experience this most basic kind of linguistic exposure. Moreover, it turns out that if children are not exposed to this fundamental kind of data, then acquisition of implicit structural knowledge is indeed seriously impaired. The well-known stories of "wild children" who never come to possess the requisite kind of linguistic knowledge have been substantiated by more systematic research on tragic cases like that of Genie, who was not exposed to language until after puberty and who has never developed the relevant kind of implicit structural knowledge (Curtiss 1977, 1980).

Linguistic Nature: What Children Know

Positive data are thus assumed to comprise the linguistic nurturing that is necessary for acquisition, and children come to possess implicit structural knowledge of their native language on the basis of this kind of exposure. More careful deliberation of this very point, though, brings out the problem of underdetermination, that is, that children come to know more than they were exposed to.

Consider again the example sentences 1–3 above, repeated for convenience here.

1. a. Where did you say who went?
   b. *Who did you say where went?
2. a. Where did you say that Mary went?
   b. *Where did you note the fact that Mary went?
3. a. John said that Jane hurt herself.
   b. *Jane said that John hurt herself.

What is it in 1–3 that children come to possess, that native speakers know? It is that the *a* sentences are well-formed in comparison to their *b* counterparts. In other words, children come to possess knowledge of structural well-formedness. How is it, though, that they come to possess this knowledge? One might imagine that children notice that their caretakers (e.g., their parents) do not use structures like those illustrated in the *b* sentences above, and, for this reason, that they do not use such structures themselves. Note, though, that this possibility amounts to the use of indirect data, which we have excluded as a necessary part of children's nurturing experience. Yet another possibility would be that children actually produce the ill-formed *b* sentences during the course of acquisition, and that they come to know the ill-formedness of these sentences because their parents correct them. There are two problems with this possibility. First, this explanation amounts to the use of negative data, which we have also excluded as a necessary component of exposure. Second and more interestingly, the extensive data now available on native-language development (e.g., through the CHILDES database; see MacWhinney 1991) demonstrate that while children produce many structures that are different from the adult model, they do not produce the kinds of ill-formed structures shown in the *b* examples above. Moreover, as a class, the "errors" that children do make turn out to be sanctioned in one or another of the world's languages: The missing subject-verb agreement marker ("daddy go") mentioned above, for example, is standard in languages like Swedish or Chinese, which do not have subject-verb agreement markers.

In the end, we are left again with positive data, and on the basis of exposure to this minimal kind of data, children come to know, for example, that the *b* sentences are structurally ill-formed. Crucially, positive data do not include information on ill-formedness, and so the facts requiring explanation change somewhat: Children come to possess implicit structural knowledge for which there is no model or precedent whatsoever in their linguistic environment. In sum, then, examination of the nurturing environment and of the nature of linguistic knowledge brings out the problem of underdetermination: Children come to possess more implicit structural knowledge than they are exposed to.

Solving the Underdetermination Problem

Obviously, we need an explanation for how children's implicit structural knowledge can uniformly exceed their linguistic exposure. Just as obviously, that explanation will not be one that invokes characteristics of the environment, of linguistic nurture. In other words, whatever explanation is proposed must be one that evokes the child's inherent learning capacity, the child's mind. Various proposals in the literature seek to provide such explanations. Some would argue that the child employs neo-Piagetian concepts like adjacency or simple cognitive strategies like generalization and so on (see, e.g, O'Grady 1987), but these kinds of proposals have been shown in fact to offer little explanation and often wind up predicting more errors on the part of the child than are actually made. Such proposals, moreover, generally fare very poorly when applied to the acquisition of languages other than English. (For an extensive discussion, see, e.g., Pinker 1984, 1989.)

We thus come to the explanation proposed in modern generative studies of acquisition: Children inevitably come to possess more implicit structural knowledge than they are exposed to because they are antecedently or innately equipped with most of the relevant kind of knowledge (see, e.g., Goodluck 1991; Atkinson 1992). That is, their prelinguistic endowment includes implicit and specifically linguistic knowledge, and it is this knowledge that stands behind the gross facts of language acquisition. While the concrete details of this endowment are still a matter of very intensive research, it is also fair to say that the last decade of research has provided an amazingly rich and intricate map of this innate capacity (see, e.g., Haegeman 1991; Napoli 1993)—and that this research has succeeded in providing precisely detailed explanations for the first-language (L1) acquisition of implicit structural knowledge. (See contributions in, e.g., Roeper and Williams 1987; Frazier and de Villiers 1990; Meisel 1992; Weissenborn, Goodluck, and Roeper 1992; Hoekstra and Schwartz 1993.)

There is, then, good reason for excitement and optimism among researchers doing generative work in L1 and L2 acquisition. But before turning to generative work on L2 acquisition in particular, a final note concerning the linguistic endowment is important. The general view among theoretical linguists is that this endowment is both specifically linguistic and autonomous (see, e.g., Lightfoot 1982; Newmeyer 1983). That is, this innate capacity is task-specific: It can operate only on structural data and on nothing else. Furthermore, it is not some subcomponent of general cognitive ability. Indeed, the very meaning of the autonomy thesis is that the linguistic endowment is entirely separate from other cognitive capacities, that it functions independently. We will not attempt to provide substantive evidence for this view here. Suffice it to note in passing that humans can suffer pathological dissociations in which the language capacity is severely impaired even while other cognitive factors such as intelligence and emotional well-being are spared. (See, e.g., Clahsen 1988; Gopnik 1990a, 1990b; Leonard et al. 1992; as well as the review of studies in Pinker and Prince 1991.)

Research on L2 Acquisition

Applying the insights from native language knowledge, we turn to generative work on L2 acquisition, where the investigation of the role played by the specifically linguistic endowment has become a virtual lightning rod, attracting intensive research. Before examining the kinds of studies that the idea has engendered, however, it is important to consider the work that preceded it in the 1970s. During this early period, research on L2 acquisition was often considered to be a branch of language pedagogy or applied linguistics; generative research on L2 in particular had yet to coalesce into an independent discipline. Nonetheless, the contributions of early work to present-day thought should not be underestimated. For a detailed overview of this early research, see surveys of general L2 research like Ellis (1986) or Larsen-Freeman and Long (1991). The following discussion will include only a sketch of the ideas, discoveries, and means of analysis that substantially influenced present-day thinking in generative research on L2 acquisition.

Early Second-Language Research

Interlanguage Hypothesis.

Perhaps the most important contribution of the early period was conceptual in nature. Faced with the failure of structuralist-behaviorist theory to explain learner behavior, S. Pit Corder (1967) conceived of an idea that fundamentally altered views on L2 learning. Corder proposed that L2 learning is not fundamentally different from L1 learning, and that the errors L2 learners make are manifestations of a developing L2 system. Repeated independently in work by Selinker (1972), this fundamental idea came to be known as the interlanguage hypothesis: The L2 learner has a developing interlanguage system that can be understood as a series of interim grammars that differ from the grammars both of the learner's native language and of the target language. The idea was nothing short of revolutionary for the time; indeed, it would not be unfair to say that it set the stage for nearly all subsequent research in L2 development, generative or otherwise.

Acquisition Order Studies.

In addition to new conceptualizations, early research contributed empirical findings as well. One group of studies in particular focused on the order in which L2 learners master a series of morphemes. For example, inspired by research on the L1 development of English (e.g., Brown 1973), Dulay and Burt (1973, 1974) and Bailey, Madden, and Krashen (1974) examined the order of mastery for certain English functional morphemes (e.g., prepositions, articles, "endings" for agreement and tense) by learners with different native languages, different kinds of exposure (e.g., classroom versus informal), and different ages (children and adults). These particular studies employed cross-sectional designs, in which a large number of subjects were examined across a range of proficiency levels, yielding a small number of subjects for each level of proficiency. Each L2 subject was tested only one time, the result being an aggregate picture of development.

The findings of these studies were very consistent: Nativelike mastery of the morphemes emerges in a predictable order. Moreover, the order of mastery was related neither to the nature of the learning environment (i.e., classroom versus nonclassroom learning), nor to the learners' mother tongue, nor to the learners' age. On the other hand, the L2 order was also somewhat different from the order found for L1 development.

To be sure, the early work on acquisition orders did attract a certain amount of criticism (for an overview, see, e.g., Larsen-Freeman and Long 1991). For some time, for example, it was felt possible that the Dulay and Burt findings in particular may have been an artifact of their data elicitation technique. In their studies, Dulay and Burt employed the Bilingual Syntax Measure (BSM), which involves a series of carefully designed pictures and corresponding questions to which individual subjects respond. In this regard, Porter (1977) charged that the apparent ordering of morphemes in the Dulay and Burt studies was not indicative of acquisitional facts, but only an epiphenomenon resulting from their use of the BSM.

The early morpheme-order research attracted a good number of follow-up studies that employed different elicitation techniques (e.g., spontaneous speech, free composition) and the inclusion of subjects with more varied native languages, learning environments, and ages. Some of these follow-up studies also employed not cross-sectional, but longitudinal designs, in which the language development of a small number of subjects is tracked over a long period of time, resulting in robust data on individuals. Indeed, so numerous were the morpheme-order follow-up studies that, according to Krashen (1985), major journals became reluctant to accept them for publication; Larsen-Freeman and Long (1991) count their number at "at least fifty" (p. 91). More importantly, though, the results of the follow-up studies remained consistent with the original findings: The functional morphemes do indeed appear to be acquired in a predictable order, and this order is not related to how old learners are, what native languages are involved, whether the L2 is a foreign language or a second language, whether it is learned in a classroom or not—or, contra Porter (1977), what data elicitation technique is employed.

Clearly, the acquisition-order results were surprising and very thought-provoking; they demonstrated that something more was going on in learners' heads than what simple theories could account for. In this early period, however, explanations for such orders tended toward the metaphorical. The acquisition-order data were said, for example, to show the presence of a process called "creative construction" (Dulay and Burt 1977) or the influence of a "language acquisition device" (Krashen 1982), the internal workings of which were completely enigmatic (see, e.g., the discussion in Dulay, Burt, and Krashen 1981; Krashen 1981). Indeed, it was not until the advent of far more robust generative theory in very recent times that well-motivated explanations for the orders could even be envisioned (Beck and Eubank 1993; Liceras and Zobl 1993). But the ultimate failure of early acquisition-order research to provide a coherent explanation for the order was not the only drawback of this research tradition. In addition, these studies measured only the order in which morphemes are mastered to a nativelike level, and, in doing so, took no account of the interim steps occurring prior to the acquisition of the nativelike form. In other words, as Wode et al. (1978) pointed out, the acquisition-order studies completely ignored the transitional systems of learners, their developing interlanguage grammars.

Developmental Sequence Studies.

Other early L2 studies assessed interlanguage more directly through the examination of evolving patterns of word order during interim stages of development. These so-called developmental sequence studies showed that there are certain parallels between L1 and L2 acquisition. For example, Ravem (1970) found that the interim word-order patterns in the L2 English of Norwegian-speaking children are not substantively different from the interim patterns found by Klima and Bellugi (1966) for the L1 development of English. (For summaries of other such studies, see Larsen-Freeman and Long 1991.) In addition, this type of research also demonstrated that interim stages of L2 word-order development are not determined by the age of learners (e.g., Pienemann 1981) or by the difference between second-language and foreign-language environments (e.g., Ellis 1989).

On the negative side, of course, early explanations offered to account for such developmental patterns seem, in hindsight, often *ad hoc* and without independent motivation (see, e.g., Eubank 1990). On the positive side, however, these studies brought about, in the 1970s and early 1980s, the large-scale collection of "raw" data on L2 learner language. It was in this period, for example, that Cazden et al. (1975) established the "Harvard" corpus, with longitudinal data on the L2 acquisition of English by native speakers of Spanish. It was also during this period that Jürgen Meisel and his collaborators in the project Zweitsprachenerwerb Italienischer und Spanischer Arbeiter (ZISA; see, e.g., Meisel, Clahsen, and Pienemann 1981; Clahsen, Meisel, and Pienemann 1983; Clahsen 1984) employed combined cross-sectional and longitudinal designs to establish the characteristics of German word-order development by native speakers of Romance languages. These and similar large-scale corpora have served as the crucial basis for many of the more detailed analyses of development in recent generative research on L2 acquisition. For example, Hilles (1986, 1991) and Lakshmanan (1991) look at data from the "Harvard" corpus while Clahsen and Muysken (e.g., 1986), Schwartz (1991), Meisel (e.g., 1991), and Eubank (e.g., 1992, 1993b) all examine data from the ZISA project.

Generative Research on L2 Acquisition

As the previous discussion indicates, the early period contributed not only the interlanguage hypothesis itself, but also the first empirical indications that the L2 acquisition of structural knowledge in some sense parallels L1 acquisition, that something indeed very special is going on. What was missing, then, was a theory that could explain these ideas and findings and that would show where research should proceed next. As Gregg (in press) and Eubank (in press a) point out, the initial impetus for the development of generative research on L2 acquisition as an independent discipline was the major conceptual shift brought about by Chomsky's proposal in 1981 of Government and Binding (GB) theory.[2] With GB, Chomsky abandoned the rule-based format of traditional generative-transformational grammar (e.g., Chomsky 1965), replacing it with the far more abstract, yet conceptually better motivated, principles and parameters of linguistic structure. Again, this chapter is not the proper forum to attempt a precise characterization of the GB framework; standard textbooks on recent generative syntax such as Haegeman (1991) or Napoli (1993) supply this type of information. What is important is quite simply that the new framework provided L1 and L2 acquisition researchers with explicit and falsifiable details on what we have been calling the autonomous linguistic endowment. In addition, it firmly established once and for all a common label for the endowment: Universal Grammar or simply UG.

Research Questions.

GB theory was about as close to an overnight success as one can expect of a theoretical enterprise. And because the earlier generative-transformational framework had shown itself to be difficult to connect with a theory of acquisition (see, e.g., Atkinson 1992), GB was especially welcome among generative researchers as well. For the case of L2 acquisition in particular, however, the GB framework brought up fundamental questions that are still subject to intensive investigation.

Consider again the findings of early L2 research, which seem to indicate that something special is going on in learners' heads, possibly the operation of some "creative construction" process that is involved in both L1 and L2 acquisition. Note, however, that the L2 data and resulting conclusions differ fundamentally from data and conclusions discussed earlier for L1 development. There we pointed out the underdetermination problem and how it led to the innateness solution. It is important to note that the early L2 research discussed above was not designed to evaluate whether L2 knowledge is underdetermined by the learning environment, and so we simply did not know whether L2 learners come to possess knowledge that surpasses what could be gained from the environment alone. Research that could shed light on this possibility is of crucial importance, because if it could be shown that implicit L2 knowledge is not underdetermined by exposure to the L2, then one could reasonably argue that L2 research need not concern itself with Universal Grammar.

Another question about L2 acquisition is based on a simple, yet fundamental, insight. Irrespective of the kind of exposure to the L2 (e.g., informal versus formal classroom) and irrespective of the length of exposure (e.g., years of instruction), L2 learners, especially adults, generally do not attain a state of implicit structural knowledge that is indistinguishable from that of the native speaker. Selinker (1972), for example, suggests that up to 95 percent of learners do not succeed in this way. In light of the logic behind the idea of innateness, this simple insight gains tremendous importance. Once again, the logic is based on the realization that all L1 learners inevitably come to possess more implicit structural knowledge than they are exposed to. The stark contrast between the inevitable success of attaining adultlike structural knowledge in L1 acquisition and the general failure to attain it in L2 acquisition thus yields a possibility that connects directly with the possibility mentioned above: Perhaps Universal Grammar does not guide L2 acquisition. Indeed, in a manuscript widely circulated in the research community in 1985, Robert Bley-Vroman (1990) argued that the mental mechanisms standing behind L2 acquisition, especially adult L2 acquisition, are perhaps fundamentally different from the UG-based mental mechanisms involved in L1 acquisition.

Following this line of thinking, the agenda for much subsequent generative research on L2 was clear: Do L2 learners come to know more than what they could have gained from exposure alone? What explains the general failure of L2 learners to reach a state of implicit structural knowledge that is indistinguishable from that of native speakers? Ultimately, these questions boil down to this: Do L2 learners have access to Universal Grammar, or is implicit structural knowledge of an L2 necessarily of an entirely different kind, perhaps more comparable to the pathological state of the "wild child" Genie? These, then, are some of the principal questions that have been pursued in recent generative research on L2 acquisition. Of course, this introduction is not the proper forum to attempt a comprehensive discussion of L2 research bearing on these questions; for that type of information, we recommend several sources at the conclusion of the chapter. For the present, what we provide instead is a more limited review of means of analysis, ways of looking at the problem, and, of course, selected results.

UG-Access Studies.

Perhaps the most widely known generative research on L2 has concentrated on whether learners' implicit structural knowledge of the L2 is underdetermined by their exposure, in other words, whether they have "access" to Universal Grammar, allowing them to know more than they were exposed to. Generally speaking, these studies have employed broadly similar data elicitation techniques, namely, acceptability judgment tasks. For this task, the researcher constructs a series of sentences that exhibit UG-possible versus UG-impossible contrasts much like those in the *a* versus *b* examples in 1–3 above. (The series of sentences is, of course, much longer and includes distractors.) Subjects (L2 learners and native-speaking controls) are then asked to determine whether such sentences are possible or impossible, and results are tallied on the basis of these responses. In addition, researchers collect background data on, for example, type of exposure to the L2, length of exposure, age, and so forth.

Such a portrayal masks the complexity of these experiments, however. The question is, if L2 speakers judge test sentences in a way that matches that of the native-speaking controls, where did they obtain this knowledge? Of course, the goal of such studies is to assess the involvement of UG, so if L2 speakers do judge sentences like those in 1–3 in a way that does not differ from the judgments of native speakers, then one might conclude that their knowledge is based on UG. L2 speakers, however, have a source of knowledge that native-speaking controls do not have, namely, their mother tongue. For instance, Korean-speaking L2 learners of English might well be tempted to employ their implicit knowledge of Korean to judge the acceptability of English test sentences. Moreover, many L2 speakers have gone through years of formal instruction, and in this type of task they may well attempt to use in their judgments the knowledge they gained from their experience with formal instruction. Thus, the Korean-speaking learners of English might be expected to attempt to perform acceptability judgments of the English test sentences on the basis of the instruction they received in their English classes.

Clearly, such factors have the potential of compromising the results of otherwise well-intentioned research. Those engaging in this type of research have, therefore, attempted to design experiments that control for such confounding factors. Consider, for example, the study reported by Bley-Vroman, Felix, and Ioup (1988), who employed L2 speakers of English whose native language was Korean. Bley-Vroman, Felix, and Ioup developed test sentences not unlike the ones shown in 4a and b below.

4.   a.   Who did Mary say that John will visit?
     b.   *Who did Mary wonder whether John will visit?
     c.   Mary wondered whether John will visit who?

As shown by the well-formedness of 4c, it is the placement or fronting of the WH-word *who* at the beginning of 4b (technically known as WH-movement) that causes the sentence to be ill-formed. It is important to note that languages that do *not* employ WH-movement form questions with a meaning analogous to 4b by leaving the WH-word in a position analogous to that shown in 4c. Korean happens to be one of the languages that does not employ WH-movement, and it is for this reason that Bley-Vroman, Felix, and Ioup chose L2 speakers of English with Korean as a native language. Would these subjects notice the contrast between sentences like 4a and 4b? Obviously, in attempting to judge such sentences, they could not use their implicit structural knowledge of Korean, since Korean does not have an analogous structure. Moreover, it is very doubtful that they could employ knowledge gained from their experience of formal classroom instruction in English since the instructional experience (e.g., rules and practice on question formation) does not include information relevant to sentences like 4b. (If they were to use this kind of knowledge, then one would expect them to judge both 4a and 4b as acceptable, since both correctly follow pedagogical rules on WH-word selection and fronting and on English do-support.) In other words, to judge the acceptability of sentences like 4b, these subjects' only source of internal knowledge would be Universal Grammar, that is, if they have access to this source.

The findings of such UG-access studies are at once interesting and puzzling. Consider first, though, potential experimental outcomes and the conclusions that one might draw from them. If L2 speakers perform on these tasks essentially as native speakers do, then one could conclude that UG does underlie L2 knowledge; if, on the other hand, L2 speakers should perform more or less randomly on such tasks, yielding "chance" performance, then one could conclude that UG does not underlie L2 knowledge. The results of such experiments have shown, however, that L2 speakers generally perform significantly worse than native-speaking controls, yet significantly better than chance. The initial judgment studies of, for example, Bley-Vroman, Felix, and Ioup (1988) and White (e.g., 1988) have been repeated many times, with some yielding L2 judgments that more closely match those of native speakers (e.g., White and Genesee 1992; Birdsong 1992; Beck 1992) and others yielding L2 judgments that are closer to chance (e.g., Schachter 1989). Seen broadly, the results of such studies seem only to have substantiated the original, guarded conclusion of Bley-Vroman, Felix, and Ioup: "adults appear to have some sort of access to knowledge of UG, and this knowledge is used in the development of foreign language competence" (1988: 27).

Much as one might expect, such UG-access studies have been subject to a number of methodological criticisms (for discussion, see, e.g., Birdsong 1989; White 1989). There is, however, also a conceptual problem with studies like those of Bley-Vroman, Felix, and Ioup (1988) or Schachter (1989), a problem that is similar in kind to one of the shortcomings of the acquisition-order studies discussed above. Recall that the acquisition-order studies measured only when the various morphemes are mastered to a nativelike level, hence ignoring the learners' interim systems, their interlanguage. As Schwartz (1993) points out, the same comment applies to the UG-access studies. In these studies, the test sentences that are provided to subjects for judgment show contrasts in acceptability; crucially, however, these particular contrasts will obtain if and only if the L2 speaker performing the judgment has a grammar that is, in the relevant respects, identical to that of a native speaker. The native-speaking controls thus perform on the task much as the researcher expects, but the L2 speakers do not. But should they? In fact, if the interlanguage hypothesis is correct, then L2 speakers have an interlanguage grammar that may well yield judgments that differ from those of the native speaker. In this sense, some of the judgment studies may have misconceptualized the developing nature of implicit structural knowledge on the part of L2 learners, and, if so, this misconception would undermine the conclusions one could otherwise draw from experimental outcomes indicating a difference between native and nonnative speakers.

Studies on UG-Constrained Interlanguage.

Studies examining the UG-access question such as Bley-Vroman, Felix, and Ioup (1988) have by no means been the only ones conducted in generative research on L2. In contrast to the UG-access studies discussed in the previous section, other generative work has focused directly on developmental phenomena, thereby avoiding the conceptual pitfall pointed out above. In other words, these studies have attempted to assess interlanguage itself, capturing the developing L2 systems "in action."

Many generative studies of interlanguage have also employed experimental designs in which groups of L2 learners and native-speaking controls are asked to perform in carefully fashioned situations. Some of these studies (e.g., White 1991, 1992a) have employed varieties of the acceptability judgment task described above, but other designs and elicitation techniques have been employed as well. For example, in addition to judgment tasks, White (1991, 1992a) also elicits interlanguage judgments through the use of relatively simple sentence-manipulation tasks (e.g., asking subjects to rewrite sentences they do not find acceptable). By contrast, subjects in the experiments reported by Bley-Vroman and Masterson (1988) and Eubank (in press b) are not asked to perform judgments or to manipulate sentences in any way. The essential idea behind their experiments is that, all other factors (e.g., sentence length, vocabulary) held equal, sentences that violate UG constraints take longer to read than sentences that do not. To exploit this idea, these researchers employ computers to present sentences on a video monitor. The subject reads from the monitor and presses a key to go on to another sentence. For each sentence so presented, an internal clock in the computer begins when a sentence is displayed and stops when the subject presses a key. The resulting measurements (in milliseconds) comprise the data these researchers examine to make determinations about subjects' implicit structural knowledge. Again, these measurements are not based on subjects' manipulations or judgments of test sentences; the only factor involved is how long it takes subjects to read test sentences.

The elicitation techniques described above all involve experimental designs, which, again, involve the use of groups of L2 subjects and native-speaking controls. But experimental designs are not the only means by which generative research in L2 is carried out. Other generative studies of interlanguage examine spontaneous production data such as those from the "Harvard" and ZISA projects (see references above).

It is worthwhile to consider in somewhat more detail the logical thinking behind these nonexperimental studies. To assess the role played by UG, these studies have taken advantage of the explicit and falsifiable detail of recent theory. In languages like French or German, for example, traditional descriptive grammars inform us that inflected verbs have a location in sentences that differs from that of uninflected verbs such as infinitives or past participles. Recent generative theory has shown, however, that inflection itself actually *causes* inflected and uninflected verbs to appear in different locations (see, e.g., Pollock 1989; Chomsky 1991). In other words, UG is structured so that the acquisition of inflection forces verbs to appear in different locations within sentences. This is not only a falsifiable prediction, but one that can be tested against the spontaneous data from longitudinal corpora: At the very point in time at which the learner acquires the relevant inflection, one should be able to observe a change in verb placement characteristics. If the causal relation can be observed in the data, then one might claim that UG does indeed underlie L2 acquisition; if, however, the spontaneous data show no indication of a temporal connection between the acquisition of inflection and verb placement, then one might conclude that UG does not constrain L2 acquisition.

Studies testing the highly specific predictions of recent theoretical work have been numerous; however, the results of these studies have not yielded uncontested evidence for a role of UG in L2 development. For example, a number of studies have examined the so-called "null-subject parameter," which divides languages into those that require grammatical subjects (e.g., French, German, English) and those that allow grammatical subjects to be omitted (e.g., Spanish, Italian, Chinese). While some of these studies have suggested a guiding role for UG in L2 development (e.g., White 1985; Hilles 1986; Lakshmanan 1991), others have suggested that UG plays no role at all, at least among adult L2 learners (Hilles 1991). In a similar vein, a number of studies have focused on verb placement in the L2 acquisition of Germanic languages like German and Dutch.

Again, results have been somewhat mixed: Some indicate the presence of UG (e.g., duPlessis et al. 1987; Tomaselli and Schwartz 1990; Schwartz 1991; Eubank 1992); others suggest just the opposite (e.g., Clahsen and Muysken 1986, 1989; Meisel 1991).

Generative Perspectives on Transfer.

It is well known that learners sometimes employ structures from their native languages in the L2. The problem here is the term *sometimes*. As Dulay, Burt, and Krashen (1981) made clear, if it is difficult to determine that transfer has in fact taken place, it is even more difficult to discern a theory for L2 that predicts in advance when transfer will take place. Of course, a good deal of general L2 research has concentrated on this problem (see Gass and Selinker 1983 and 1992 and references cited therein); needless to say, generative research on L2 has concentrated on the problem as well.

The general idea behind the generative perspective is that it is not surface language patterns that transfer, but particular choices of parameterized principles (White 1992b). To understand this notion, consider a simple example first. One of the principles of UG specifies the order of, for example, verbs and their object complements with a parameter having two options, "left" and "right." Hence, Japanese has the order OV (object-verb) because it chooses the parametric option "right"; by contrast, English has the order VO (verb-object) because it chooses the parametric option "left." What occurs when a speaker of English learns Japanese as L2? The generative view of transfer would be that a learner initially employs the parametric option relevant to the native language, in this case, "left." As a result, we might expect the English-speaking learner of Japanese initially to produce VO (rather than OV) utterances.

The simple OV-VO example above does not, however, do justice to the full complexity of the potential effects of transferred UG parameter settings. For instance, it may well be the case that transferring certain parameter settings from the native language to the L2 can cause severe impediments to acquisition. To see this, consider the interpretation of reflexive anaphors such as *herself* as in 5 below; following standard practice, we annotate the sentence in 5 with subscripts to indicate coreferential elements (same subscripts) and noncoreferential elements (different subscripts).

5. Mary$_j$ knows that Jane$_i$ cut herself$_i$.

As the subscripts in 5 indicate, native speakers of English know that *herself* refers to *Jane* and that it cannot refer to *Mary*. We can say that the interpretation of such anaphors is clause-bound in that the antecedent of the anaphor (*Jane* in 5) must appear within the clause that contains the anaphor itself. This condition is shown by the brackets in 6 below.

6. Mary$_j$ knows that [Jane$_i$ cut herself$_i$].

As the brackets in 6 show, the anaphor is contained within the domain of the lower clause; for this reason, the anaphor cannot refer past this clausal domain to relate to Mary. The clause-boundedness of anaphors is not universal, however; other languages may allow the antecedents of anaphors to appear either inside or outside the clausal domain, hence allowing interpretations of sentences analogous to 5 in which *herself* can refer to either *Jane* or *Mary*.

In the generative framework, the variation on the structural domain for anaphoric interpretation is assumed to be governed by a principle of UG that has a parameter allowing for the different domains (see, e.g., Wexler and Manzini 1987). It is significant that the Wexler and Manzini analysis also makes predictions about the course of acquisition. In this regard, consider a child learning her native language. Simplifying for presentational purposes, we assume that the relevant principle allows only two parametric options for anaphors, one allowing only clause-bound (CB) interpretations and the other allowing what we can call long-distance (LD) interpretations. As explained earlier, we restrict the child to the use of only positive data; negative and indirect data are excluded. The child's task is thus to select the correct parameter setting, CB or LD, on the basis of positive data alone.

Suppose this child is learning Japanese, one of the languages that takes the LD setting. Suppose further that the child tries, at random, the CB option first. Exposure to positive data from Japanese will disconfirm this option since the child will eventually be exposed to utterances in context (i.e., positive data) that require the LD interpretation. As a result, the child can successfully turn to the LD option, which will (obviously) not be disconfirmed by positive data. However, suppose that the child is learning not Japanese, but English, which requires the CB setting. If the child's initial guess is the CB option, then all is well, since no positive data will disconfirm this choice. If the child happens to select the LD option of the parameter first, however, then we find a problem. In this case, exposure to positive data from English (e.g., sentences like 5) will not disconfirm the LD option, since this choice allows both clause-bound and long-distance interpretations. Indeed, there are no positive data from English that could disconfirm the LD choice; the only data that could disconfirm this option are negative data or indirect data, both of which we exclude from consideration. In effect, then, if the child learning English were to try the LD option before trying the CB option, she would be caught in a kind of "never-never land," unable to escape from an incorrect parametric choice. More generally, then, no matter what the correct parametric option for anaphoric interpretation is for a particular language, the only way to guarantee successful acquisition is to require all children to begin with the CB choice.

Recognizing this problem, Wexler and Manzini (1987) propose that certain parametric choices must always be tried out by the child before other options are tried. To accomplish this, they point out that such parametric choices fall into proper subsets. To see such a relationship in terms of our simple LD and CB choices above, examine 7 below.

7. LD allows both: Mary says that Jane$_i$ cut herself$_i$.
   and: Mary$_i$ says that Jane cut herself$_i$.
   CB allows only: Mary says that Jane$_i$ cut herself$_i$.

As 7 shows, LD is a superset of CD in that LD includes a possibility that CB does not. To guarantee that all children will initially try the smaller, subset choice (here, CB) before turning to the larger, superset choice (LD), Wexler and Manzini propose a UG-associated mechanism known as the Subset Principle, which imposes a restriction requiring the subset option to be tried before any superset option.

We now return to L2 acquisition and the transfer problem. Consider, as several generative researchers have (e.g., Finer 1991; Finer and Broselow 1991; Thomas 1991), learners whose native language has the superset LD option and whose L2 takes the subset CB option. If learners transfer the superset option from the native language into the L2, they will presumably be caught in the problematic "never-never land," because they will be unable to change over to the appropriate CB choice on the basis of exposure to positive data from the L2.

To test this possibility, Finer (1991) employs a design more commonly seen in L1 acquisition research. In his design, subjects are given a sentence that may have different anaphoric interpretations, depending on the exact nature of their implicit grammar. Subjects are then shown a series of pictures, each associated with one of the possible interpretations of the test sentence. They simply select the one picture they think is associated with the meaning of the test sentence, and on the basis of their responses, the researcher draws conclusions about the subjects' implicit grammar.

Using this design, Finer (1991) shows that the superset choice of the principle does apparently transfer from the native language into the L2, and, further, that his subjects have not acquired the subset choice of English. More generally, what the generative analysis has suggested here is that transfer may, in such situations, lead to impossible learning situations. As White (1989) suggests, transfer of superset parameter choices from the native language into a second language that requires the subset choice seems to preempt the function of the Subset Principle.

Generative Research on L2 and Formal Instruction.

We would be remiss if we were not to mention the generative studies that dealt with formal instruction. The goal of such work is to ascertain whether implicit L2 grammars in particular are amenable to direct manipulation through formal instruction, which we can consider to be a kind of negative evidence. Several studies have been conducted in this framework (e.g., White 1991, 1992a; Carroll and Swain 1992), though the work of White is perhaps the best-known treatment. In these works, White examines the "verb movement parameter," which determines the placement of inflected verbs relative to elements such as medial adverbs (i.e., adverbs that appear in the middle of sentences rather than in initial or final positions). English and French differ on just this parameter, as shown below in 8a-d.[3]

8. a. Marie always takes the metro.

    b. *Marie takes always the metro.

    c. *Marie toujours prend le métro.

    d. Marie prend toujours le métro.

White (1991) focuses on verb placement vis-à-vis the medial adverb among native speakers of French learning English as a foreign language. Following standard practice, White divided her subjects into several groups, including one group that received form-focused instruction and practice on adverb placement, another group that received no pedagogical treatment on adverb placement, and a group of native-speaking controls. At pretesting, the two learner groups performed equally on White's various tests: Neither group showed evidence of having acquired the English placement of the verb. After the one group received instruction and practice, White followed up with several posttests. In the initial posttests, the instructed group seemed to show significant improvement, suggesting that the implicit grammars of L2 learners, unlike those of child L1 learners, may indeed be amenable to instructional manipulation, that is, through negative evidence.

Such, at least, was the initial result. However, in a last posttest one year later to determine long-term effects, the instructed group failed to show the same improved performance on verb placement, a finding that suggested only short-term effects from external manipulation. Yet even the possibility of short-term effects from negative evidence was soon challenged. In a careful scrutiny of White's initial posttest data, Schwartz and Gubala-Ryzak (1992) showed that instruction and practice did not have any effect at all on the implicit knowledge of the instruction group—a finding that White (1992a) acknowledges. Thus, the only conclusion that can be drawn at the present time is that formal instruction and practice may have a short-term effect on the language *behavior* of L2 learners, but it remains unclear whether and how such manipulation can cause changes to learners' implicit structural *knowledge*.

Conclusion

Surveying these kinds of results, one might conclude that unequivocal findings are, at best, very slow in forthcoming. In fact, however, the conflicting results of previous studies have had a very constructive effect on the discipline, causing constant reevaluation of the questions that are asked. Indeed, in reexamining previous work and in keeping abreast of recent advances in generative thought in linguistics, L2 researchers have come to a far deeper understanding of our object of inquiry. From the perspective of present-day thinking, for example, it seems highly unlikely that UG would be either completely "accessible" to the L2 learner or completely "inaccessible," as if UG were some indivisible, monolithic entity.

And so we end where we began: For those in generative research on L2, these are exhilarating times. Our goal here was simply to convey some of this excitement: to let others know of the kinds of research questions being asked and of some of the ways in which these questions have been pursued. Of course, in such a short survey, we could not hope to present anything like a comprehensive review of research. We have not discussed, for example, some of the recent studies that question the idea that all parametric values from the native language transfer into the L2 (see, e.g., Eubank 1993a; Schwartz and Sprouse in press; Young-Scholten and Vainikka in press). Nonetheless, if we have succeeded in conveying the excitement surrounding this research, perhaps the reader will find the list of information sources in Appendix 2A to be useful as well.

Notes

1. We would like to thank Robert Bley-Vroman, Alice Omaggio Hadley, Elizabeth Martin, and two anonymous reviewers for their helpful comments. As usual, all errors are to be credited to our own account.

2. The acronym GB refers informally both to the particular theory of Universal Grammar proposed in Chomsky's (1981) *Lectures on Government and Binding* and to the research tradition in linguistics that followed the publication of this volume. Because of this ambiguity, some favor referring to the research tradition more neutrally as "Principles and Parameters" (P&P) theory. For present purposes, we will maintain the common (though ambiguous) term, GB theory.
3. Some readers may be familiar with White's earlier treatment of adverb placement among native speakers of French learning English as L2. (See White 1989 for a review.) There, White suggested that the French-English data (see 8a-d in the text) fall into a subset-superset relation and, hence, that the Subset Principle may be involved. The problem is that it is not clear that these data do in fact fall into a proper subset relation (see, e.g., Eubank 1993b). Regardless, the more recent analysis in terms of verb movement supersedes the older analysis and does not implicate the Subset Principle.

References

Generative Research on Second-Language Acquisition

Atkinson, Martin. 1992. *Children's Syntax.* Oxford, Eng.: Blackwell.

Bailey, Nathalie, Carolyn Madden, and Stephen Krashen. 1974. "Is There a 'Natural Sequence' in Adult Second Language Learning?" *Language Learning* 24,2: 235–43.

Beck, Maria. 1992. "Grammaticality Judgments: What Subjects Could Have Told Us If We'd Only Bothered to Ask." Paper presented at the 12th Second Language Research Forum, Michigan State Univ.

———, and Lynn Eubank. 1993. "Are There Rules in L2?" Paper presented at the 13th Second Language Research Forum, Univ. of Pittsburgh and Carnegie-Mellon Univ.

Birdsong, David. 1989. *Metalinguistic Performance and Interlinguistic Competence.* Berlin, Ger.: Springer Verlag.

———. 1992. "Ultimate Attainment in Second Language Acquisition." *Language* 68,4: 706–55.

Bley-Vroman, Robert. 1990. "The Logical Problem of Foreign Language Learning." *Linguistic Analysis* 20: 3–49.

———, Sascha Felix, and Georgette Ioup. 1988. "The Accessibility of Universal Grammar in Adult Language Learning." *Second Language Research* 4,1: 1–32.

———, and Deborah Masterson. 1988. "Reaction Times as a Supplement to Grammaticality Judgments in the Investigation of Second Language Learners' Competence." *University of Hawai'i Working Papers in ESL* 8,2: 207–37.

Bohannon, John Neil, B. MacWhinney, and C. Snow. 1990. "No Negative Evidence Revisited: Beyond Learnability, or Who Has to Prove What to Whom?" *Developmental Psychology* 26: 221–26.

Bohannon, John Neil, and Laura Stanowicz. 1988. "The Issue of Negative Evidence: Adult Responses to Children's Language Errors." *Developmental Psychology* 24: 684–89.

Brown, Roger. 1973. *A First Language.* Cambridge, MA: Harvard Univ. Press.

———, and C. Hanlon. 1970. "Derivational Complexity and Order of Acquisition in Child Speech," in J. R. Hayes, ed., *Cognition and the Development of Language.* New York: Wiley.

Carroll, Susanne, and Merrill Swain. 1992. "Explicit and Implicit Negative Feedback: An Empirical Study of the Learning of Linguistic Generalizations." Unpublished ms., Ontario Institute for Studies in Education, Toronto, Can.

Cazden, Courtney, Herlinda Cancino, Ellen Rosansky, and John Schumann. 1975. "Second Language Acquisition Sequences in Children, Adolescents and Adults." Final report submitted to the National Institute of Education, Washington, D.C.

Chomsky, Noam. 1965. *Aspects of the Theory of Syntax.* Cambridge, MA: MIT Press.

―――. 1981. *Lectures on Government and Binding.* Dordrecht, Neth.: Foris.

―――. 1991. "Some Notes on Economy of Derivation and Representation," in Robert Freidin, ed., *Principles and Parameters in Comparative Grammar.* Cambridge, MA: MIT Press.

Clahsen, Harald. 1984. "The Acquisition of German Word Order: A Test Case for Cognitive Approaches to L2 Development," in Roger Andersen, ed., *Second Languages: A Crosslinguistic Perspective.* Rowley, MA: Newbury House.

―――. 1988. *Normale und gestörte Kindersprache.* Amsterdam, Neth.: Benjamins.

―――, Jürgen Meisel, and Manfred Pienemann. 1983. *Deutsch als Zweitsprache.* Tübingen, Ger.: Narr.

―――, and Peter Muysken. 1986. "The Availability of Universal Grammar to Child and Adult Learners." *Second Language Research* 2,2: 93–119.

―――, and Peter Muysken. 1989. "The UG Paradox in L2 Acquisition." *Second Language Research* 5,1: 1–29.

Corder, S. Pit. 1967. "The Significance of Learners' Errors." *International Review of Applied Linguistics* 4. Reprinted in Jack Richards, ed., *Error Analysis.* London, Eng.: Longman, 1974.

Curtiss, Susan. 1977. *Genie, a Psycholinguistic Study of a Modern-Day "Wild Child."* New York: Academic Press.

―――. 1980. "The Critical Period in Feral Children." *UCLA Working Papers in Cognitive Linguistics* 2: 22–31.

Dulay, Heidi, and Marina Burt. 1973. "Should We Teach Children Syntax?" *Language Learning* 23: 245–58.

―――. 1974. "Natural Sequences in Child Second Language Acquisition." *Language Learning* 24: 37–53.

―――. 1977. "Remarks on Creativity in Second Language Acquisition," in M. Burt, H. Dulay, and M. Finocchiaro, eds., *Viewpoints on English as a Second Language.* New York: Regents.

―――, and Stephen Krashen. 1981. *Language Two.* New York: Oxford Univ. Press.

duPlessis, Jean, Doris Solin, Lisa Travis, and Lydia White. 1987. "UG or Not UG: That's the Question." *Second Language Research* 3,1: 56–75.

Ellis, Rod. 1986. *Understanding Second Language Acquisition.* Oxford, Eng.: Oxford Univ. Press.

―――. 1989. "Are Classroom and Naturalistic Acquisition the Same? A Study of the Classroom Acquisition of German Word Order Rules." *Studies in Second Language Acquisition* 11,3: 305–28.

Eubank, Lynn. 1990. "Linguistic Theory and the Acquisition of German Negation," in Bill VanPatten and James F. Lee, eds., *Second Language Acquisition/Foreign Language Learning.* Clevedon, Eng.: Multilingual Matters.

―――, ed. 1991. *Point Counterpoint.* Amsterdam, Neth.: Benjamins.

―――. 1992. "Verb Movement, Agreement and Tense in L2 Acquisition," in Jürgen Meisel, ed., *The Acquisition of Verb Placement.* Dordrecht, Neth.: Kluwer.

―――. 1993a. "On the Transfer of Parametric Values in L2 Development." Unpublished ms., Univ. of North Texas.

―――. 1993b. "Optionality and the 'Initial State' in L2 Development," in Teun Hoekstra and Bonnie Schwartz, eds., *Language Acquisition Studies in Generative Grammar.* Amsterdam, Neth.: Benjamins. [In press]

————. In press a. "Syntactic Parameters, Lexical Parameters, and L2 Competence," in Alan Beretta, Rod Cocking, and Howard Kurtzman, eds., *Psycholinguistic Approaches to SLA: Issues and Agendas.* Cambridge, Eng.: Cambridge Univ. Press.

————. In press b. "Sentence Matching and Processing in L2 Development." *Second Language Research.*

Finer, Dan. 1991. "Binding Parameters in Second Language Acquisition," in Lynn Eubank, ed., *Point Counterpoint.* Amsterdam, Neth.: Benjamins.

————, and Ellen Broselow. 1991. "Parameter Setting in Second Language Phonology and Syntax." *Second Language Research* 7,1: 35–59.

Frazier, Lyn, and Jill de Villiers, eds. 1990. *Language Processing and Language Acquisition.* Dordrecht, Neth.: Kluwer.

Gass, Susan, and Larry Selinker, eds. 1983. *Language Transfer in Language Learning.* Rowley, MA: Newbury House.

————. 1992. *Language Transfer in Language Learning.* Amsterdam, Neth.: Benjamins.

Goodluck, Helen. 1991. *Language Acquisition: A Linguistic Introduction.* Oxford, Eng.: Blackwell.

Gopnik, Myrna. 1990a. "Dysphasia in an Extended Family." *Nature* 344: 715.

————. 1990b. "Feature Blindness." *Language Acquisition* 12: 139–64.

Gregg, Kevin. In press. "UG and SLA Theory: The Story So Far" (provisional title), in Alan Beretta, Rod Cocking, and Howard Kurtzman, eds., *Psycholinguistic Approaches to SLA: Issues and Agendas.* Cambridge, Eng.: Cambridge Univ. Press.

Haegeman, Liliane. 1991. *Introduction to Government and Binding Theory.* Oxford, Eng.: Blackwell.

Hilles, Sharon. 1986. "Interlanguage and the Pro-Drop Parameter." *Second Language Research* 2,1: 33–52.

————. 1991. "Access to Universal Grammar in Second Language Acquisition," in Lynn Eubank, ed., *Point Counterpoint.* Amsterdam, Neth.: Benjamins.

Hoekstra, Teun, and Bonnie D. Schwartz, eds. 1993. *Language Acquisition Studies in Generative Grammar: Papers in Honor of Ken Wexler from the GLOW 1991 Workshops.* Amsterdam, Neth.: Benjamins. [In press]

Hornstein, Norbert, and David Lightfoot, eds. 1981. *Explanations in Linguistics.* London, Eng.: Longman.

Juffs, Alan. 1992. "Review of Larsen-Freeman and Long's *Introduction to Second Language Acquisition Research.*" *Second Language Research* 8,2: 161–66.

Klima, Edward, and Ursula Bellugi. 1966. "Syntactic Regularities in the Speech of Children," in J. Lyons and R. J. Wales, eds., *Psycholinguistic Papers.* Edinburgh, Scot.: Edinburgh Univ. Press.

Krashen, Stephen. 1981. *Second Language Acquisition and Second Language Learning.* Oxford, Eng.: Pergamon.

————. 1982. *Principles and Practice in Second Language Acquisition.* Oxford, Eng.: Pergamon.

————. 1985. *The Input Hypothesis: Issues and Implications.* London, Eng.: Longman.

Lakshmanan, Usha. 1991. "Morphological Uniformity and Null Subjects in Child Second Language Acquisition," in Lynn Eubank, ed., *Point Counterpoint.* Amsterdam, Neth.: Benjamins.

Larsen-Freeman, Diane, and Michael H. Long. 1991. *An Introduction to Second Language Acquisition Research.* London, Eng.: Longman.

Leonard, Laurence, Umberta Bortolini, M. Cristina Caselli, Karla K. McGregor, and Letizia Sabbadini. 1992. "Morphological Deficits in Children with Specific Language Impairment: The Status of Features in the Underlying Grammar." *Language Acquisition* 2,2: 151–79.

Liceras, Juana, and Helmut Zobl. 1993. "Functional Categories and Acquisition Orders, with Particular References to the Morpheme Studies in English L2 and Spanish L2." Paper presented at the 13th Second Language Research Forum, Univ. of Pittsburgh and Carnegie-Mellon Univ.

Lightfoot, David. 1982. *The Language Lottery.* Cambridge, MA: MIT Press.

MacWhinney, Brian. 1991. *The CHILDES Project.* Hillsdale, NJ: Erlbaum.

Marcus, Gary F. 1993. "Negative Evidence in Language Acquisition." *Cognition* 46: 53–85.

Meisel, Jürgen. 1991. "Principles of Universal Grammar and Strategies of Language Learning: Some Similarities and Differences between First and Second Language Acquisition," in L. Eubank, ed., *Point Counterpoint.* Amsterdam, Neth.: Benjamins.

————, ed. 1992. *The Acquisition of Verb Placement.* Dordrecht, Neth.: Kluwer.

————, Harald Clahsen, and Manfred Pienemann. 1981. "On Determining Developmental Stages in Natural Second Language Acquisition." *Studies in Second Language Acquisition* 3,1: 109–35.

Napoli, Donna Jo. 1993. *Syntax.* New York: Oxford Univ. Press.

Newmeyer, Fritz. 1983. *Grammatical Theory.* Chicago: Univ. of Chicago Press.

O'Grady, William. 1987. *Principles of Grammar and Learning.* Chicago: Univ. of Chicago Press.

Pienemann, Manfred. 1981. *Der Zweitsprachenerwerb ausländischer Arbeiterkinder.* Bonn, Ger.: Bouvier.

Pinker, Steven. 1984. *Language Learnability and Language Development.* Cambridge, MA: Harvard Univ. Press.

————. 1989. *The Acquisition of Argument Structure.* Cambridge, MA: MIT Press.

————, and Alan Prince. 1991. "Inflectional Morphology and the Psychological Status of Rules of Grammar." Unpublished ms., Massachusetts Institute of Technology and Brandeis Univ.

Pollock, Jean-Ives. 1989. "Verb Movement, Universal Grammar, and the Structure of IP." *Linguistic Inquiry* 20,3: 365–424.

Porter, J. 1977. "A Cross-Sectional Study of Morpheme Acquisition in First Language Learners." *Language Learning* 27,1: 47–62.

Ravem, Roar. 1970. "The Development of WH-Questions in First and Second Language Learners." Occasional Papers, Univ. of Essex. [Reprinted in J. Richards, ed., *Error Analysis.* London, Eng.: Longman, 1974.]

Roeper, Thomas, and Edwin Williams, eds. 1987. *Parameter Setting.* Dordrecht, Neth.: Reidel.

Schachter, Jackie. 1989. "Testing a Proposed Universal," in Susan Gass and Jackie Schachter, eds., *Linguistic Perspectives on Second Language Acquisition.* Cambridge, Eng.: Cambridge Univ. Press.

Schwartz, Bonnie D. 1991. "Conceptual and Empirical Evidence: A Response to Meisel," in Lynn Eubank, ed., *Point Counterpoint.* Amsterdam, Neth.: Benjamins.

————. 1993. "On Explicit and Negative Data Effecting and Affecting Competence and Linguistic Behavior." *Studies in Second Language Acquisition* 15: 147–63.

————, and Magda Gubala-Ryzak. 1992. "Learnability and Grammar Reorganization in L2A: Against Negative Evidence Causing the Unlearning of Verb Movement." *Second Language Research* 8,1: 1–38.

————, and Rex A. Sprouse. 1993. "Word Order and Nominative Case in Nonnative Language Acquisition: A Longitudinal Study of (L1 Turkish) German Interlanguage," in Teun Hoekstra and Bonnie D. Schwartz, eds., *Language Acquisition Studies in Generative Grammar.* Amsterdam, Neth.: Benjamins. [In press]

Selinker, Larry. 1972. "Interlanguage." *International Review of Applied Linguistics* 10: 209–31.

Slobin, Dan. 1972. "Children and Language: They Learn the Same Way All around the World." *Psychology Today* 6: 71–82.

Thomas, Margaret. 1991. "Universal Grammar and the Interpretation of Reflexives in a Second Language." *Language* 67,2: 211–39.

Tomaselli, Alessandra, and Bonnie D. Schwartz. 1990. "Analysing the Acquisition Stages of Negation in L2 German: Support for UG in SLA." *Second Language Research* 6,1: 1–38.

Weissenborn, Jürgen, Helen Goodluck, and Thomas Roeper, eds. 1992. *Theoretical Issues in Language Acquisition.* Hillsdale, NJ: Erlbaum.

Wexler, Kenneth, and Peter W. Culicover. 1980. *Formal Principles of Language Acquisition.* Cambridge, MA: MIT Press.

Wexler, Kenneth, and Rita Manzini. 1987. "Parameters and Learnability in Binding Theory," in Thomas Roeper and Edwin Williams, eds., *Parameter Setting.* Dordrecht, Neth.: Reidel.

White, Lydia. 1985. "The 'Pro-Drop' Parameter in Adult Second Language Acquisition." *Language Learning* 35,1: 47–62.

———. 1988. "Island Effects in Second Language Acquisition," in S. Flynn and W. O'Neil, eds., *Linguistic Theory in Second Language Acquisition.* Dordrecht, Neth.: Kluwer.

———. 1989. *Universal Grammar and L2 Acquisition.* Amsterdam, Neth.: Benjamins.

———. 1991. "Adverb Placement in Second Language Acquisition: Some Effects of Positive and Negative Evidence in the Classroom." *Second Language Research* 7,2: 133–61.

———. 1992a. "On Triggering Data in L2 Acquisition: A Reply to Schwartz and Gubala-Ryzak." *Second Language Research* 8,2: 120–37.

———. 1992b. "Universal Grammar: Is It Just a New Name for Old Problems?" in Susan Gass and Larry Selinker, eds., *Language Transfer in Language Learning.* Amsterdam, Neth.: Benjamins.

———, and Fred Genesee. 1992. "How Native Is a Near-Native Speaker?" Paper presented at the 17th Boston University Conference on Language Development, Boston Univ.

Wode, Henning, J. Bahns, H. Bedey, and W. Frank. 1978. "Developmental Sequence: An Alternative Approach to Morpheme Order." *Language Learning* 28: 175–85.

Young-Scholten, Martha, and Anne Vainikka. 1993. "Direct Access to X-bar Theory: Evidence from Korean and Turkish Adults Learning German," in Teun Hoekstra and Bonnie D. Schwartz, eds., *Language Acquisition Studies in Generative Grammar.* Amsterdam, Neth.: Benjamins. [In press]

Appendix 2A: Sources of Information

White's *Universal Grammar and L2 Acquisition* (1989) provides a useful and comprehensive overview of background issues and studies in theoretical L2 research.

Goodluck's *Language Acquisition* (1991) is a well-written introductory undergraduate text on theoretical studies in L1 development.

Atkinson's *Children's Syntax* (1992) is an examination of conceptual/theoretical issues in L1 development. Not recommended for the faint of heart, but very informative for those who desire to know more.

Lightfoot's *Language Lottery* (1982) introduces many of the topics pursued in generative linguistics. As Lightfoot makes clear in the dedication, his intended readership is a general one: "This book is dedicated to anybody whoever met a couple of linguists in a bar and asked them what they did for a living."

All the papers in Eubank's *Point Counterpoint* (1991), and a number of the papers in the volume edited by Hoekstra and Schwartz, *Language Acquisition Studies in Generative Grammar* (1993), deal with theoretical issues in L2 knowledge. Both volumes are recommended reading.

It is perhaps also important to recommend what not to read for further information on generative work on L2 acquisition. Ellis (1986) and Larsen-Freeman and Long (1991), both introductory textbooks, present competent overviews of general studies in L2 development. As Juffs (1992) points out, however, the treatment of generative work includes a number of fundamental misconceptions.

While generative studies in acquisition appear from time to time in a number of academic periodicals, two journals in particular specialize in generative work. *Language Acquisition* accepts contributions in both L1 and L2 acquisition; *Second Language Research* specializes in L2 studies.

The most recent generative research is presented at conferences. The "Second Language Research Forum," held yearly at various universities, generally includes a few papers in generative research. For generative studies in either L1 or L2 acquisition, the yearly "Boston University Conference on Language Development" is by far the best forum in North America. In addition, a new conference, "Generative Approaches to Language Acquisition" (GALA) has recently been funded and will be held at locations in Europe. Like the BU conference, GALA will provide a forum for generative research in both L1 and L2 acquisition.

3

Language in Society

Elite Olshtain
Hebrew University, Jerusalem

Language and Communication

Communicative Competence Models

With the continuing spread of communicative approaches in language instruction during the last decades, the field of sociolinguistics has become increasingly relevant to language teaching. Whether we aim at teaching "language for communication" or "language as communication" (Widdowson 1984: 215), it is imperative that we go beyond the linguistic features of language and expand the scope of social questions of language use and language appropriateness. If learners of a foreign or second language are to become effective users of the new language, they need to become knowledgeable not only about the rules of grammar but also about the sociolinguistic rules of language use.

Canale and Swain (1980) provided researchers and practitioners in the field with both theoretical and operational definitions of *communicative competence,* the ultimate aim of communicative approaches to language teaching. Canale (1983) further developed these notions and specified the four major subcomponents of communicative competence: *grammatical competence, sociolinguistic competence, discourse competence,* and *strategic competence.* Grammatical competence can be described in terms of phonology, orthography, vocabulary, word formation, and sentence formation. Sociolinguistic competence refers to one's knowledge of the rules that map grammatical

Elite Olshtain (Ph.D., University of California) teaches Second-Language Acquisition, Discourse Analysis, Course Design and Policy Making, and Classroom Oriented Research at the schools of Education at Hebrew University and Tel Aviv University in Israel. She is presently also the Director of the NCJW Research Institute for Innovation in Education at the School of Education at Hebrew University. Elite Olshtain established the M.A. in language teaching at Tel Aviv University and headed it for ten years. From 1984 to 1989 she was Head of Teacher Education and from 1990 to 1992 she was Dean of the School of Education at Tel Aviv University. Her research focuses on language acquisition, language attrition, discourse analysis, and curriculum development. She has coordinated teams of material developers in TEFL; the teaching of Hebrew, French, and Arabic as foreign languages; and computer courseware. She has trained language teachers in various countries such as the United States, Israel, Italy, Spain, Mexico, Brazil, and Japan. She has published professional articles in journals and anthologies and is coauthor (with Fraida Dubin) of *Facilitating Language Learning* (McGraw-Hill 1977), *Reading by All Means* (Addison-Wesley 1991 and 1992) *Reading on Purpose* (Addison-Wesley 1986), and *Course Design* (Cambridge Univ. Press 1986).

forms to appropriate social meanings. Discourse competence relates to knowledge of textual conventions in oral and written discourse. Strategic competence refers to the learner's ability both to develop strategies that compensate for difficulties in any other components and to use rhetorical skills in getting meaning across effectively.

The communicative competence model suggested by Canale and Swain (1980) has contributed significantly both to research in language teaching and to teaching itself, although considerable criticism has been expressed over the last decade. One difficulty arose from the fact that the components of Canale and Swain's model were not operationally defined and both language testers and material developers had problems translating the model into functional goals formulated in performance terms (see Harley et al. 1990 and especially Schachter 1990). The shortcomings of the Canale and Swain model led to new proposals in the nineties. Thus, Bachman (1990) specifies communicative language abilities as a development of the Canale and Swain model and Bachman and Palmer (1993) propose two main categories of "knowledge types": *organizational knowledge* and *pragmatic knowledge*. Organizational knowledge relates to the formal structure of the language and consists of grammatical and textual knowledge, while pragmatic knowledge is the knowledge of how to use language in context and consists of lexical and functional knowledge. Finally, the "Pedagogical Framework for Communicative Competence," proposed by Celce-Murcia, Dornyei, and Thurrell (forthcoming) seems to be most relevant to teachers and practitioners in this decade.

Celce-Murcia, Dornyei, and Thurrell's communicative competence model consists of the following components: *discourse competence,* the pivotal center of the model, interacting with three other components—*linguistic, sociolinguistic,* and *actional competence*—and a fifth component, *strategic competence,* which refers to the various strategies that enhance interpersonal communication at all levels of competence. Celce-Murcia, Dornyei, and Thurrell provide many examples of the subcomponents for these five types of competence, but here we will address particularly the sociolinguistic and the actional competencies and some major features of the central component of discourse competence that are relevant to the present chapter. *Sociolinguistic competence* focuses on the context of communication and involves all the pragmatic and cultural factors that determine appropriateness of language use. *Actional competence* refers to the language user's ability to interpret and perform speech acts and language functions. This chapter will focus particularly on these last two components.

Communication Goals

Goffman (1976) described human communication as possessing a set of universal constraints that are part of all types of communication and therefore function in all languages. In each language, however, these constraints apply differently. It is such differences between languages that are presumed relevant to the language acquisition process. Goffman further divided these communication constraints into *system constraints*—the components required for all communication systems—and *ritual constraints,* which are the social constraints that make harmonious social interaction possible. If one aims at communicative competence when learning a new language, one needs to understand and react appropriately by complying with the idiosyncratic constraints of the particular target language.

Human communication fulfills many different goals. We communicate information, ideas, beliefs, emotions, and attitudes to one another in our daily communicative interactions. Sometimes the goal of the interaction takes on additional force and enables us to perform social acts. The use of speech acts, to be discussed in detail later in this chapter, is one such social function. The use of speech acts serves, on the one hand, to maintain the speaker's solidarity with the listener and maintain social harmony and, on the other hand, to ensure the speaker's rights and status in society.

The communicative goals of speakers and writers are achieved by using the full repertoire of the linguistic code in interpersonal situations or in written texts. The elements of this repertoire (linguistic competence) are carefully selected by the speaker/writer to suit the social and pragmatic constraints of the particular situation. In spoken interaction, for instance, the successful combination of pragmalinguistic factors (i.e., the relations holding between linguistic and pragmatic/situational factors) and sociopragmatic factors (i.e., the interface of social and particular pragmatic elements) usually results in appropriate discourse (see Leech 1983). There is often room for failure and misunderstanding, however, even in the communicative act that takes place among speakers who share the same linguistic and cultural background. The following is an example of an exchange between a university student and a clerk in a departmental office, both native speakers of English:

Woman (student):	Excuse me, where can I make some Xerox copies?
Clerk:	For?
Woman:	(silence)
Clerk:	Are you an instructor?
Woman:	No, a student.
Clerk:	We can only make Xerox copies for instructors.
Woman:	Well, I . . . OK. But where can I find a Xerox machine? (the original intention)
Clerk:	Oh, I see. Up the stairs past the bookstore.

(Example presented by a student in a course on cross-cultural interaction, Summer 1990, Michigan State University)

In the above exchange there was obviously a breakdown in communication, since the woman's first utterance, which was an information question, was misunderstood by the clerk as a request to photocopy the pages. Since the clerk did not know the woman, she wanted to check her status and the legitimacy of the request by bluntly asking "For?" The woman was, obviously, completely taken aback by such a question and did not react for a moment. Three more exchanges were necessary in order to clarify the misunderstanding. Both social and pragmatic factors were involved in this exchange. In terms of status, it was made clear that only instructors can request photocopying services. In terms of pragmatic considerations, the clerk did not expect someone to walk into the office and ask a straightforward information question about a Xerox machine.

In written communication, we tend to distinguish between writer-based and reader-based texts. In a writer-based text there is less consideration for the potential reader who will eventually read the text and attempt to interpret its meaning. Such texts place higher value on conventional and rhetorical structure. In reader-based texts, on the other hand, the writer strives to make the text accessible to the reader by planning the information and the format in such a way that potential readers will be able to reach the intended interpretation.

Cross-Cultural Research

Every traveler who has encountered other cultures and other behavioral patterns is aware of the fact that you may know a foreign language very well in terms of its grammar, but that it is only when you are familiar with the sociocultural rules pertaining to that speech community that you can hope to minimize miscommunication and pragmatic failure due to deviance from the acceptable native behavioral standards. In other words, it is certainly not sufficient to have linguistic competence in a language if one wants to become an efficient communicator in that language. The sociolinguistic and the actional competencies are extremely important in helping the learner become an appropriate language user.

A group of students in a cross-cultural seminar held during the 1990 TESOL Summer Institute at Michigan State University reported on the following insights derived from experiences they had when they came into contact with another culture:

1. A young American woman who spent a year in Greece reported that it took her a long time to realize the rule of speaking that controlled interactions between men and women. According to her report, it was acceptable (in Greek) for the taxi driver to ask a lot of personal questions of a woman passenger, but she was not expected to give explicit and full answers to such questions. Before she realized this, she would get annoyed at the "impertinence" that these drivers had, and did not want to answer any of these questions. Later she understood that this was only a polite way of keeping up the conversation.

2. An Egyptian student was told, before he left for the States, never to ask personal questions since "Americans don't like personal questions." He maintained this policy for years in the States and only in a cross-cultural seminar did he realize that he had given his American friends the impression that he was uninterested and indifferent toward them.

3. A young Japanese woman explained why it was impossible for her to ask questions during the lesson—in Japan she had been taught never to interrupt a professor.

The above are a few random examples of cross-cultural stereotypes that the students in the seminar recounted. As a result of their travels abroad and their encounter with another culture, they had discovered important differences between their own culture and the new one. Cultures tend to exhibit differences in the perception of what are relevant or acceptable topics of conversation as well as who can address whom under what circumstances. Effective use of a language that we know is based on cultural presuppositions about the kinds of language behavior that are appropriate for particular situations and the expectations people have regarding effective structuring of information.

Cross-cultural research can be viewed as an extension of the traditional contrastive linguistic analyses. The latter focused mainly on the comparison of linguistic levels of different languages, although the very early work of Lado (1957) already advocated concern with cross-cultural comparisons centering on cultural perspectives. Still, until well into the 1980s, most of the contrastive approaches were limited to linguistic issues (James 1980; Sajavaara et al. 1980). During the 1980s we saw the beginnings of pragmatic contrastive work such as that done on English-German analyses of discourse phenomena, conversational strategies, and everyday gambits. These features in the two languages were compared in the framework of a project investigating the development of learners' communicative competence (Edmondson et al. 1984). Other such contrastive work developed in the 1980s: an analysis of the use of gambits in Danish and German conversations was carried out by Faerch and Kasper (1983), speech acts in English and Japanese were studied by Coulmas (1981), German and British English were compared in the work of House and Kasper (1981), Swedish and English were compared by Stenstrom (1984), and a series of studies dealt with Hebrew and English contrastive pragmatics and speech-act behavior—Blum-Kulka (1982), Olshtain (1983), Cohen and Olshtain (1985), Olshtain and Weinbach (1986), and others. Blum-Kulka, House, and Kasper (1989) published an extensive work on the cross-cultural pragmatic comparison of requests and apologies in a number of different languages at the end of the decade, making the 1980s a significant period for the advancement of cross-cultural pragmatics.

The accumulation of cross-cultural studies on perspectives of pragmatic and speech-act behavior has intensified the quest for better research methodologies and techniques of data analysis and data collection. In addition to contributing to the research base, these studies have enhanced the general awareness of cultural differences. Teachers, material developers, and curriculum designers are aware today that the sociolinguistic perspective is a necessary component of any course of language study. Furthermore, many language learners have become aware of cultural differences and have begun paying attention to them, a fact that will in itself improve their acquisition of appropriateness rules in addition to linguistic rules.

Sociolinguistic Features

In recent years, the field of pragmatics has come to be viewed as the study of the use and meaning of linguistic utterances in relation to the social situations within which they are produced. Leech (1983) perceives general pragmatics as consisting of two subfields: pragmalinguistics, which is related to linguistics, and sociopragmatics, which is related to sociology and societal rules of behavior. The sociolinguistic competence component identified by Canale and Swain (1980) and Canale (1983) and rephrased by Celce-Murcia, Dornyei, and Thurrell (forthcoming), consists of the pragmalinguistic and sociopragmatic rules of the target language to be acquired.

The sociolinguist, who studies pragmalinguistic and sociopragmatic phenomena, will be concerned with (1) features of the individuals who take part in the communicative exchange, (2) features of the situation within which this exchange takes place, (3) the goal of the exchange, and (4) features of the communicative medium by which it is carried out. In other words, the variation that is likely to occur in the utterance used may be related in one way or another to any of these sets of features. It is the object of sociolinguistic investigation to identify and explain the systematic relationships that hold among these variables within a particular language or within the communicative exchange in general.

Individual features include variables such as sex, age, social status, social distance, and the specific role the participant has within the situation. These features of the participant are referred to as social factors. In some cultural contexts, rules of speaking might be somewhat different for women than for men, while in other cultures there may be significant differences related to age. It seems reasonable to assume that in all cultures, social status and social distance will play some role. Social status will take on different definitions in different cultures but will be easily recognized by the members of any one culture. For example, in some cultures, government officials carry very high status; in other cultures, individuals with high educational and professional knowledge enjoy high status. Effective users of the language in each culture are aware of ways to adjust the rules of speaking when interacting with a person of higher social status. Yet any person may take on different roles according to their function in different situations. Thus, a judge, who may have a very high social status in society in general, will become merely a passenger on a bus, where the bus driver plays a role of authority. Similarly, social distance, which is usually defined as how well the interactors know each other, can be viewed on a continuum from strangers (+social distance) to very close friends or relatives (−social distance).

When social factors play a significant role in a culture, the fact is realized in the choice of grammatical forms, words, expressions, or topics used in the interaction. In certain cultures, women may tend to use more softening expressions than men when reproaching another individual. This is not necessarily the case, however, when they fulfill the role of mother in a family or teacher in a classroom. In other words, in the interaction among various social factors, sometimes one factor is stronger than others, and one's social status may therefore be more important than sex differences. Age is another factor that may play a very significant role in some societies: A request for help, for instance, might result in different utterances when addressed to an older person than when addressed to a younger one. In some cultures, higher social status of the addressee requires the speaker or writer to use special terms of deference—honorifics— or a higher, more formal register. *Register* is a term referring to the level of formality or "educated" language that is used. Every speaker, in any language, uses more than one register—the more intimate and casual register is used in immediate and familiar contexts, while the higher and more formal register is used in formal situations with interactors that the speaker doesn't know well or who are of a higher status. Register is therefore a general feature of language that reflects the role played by these social factors. The interaction between social factors and speech behavior in a culture provides the basis for speech-act realizations in that culture and, to a lesser extent, also affects written interaction—to be discussed later in this chapter.

The situation within which an interaction takes place presents another set of parameters that will affect the choice of linguistic realizations. Thus, people behave differently and use different language styles and register at work, at a family birthday party, or while waiting in line for a train or a bus. The contextual circumstances of such encounters together with the social parameters discussed above affect the speaker's choice of utterance.

Social and contextual factors play a more significant role in spoken interaction than in written interaction, since much spoken interaction is not carefully preplanned. Written interaction, on the other hand, is often planned in advance and rewritten before a final version is produced and conventional features of written texts guide writers in their composition of the text. Features of written texts will be described in the last section of this chapter.

Speech Acts

Speech-Act Behavior

It seems that every culture and, consequently, every language develops a set of patterned, routinized utterances that its speakers use to perform a variety of functions such as apologies, requests, complaints, refusals, compliments, and so forth. Patterned routines, when paired up with written conventions, are utilized in a similar fashion in written communication. By using a routinized utterance of this kind in the appropriate situation, the speaker carries out an act with respect to the addressee. In formal terms, a routinized utterance carries both a basic, propositional meaning (e.g., "It's terribly cold in here," which may be a simple statement about the condition in the room) and an intended illocutionary meaning (e.g., "It's terribly cold in here," which, given the proper circumstances, such as an open window, may actually be a request for someone to close the window). Speakers of the language recognize the illocutionary force of an utterance by pairing up the situational information within which the utterance was produced with the content of the utterance. Such conventionalized utterances function and are recognized as *speech acts.*

Speech acts have been investigated and described from a variety of perspectives: philosophical, social, linguistic, and cultural. They have been claimed by Austin (1962) and Searle (1969, 1975) to operate by universal pragmatic principles and by Green (1975) and Wierzbicka (1985) to vary in conceptualization and realization across cultures and languages. The various studies carried out to date have seemed to reinforce the notion that speech acts are ruled by universal principles of cooperation and politeness (Grice 1975; Brown and Levinson 1978; Leech 1983), although cultures vary greatly in their interactional styles and preferences for certain realization patterns.

In the study of speech acts, a number of central issues seem to play a major role: (1) the issue of *universality* as contrasted with *language specificity,* (2) the strength of social status versus the pragmatic component, and (3) the development of research methodologies to focus on the first two issues. The question of universality can be approached from a theoretical perspective revolving around an attempt to validate claims of universality in the basic structure of the speech acts. This represents a theory-driven approach. It can also be investigated from an anthropological, ethnographic point of view—a data-driven approach—in an attempt to pinpoint the difference in conceptualization and realization of speech acts across cultures.

One of the most influential studies of speech acts from both the universal and the language-specific perspectives has been that of the CCSARP (Cross-Cultural Speech Act Realization Patterns) project (Blum-Kulka and Olshtain 1984), which compared speech-act behavior in a number of different languages and as exhibited by learners of those languages. The CCSARP project has also produced useful instruments for data collection and a coding scheme that has been widely replicated in other speech-act studies throughout the world.

Researching Speech-Act Behavior

The study of speech-act behavior requires careful considerations of research methodologies and research instruments in order to incorporate the social and pragmatic predictor variables with the linguistic production variables. A basic requirement for such research is the development of comparable units of analysis. Olshtain and Cohen (1983) propose the notion of a *speech-act set* to encompass the major linguistic and pragmatic strategies, any one of which would suffice as a minimal element to represent any particular speech act. Such a speech-act set consists of the explicit and conventional patterns of realization as well as the more implicit or indirect ones (Searle 1975). It provides the researcher with (1) a framework for defining the relationships between illocutionary intent and linguistic repertoire in a specific language and (2) the possibility of comparing speech-act sets across languages.

Speech-act sets encompass the routinized realization patterns of speech acts related to the semantic criteria and the illocutionary intent relevant to the particular speech act. These patterns need to be further matched to sets of sociopragmatic features in order to set up preferences and appropriateness rules for the selection of any particular realization in a given context. The basic components of the speech-act set have universal potentials, while preferences and appropriateness to contextual features are language- and culture-specific.

Apologies.

The speech-act set for an apology, for example, is related first and foremost to the inherent goal of an apology act: to provide support and to placate the hearer (apologizee) who has been negatively affected by some violation for which the speaker is or feels at least partially responsible. When apologizing, the speaker is willing to humiliate himself or herself to some extent and to admit to fault or responsibility for the offense. This apology goal has universal validation. The semantic criteria that need to be met by the act of apologizing are an expression of regret and an acknowledgment of responsibility on the part of the speaker/offender. Accordingly, the apology speech-act set needs to include linguistic formulas that meet these semantic criteria. Notwithstanding the fact that the semantic criteria hold true across cultures, the appropriateness of the apology act to certain situations and the degree of apology in relation to any type of violation may differ considerably among languages and cultures. Thus, in one culture "coming late to a meeting" might be considered a much graver offense than in another, and the preferred apology realization in each of these cultures will reflect this difference accordingly. In the case where it is considered a serious offense, the speaker will need to intensify the apology by using more than one apology strategy as well as special intensification elements: "I'm terribly sorry to be late. There was an unbelievable traffic jam" as opposed to a brief and unintensified apology such as "I'm sorry I'm late."

Complaining.

The speech act of complaining is quite different from that of apologizing. In fact, in terms of Leech's (1983: 107) *cost-benefit continuum,* they are at opposite ends. On this continuum we can perceive of one end as being highly beneficial to the hearer and rather costly to the speaker, whereas at the other end we have acts that are beneficial to the speaker and costly to the hearer. The speech act of apology can be considered beneficial to the hearer since it is intended to placate him or her, and costly to the speaker who needs to humiliate himself or herself to a certain extent. Complaining, on the other hand, is costly to the hearer, who is being reproached, and beneficial to the speaker, who manages to express some frustrations and discomfort. In other words, the speech act of complaining aims at bringing some conflict or violation into the open at the cost of the hearer. In terms of politeness rules, we need to look for interactions that are beneficial to the hearer, since this maintains harmony in the social sense. In Leech's terminology, the apology can be considered a convivial type of speech act, while complaining is a conflictive one.

The speech act of complaining is a *hearer face-threatening* act by definition (Brown and Levinson 1978), since its major goal is to "attack" the hearer, who is considered responsible for some violation. The expression of the complaint threatens the public and social face of the addressee. When complaining, the speaker expresses displeasure or annoyance verbally as a reaction to a past or ongoing violation (Olshtain and Weinbach 1986). Such a complaint may be addressed to the hearer as the person responsible for the act that caused the annoyance, or it may concern a third or unavailable party, in which case it is much less face-threatening. For example, if someone pushes in front of the speaker in a line at the post office, the speaker may say: "Excuse me, I am the last person in line." This is a statement that functions as a mild complaint. If, on the other hand, the service at the post-office is slow, one person may address another person in line and say: "Lately the service here has become quite inefficient." The latter is often referred to as a gripe.

The speech act of complaining has two major goals: One is to point out the violation in behavior and thus relieve one's own frustration and anger, and the second, when such a possibility exists, to request repair. Since this is a face-threatening act toward the hearer, however, some speakers may prefer to avoid the potential confrontation and never seek the goal of the complaint. The speech-act set for complaints will therefore include the possibility of opting out entirely and avoiding social conflict, even if the situation calls for a complaint. If a speaker chooses the option to express a complaint, then the semantic criteria include two important features: (1) reference to the violation that brought about the need to complain and (2) the responsibility of the hearer for the violation. The explicit or implicit reference to these two criteria results in various degrees of complaining, allowing speakers to make their choices according to the contextual circumstances. Let us assume a situation in which two students were supposed to meet and work together on some assignment, which they had often done before, but one of them is quite late (more than usual), creating a legitimate reason for complaint. The type of complaint expressed would depend on how the other student perceives the situation and the relationship with his or her friend. In other words, both the pragmalinguistic and sociopragmatic considerations play a significant role here. The speaker might choose any one of the following realization patterns:

1. "No harm done. Let's meet some other time."
2. "It is a shame that we have to work under pressure now."
3. "You are always late for our meetings. It's annoying!"
4. "Next time don't expect me to sit here and wait for you."
5. "If you don't pull yourself together, I don't think we can continue working together."

Each of the above utterances corresponds to one of five semantic formulas that make up the speech-act set for complaining (Olshtain and Weinbach 1986). The first is a mild complaint that only vaguely hints at the offense. The second expresses disapproval without directly mentioning the hearer as responsible. The third is a more direct complaint with explicit reference to both the hearer and the violation. The fourth is even stronger, expressing accusation and warning, while the fifth is a straightforward threat. The speech-act set for complaining, with its five semantic formulas, can be used for cross-cultural studies but will most probably be realized linguistically somewhat differently in different languages. It is, however, reasonable to expect all languages to have some kind of a continuum of realizations moving from the least incriminating complaint to a very strong threat and warning.

Requesting.

A rather different speech-act set represents the speech act of requesting. A request is inherently a *face-threatening* speech act, although it is less conflictive than the speech act of complaining. By making a request, the speaker impinges on the hearer's freedom of action, since by complying the hearer follows the speaker's direction. Furthermore, a request is usually viewed as being beneficial to the speaker. All languages have developed indirect ways to express requests so as to allow the speaker to carry out the act and still leave some freedom of action for the hearer. Thus, if the speaker produces a direct and blunt request such as "Open the window," there is very little room for any further negotiation. But if the speaker chooses a more conventional request form such as "Could you please open the window?" the hearer might have a feeling that it is up to him or her to carry out the act and the intensity of the face-threatening perspective is lowered. The speaker could choose an even less direct form for the same request— "It is very warm in this room"—which allows the hearer to interpret the utterance as a general statement or as a request for something, perhaps the opening of a window. The latter realization of the request is indirect, leaving considerable freedom for the hearer, while the speaker is taking a deliberate risk that the request may not be interpreted as such and therefore not carried out. There seem to be three major levels of directness that one can expect to be manifested universally by requesting strategies (Blum-Kulka and Olshtain 1984) and which make up the requesting speech-act set:

1. The most direct, explicit request, often expressed by an imperative.
2. The conventionally indirect forms, which are most commonly used for requesting. In English the use of "Could you" or "Would you" is common.
3. Unconventional indirect requests, which rely heavily for their illocutionary interpretation on contextual information.

Complimenting.

The speech act of complimenting is yet another type of speech act. Complimenting can be viewed as a most suitable candidate for Leech's (1983: 104–5) category of *convivial acts* whose illocutionary goal coincides with the social goal of establishing and maintaining comity (i.e., social harmony). Convivial acts, according to Leech, are intrinsically courteous and enable the speaker to make use of available opportunities to express politeness and interest in the hearer. A number of studies on compliments in American English (Wolfson and Manes 1980; Manes and Wolfson 1981; Wolfson 1981) have suggested *solidarity* as the main goal of the speech act of complimenting. Solidarity can mean the creation of a positive feeling between the speaker and the hearer in an interaction, or, in other words, the creation of social comity.

Manes and Wolfson (1981) emphasize the fact that American compliments are highly formulaic; although there are circumstances in which they might be strongly expected, they are never really obligatory. Accordingly, the reaction to a compliment in American English is usually a simple "Thank you," since it is not the content of the compliment that carries significance but the actual act of complimenting that is important. In other languages the "truth value" of the compliment may carry more importance, as it happens in Hebrew, for instance. In a comparison of reactions to compliments in English and in Hebrew (Olshtain in press), it was found that reactions in Hebrew are much more varied and relate to the content of the compliment in each case, while in English, the reaction in approximately 90 percent of the cases was "Thank you."

Chapter 4 of Wolfson (1989) discusses various speech acts; in addition to requests and apologies, she analyzes *disapprovals, refusals, expressions of gratitude,* and *greetings.* More work needs to be done on all speech acts, especially from a cross-cultural perspective, and speech-act sets need to be established. The speech-act set for any particular speech act needs to be paired up with a sociopragmatic set, consisting of two major components: (1) the social factors that are external to the context and which would affect any speech-act realization within the same culture, and (2) the contextual features relevant to the particular speech act and specific to the given situation. The social factors include sex, age, social status, and social distance, as discussed earlier in this chapter. The contextual factors include the role relationship between the participants in the situation, the necessary context preconditions for the speech act to occur (a perceived violation for the apology or the complaint), and the intensity of such preconditions (the severity of the offense). A description of the interaction between the factors included in the sociopragmatic set and the strategies making up the speech-act set is the main object of the study of speech-act behavior.

Research Methodology

The complexity of speech-act behavior and the variation of realization patterns in different contextual settings places considerable constraints on the research methodology that needs to be developed for this area. The first consideration relates to data collection: Do the researchers prefer ethnographic data collection during spontaneous interactions or do they prefer to work with elicited data? Obviously each data-collection technique has its advantages and disadvantages and therefore it is usually necessary to combine the two. An effective solution is derived from a cycle of data-collection methods that complement each other (Olshtain and Blum-Kulka 1983, 1985a; Cohen 1986; Cohen and Olshtain 1991) and create an alternating sequence between ethnographic and structured data collection.

The cycle of data collection should ideally begin with ethnographic collection of speech acts as used in natural situations by speakers of the language. Such initial data are useful in leading the researcher toward the generation of initial hypotheses about the studied speech-act behavior. Further reinforcement for these hypotheses can be acquired through simulated speech such as role-plays. The advantage of role-play is that it resembles natural interaction since its simulation is as close to the real situation as possible. Furthermore, during the role-play it is possible to manipulate some of the social and pragmatic features relating to the speech act and thus have more control over the data.

There is no doubt that ethnographic data or even role-play simulations can provide researchers with more authentic and natural speech-act behavior, but such data make it more difficult to focus on the frequency and dominance of the major strategies that make up the speech-act set. Here a paper-and-pencil test such as the Discourse Completion Test (Blum-Kulka 1982) can be very effective. In such a test, the social and pragmatic variables can be manipulated systematically in order to isolate their specific impact. Furthermore, the test can be administered to a large number of people, enabling the researcher to work with frequencies of realization patterns and their relation to the manipulated variables. If we look at the following item as an example, we can see the potential for analysis embedded in such a test:

You promised you'd buy your neighbor medicine for her sick child while in town but you forgot.

        Your neighbor: Did you get the medicine?
                You: _____
        Your neighbor: Don't worry. I'll get it later today.

(Cohen, Olshtain, and Rosenstein 1986)

The respondents in this situation take into account that an intensified apology is called for, since there was a promise for something important that was not fulfilled (Cohen, Olshtain, and Rosenstein 1986). However, the violation was not deliberate, and there was no prescribed obligation to carry out this act. Furthermore, the interactors are equals and there will certainly be room for repair and other exchanges in the future. Such a test item can later be compared with a promise made by the respondent to the boss (higher status), or by specifying different types of offenses calling for lesser or stronger complaints. Such a data-collection technique enables the researcher to identify the most frequent strategies for apologizing as well as situation-specific effects. Most of the studies presented in Blum-Kulka, House, and Kasper (1989) used the same Discourse Completion Test for the data collection from the different languages studied, which enabled the researchers to compare the data across languages.

In the sequence of data-collection techniques, the next procedure might be another paper-and-pencil test focusing this time on the reaction of the hearer, or, more precisely, on the perlocutionary aspect of the speech act, which refers to the effect that the particular speech-act realization has on the hearer. This could be in the form of an acceptability test to validate the range of acceptability of the strategies identified in the earlier phase of the study. At this point the researcher can come up with a reasonably good definition of the speech-act set. Such a study was carried out for speakers of Hebrew as a native language and for immigrants to Israel at various stages of their acquisition of Hebrew (Olshtain and Blum-Kulka 1985b). The important finding of this study was the fact that learners of Hebrew reacted quite differently than native speakers to the given speech-act realizations, except for those who had lived in the country for eight years or more. The latter had fully acquired the perception of speech-act realizations in Hebrew and therefore reacted in a manner very similar to that of the native speakers.

Assuming that researchers have carried out the full sequence of data-collection techniques described above for any given speech act as used in a particular speech community, it is now desirable to continue work in the same speech community with additional ethnographic data collection for a variety of contexts, ethnic groups, subcultures, age groups, professional groups, and others. Furthermore, with the instruments that have been developed, it would be possible to engage in cross-cultural research.

Teaching Speech Acts in the Foreign or Second Language

In developing a teaching program that incorporates sociolinguistic rules and speech-act behavior, the first consideration must be the expected objectives. An important distinction has to be made from the start between reaction to speech acts and their production. Though it may not be realistic to expect students to start behaving like native speakers, it would be most important for them to become aware of differences and potential "pitfalls" that may cause misunderstanding.

For beginners in a second- or foreign language course of study, we may want to limit our goals to the most prominent realization patterns for a number of important speech acts. On the one hand, language learners need to be aware of the variety of possibilities that the new language offers so that they can react properly as hearers in an interaction. On the other hand, it may be sufficient for students to master one or two major strategies and limit themselves to those for production purposes. Whatever objectives are specified for a particular course of study, the focus must be on cross-cultural awareness.

A variety of teaching techniques can be developed for the teaching of speech acts. What all the different ways of teaching should have in common is the specification of situational and social factors matched with the most prominent realization patterns. It is important for learners to realize, for instance, that in English (if that is the target language) an expression of an apology with no intensification ("I'm sorry") would not be considered a very sincere apology and is therefore not appropriate for interaction with friends or interlocutors that are at a higher status than the speaker. Such unintensified apologies are most common with strangers and in cases where the infraction is not severe. A similar situation would probably be true for the teaching of apologies in French or German as target languages.

At a more advanced stage of language acquisition, learners of any target language need to become aware of the more subtle ways used by native speakers to intensify and give a feeling of sincerity to their speech acts. In English, for instance, the word "very"—a typical intensifier used in textbooks—is not always perceived as true intensification. The more common intensifiers in colloquial American English are "terribly" and "really." In order to help students become aware of such variation in apology use, they need to be given the chance to compare apologies in a variety of target language contexts, while carefully considering the differences and similarities.

The communicative approach to language teaching places awareness and sensitivity to cross-cultural differences at a high level of priority. Such awareness should be shared by teachers and students and should be exhibited in the teaching materials. It is the sensitivity to cultural differences that will often explain to both teachers and learners why unintended pragmatic failure and a subsequent breakdown in communication sometimes occur. Being aware of differences may help us become more open to other ways of speech behavior and, as a result, ensure better communication across cultures, and more tolerance and understanding in interpersonal interaction.

Written Communication

The Communication Model

Communication is a process of transmitting information, propositions, thoughts, ideas, beliefs, attitudes, and emotions from one person to another. In oral communication, the *speaker* initiates the process and the *hearer* receives the information. In written communication, the *writer* produces the text that carries the message and the *reader* decodes and interprets the message in its written form.

The basic communication model that underlies both types of communication is very similar: the *speaker/writer* starts out with a set of presuppositions about the relations, the expectations, and the context shared with the *hearer/reader*. On the basis of these presuppositions, a text (verbal or written) is produced. The *hearer/reader* also brings a set of presuppositions to the interpretation process of the message. Both interactors need to rely on the linguistic code and on social and cultural conventions in order to carry out the communication process successfully.

A number of important factors distinguish spoken and written communication. Spoken communication is seldom planned and usually develops through the various steps in the oral interaction. Written communication, on the other hand, is usually carefully planned and edited. Since spoken communication occurs mostly when the interactors see each other (except, of course, for such instances as telephone conversations), share time and space during the process of communication, and can appeal to contextual elements immediately available to them, we think of it as context-embedded interaction. Such communication relies more heavily on the immediate context and on information shared by the interactors than on linguistic and conventional rules.

Written communication has to overcome the distance of time and place between the interactors and the fact that the writer never really knows who the reader might be (unless specifically addressed). The writer cannot rely too heavily on shared knowledge or on contextual features and needs to adhere to conventions of writing in order to ensure that the message is well understood. Most people become successful communicators in the oral exchange, but in order to become an effective writer, one needs considerable practice and training. Similarly, most speakers are also effective listeners, but readers need to become proficient in decoding the written message and in utilizing their linguistic and textual knowledge while doing so.

In real-life situations, there is a continuum of oral communication that can move from the immediate and most familiar environment to a more formal and decontextualized situation. Thus, all conversations taking place at home, with close friends, and in other familiar contexts are contextually supported. If, however, we attend a public lecture or some formal speech or presentation, such an oral interaction is unidirectional and relies more heavily on linguistic and conventional codes. In that respect it is more similar to written communication. Similarly, writing a note to another member of the family is in many ways similar to oral communication because it also relies heavily on shared knowledge and contextual information. Writing an official letter, an assignment for an academic course, or an article, however, will require writing proficiency of the kind mentioned above. We can therefore perceive a *literacy continuum* for both oral and written communication, where one end is more context-embedded and relies heavily on shared knowledge and the other end is context-reduced and relies more heavily on linguistic and textual conventions. Along the whole continuum, we might have either oral or written communication.

The Interactive Nature of the Reading Process

Written communication consists of three basic components: the writer, the text, and the reader. The reader can approach the interpretation process from a top-down or bottom-up perspective. The top-down approach is also referred to as the knowledge-driven or concept-driven approach, since it is based on the knowledge and background the reader brings to the process. Thus the top-down approach relates to the written text from a global point of view and utilizes the reader's previous experience, knowledge, and expectations. The bottom-up approach, on the other hand, is also known as the data-driven approach, since it is text-bound and relies heavily on local clues found in the text (Grabe 1991; Swaffar and Bacon, this volume).

Good and effective reading is usually a combination of rapid and accurate feature recognition of letters, words, collocations, and other local forms without depending on context (bottom-up processing), together with global predictions and overall perceptions of the text as a whole (top-down processing). The interactive approach to reading focuses on the interaction that takes place during the reading process between the reader and the text.

A reader faced with a written passage that she or he is willing to interpret goes through a sequence of decisions before reading and again during the reading of the text. Before reading, the individual might consider the necessity and efficacy of reading the particular passage and his or her purpose in doing so. During the reading itself, the reader might ask herself or himself whether she or he is following the message and the thread of thought presented by the writer. If this is a "good" reader, there is probably a close match between the reader's expectations and the actual content of the text; for many readers or for many texts, however, there might be mismatches between the reader's expectations and the text realization. Good readers are quick in changing and adjusting their reading strategies to adjust to the features of the text, constantly switching back and forth between top-down and bottom-up processing.

In the second- or foreign language reading lesson, special attention needs to be given to the integration of top-down and bottom-up strategies. Teachers can encourage learners to tackle some of the top-down strategies before reading by prediction and hypothesis-making steps. This can often be done via techniques such as "brainstorming" with the whole class and tapping the students' relevant prior knowledge, which helps the reading process. During the reading itself, students need to test their predictions against the information presented in the text. After the first reading of a text, students can be encouraged to carry out some bottom-up tasks, which will help them become more efficient decoders at the local level. It is this combination of bottom-up and top-down subskills that will facilitate the development of successful readers.

Features of the Text

A well-written text has two important features: coherence and cohesion. It is the re-sponsibility of the writer to make a text coherent and cohesive in order to facilitate the reader's interpretation of the text. *Coherence* is a quality that makes the text conform to conventional ways of organizing ideas and thoughts in a logical manner. Such a "logical manner" is actually a conventionally and culturally acceptable rhetorical or-ganization. Widdowson (1978) perceives coherence of a text through the interpretation of the particular *illocutionary* act or acts and through the illocutionary development of the conversation or the written text.

One genre of writing with a specific prescribed and conventional format is the business letter. The format of a business letter supplies part of its coherence. While the basic function of the business letter is universal and incorporates relevant illocutionary acts such as requesting information, placing orders, apologizing, persuading, etc., the actual format is different in different cultures.

Cohesion is an overt feature of the text providing surface evidence for the text's unity and connectedness. Cohesion is realized linguistically through devices that connect and arrange the elements of the text (spoken and written). In the written text, cohesion relies heavily on grammatical devices, while in the spoken text one often relies on contextual information. The foreign language reader's limited grammatical knowledge in the target language often causes difficulties in the interpretation of the cohesive links within the text.

Carrell (1988) discusses two types of difficulties that foreign language learners may encounter while reading: first, there may be too much reliance on text-based, bottom-up processing, which creates text-boundedness; alternatively, there might be too much reliance on knowledge-based processing, allowing inappropriate schemata and irrelevant extratextual knowledge to interfere with proper text interpretation. The foreign language curriculum needs, therefore, to provide students with ample experience in reading a variety of texts from different genres with various interpretation tasks in order to become efficient in choosing and adapting reading strategies to reading texts.

It is important to view the reading process in both the first and the foreign language as a communicative activity in which the reader plays an important role in the inter-pretation process and in which the text, as produced by the writer, includes both facilitating and complicating features that need to be utilized and tackled.

This chapter has presented some of the important functions that language plays in society, focusing specifically on the act of communication. The discussion has taken us from spoken to written communication, with special emphasis on the responsibility that the speaker/writer and hearer/reader have in ensuring successful communication.

References

Language in Society

Austin, John L. 1962. *How to Do Things with Words.* Oxford, Eng.: Calderon.

Bachman, Lyle F. 1990. *Fundamental Considerations in Language Testing.* Oxford, Eng.: Oxford Univ. Press.

———, and Adrian Palmer. 1993. *Language Testing in Practice.* Oxford, Eng.: Oxford Univ. Press. [In press]

Blum-Kulka, Shoshana. 1982. "Learning to Say What You Mean in a Second Language: A Study of the Speech Act Performance of Learners of Hebrew as a Second Language." *Applied Linguistics* 3,1: 29–59.

———, Juliane House, and Gabriele Kasper. 1989. *Cross-Cultural Pragmatics: Requests and Apologies.* Norwood, NJ: Ablex.

———, and Elite Olshtain. 1984. "Requests and Apologies: A Cross-Cultural Study of Speech Act Realizations Patterns (CCSARP)." *Applied Linguistics* 5,3: 196–213.

Brown, Penelope, and Stephen Levinson. 1978. "Universals of Language Usage: Politeness Phenomena," pp. 56–324 in E. Goody, ed., *Questions and Politeness.* Cambridge, Eng.: Cambridge Univ. Press.

Canale, Michael. 1983. "From Communicative Competence to Communicative Language Pedagogy" in J. Richards and R. Schmidt, eds., *Language and Communication.* London, Eng.: Longman.

———, and Merrill Swain. 1980. "Theoretical Bases of Communicative Approaches to Second Language Teaching and Testing." *Applied Linguistics* 1,1: 1–48.

Carrell, Patricia L. 1988. "Interactive Text Processing: Implications for Second Language Reading Classrooms," in P. Carrell, J. Devine, and D. Eskey, eds., *Interactive Approaches to Second Language Reading.* New York: Cambridge Univ. Press.

Celce-Murcia, Marianne, Z. Dornyei, and S. Thurrell. Forthcoming. "A Pedagogical Framework for Communicative Competence: Content Specifications and Guidelines for Communicative Language Teaching." Unpublished ms., Univ. of California–Los Angeles.

Cohen, Andrew D. 1986. "Researching the Learning of Speech Act Sets." Revised version of a paper presented at the TESOL and Sociolinguistics Colloquium, 20th Annual Convention, Anaheim, CA.

———, and Elite Olshtain. 1985. "Comparing Apologies across Languages," in K. R. Jankowsky, ed., *Scientific and Humanistic Dimensions of Language—A Festschrift for Robert Lado.* Amsterdam, Neth.: Benjamins.

———, and Elite Olshtain. 1991. "The Production of Speech Acts by Nonnatives." Jerusalem, Isr.: Hebrew Univ., School of Education.

———, Elite Olshtain, and D. S. Rosenstein. 1986. "Advanced EFL Apologies: What Remains to Be Learned?" *International Journal of the Sociology of Language* 62: 51–74.

Coulmas, Florian. 1981. "Poison to Your Soul: Thanks and Apologies Contrastively Viewed," pp. 69–91 in Florian Coulmas, ed., *Conversational Routines.* The Hague, Neth.: Mouton.

Edmondson, Willis, Juliane House, Gabriele Kasper, and B. Stemmer. 1984. "Learning the Pragmatics of Discourse." *Applied Linguistics* 5,2: 113–27.

Faerch, Claus, and Gabriele Kasper. 1983. "Ja und —og Hva Sa? A Contrastive Discourse Analysis of Gambits in German and Danish," in J. Fisiak, ed., *Contrastive Linguistics.* The Hague, Neth.: Mouton.

Goffman, Erving. 1976. "Replies and Responses." *Language in Society* 5,3: 254–313.

Grabe, William. 1991. "Current Developments in Second Language Reading Research." *TESOL Quarterly* 25,3: 375–406.

Green, G. 1975. "How to Get People to Do Things with Words," pp. 107–42 in P. Cole and J. Morgan, eds., *Syntax and Semantics 3: Speech Acts.* New York: Academic Press.

Grice, H. P. 1975. "Logic and Conversation," pp. 41–58 in P. Cole and J. Morgan, eds., *Syntax and Semantics 3: Speech Acts.* New York: Academic Press.

Harley, Birgit, Patrick Allen, Jim Cummins, and Merrill Swain, eds. 1990. *The Development of Second Language Proficiency.* New York: Cambridge Univ. Press.

House, Juliane, and Gabriele Kasper. 1981. "Politeness Markers in English and German," pp. 157–85 in Florian Coulmas, ed., *Conversational Routine.* The Hague, Neth.: Mouton.

James, Carl. 1980. *Contrastive Analysis.* London, Eng.: Longman.

Lado, Robert. 1957. *Linguistics across Cultures.* Ann Arbor: Univ. of Michigan Press.

Leech, Gregory N. 1983. *Principles of Pragmatics.* London, Eng.: Longman.

Manes, Joan, and Nessa Wolfson. 1981. "The Compliment Formula," in Florian Coulmas, ed., *Conversational Routines.* The Hague, Neth.: Mouton.

Olshtain, Elite. 1983. "Sociocultural Competence and Language Transfer: The Case of Apology," pp. 232–50 in Susan Gass and Larry Selinker, eds., *Language Transfer in Language Learning.* Rowley, MA: Newbury House.

———. In press. "Compliments and Reactions to Compliments in American and Israeli Interactions." Unpublished ms., Hebrew Univ., School of Education, Jerusalem, Isr.

———, and Shoshana Blum-Kulka. 1983. "Cross-Linguistic Speech Act Studies: Theoretical and Empirical Issues," in L. Mac Mathuna and D. Singleton, eds., *Language across Cultures.* Dublin, Ire.: Irish Association for Applied Linguistics.

———, and Shoshana Blum-Kulka. 1985a. "Cross-Cultural Studies and Testing for Communicative Competence." *Language Testing* 2,1 (June): 16–30.

———, and Shoshana Blum-Kulka. 1985b. "Degree of Approximation: Nonnative Reactions to Native Speech Act Behavior," in S. Gass and C. Madden, eds., *Input in Second Language Acquisition.* Rowley, MA: Newbury House.

———, and Andrew Cohen. 1983. "Apology: A Speech Act Set," in N. Wolfson and E. Judd, eds., *Sociolinguistics and Language Acquisition.* Rowley, MA: Newbury House.

———, and Andrew Cohen. 1991. "Researching the Production of Speech Acts." Paper presented at the Conference on Theory Construction and Methodology in SLA Research, Michigan State Univ.

———, and L. Weinbach. 1986. "Complaints—A Study of Speech Act Behavior among Native and Nonnative Speakers of Hebrew," in M. B. Papi and J. Verschueren, eds., *The Pragmatic Perspective: Selected Papers from the 1986 International Pragmatics Conference.* Amsterdam, Neth.: Benjamins.

Sajavaara, Kari, Jaakko Lehtonen, and L. Korpimies. 1980. "The Methodology and Practice of Contrastive Discourse Analysis," pp. 27–55 in Kari Sajavaara and Jaakko Lehtonen, eds., *Papers in Discourse and Contrastive Discourse Analysis.* No. 6. Jyvaskyla, Finland: Univ. of Jyvaskyla.

Schachter, Jacqueline. 1990. "Communicative Competence Revisited," pp. 39–49 in B. Harley et al., eds., *The Development of Second Language Proficiency.* Cambridge, Eng.: Cambridge Univ. Press.

Searle, John R. 1969. *Speech Acts.* Cambridge, Eng.: Cambridge Univ. Press.

———. 1975. "Indirect Speech Acts," pp. 59–82 in P. Cole and J. Morgan, eds., *Syntax and Semantics 3: Speech Acts.* New York: Academic Press.

Stenstrom, Anna-Brita. 1984. "Questioning Strategies in English and Swedish Conversation." Paper presented at AILA (Association International de Linguistique Appliquée), Brussels, Belg., August.

Widdowson, Henry G. 1978. *Teaching Language as Communication.* Oxford, Eng.: Oxford Univ. Press.

———. 1984. *Explorations in Applied Linguistics 2.* Oxford, Eng.: Oxford Univ. Press.

Wierzbicka, Anna. 1985. "Different Cultures, Different Languages, Different Speech Acts." *Journal of Pragmatics* 9: 145–78.

Wolfson, Nessa. 1981. "Compliments in Cross-Cultural Perspective." *TESOL Quarterly* 15,2: 117–24.

———. 1989. *Perspectives: Sociolinguistics and TESOL.* New York: Newbury House.

———, and Joan Manes. 1980. "The Compliment as a Social Strategy." *International Journal of Human Communications* 13,3.

4

Cognitive Processes in Language Learning[1]

Evelyn Hatch
University of California–Los Angeles

Asako Yoshitomi
Keio University, Japan

Introduction

Cognitive scientists study perception (visual, auditory, kinesthetic, olfactory) and cognition, the processes whereby we understand, remember, recall, and use this information in our everyday lives. Linguists, too, study perception—particularly auditory perception—and cognition, processes that enable us to acquire and use language. One might assume, therefore, that there would be a great deal of overlap. However, a basic tenet of modern American linguistics has been that general cognitive processes cannot explain language acquisition. In linguistics, language acquisition is explained by a theory of competence that is thought to result from an innate human genetic endowment. In initial forms of the theory, this was called a "language acquisition device" and more recently "universal grammar."

Nevertheless, whether we can or should separate linguistic processes from general cognitive processes continues to be questioned both in applied linguistics and in cognitive science. Our position is that language learning reflects the acquisition of social, cognitive, and linguistic knowledge in a gradually integrated system, and that any comprehensive description of that learning must be "neurally plausible," i.e., consistent with what is known about the physiology of the brain. In this chapter we will review research that flows from this argument.

Evelyn Hatch (Ph.D., University of California–Los Angeles) is Professor Emerita in the TESL/ Applied Linguistics Department at UCLA. Her most recent publications include *The Research Manual* (coauthored with Anne Lazaraton) and *Discourse and Language Education.* She is currently working on a book about semantics and lexicon in cross-linguistic settings.

Asako Yoshitomi is a Ph.D. candidate in Applied Linguistics at University of California–Los Angeles, where she has taught Japanese as a foreign language. Her major areas of interest are language acquisition and attrition, foreign language teaching, and the neurobiology of language. She is currently teaching EFL at Keio University in Japan.

Our view is admittedly at odds with linguistic theory, which assumes that cognitive and linguistic systems are fundamentally different and separate. One argument for this division is the complexity and abstract quality of linguistic systems (i.e., we fail to recognize the importance of universal grammar as distinct from general cognitive capacity because we underestimate the abstractness and complexity of language). A second argument derives from the study of language disorder data. The most relevant case for us, since it includes some limited second language learning, is that of Marta, a woman with a documented mental age of 2½ years (with some variability across the battery of tests). Yamada (1981, 1983) convincingly demonstrates Marta's excellent linguistic development yet retarded cognitive development. For example, Marta's poor numerical *concepts* are reflected in the inaccurate information she gives in *linguistically* correct responses. Though Marta can "count" and knows she should point to items as she counts them, she may assign two numbers to a given item or count the same item several times. In cases where she has correctly counted an array of items, she is not then able to say how many items there are. Marta has neither grasped the 1-to-1 principle in counting nor the cardinal principle in telling how many items there are, revealing a clear deficit in cognitive ability. Yet, in spontaneous speech, her temporal and numerical expressions fall within the appropriate semantic field: "I was like fifteen or nineteen when I started moving out o' home, so now, I'm like fifteen now, and I can go." She is also able to produce numbers in appropriate places (and even to use ordinals such as *second friend, third school*). In addition, Marta is reported to have acquired some French during a short stay in France.

Case studies such as Yamada's study of Marta and Smith and Tsimpli's (1991) study of a severely retarded adult who can translate sixteen languages into English with ease are important. They reveal differences between cognitive and linguistic *knowledge,* but do not clarify whether these two types of knowledge involve the same or very different learning *processes.* That is, while there is agreement that there are differences in cognitive and linguistic skills, linguists and cognitive psychologists are only now beginning to explicate this agreement in terms of the mechanisms that connect language and thought.

How does this argument relate to second- and foreign language learning? If success in one area of learning and failure in another is to be taken as evidence for specialized processes, then must we propose specialized processes for all areas where success is variable? If so, it is understandable that there is so much disagreement about the processes involved in L1 vs. L2 acquisition, in child bilingualism vs. adult language learning, in second language vs. foreign language learning, and those that result in unequal performance across language skills.[2]

The research projects discussed in this chapter, however, question whether special processes other than those used for all learning are needed to account for the acquisition of languages. The methods used in the research are wide-ranging. Some are accessible to anyone, while others are limited to researchers with considerable familiarity with computer technology. Methods include theoretical modeling, computer modeling, classical experimental testing, the use of descriptive statistics with natural language data, introspection and retrospection (whereby learners comment on their performance either during or after the task), error analysis, and contextual analysis.

There are several different approaches to modeling. By far the most common is a deductive approach, in which the researcher proposes a theoretical model (e.g.,

Schumann's acculturation model or Krashen's monitor model) and then searches for data that support the model. This may include library research, where previous findings that fit the model are highlighted. Serious study of neurobiological details related to learning may be carried out to show the neural plausibility of the model. Or the researcher may carry out experimental research to test the model. A second, more inductive, approach is to examine the stages in acquisition of a cognitive concept and build a theoretical model that explains the stages. A third, more recent, method is to program the model on the computer and then subject it to rigorous testing, asking the computer to respond correctly to new data by using the model. An example of this is the modeling of scripts. A related method is to model learning itself by asking the computer to sense patterns in data and arrive at a solution, a process that researchers hope might parallel that of a human learner. These approaches can be further differentiated in terms of *what* is described or modeled—stages of acquisition (stage models), mental processes (process models, neurobiological investigations), mental representations of information (most formal linguistic theories, scripts, and connectionist models), or learning itself (connectionist experiments and neurobiological investigations).

The basic question to be answered in cognitive modeling is how language knowledge is represented in or acquired by the brain. We are blessed with the ability to learn. In cognitive terms, learning is the ability to adapt, change, or modify connections of the nervous system in the brain so that it will later behave differently. This ability (modifying connections) is basic to learning (behaving differently) and remembering.

The remainder of this chapter introduces some of the main models of cognition and language that have been proposed thus far. Each model looks at learning as a cognitive process where changes take place over time. They differ, however, in terms of what is modeled and how (and why) the changes we call "learning" take place. The models are grouped in the following categories: (1) stage models of cognitive concepts; (2) models related to memory consolidation; (3) neuroscience models; (4) connectionist models; and (5) script models. The five types of model will be briefly summarized and each summary will be followed by a discussion of its strengths and weaknesses. We conclude the chapter with a discussion of prospective directions for future research on cognition and language.

Stage Models of Cognitive Concepts

Stage models are models that describe acquisition "stages" that are induced from language acquisition data. If no special processes are involved in language learning, we would expect that linguistic forms for any cognitive concept would be acquired in relation to the simplicity of correspondence between the forms and the concept. There is a long history of research describing stages in the acquisition of L2 forms (see, for example, studies in Hatch 1978). More recently, researchers such as Andersen (1984, 1988) and Schumann (1987) have charted the acquisition of the forms for cognitive concepts in the L2, specifically the concepts of temporal and spatial relations. Forms for temporality as a cognitive concept include adverbs (e.g., *now, then*), prepositional phrases (e.g., *in a minute, in three years),* verb tense/aspect markers (e.g., *-s, -ed, -ing, -en*) and the question form, *when.* Spatial markers include adverbs (e.g., *here, there*), prepositional phrases (e.g., *in front/back),* and the question form *where.* All forms for the concepts were pulled from interview and narrative data obtained from adults (primarily immigrants who acquired the language without formal instruction but who had lived for many years in the United States). The data were then described in terms of "stages" that contrast the forms used by the least proficient with those used by the most proficient learners.

A group of eminent scholars from the European Science Foundation project has also examined the development of linguistic forms for particular cognitive concepts. The data are from uninstructed adults, learners from a wide variety of L1 groups learning a variety of L2 target languages. The research tasks include narration of a silent film, the telling of autobiographical stories, conversational interviews, and role play. The data are typically displayed using descriptive statistics (since the goal is to describe the stages, not to test hypotheses).

Though this research identifies and describes stages in language acquisition rather than cognitive processes, the results are typically discussed in terms of acquisition principles (see Andersen 1988; Long 1990). These include reliance on pragmatic cues and real-world plausibility, attention to usual (canonical) word order and preference for minimal changes in that order, simplicity and one-to-one mapping between forms and meanings, perceptual saliency and transparency, and so forth. The principles have also led to hypotheses about learning, for example, Clahsen's (1984) and Pienemann's (1984) learnability and teachability hypotheses. Examples of resulting hypotheses include

Word order—canonical order is preferred over optional variants of that order (German SL word-order studies).

Minimal changes—canonical order is preferred over (1) structures requiring several word-order changes (e.g., AUX movement in question formation) and (2) structures, such as embedded clauses, which have to be held in memory while the major clause is processed.

Simplicity and one-to-one mapping—one basic form for a function will be adopted and used in early stages of learning (e.g., the use of adverbs such as *now, before, tomorrow* for temporality before verb tense/aspect).

Saliency and transparency—stressed content words are easier to perceive than function words and, if their reference is to concrete objects in the immediate environment, they should be easily acquired.

Acquisition principles explain what it is about certain forms that allows them to be acquired early and others later. The hypotheses expand these principles to predictions about learnability and teachability. While the principles are not descriptions of internal processes, it is assumed that the descriptions of stages in learner behavior reflect cognitive processes at work.

Figure 4-1. Stage Models

Strengths

- Acquisition principles inform us which language forms for a particular cognitive concept are first registered in memory and which ones are acquired much later.

- Many types of analyses and comparisons can be drawn across many language groups learning different languages in group research efforts such as those of the European Science Foundation.

- Uninstructed learners give us baseline data against which to compare instructed learners.

- Instruction can be made more sensitive to findings about natural stages of acquisition. Information about stages can be useful in planning cyclical review in instruction.

Weaknesses

- While deictic reference terms (such as those used in temporal and spatial relations) are both cognitive and linguistic, the descriptions are only concerned with linguistic stages (not cognitive). For a cognitive description that links spatial forms to sensorimotor data, see Lakoff (1987, 1989).

- Principles, maxims, and learnability hypotheses relate to internal cognitive processes but do not attempt to describe them directly.

Models Related to Memory Consolidation

In contrast to stage descriptions, cognitive phase models (such as those of Karmiloff-Smith, Berman, and others for first language learning and McLaughlin and Bialystok for second-language learning) attempt to describe internal processes. These descriptions do not directly reflect neurobiology, but draw on psychological constructs that are presumably neurally plausible. To make the models more explicit, we will relate each to descriptions of learning and memory.

Learning, as we have said, is the ability to adapt, change, or modify the nervous system so that it will later behave differently. Changes in memory occur as the connections between neurons are altered. That is, the neural connection may become stronger, be reorganized, or disappear altogether. If the connection "dies," then "forgetting" occurs. If it becomes stronger and is altered for a "better fit" through reorganized and consolidated interconnections, then learning continues. This notion that, after initial learning, the quality of memory storage changes in a gradual process of reorganization is called "memory consolidation." Initial language learning, such as a learner's chunk-learning of phrases ("My name is . . . ," "What is your name?"), requires the formation of connections. It is memory consolidation—the reorganization of these connections—however, that is basic to language acquisition.[3]

Karmiloff-Smith (1985) has proposed a three-phase model of learning. In phase one, called *implicit,* learning is *data-driven.* What is learned is not necessarily analyzed but reflects matching of input in memory. Phase two, called *explicit 1* in Karmiloff-Smith's model, is *internally driven.* That is, memory consolidation is going on as the learned material is reorganized into a "better" system of connections. The third phase involves both data-driven and internally driven processes. Here memory consolidation includes further restructuring and/or automatization.

The research that supports such phase models is both anecdotal and empirical. U-shaped learning curves are often cited as supporting evidence. An example is the child's early use of correct irregular forms such as *went* and *feet.* This is the initial, phase-one matching of the input in memory. Then, as the connections are modified in phase two to handle more and more data, the child produces incorrect forms, *goed* and *foots,* in line with the major pattern found in memory. In phase three, the connections continue to be refined so that the child again produces *went* and *feet* in addition to regular forms such as *liked* and *books.* Memory consolidation thus refers to the grouping of previously unintegrated features into one assembly, which subsequently forms the basic unit of further reorganization and integration. Each restructuring allows more and more complex learning (and memory building) to take place.

There is a wealth of evidence that beginners in and out of language classes learn phase-one chunk utterances such as "I don't know." The forms are not integrated, analyzed features of the interlanguage. As the learner acquires more and more "I don't VERB" forms, the "I don't know" can be reorganized in memory (phase two) with many more forms of this pattern. Only later, however, can we say that the learner has phase-three "analyzed DO"—with the forms *do, does, did* consolidated within the total system. Initial and final phase data may look alike. That is, the learner may produce correct forms at both times, but the connections and memory that allow this production are very different. The many errors found at the intermediate level show the process of reorganization. Phase two forms the bottom of the U-shaped learning curve.

Not satisfied with such anecdotal evidence, Karmiloff-Smith (1985) and her associates turned to experimental research to validate the model. Data were collected from young children (4 to 10 years of age, English and French speakers) using many different experimental tasks. One task that illustrates reorganization of linguistic forms involves storytelling. Children were asked to tell stories in response to sets of sequenced pictures. Each story was analyzed separately according to the number of children at each age level who did or did not show sensitivity to discourse in selecting forms to refer to the main protagonist rather than other characters in the story. A statistically significant U-shaped curve was substantiated across the age range. The three-phase model was further validated across an array of linguistic *and* cognitive experiments. This led to Karmiloff-Smith's claim that the data support a general three-phase model for *all* types of learning.

In this model, it is memory consolidation, the point at which the learner has automatic control, that distinguishes one phase from the next. Instead of using phase numbers to refer to processes of memory consolidation, McLaughlin (1987, 1990) uses the terms *restructuring* and *automaticity.* His notion is that adult language learners begin slowly, haltingly, and, if they are taking language classes, with a good deal of conscious awareness of what they are trying to learn. Practice, however, has two benefits. First, it allows memory consolidation to take place. McLaughlin calls this *restructuring,* since there is a qualitative shift whereby the representation of information is changed. Second, practice promotes automaticity. Over time, the learner needs to attend less and less to areas that were originally difficult, less and less control is needed, and the material becomes automatized. When that happens, the learner can use the forms without reflection.

Bialystok's (1982, 1988, 1991) framework differs somewhat. She claims that proficiency develops along two dimensions: *analyzed* and *automatic.* In *nonanalyzed* language (like the chunk "I don't know"), the underlying formal constituents are not controlled. In *analyzed* language, however, the learner has control of the structural properties (in the "I don't know" example, the learner controls negation and the present-tense forms of *do*). This is similar to the end points of phase one and phase three of the Karmiloff-Smith model. Bialystok's framework, however, has no phase two. Rather, the change is viewed as a continuum.

Automatic access, for Bialystok, is an independent dimension. That is, analyzed language is not necessarily accessed in fluent performance. Bialystok makes three predictions on the basis of analyzed and automatic access: (1) Learners begin with "unmarked" nonanalyzed language and nonautomatic access to that language. (2) Control of the two dimensions develops in a relatively independent fashion. An adult foreign language learner might move rapidly from nonanalyzed language to analyzed language but still have problems with fluency. (3) While a learner may exhibit both analyzed language and automatic performance, the combination of analyzed and automatic control varies across situations. That is, a learner may not be able to combine them equally well in all contexts. For example, a learner may be able to use correctly the analyzed form *doesn't* automatically in an informal, relaxed situation, whereas the same learner may have to monitor his or her use of the form in a formal situation in order to avoid mistakes. Tarone (1983) describes the effects of situational context on interlanguage variability. Ellis (1986) also provides a comprehensive account of the variability observed in interlanguage data.

Bialystok (1982) asked native speakers and language learners at different levels of proficiency to complete a series of tasks, ranging from discrete-point grammar tests to relaxed conversations. Her methodology combines proficiency testing and tests that might make different demands on the learner's fluent, automatic control and analyzed language. Though the findings from this research are complex, Bialystok believes that they do establish the claim that control in terms of analysis and control in terms of access as reflected in fluency are separate dimensions of language proficiency.

Karmiloff-Smith, McLaughlin, and Bialystok all believe that common cognitive processes underlie all learning. Their opinions differ, however, on the nature of automaticity. For Karmiloff-Smith and McLaughlin, automaticity appears to be a by-product of memory consolidation. For Bialystok, automaticity is an independent dimension. Therefore, she claims that there is a separation between how well the brain consolidates information and how easily that information can be retrieved for use.

Part of McLaughlin's work was to note explicitly different types of processing that need to be accomplished in L2 learning. These include semantic, syntactic, and phonological processing across skill areas. The question then arises as to how these different types of processing are to be carried out by "common cognitive processes." While the models discussed so far offer no explanation, parallel distributive processing (PDP) models, which we will discuss in a moment, offer some solutions. The basic idea is that memories are *simultaneously* accessed across *parallel* networks of connections. Thus, although the same process may underlie all learning, language might be redundantly represented in parallel networks that act in concert. Some of these connections might be relatively weak while others are highly developed. We would not be surprised, then, to find differences across skill areas and in analyzed and automatic performance.

Figure 4-2. Models Related to Memory Consolidation

Strengths

- Process models explain U-shaped curves in L1 acquisition and account for the shift from chunk-learned utterances in early second-language learning to more analyzed forms of the language.
- Cognitive phase models have been tested in a variety of experimental tasks.
- The models (as described above) can be interpreted in a way that gives them some neural plausibility. (See the next section, "Neuroscience and Language Learning.")

Weaknesses

- There is growing evidence that U-shaped curves such as those described in the *feet-foots-feet* and *went-goed-went* examples apply only to a few nouns and verbs. Some children never exhibit these "phases." Others show them for a few verbs but not on a principled basis (perhaps only a few times over many months of development). One could argue that cognitive models are describing patterns that are limited and fleeting, if they exist at all.
- In second-language acquisition, case data reveal that learners acquire chunk-learned routines, which are then gradually reorganized into analyzed forms (see, for example, Wong Fillmore 1976; Huang and Hatch 1978; Hakuta 1978; Itoh and Hatch 1978). These data also show, however, early production of forms that do not look like matches of the input (i.e., do not look like phase-one correct forms). Process models do not explain why this should be. Acquisition principles such as those offered in stage models (see Clahsen 1984 and those detailed by Andersen 1988) may be more successful in this regard.
- Models need to be more detailed in order to account for the multistage data (see Berman's 1986 five-phase model) often found in L1 and L2 acquisition.
- Attempts to replicate Karmiloff-Smith's experimental methodology with bilingual children (e.g., Hatch and Hawkins 1991) have not been successful. First, it is almost impossible to obtain reliable data. For example, children

may show phase-one behavior in telling one story and phase-three behavior in telling another. Unfortunately, reliability figures from story to story are not available in Karmiloff-Smith's experiments. In addition, some bilingual children told a story within which they showed phase-one, phase-two, and phase-three behavior. Such stories could not be scored. If the methodology results in discarding one-third of the data, we need to understand why so much variation occurs.

- The methodology in support of dimensions is also problematic from the standpoint of analyzing conversations. It isn't clear that interactive tasks (informal relaxed conversation vs. conversation with other learners on an abstract topic vs. an interview with a native speaker) can be classified as requiring nonanalyzed vs. analyzed language or nonautomatic vs. automatic access. Nevertheless, teachers would intuitively agree that one can have control of grammar structures but not be able to use this knowledge in fluent performance. Whether fluent and accurate performance requires two dimensions (Bialystok) or is something that happens in the consolidation of phase-three behavior (Karmiloff-Smith) or over time (McLaughlin) is not yet clear.

- If cognitive processes are the same for all learning, how can there be substantial differences in acquisition of language skills and cognitive concepts (as in the Yamada 1981 example in the introduction or Smith and Tsimpli's 1991 study of a severely retarded adult who can translate sixteen languages to English with ease)? How do we account for differences across skill areas (i.e., listening vs. speaking, reading vs. writing) in second- and foreign language learning? Are differences in the Yamada study simply another example of different types of information (cognitive vs. linguistic information) being more or less successfully stored and reorganized in the neural system? Or are there genuine differences between the processes used in consolidating linguistic information and those used in consolidating conceptual information?

- Phase models leave us with very general models of the learning process, so general as to be of limited use. More specific models are needed.

Neuroscience and Language Learning

Jacobs (1988), Schumann (1990a), Jacobs and Schumann (1992), Sato and Jacobs (1992), Yoshitomi (1992b) and others argue that an understanding of neurobiology is needed in order to explain language-learning behaviors. Neurobiological research provides evidence for the reality of such constructs as affect, intake vs. input, critical periods, critical threshold, language learning, and language loss—metaphorical constructs that form the basis of much of our thinking about language learning.

We are all familiar with the notion of short-term memory, or working memory, as that which very quickly decays, but which may or may not allow information to be stored and become consolidated, long-term memory. In his early model of language learning, Schumann (1975, 1978) proposed that affective factors play a very important role in determining what (if any) of the input is actually held in memory long enough to become intake for the system. (This became the "affective filter" in Krashen's 1982 model.)

While others despaired of ever being able to define *affect,* Schumann turned to neuroscience to validate the construct. Schumann (1990b) and Jacobs and Schumann (1992) demonstrate that affect in L2 acquisition has a neurobiological basis. The amygdaloid complex in the limbic system of the brain is the mediator of association memory formed through the senses (visual, auditory, kinesthetic, and so forth). It links stimuli through its direct and extensive connections with the sensory systems in the cortex *and* attaches emotional evaluation to the stimuli. When the evaluation is strong, more efficient information processing takes place. Thus, the amygdala is a critical source of "selective attention" that is needed for learning. It adjusts attention to novel, emotionally significant information. Sato and Jacobs (1992) argue that the nucleus reticularis thalami (NRT, a part of the thalamus through which all sensory information aside from olfaction passes before being further processed by the cerebral cortex) is a structure crucial to selective attention as well. Affect may "protect" some information by strengthening connections until the information can be consolidated into more permanent memory. Thus, it is claimed that these important structures of the brain not only influence what one perceives, pays attention to, and thus learns (Jacobs and Schumann 1992 and Sato and Jacobs 1992), but, by strengthening connections, may also "protect" what one learns from loss (Yoshitomi 1992a, 1992b).

There is also some evidence, though it is as yet very tentative, that the low success rates of older, senior citizens as language learners may relate to the areas of the brain that control selective attention. In her study of the effects of aging on second-language auditory memory and perception, Scott (1992) demonstrates that short-term memory does not decline for older learners (50–79 years old with normal hearing), but that perception definitely changes. Elderly adults have no difficulty in recalling chains of numbers or sentences (even under noise conditions) in a language they know. They have much more difficulty than younger language learners, however, in perceiving and discriminating items in a second language. One explanation (Geschwind 1980) is that aging brings about a change in attentional systems. (As we have already seen, this is controlled at least in part by the NRT and the amygdaloid complex which assigns affect to a stimulus.) If the attentional system has changed for older adults and affect can no longer "protect" information by boosting the strength of connections, we can see why Craik and Simon (1980, cited in Scott 1992) believe that the elderly do not process new information deeply at the time of acquisition. If the connections are weak, items may not be retained in memory long enough for learners to reorganize and consolidate them. Scott is skeptical whether such an explanation is justified given the problem of finding reliable and valid measures of perception, memory, and depth of processing for use in second-language research.

In summary, affect is seen as crucial for moving information from short-term memory into intermediate-memory connections. (Sato and Jacobs 1992 relate the selective attention function of the NRT to the input/intake construct in second-language theory.) In intermediate memory, structures are reorganized and consolidated and gradually automatized as competing connections are eliminated. As information "collects" in connections, reorganization and consolidation take place. As knowledge is consolidated and automatized, a "critical threshold" is reached. This allows the information to be transformed into long-term memory connections. Perhaps it is this transformation, itself, which is reflected in McLaughlin's "automatized" performance.

In foreign and second-language acquisition theory, the notion of critical thresholds is well known. We talk about the need for a certain number of courses in order to reach this critical threshold that will allow students to learn and retain the language over time. In bilingual education, the critical threshold refers to a consolidation of first language knowledge prior to the start of second-language instruction. Language knowledge that has gone through restructuring and consolidation should naturally be less vulnerable to attrition. In other words, there should be less danger of L1 loss, and the knowledge gained through the L1 system should be solid once it has been transformed to long-term memory connections. There may be several levels of long-term memory while information is still open to more restructuring. Genuine long-term memory should be "permanent" (though permanence is relative) and automatized. The term *permastore,* coined by Bahrick (1984a, 1984b), is sometimes used for long-term memory, which seems impervious to change.

Yoshitomi (1992a, 1992b) notes that there is some neurobiological support for the notion of permastore. She draws on Squire (1985) who suggests that memory storage in the medial temporal lobe might be considered intermediate memory. Once these connections are reorganized and automatized, they can be transmitted into the neocortex, which might be considered permanent memory. This transfer frees up the medial temporal lobe to work on new material. These parts of the brain are phylogenetically different. Simpler processing seems to be a function of older parts of the brain whereas more complex processing depends on the neocortex.

The maturation of the attention system of the brain coordinated by the NRT may also relate to the notion of critical periods. According to Sato and Jacobs (1992), there are two types of attention systems coordinated by the NRT: one that is involved in a primitive type of attention (general arousal), and the other in a higher-order type of attention (selective attention). Sato and Jacobs maintain that the latter type of attention system is controlled by the cerebral cortex, especially by an association area called the prefrontal cortex, which does not mature until the second decade of life. It is likely, therefore, that the time at which intake or discontinuance of a language takes place (i.e., before or after the functional maturation of the higher-order attention system) will greatly influence the degree of acquisition and attrition of that language.

When attrition occurs, neuroscientists believe that there is actual loss of some of the neural connections that originally represented acquired knowledge. This attrition depends, at least in part, on how well the information has been consolidated. If it has not become part of permastore, it is more vulnerable to loss, although connections may not be totally lost but rather gradually weakened. Retrieval of information in weakening connections would be reflected in difficulty of access rather than loss. Relearning of languages, such as that documented in Celce-Murcia and Vialla's fascinating study (1983) of a six-year-old's alternate relearning of English and French as she moved from the United States to France and then back again, may be the result of restrengthening connections that were considerably weakened though not completely lost.

The hypothesis that language loss may continue over time with ever-weakening connections is the mirror-image of language acquisition over time with ever-strengthening consolidation of information in neural connections. The idea that memory consolidation proceeds over time is supported by a number of studies (Scherer 1957; Cohen 1974, 1975) that indicate that a student's "mental metabolism" continues to work after a language course is over. In these studies, data are typically collected at the end of the course and then again at the end of summer vacation. While some connections are eroded and information forgotten, in other cases, students actually improve over vacation. For example, one of the subjects in Cohen's (1975) study demonstrated "residual learning," in which incorrect Spanish patterns became "unlearned" and errors disappeared after the recess. Such cases of residual learning can be explained in terms of ongoing memory consolidation.

It is not possible, however, to predict exactly what parts of language or what skills in language use will have the highest rate of attrition. Differences in attrition, as well as in learning, may be linked in some way to the limbic structures of the brain that relate to attention and affective evaluation. The nature of consolidation may also explain differences in attrition. If consolidation were a simple linear process, we would expect uniformity of loss across skills and that the material learned last would be the first forgotten. However, consolidation of complex interlinking connections in some circumstances may be swift and in others require an extended period of time. A student encounters an array of vocabulary and grammar *early* in the learning process. Some of these words or structures may exist in a few networks, but the interconnections between the networks may be incompletely established or otherwise be quite weak. Other vocabulary and structures, even those encountered much later, may be represented in many networks with strong interconnections between them. This makes a simple "last learned, first lost" prediction very shaky. Still, this prediction matches the general pattern found in many studies. Vulnerability to loss is greatest in recently acquired, unconsolidated knowledge.

Recent studies of L2 English attrition of children and adults offer findings that can be viewed from the neurobiological perspective presented above. Bahrick (1984a, 1984b) examined loss patterns of 733 students of Spanish. The time elapsed since the completion of their coursework varied from 1 to 50 years. A large portion of Spanish knowledge was lost within a few years after training, while the remainder was immune to further loss for as long as 25 years, and much of that content survived for 50 years. Bahrick calls the knowledge retained after 25 years the permastore content. Moorecroft and Gardner (1987), in their study of 114 high school learners of French, argue that less proficient learners have a relatively unstable knowledge of grammar and, therefore, are more likely to lose structures. Once again, more recently learned structures are quickly forgotten. In a series of longitudinal studies of L2 loss, Berman and Olshtain (1983), and Olshtain (1986) report on the loss of L2 English by learners who returned to Israel. Older children (8 to 14) showed less loss than younger children of irregular forms of nouns and verbs. Olshtain (1986) claims the older children showed less attrition because they had reached a level of stability (i.e., these forms had passed the critical threshold, becoming part of genuine long-term memory).

Yoshida (1989), in one of the attrition studies of the JOSEF (Japan Overseas Student Education Foundation) project in Japan, examined L2 attrition of 44 returnee children who had lived in English-speaking countries for more than four years. While there was a deterioration of some grammar skills (e.g., decreased use of complex syntactic structures with embedding, misuse of prepositions), learners retained emotional expressions such as interjections and fillers, which play a role in social interaction. Like Berman and Olshtain (1983), they found that some types of knowledge are, indeed, deeply entrenched. If this knowledge is primarily pragmatic and used for important status relationships, then perhaps it is well protected by affect. It may also be true that the knowledge has been coded across several different parallel networks so that the structures are particularly strong.

Both language learning and language loss seem to be influenced by age. Berman and Olshtain (1983) found the greatest language loss in young children, aged 5 to 8. Yoshida's (1989) studies found children under age 9 much more vulnerable to loss than older children. And Nakazawa (1989) reported that children under 5 years of age showed the greatest loss of the L2. Yoshitomi comments that if there are sensitive periods for acquisition of certain types of information, it would be interesting to know if the same sensitive periods exist for attrition.

The studies mentioned above are but a few that support a developing model of language acquisition and attrition within a neurobiological approach. The research reported in the 1992 volume of *Issues in Applied Linguistics* further validates this approach.

Figure 4-3. Neuroscience and Language Learning

Strengths

- The study of neurobiology is the only approach that attempts to understand the physical biology that underlies human language behavior. This approach has significant consequences for our understanding of the mechanisms of language as it affects our perspective on the language acquisition process. It considers language as embodied in the human nervous system. Since the nervous system collects sensory information, stores and restructures it, and retrieves it for use, it is impossible to see how any comprehensive theory of language acquisition could ignore or contradict the findings of neurobiological research.

- The study of neurobiology gives us some understanding of why students forget some less-consolidated language features and yet continue to improve performance for other parts of the language even after instruction ceases.

- The research gives neurobiological evidence for the reality of a variety of constructs that appear in theoretical models of language learning: affect, intake vs. input, critical threshold, critical periods, language learning, and language loss.

- The research demonstrates variation in acquisition of different types of information as well as attrition of that information. This supports the notion that information is handled in parallel distribution.
- The research gives further credence to phase models, since storage in initial to permastore memory resembles that described in such models.

Weaknesses

- Neurobiology and language acquisition are two fields in which it is easier to speculate about how things work than to find incontrovertible evidence of how they work. Bringing the fields together may or may not illuminate our understanding of each of them. Perhaps neurobiological evidence should be used as only one of several types of evidence in support of theoretical constructs. (Statistical construct validation is another alternative.)
- Neurobiology has yet to answer questions about how different types of information are represented in memory connections. How do the networks differ, overlap, or work in parallel (*if* they do)? Are networks organized and specialized according to linguistic (phonology, morphology, syntax, semantics, discourse), cognitive, and social information? If so, does this differentiation remain isolated in these networks or does it reappear in other more integrated networks (multiple representation of information in parallel networks)?
- There is little agreement in the literature about whether L1 and L2 networks are or are not differentiated. In some accounts of early child bilingualism, the languages are seen as originally undifferentiated, gradually becoming differentiated. In neural probe research, L2 representation is seen as being widely distributed across large areas of the cortex and separate from the L1, before gradually becoming more consolidated in a smaller area (diminishing concentric circles) with strong links between languages. Bilingual aphasia studies also present conflicting pictures of L1 and L2 representation. L1 learning is difficult to explain; bilingualism and multilingualism further complicates the difficulty. The hope in turning to neurobiology has been to find answers. Instead, the research presents many intriguing ideas that may or may not lead to answers.

Connectionism and Language Learning

After decades of learning about symbolic models of linguistic knowledge, and being fascinated and frustrated by the scope and claims of generative grammar and Government and Binding theory, applied linguists approach connectionist models with expectations tempered by healthy skepticism.

Connectionism takes its name from the notion that it is the formation and consolidation of neural connections that makes learning possible. Connectionists believe that patterned behavior (and the fascinating variation in patterns that occurs in all language use) is the result both of the way connections are established and consolidated and of the way they are activated and used. The position we have taken throughout this chapter is that no special neural mechanisms are needed for language beyond those already in place for general cognitive processing. (Although there are initially no specialized "language mechanisms," after training and learning certain networks clearly take on specializations.) Connectionists, in general, attempt to simulate neural networks in parallel distributed processing (PDP) models. In language learning, this means that language will be redundantly represented and processed across parallel networks of connections as described in the previous sections.

Linguists and applied linguists working on connectionist models have, of course, had a great deal of experience with symbolic models (e.g., various transformational-generative models or Government and Binding theory where units are identified and manipulated in a rule-based approach). They do not all necessarily feel that the two approaches are entirely incompatible. Linguists interested in connectionism, however, want to test the hypothesis that it is possible to *learn* from input using the same processes that work for other kinds of information.[4]

To test this, connectionists have fed linguistic input to computers and asked them to "learn" such things as past tense from the linguistic data. The findings show that it is possible to simulate learning of small parts of language such as parts of phonology, morphology, noun gender, and so forth (see e.g., Sokolik and Smith 1988; Sokolik 1990). The computer is able to sense patterns in the data with a fair degree of accuracy and, while learning, produces errors, some of which are similar to those of human learners (for example, producing data that forms the *went-goed-went* U-shaped curve for irregular past tense verbs).

It is also possible to use connectionist modeling to investigate language transfer. Gasser (1990) wondered what the outcome would be if he "taught" simple forms of an L1 to a computer and then introduced it to forms from a second language. And, if he gave the computer forms in two other languages—one of which was similar to the L1 and one that was not—what might the outcome be? Gasser reports interesting findings, some of which match those of human learning: The L2 was never as well learned as the L1, but learning was initially easier in the L2 than it was at the beginning of L1 learning. There was less "interference" when the L2 was similar in word order to that of L1. As more and more L2 patterns were learned, the initial difference in favor of the similar L2 washed out. Thus, the findings provide additional support for Kellerman's (1977) hypothesis that perceived "language distance" influences the amount and type of transfer. The "language distance" hypothesis has, of course, been invoked as an explanation for data obtained in more traditional ways; for example, in Ringbom's (1987) comparison of the amount and types of transfer in the natural language use of speakers of similar languages (Swedish and English) and dissimilar languages (Finnish and English).

Further validation of the connectionist approach comes from another type of research methodology—introspection and retrospection. Haastrup (1991) analyzed "think-aloud" (i.e., introspection) and "retrospect" protocols in which paired Danish learners of English discussed test words in reading passages. Haastrup builds her work on Flores d'Arcais and Schreuder's (1983) cross-talk model. This model assumes that processing works in a parallel fashion across all levels of connections and that all levels communicate with each other directly. The following record of a think-aloud conversation illustrates that lexical, morphological, semantic, and text processing are accessed in a simultaneous parallel fashion (i.e., the data do not suggest serial, unidirectional processing). The passage is about a military leader with *insatiable* political ambitions.

Text 9.5 Test word: *insatiable*

Think-aloud

A: able means being able to—insane—ins
B: I think it is a positive word—something with extremely great
A: what does sati mean
B: satanic
B: there is also a negation—it is something with in——they couldn't be calmed down
A: why do you think it is a negation?
B: it usually is with in——I mean the prefix
A: he sounds as if he is rather single-minded
A: in-sa-ti- okay—in- is something with
B: it is a negation—it is something with u-
B: this is a good word—oh by the way sati is related to satisfy
A: yes he has not yet been satisfied.

(They agree on) not satisfied.

(Haastrup 1991: 127)

Connectionism gives us a welcome framework for dealing with data that is, by its very nature, messy, redundant, and nonlinear in many respects. Each month, new research reveals even more methods that might be used to test or give support to nonrule models of language learning, language attrition, and language performance. (For example, see Skousen's 1992a, 1992b analogic modeling of the linguistic variation found in actual use of *an* in contrast to rules on the use of *a/an*, variation in the use of the two greeting forms of "my brother" in Arabic [*ya/axi* and *yaxuuya*], and the variation in the use of Finnish past tense forms.)

Figure 4-4. Connectionism and Language Learning

Strengths

- Connectionist experiments are promising because they are designed to model learning without special innate linguistic preprogramming.
- The computer is relatively tireless, so experiments can be run indefinitely without damage to reliability. The computer can go back to "square one" at the start of each test.

- The finding that computers make errors in learning, some of which are similar to errors made by humans while acquiring the same material, attests to their potential for modeling human learning.
- Connectionist experiments that contrast the test results of humans and computers (e.g., Sokolik 1990) are especially useful in helping us understand the problems and potentials of modeling.
- Connectionist PDP models can also serve as the framework for analysis of think-aloud and retrospection protocols.

Weaknesses

- At this point in time, each experiment in computer modeling must, by its nature, be extremely limited in scope. (The numerous computer calculations and the inordinately long time it takes to train a network is a problem that Skousen's 1992 analogic method claims to overcome. While it is true that the computer can go back to "square one," the programmer must rework— untrain and retrain—the program to make this possible.)
- The "learning" that the computer is doing is mainly that of matching and sensing patterns in input lists. This is similar to phase-one matching and perhaps the beginning of phase-two restructuring in Karmiloff-Smith's terms.
- While much has been said to highlight the humanlike errors the computer makes, little has been said about the computer-generated errors that are unlikely if not impossible responses from humans. What prevents people from making errors similar to those generated by the computer?
- The "teaching" input is in no way similar to that given to humans. In natural language acquisition situations, people do not receive lists of words, phrases, or sentences completely out of context.
- While think-aloud and retrospection data can be better understood within the PDP model, such data do not test the model. That is, the data could be used as support for other models as well.
- It is important to remember that simulated neural networks are not the same as physical neural networks of the human body.

Modeling Scripts as Cognitive-Linguistic Structures

One of the criticisms of connectionism is that it models learning of some very small piece of language while learners, of course, must be able to use language in ordinary communication. Sharwood Smith (1988), in a discussion of how learners gain automatic control of language, offers an explanation that sounds like a combination of cognitive-process models and script theory. Imagine, he says, that you are about to take part in some event in the new language, an event *"where certain things can be predicted in advance"* (p. 57, our italics). You know what needs to be said. You may have attended language classes and have the ability to put utterances together in a conscious manner.

Then suppose that you repeat this activity again and again. It is, Sharwood Smith says, quite possible that what began as uncertain and conscious performance can eventually develop into automatized behavior.

When we imagine an event, according to Sharwood Smith's description, we may activate a skeleton script of all the *things that can be predicted* about that event. That script has evolved in much the same way as all our other knowledge. In response to a need, we form a plan to meet the need. We observe and see how X is done, do it, and refine and extend it to new instances. (This move from goal to plan to script, discussed in Schank and Abelson 1977, sounds very much like a three-phase process model.) When the plan is refined and consolidated, the end result is an abstract script. There are many different conceptual theories of script representation. The following description builds on Schank's (1984) conceptual dependency theory and the work of Anderson (1983) on augmented transition networks. The general notion is that we can model a representation of our knowledge of any event—model eating at a restaurant, a visit to the dentist, painting the hallway, or any of the myriad events we do in life to meet specific needs. This script is modeled by writing a computer program for it. The program is then tested by asking the computer questions that require script comprehension.

All scripts have roles, props, actions, and evaluation. If you want to model a language classroom, you must establish the *roles* people play within the script. TEACHER, STUDENT, TEACHER'S ASSISTANT, PRINCIPAL, CUSTODIAN are examples of such roles. These roles are placed in capital letters because they represent *cognitive concepts,* not *linguistic vocabulary* items. (In a courtroom, the roles include those of JUDGE, DEFENDANT, and so forth. In the hospital, DOCTOR, NURSE, PATIENT, and other roles are found.) The vocabulary items (*teacher, student,* and so forth) that represent these role concepts are activated along with the script. The connection between concepts and instances of concepts is modeled on the computer using an ISA link so that '*teacher* ISA TEACHER' shows that the lexical item *teacher* is an instance of the concept TEACHER and "inherits" all the characteristics of that role. Motives associated with actions are linked to roles. If the teacher holds up her hand, we do not expect students to interpret this as a signal that the teacher wishes to recite. Instead, the sign is recognized as a call for attention and quiet. The motive for the action is bound up with the role. Unmotivated actions are usually quite disturbing because we do not know exactly how to interpret them within the script.

In some scripts, the role has dress requirements, so 'JUDGE HASA ROBE,' 'NURSE HASA UNIFORM' would also be modeled. Roles also have particular *props* assigned to them. 'TEACHER HASA DESK,' 'JUDGE HASA GAVEL,' 'NURSE HASA CHART' are examples of props assigned to roles. (Notice that the relation of props and clothing is formalized with the HASA link.)[5]

In addition to having props, roles carry out *actions* that are usually modeled in temporal order. If you think of all the things that you do in the classroom, and place these actions in chronological order, you might have a set of acts similar to those modeled for a teacher to DO. These actions form the backbone of the script.

Some of the actions in scripts are physical. For example, the teacher may walk about the room. The MOVE concept can spread activation to the parallel semantic schema. There are many choices that mean to move "in a certain way."

Figure 4-5. A Semantic Analysis of MOVE

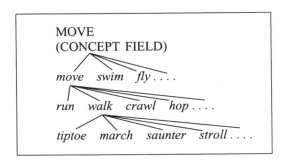

Research in semantics (e.g., Rosch 1978) shows that some terms are more basic than others. In this schema, the default basic term would be *walk*. "The teacher walked around the room." If the computer encounters a passage where "The teacher tiptoed around the room," it would be able to retrieve it through the MOVE options, but since it is a more specific form, it would also look for the role motivation of tiptoeing about. Perhaps that is something teachers do at specific times.

Other actions include the physical transfer (PTRANS) of objects, such as when the teacher moves books to a table. The actual movements within PTRANS are then further specified. The schema for GRASP involved in taking CONTrol of an object to be transferred might give us *pick up*. *Put* is the most basic term for PTRANS of an object to a flat surface. These choices give us "The teacher picked up the book" and "The teacher put the book on the table." In the case of teachers handing papers back to their students, however, the PTRANS of moving the object from one place to another is accompanied by an ATRANS, a transfer of ownership. The converses *give to/take from* and *give/receive* are typical verb choices for the transfer-of-ownership schema.

In classrooms, we hope that there is a healthy exchange of ideas. Ideas are not objects that can be picked up and moved from place to place. MTRANS is the concept for mental transfer of information. Possible vocabulary converses for this concept include *teach/learn from, ask/answer, tell/listen, say/hear, explain/understand*. For further explication of other action concepts, see Schank (1984).

EVALUATION is ongoing in all scripts. In a restaurant, we evaluate the service by judging the meal, its presentation, the service, the cost, and so forth in terms of how well it matches the script and how well it meets our goals in participating in the script (e.g., are we still hungry?). EVALUATION calls up evaluation terms, which may be arranged on a scale from positive to negative. Teachers constantly evaluate in the classroom and there are readily available formulaic utterances ("good," "right," "fantastic") for this function.

Formulaic utterances go with role actions in the script. "Time to turn in your papers," is a formulaic teacher utterance. "May I be excused?" is a formulaic student utterance. Much of the language of the script is predictable. Whether utterances, phrases, or individual lexical choices, these are activated as we move from concepts to the words that express them.

The language that is not formulaic needs to be specified in semantic schemas such as that illustrated above for MOVE. While there are not an enormous number of actions involved in scripts (Schank lists eleven), these action concepts activate semantic schemas that may be quite complex. Syntax is modeled to show cognitive relations. This should already be clear in the ISA and HASA link examples above. MOVE, PTRANS, ATRANS, and MTRANS are readily available in prototype patterns, but the pattern is a syntactic schema that links cognitive concepts. For example, the change of ownership schema might activate a pattern such as:

Figure 4-6. A Transfer-of-Ownership Schema

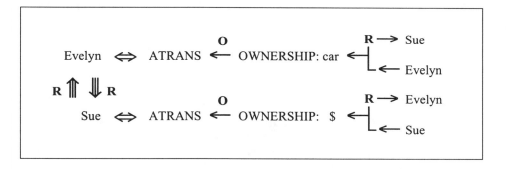

Following the arrows, Evelyn transfers ownership of the O (object) car to the R (recipient) Sue and Sue transfers ownership of the O (money) to R (Evelyn). That the exchange is reciprocal is shown by the triple-line arrows.

Once the researcher has succeeded in programming the model, it is tested to see whether the computer can answer questions on data in a way that shows "comprehension." This process of modeling and testing is cyclical. The model is revised after each test to fix any problems that remain.

If the program succeeds during tests, the second question is whether it is a plausible model of human cognitive processing. As we have described it, it certainly is not. It makes little sense to think that each time we take part in an activity, we have to check through hundreds of "files" trying to find the classroom script, the courtroom script, or the restaurant script. Schank and his colleagues agree. They have grouped scripts that share features to arrive at a hierarchy of overlapping scripts. The lower-level scripts inherit the shared features from the more general, higher levels. Thus, PAY for service is part of all service-encounter scripts and would be inherited by the restaurant, the grocery store, or the doctor's office visit. A WAITING ROOM would appear in professional office encounters, but not in all service encounters. It is inherited in all professional office visits—the doctor's, the dentist's, the lawyer's. Thus, when problems arise in comprehension within a script, one can check through a whole series of branching networks to find solutions.

Script models are written with the hope that they have neurobiological plausibility and reflect cognitive processing at least to some extent. The higher-level, more general scripts at the top of the hierarchy are called *memory organization packets,* a term that makes implicit reference to the goal of modeling human cognitive processes. Script builders talk about spreading activation across networks (as though they were parallel processing neural networks), about making choices among semantic fields where many are possible but the "winner takes all" once an item is selected. "Winner takes all" is a term used to explain inhibition of competing neural signals in cognitive science. Obviously, the researchers are attempting to present neurally plausible models. Terms, however, do not necessarily change a computer model into a model of cognitive processes. Still, the approach is attractive if one believes that language learning involves the acquisition of social, cognitive, and linguistic knowledge in a gradually integrated system, because scripts are a first step toward modeling such integrated knowledge.

Figure 4-7. Scripts as Cognitive Structures

Strengths

- Script modeling allows the researcher to begin with a conceptual base containing social information and integrate linguistic forms with it. Thus, the description is social-cognitive-linguistic rather than one or the other.
- Modeling is flexible in scope. You can model some very small aspect of language such as a semantic field taxonomy (e.g., legal terms to be used in a will). Or you can model a fairly simple script (e.g., the will itself), a more complex script (e.g., consulting a lawyer about a will), or a higher-level script (a professional office visit) that can then branch off to more specific instances (lawyer, doctor, dentist, teacher, psychologist visit). In addition to modeling scripts and semantic schemas, there is interest in modeling conceptual metaphor since creative, figurative use of language is so pervasive in all languages. Space does not permit further documentation of that work here, but Lakoff (1987) and Lakoff and Turner (1989) provide a good theoretical introduction to conceptual semantics and figurative language.
- Since the work is done on the computer, the researcher does not need to worry about the multitude of factors that affect reliability when human subjects are repeatedly tested. The number of tests that can be run are determined by the programmer's patience and skill.
- Because "what is modeled" includes event scripts and rhetorical structures, the "what" is very familiar to teachers and textbook writers. LSP (language for specific purposes) courses select from a variety of scripts and schemas according to the needs of students. Survival language courses and the situational approach in language teaching center on the language of ordinary social scripts such as going to the bank, getting a driver's license, and doing grocery shopping. There may be some universal set of scripts, but the roles,

props, actions, and evaluation in each will vary from culture to culture. Cognitive script models must reflect those differences. In contrast to script models, which have generally ignored this problem, schema modeling and modeling of rhetorical structures (e.g., the structure of narratives) have been much concerned with cross-language structures and the influence of the L1 on target language performance.

- The modeling of semantic schema relates to language acquisition theory and to situated teaching of vocabulary. Basic prototype terms are chosen for a script from the schema unless the script itself (or the evaluation component within the script) requires an alternative. So, for example, the most common change-of-ownership terms would be *give* when the focus is on the giver and *take* if the focus is on the taker. Thus, script modeling reflects human behavior: Language learners first acquire such unmarked, prototype vocabulary. If the script is a robbery, however, these unmarked terms would not be selected. Rather, the major focus is the robber role and, given the motives of robbers, *steal* would be the choice. *If* the original owner is mentioned in the exchange, the choice might be *hand over, give up,* or *relinquish.*[6]

Weaknesses

- Criticisms can be summarized in two general points: Modeling is difficult to do and, even when one is successful, the result may not tell us much about human cognitive processing.
- Modeling of scripts and semantic schemas takes considerable computer programming skill. Since it is so time-consuming, it is not something the ordinary researcher or classroom teacher would do. See, however, Gasser (1988, 1990), Zernik and Dyer (1986), and Zernik (1987).
- Many models are simply descriptive taxonomies (i.e., a semantic schema of kinship terms, clothing terms, or cooking terms in a hierarchically arranged taxonomy). If the goal is to model and test a schema description with the hope of linking it to a variety of scripts, that may be sufficient, but taxonomies, even if they are hierarchically arranged, are weak as models of cognitive processes.
- Unless the researcher is extremely skilled, the program may contain too much information. The result is sometimes referred to as "rabbits in, rabbits out." That is, any spectacular results that appear to be magic are simply the result of putting everything in and then displaying everything out.
- Language acquisition is not being modeled. Rather the researcher is writing a program. Once the program is completed, the researcher tests it to see whether the computer can use the program accurately to "comprehend" new language data and produce appropriate responses. The computer does not acquire the language; it simply uses the program it has been given. The same criticism, of course, has been leveled at innateness claims (the language acquisition device) of more traditional linguistic models.

Conclusion

We began this chapter by stating our position that language learning is the gradual integration of cognitive, social, and linguistic knowledge. In acquisition studies, researchers have traditionally taken a modular approach, examining areas of linguistic knowledge. We have pointed out that this leads to potential error in interpretation (Hatch, Shirai, and Fantuzzi 1990). We would argue further that not only is it misleading to carry out modular research of linguistic forms without considering cross-module influence but that it is misleading to carry out research on linguistic forms without considering the interlocking systems of cognitive and social knowledge. This position has important consequences in determining the scope of research. Each time we look at data that addresses a particular isolated piece of language, we must remember that it is but part of a much larger integrated system of social, cognitive, and linguistic knowledge. Our interpretation of the data may begin with our claims about the isolated piece, but we should then look at our data again from a more unified perspective. A final example might make this clear.

Many researchers have been interested in the acquisition of logical markers (e.g., *if, and, since, because, however*) by L1 learners of English. Logical markers explicitly signal the relation that the speaker or writer wants to draw in linking pieces of information. These are, then, *linguistic* instructions to the listener to perform certain types of *cognitive* operations in linking the information (e.g., assign causality, assign contrast, and so forth). A research team might collect natural language data from L2 learners and then build a stage model showing the order in which particular markers are acquired, what the functions of the markers are, and whether the order is the same for students from different first language groups. The stages might lead us to a set of acquisition principles that explain why particular markers are easier or more difficult for L2 learners. A second team might examine the data from a *process* model perspective, trying to discover evidence of memory consolidation in the use of markers. Since phase one, in Karmiloff-Smith's terms, requires matching of input, the team might need to do a contextual analysis in order to discover the frequency of different types of logical markers in the input. This analysis would look at frequency across many different genres of oral and written language (see Celce-Murcia 1990, 1991 for a description of this methodology). It might show us which types of markers are used in various scripts or by certain script roles. A third group, trained in the techniques of conversation analysis, could look at how markers are or are not used to promote collaborative construction of conversation or coherence in monologues (see Ford and Thompson 1986; Ford 1988; Lazaraton 1992 for examples). A fourth team might carry out a rhetorical structure analysis using Mann and Thompson's (1988) rhetorical structure theory (RST) methodology. This would give us further information about why we select certain markers to show the relations between ideas expressed in clauses. Students might be asked to "think-aloud" or "retrospect" about their use of markers (see Johns 1980, 1984). This might give evidence to parallel the RST information about how arguments are built within an extended text. The recorded introspections and retrospections might also be analyzed for conscious affective reactions to particular markers (are some viewed as positive, novel, interesting, and pleasurable and others as negative, vague, dull, and boring?). These tapes and natural language data might also be used to look for evidence of separate automatic and analyzed dimensions. A comparison could be made between oral and written language data to discover when and how markers are used to make the nature of the relationship between clauses more explicit. To investigate the effect of L1 on the use of markers, a team could begin by reviewing Scarcella's (1984) study of the frequency and forms of markers used as cohesive ties in the academic writing of native speakers and university foreign students. Each member of the team might select a different first language group. Teacher researchers (Curran 1983; Carter 1992) have noticed that Korean students show atypical use of logical markers such as "that's why" and "so." An analysis of clause chaining in Korean and other languages using the RST model might be done. Furthermore, findings from neurobiological investigations can be consulted to check neural plausibility of models and theories derived from such an array of studies. Neurobiology may also provide us with insights of different ways of looking at linguistic data, which will in turn stimulate new approaches to research. The list of possibilities is unending.

Obviously, each of these studies would give us one piece of the puzzle. However, with a group research effort (such as that of ZISA in Europe or the JOSEF group in Japan), a more comprehensive, integrated approach is possible. To use memory consolidation as a metaphor, each piece of information provided by a given study is represented in connections. These connections will be consolidated and streamlined each time the research team meets. Parallel networks will be established as more and more studies are under way, each with cross-network connections. These connections will gradually consolidate until some critical threshold is reached. At that point, the findings of the studies will have promoted an integrated understanding of the use of markers in parts of the cognitive, linguistic, social system. That understanding would then form an integrated system on which we could build further understanding of language learning.

This may sound like "pie in the sky," but all it takes is an announcement at TESOL, ACTFL, or AAAL that research is going to be carried out on a selected topic with an invitation to all interested parties to join. Teachers and teacher trainers often search for new projects for students in their courses, projects that are related to course content. Anyone teaching a composition course, a methods course, a language acquisition course, a language analysis class, or a course in contrastive analysis could easily fit such a project into a syllabus. The organizers should be prepared with ideas about what should be researched, offer suggestions about the type of data that might be collected, the kinds of research methods that might best suit the interests and talents of the volunteer researchers, and offer help with analyses. With easier access to e-mail internationally, the group can schedule "meetings" every day if they wish. With a communications network, everyone would "hear" the questions and either offer or critique advice. They could comment on conflicting or similar findings in their data, offer to share data, take each other to task on statistical methods used, and so forth. What it takes is a few people willing to start the process, organize the network, and help guide the effort. The results, however, would be worth the effort, for they would illustrate the possibility of integrated research on cognitive-social-linguistic processes. (For a description of one possible implementation plan, see Clark and Davidson, this volume.)

Notes

1. We thank Bob Jacobs, Alice Hadley, Anne Lazaraton, Elizabeth Martin, Barry McLaughlin, Mary Lee Scott, and two anonymous readers for their comments and suggestions. The errors that remain are ours alone.

   We regret that we have only lightly touched on the importance of prior knowledge structures (L1 linguistic, cognitive, and social information) on the learning of additional languages. The vast research on L1 influence (transfer and interference) shows how important prior knowledge is. To adequately discuss cognitive processes *and* the importance of prior knowledge in shaping those processes would require at least another chapter, if not a book.

2. Applied linguists generally believe that cognitive processing (rather than strictly linguistic processing) is fundamental to adult and foreign language learning. For the adult, these processes are strengthened, in part, because they have already been established in first language use. There is considerable argument about whether different language-specific (i.e., specifically linguistic) processes are used in L1 acquisition and early child bilingualism. There is perhaps less argument about adult language learning. Bley-Vroman (1988) charts possible differences between child and adult learning as:

Child	Adult
Universal grammar	Native language knowledge
Domain-specific learning procedures	General problem-solving systems

3. In neurobiological terms (see Squire 1985), this means that synaptic connections are formed as the axon of the neuron makes contact with its postsynaptic partners. These connections stabilize as the synaptic transmitter is released from the nerve terminal and received by the target cell. The connections may then become modified as synapses are rearranged or eliminated in certain regions of the nervous system. Increases in synaptic strength are typically accompanied by decreases in the strength of competing connections and processing becomes more efficient.

4. This, of course, is in sharp contrast to the notion of an innate "language acquisition device," an in-place universal linguistic program set for a particular language via a series of "parameters." The symbolic view of language learning assumes that the program, once the parameters are set, begins to work out "rules" that operate on linguistic units or symbols. In symbolic models, language learning is the result of "rule-governed" mental behavior. In connectionist models, patterned behavior results from neural firing across networks of connections.

5. This explains why a definite rather than an indefinite article is used for props: Both roles and props are "known" items once a script is activated. We wouldn't say "A teacher erased a blackboard" in describing a classroom. Instead, we would use definite articles even though neither *teacher* nor *blackboard* has been given previous mention: "The teacher erased the blackboard."

6. It's clear that the same structure works in athletics. An athlete can *take away* a record or even *steal* it if it is won by the slightest of margins. The former record *holder,* who may not even be there, reluctantly *relinquishes* the record. And the change of ownership does not involve a physical object but an abstract idea of being the best in the world. No one *holds* anything. In interviews, Olympic athletes repeatedly commented on this difference by saying they value their medals because no one can take them away from them.

References

Cognitive Processes in Language Learning

Andersen, Roger. 1984. "The One-to-One Principle of Interlanguage Construction." *Language Learning* 34: 77–95.

———. 1988. "Models, Processes, Principles, and Strategies: Second Language Acquisition in and out of the Classroom." *IDEAL* 3: 111–38.

Anderson, James A. 1983. *The Architecture of Cognition.* Cambridge, MA: Harvard Univ. Press.

Bahrick, Harry P. 1984a. "Semantic Memory Content in Permastore: 50 Years of Memory for Spanish Learned in School." *Journal of Experimental Psychology: General* 113,1: 1–31.

———. 1984b. "Fifty Years of Second Language Attrition: Implications for Programmatic Research." *Modern Language Journal* 68: 105–18.

Berman, Ruth. 1986. "A Step-by-Step Model of Language Learning," in Iris Levin, ed., *Stage and Structure: Reopening the Debate.* Norwood, NJ: Ablex.

———, and Elite Olshtain. 1983. "Features of First Language Transfer in Second Language Attrition." *Applied Linguistics* 4: 222–34.

Bialystok, Ellen. 1982. "On the Relationship between Knowing and Using Linguistic Forms." *Applied Linguistics* 3,3: 181–206.

———. 1988. "Psycholinguistic Dimensions of Second Language Proficiency," in William Rutherford and Michael Sharwood Smith, eds., *Grammar and Second Language Teaching: A Book of Readings.* New York: Newbury House.

———. 1991. "Achieving Proficiency in a Second Language: A Processing Description," in Robert Phillipson, Eric Kellerman, Larry Selinker, Michael Sharwood Smith, and Merrill Swain, eds., *Foreign/Second Language Pedagogy Research.* Clevedon, Eng.: Multilingual Matters.

Bley-Vroman, Robert. 1988. "The Fundamental Character of Foreign Language Learning," in William Rutherford and Michael Sharwood Smith, eds., *Grammar and Second Language Teaching.* New York: Newbury House.

Carter, Elizabeth. 1992. "A Korean Student's Oral and Written Discourse." Unpublished paper.

Celce-Murcia, Marianne, and Gabriel Vialla. 1983. "The Second French Immersion Experience of an English-Speaking Child," in Kathleen Bailey, Michael Long, and Sabrina Peck, eds., *Second Language Acquisition Studies.* Rowley, MA: Newbury House.

———. 1990. "Data-Based Language Analysis and TESL," in James E. Alatis, ed., *Linguistics, Language Teaching and Language Acquisition: The Interdependence of Theory, Practice, and Research.* Georgetown University Round Table on Language and Linguistics. Washington, DC: Georgetown Univ. Press.

———. 1991. "Discourse Analysis and Grammar Instruction," *Annual Review of Applied Linguistics* 11: 135–51.

Clahsen, Harald. 1984. "The Acquisition of German Word Order: A Test Case for Cognitive Approaches to L2 Development," in Roger Andersen, ed., *Second Language: A Crosslinguistic Perspective.* Rowley, MA: Newbury House.

Cohen, Andrew D. 1974. "The Culver City Spanish Immersion Program: How Does Summer Recess Affect Spanish Speaking Ability?" *Language Learning* 24,1: 55–68.

———. 1975. "Forgetting a Second Language." *Language Learning* 25,1: 127–38.

Craik, Fergus, and E. Simon. 1980. "Age Differences in Memory: The Roles of Attention and Depth of Processing," in Leonard Poon, John Fozard, Laird Cermak, D. Arenberg, and L. Thompson, eds., *New Directions in Memory and Aging: Proceedings of the George A. Talland Memorial Conference.* Hillsdale, NJ: Erlbaum.

Curran, Susan. 1983. "Transfer and Topic Prominence in Korean-English." M.A. thesis, Dept. of Linguistics, Univ. of California–Los Angeles.

Ellis, Rod. 1986. *Understanding Second Language Acquisition.* Oxford, Eng.: Oxford Univ. Press.

Flores D'Arcais, Giovanni, and R. Schreuder. 1983. "The Process of Language Understanding: A Few Issues in Contemporary Psycholinguistics," in Giovanni Flores D'Arcais and Robert Jarvella, eds., *The Process of Language Understanding.* New York: Wiley.

Ford, Cecilia. 1988. "Grammar in Ordinary Interaction: The Pragmatics of Adverbial Clauses in Conversational English." Unpublished Ph.D. diss., Dept. of Linguistics, Univ. of California–Los Angeles.

———, and Sandra Thompson. 1986. "Conditionals in Discourse: A Text-Based Study from English," in Elisabeth Traugott, Alice ter Meulen, Judy Reilly, and Charles Ferguson, eds., *On Conditionals.* Cambridge, Eng.: Cambridge Univ. Press.

Gasser, Michael. 1988. *A Connectionist Model of Sentence Generation in a First and Second Language.* Tech. Report No. UCLA-AI-88-13. Los Angeles: UCLA, Computer Science Department.

———. 1990. "Connectionism and Universals of Second Language Acquisition." *Studies in Second Language Acquisition* 12: 179–99.

Geschwind, Norman. 1980. "Language and Communication in the Elderly: An Overview," in Loraine Obler and Martin Albert, eds., *Language and Communication in the Elderly.* Lexington, MA: Lexington.

Haastrup, Kirsten. 1991. "Developing Learners' Procedural Knowledge in Comprehension," in Robert Phillipson, Eric Kellerman, Larry Selinker, Michael Sharwood Smith, and Merrill Swain, eds., *Foreign/Second Language Pedagogy Research.* Clevedon, Eng.: Multilingual Matters.

Hakuta, Kenji. 1978. "A Report on the Development of Grammatical Morphemes in a Japanese Girl Learning English as a Second Language," in Evelyn Hatch, ed., *Second Language Acquisition: A Book of Readings.* Rowley, MA: Newbury House.

Hatch, Evelyn. 1978. *Second Language Acquisition: A Book of Readings.* Rowley, MA: Newbury House.

———, and Barbara Hawkins. 1991. "Participant Tracking and the Question of U-Shaped Learning Curves." Paper presented at AAAL, Seattle, WA.

———, Yasuhiro Shirai, and Cheryl Fantuzzi. 1990. "The Need for an Integrated Theory: Connecting Modules." *TESOL Quarterly* 24,4: 697–716.

Huang, Joseph, and Evelyn Hatch. 1978. "A Chinese Child's Acquisition of English," in Evelyn Hatch, ed., *Second Language Acquisition: A Book of Readings.* Rowley, MA: Newbury House.

Itoh, Harumi, and Evelyn Hatch. 1978. "Second Language Acquisition: A Case Study," in Evelyn Hatch, ed., *Second Language Acquisition: A Book of Readings.* Rowley, MA: Newbury House.

Jacobs, Bob. 1988. "Neurobiological Differentiation of Primary and Secondary Language Acquisition." *Studies in Second Language Acquisition* 10: 303–39.

———, and John Schumann. 1992. "Applied Linguistics, Language Acquisition, and Neuroscience: Towards a More Integrative Perspective." *Applied Linguistics* 13,3: 282–301.

Johns, Ann. 1980. "Cohesive Error in the Written Discourse of Nonnative Speakers." *CATESOL Occasional Papers* 8: 65–70.

———. 1984. "Textual Cohesion and the Chinese Speaker of English." *Language Learning and Communication* 3: 1–92.

Karmiloff-Smith, Annette. 1985. "Language and Cognitive Processes from a Developmental Perspective." *Language and Cognitive Processes* 1,1: 60–85.

Kellerman, Eric. 1977. "Toward a Characterization of the Strategy of Transfer." *Interlanguage Studies Bulletin* 2: 59–92.

Krashen, Stephen. 1982. *Principles and Practice in Second Language.* New York: Pergamon.

Lakoff, George. 1987. *Women, Fire, and Dangerous Things: What Categories Reveal about the Mind.* Chicago: Univ. of Chicago Press.

———. 1989. "A Suggestion for a Linguistics with Connectionist Foundations," in D. Touretsky, G. Hinton, and Terrence Sejnowski, eds., *Proceedings of the 1988 Connectionist Models Summer School.* San Mateo, CA: Morgan Kaufmann.

———, and Mark Turner. 1989. *More than Cool Reason.* Chicago: Univ. of Chicago Press.

Lazaraton, Anne. 1992. "Linking Ideas with AND in Spoken and Written Discourse." *International Review of Applied Linguistics* 30: 191–206.

Long, Michael. 1990. "The Least a Second Language Acquisition Theory Needs to Explain." *TESOL Quarterly* 24: 649–66.

Mann, William, and Sandra Thompson. 1988. "Rhetorical Structure Theory: Towards a Functional Theory of Text Organization." *TEXT* 8,3: 243–81.

McLaughlin, Barry. 1987. *Theories of Second Language Learning.* London, Eng.: Edward Arnold.

———. 1990. "Restructuring." *Applied Linguistics* 11,2: 113–28.

Moorecroft, R., and Robert Gardner. 1987. "Linguistic Factors in Second Language Loss." *Language Learning* 37,3: 327–40.

Nakazawa, Yasuo. 1989. "Kikoku shijo no nihon kikokugo no gaigokugo ijiteedo o ketteesuru yooin ni tuiteno choosa" [A Report on the Factors That Determine Foreign Language Retention of Returnees after Returning to Japan], in *Kikoku shijo no gaikokugo hoji ni kansuru chosa kenkyu hokokusho* [A Survey on the Foreign Language Retention of Returnees], Vol. 1. Tokyo: Kaigai shijo kyoiku shinko zaidan [Japan Overseas Student Education Foundation].

Olshtain, Elite. 1986. "The Attrition of English as a Second Language with Speakers of Hebrew," in Bert Weltens, Kees De Bot and Theo Van Els, eds., *Language Attrition in Progress.* Dordrecht, Neth.: Foris.

Pienemann, Manfred. 1984. "Psychological Constraints on the Teachability of Languages." *Studies in Second Language Acquisition* 6,2: 186–214.

Ringbom, Hakan. 1987. *The Role of the First Language in Foreign Language Learning.* Clevedon, Eng.: Multilingual Matters.

Rosch, Eleanor. 1978. "Principles of Categorization," in Eleanor Rosch and Barbara Lloyd, eds., *Cognition and Categorization.* Hillsdale, NJ: Erlbaum.

Sato, Edynne, and Bob Jacobs. 1992. "From Input to Intake: Towards a Brain-Based Perspective of Selective Attention." *Issues in Applied Linguistics* 3: 267–92.

Scarcella, Robin. 1984. "Cohesion in the Writing Development of Native and Non-Native English Speakers." Unpublished Ph.D. diss., Dept. of Linguistics, Univ. of Southern California.

Schank, Roger. 1984. *Conceptual Information Processing.* Amsterdam, Neth.: North Holland.

————, and Robert Abelson. 1977. *Scripts, Plans, Goals and Understanding*. Hillsdale, NJ: Erlbaum.

Scherer, George. 1957. "The Forgetting Rate of Learning German." *German Quarterly* 30: 275–77.

Schumann, John. 1975. "Affective Factors and the Problems of Age in Second Language Acquisition." *Language Learning* 26: 135–43.

————. 1978. "The Acculturation Model for Second Language Acquisition," in Rosario Gingras, ed., *Second Language Acquisition and Foreign Language Teaching*. Washington, DC: Center for Applied Linguistics.

————. 1987. "Acquisition of Temporality in Basilang Speech." *Studies in Second Language Acquisition* 9: 21–42.

————. 1990a. "Extending the Scope of the Acculturation/Pidginization Model to Include Cognition." *TESOL Quarterly* 24,4: 667–84.

————. 1990b. "The Role of the Amygdala as a Mediator of Affect and Cognition in Second Language Acquisition," in James E. Alatis, ed., *Linguistics, Language Teaching and Language Acquisition: The Interdependence of Theory, Practice and Research*. Georgetown University Round Table on Languages and Linguistics. Washington, DC: Georgetown Univ. Press.

Scott, Mary Lee. 1992. "Auditory Memory and Perception in Younger and Older Adult Second Language Learners." Unpublished ms., Linguistics Department, Brigham Young Univ., Provo, UT.

Sharwood Smith, Michael. 1988. "Consciousness Raising and the Second Language Learner," in William Rutherford and Michael Sharwood Smith, eds., *Grammar and Second Language Teaching*. New York: Newbury House.

Skousen, Royal. 1992a. *Analogy and Structure*. Dordrecht, Neth.: Kluwer.

————. 1992b. "Analogy: A Non-Rule Alternative to Neural Networks." Paper presented at the 21st Annual Linguistic Symposium, Univ. of Wisconsin at Milwaukee. [Paper can be obtained from the author, Department of English, Brigham Young University, Provo, UT 84602.]

Smith, Neil, and Ianthi Tsimpli. 1991. "Linguistic Modularity? A Case Study of a 'Savant' Linguist." *Lingua* 84: 315–51.

Sokolik, Margaret. 1990. "Learning without Rules: PDP and a Resolution of the Adult Language Learning Paradox." *TESOL Quarterly* 24,4: 685–96.

————, and M. E. Smith. 1988. "French Gender Recognition: A Network Model and Implications for SLA." Paper presented at the Ninth Second Language Research Forum, Los Angeles.

Squire, Larry. 1985. "Memory: Neural Organization and Behavior," in John Brookhart and Vernon Mountcastle, eds., *Handbook of Physiology: The Nervous System V*. American Physiological Society.

————. 1986. "Mechanisms of Memory." *Science* 232: 1612–19.

Tarone, Elaine. 1983. "On the Variability of Interlanguage Systems." *Applied Linguistics* 4,2: 143–63.

Wong Fillmore, Lily. 1976. "The Second Time Around." Unpublished Ph.D. diss., Stanford Univ.

Yamada, Jun. 1981. "Evidence for the Independence of Language and Cognition: Case Study of a 'Hyperlinguistic' Adolescent." *UCLA Working Papers in Cognitive Linguistics* 3: 121–60.

————. 1983. "The Independence of Language." Unpublished Ph.D. diss., Dept. of Linguistics, Univ. of California–Los Angeles.

Yoshida, Kensaku. 1989. "Kikoku shijo no gaikokugo hoji nikansuru ichi kosatu" [A Consideration on the Retention of a Foreign Language by Returnees], in *Kikoku shijo no gaikokugo hoji ni kansuru chosa kenkyu hokokusho* [A Survey on the Foreign Language Retention of Returnees], Vol. 1. Tokyo: Kaigai shijo kyoiku shinko zaidan. [Japan Overseas Student Education Foundation.]

Yoshitomi, Asako. 1992a. "Second Language Attrition: A Review of Literature and Considerations for Future Research." Qualifying paper, Applied Linguistics, Univ. of California–Los Angeles.

————. 1992b. "Towards a Model of Language Attrition: Neurobiological and Psychological Contributions." *Issues in Applied Linguistics* 3: 293–318.

Zernik, Uri. 1987. *Failure-Driven Acquisition of Figurative Phrases by Second Language Speakers.* Los Angeles: UCLA, Computer Science Department.

————, and Michael Dyer. 1986. *Disambiguation and Language Acquisition through the Phrasal Lexicon.* Tech. Rep. No. 86-2. Los Angeles: UCLA, Computer Science Department.

5

Learner Characteristics in Second-Language Acquisition

J. Michael O'Malley
Prince William County Public Schools

Anna Uhl Chamot
Georgetown University

Introduction

This chapter focuses on learner characteristics that can contribute to our understanding of individual differences in second-language acquisition. The range of learner characteristics considered as potentially influential in second-language acquisition is extremely broad and includes exhaustive listings of variables such as age, gender, attitude, aptitude, personality, and cognitive style (e.g., see Galloway and Labarca 1990; Larsen-Freeman and Long 1991 for recent comprehensive reviews). These listings are typically accompanied by an analysis of why each characteristic is thought to influence second-language acquisition and a discussion of correlations between one or more learner characteristics and second-language outcomes. While interesting, these analyses have not provided an integrated view of learner characteristics that influence learning outcomes and are responsive to instruction.

One approach not yet taken in these and other reviews (e.g., Skehan 1989; Parry and Stansfield 1990) is to advance a central theoretical position at the onset that will be used to select learner characteristics, indicate why the characteristics are expected to influence language-learning outcomes, and then examine research evidence to suggest their level and type of influence. We build the foundation for this review by describing

J. Michael O'Malley (Ph.D., George Peabody College) is Supervisor of Assessment and Evaluation in the Prince William County Schools in Virginia. He has published the results of his research on learning strategies in second-language acquisition in journals such as *Applied Linguistics, Studies in Second Language Acquisition, TESOL Quarterly,* and *Language Learning* in addition to authoring two books and various instructional materials with Dr. Chamot.

Anna Uhl Chamot (Ph.D., University of Texas at Austin) is Director of Language Research Projects at Georgetown University and Adjunct Professor of Linguistics. Her research on language-learning strategies has appeared in *Foreign Language Annals, Applied Linguistics, TESOL Quarterly, Studies in Second Language Learning,* and *Language Learning.* She is author and co-author of instructional materials and has also published two books with Dr. O'Malley.

a cognitive-theoretical view of second-language acquisition in some detail. We then specify theory-derived learner characteristics that should influence learning outcomes and use the theory to examine other representative learner characteristics that may be important for instruction. Finally, we identify research methods that have promise for analyzing these learner characteristics and draw instructional implications from the theory that describes them.

Learner characteristics have significance in second-language acquisition because of their purported relationship to individual differences in the rate of learning and level of proficiency individuals attain. That is, variables such as age, motivation, learning style, or aptitude may influence the ways in which individuals go about learning a second language, their rate of learning, or their ultimate proficiency in using the language effectively. Individual characteristics of learners may influence acquisition even in varying learning contexts and for different language tasks. Moreover, learner characteristics may be used in selecting individuals for language study who are most likely to succeed or for adapting instructional methods to individual styles or aptitudes of learners (Parry and Stansfield 1990). Learner characteristics also have interest as a way for research and theory to improve our understanding of these variables and the ways in which they are interrelated in conceptual models of second-language acquisition.

A Cognitive-Theoretical View of Learning

Cognitive models of learning indicate that learning is an active, dynamic process in which learners select information from their environment, organize the information, relate it to what they already know, retain what they consider to be important, use the information in appropriate contexts, and reflect on the success of their learning efforts (Gagné 1985; Shuell 1986). Cognitive theories of learning begin with a distinction among three types of functions in memory (Lachman, Lachman, and Butterfield 1979; Anderson 1985; Shuell 1986). There appears to be a *long-term memory* in which the information stored is derived from personal experience and education. A *short-term memory* is used to briefly remember information that is unimportant to retain more than a few moments or is easily forgotten. There also seems to be a *working memory* in which we manipulate information as in performing mathematical calculations, solving problems, reorganizing information, or comparing what we already know with new information just presented. We modify and expand on information in long-term memory based on new information that is stored temporarily in short-term memory and manipulated while in working memory. The information manipulated in working memory can be drawn not only from short-term memory but also from long-term memory, enabling learners to compare new and former learning contents and processes.

Because learning is an active, dynamic process, we believe that second-language acquisition will occur most effectively with high degrees of learner involvement. Learners in both classroom and nonclassroom settings analyze what they are doing, think about the learning that occurs, anticipate the kinds of language demands they are likely to encounter, and marshall prior knowledge and skills to apply to new learning opportunities (O'Malley et al. 1985a). Learning a second language is therefore strategic and involves the use of higher-order thinking skills. This type of strategic learning can focus on understanding or communicating meaningful ideas orally or in writing, or can focus on discrete components of the language such as vocabulary and syntax. Once language skills are fully learned, they can be performed with reasonable accuracy and speed with little awareness (McLaughlin 1987). The cognitive view directly contradicts one prevalent view of second-language acquisition, which holds that the learning process itself is most effective when it occurs unconsciously or without awareness (e.g., Dulay, Burt, and Krashen 1982).

The particular representation of cognitive theory we have selected is based largely on the work of John Anderson (1983; 1985) with elaborations and instructional implications drawn by others (e.g., Gagné 1985; Shuell 1986; Jones et al. 1987). Anderson's work integrates other independent views of cognitive processing and has been continually updated, expanded, and refined (e.g., Anderson 1989; 1990). The theory is especially relevant in second-language acquisition because it can be used to examine complex cognitive skills and individual differences, addresses strategic learning and processing, and is adaptable to informing instructional processes.

The cognitive-theoretical framework must address how both simple and complex information and skills are stored in memory and describe how they are learned. In addition, the theory should identify the components of motivation and describe how motivation influences learning. For the theory to be useful, the implications for instruction should be explicit, suggesting what teachers should do in classrooms and what learners can do to improve their own learning.

What Is Learned?

Anderson (1983; 1985) suggests that most information is stored in long-term memory as either *declarative knowledge* or *procedural knowledge*. Declarative knowledge consists of "what" we know or can declare, and procedural knowledge consists of the things that we know "how" to do. Declarative knowledge is stored in memory frameworks or *schemata* (Minsky 1975; Norman, Rumelhart, and the LNR Research Group 1975) that consist of interconnected concepts. One example might be the concept of a household pet, with subconcepts that represent the type of pet, characteristics of different pets, and the functions pets serve in homes. A second example is the scripts and plans associated with common activities such as eating in a restaurant and going to work (Schank and Abelson 1977). The connections between these concepts are extremely complex and are often hierarchical. Schemata may result from formal education, such as the hierarchy of the animal kingdom, or other experiences, in which we sometimes link objects, people, or concepts in idiosyncratic ways. Depending on prior learning experiences, the concepts may be connected with various strengths of association such that the recall of one concept will evoke the recall of others, depending on the strength of association (Anderson 1983).

Language pervades schemata through *propositional representations* (see Kintsch 1974) or abbreviated language that represents the original textual information. These language-based representations maintain essential meanings by abstracting the complete language used to express the original concepts (Stillings et al. 1987). Essential meanings may include the subject and object of a sentence, the ways in which concepts are related in the sentence, a causal sequence, or a hierarchical relationship. Objects might be related in the household pet example in that the person speaking a sentence might express *liking* a particular household animal or *petting* it affectionately. Unimportant information not retained in the propositional representation might include incidental details, connecting words, or other elements that are not the focus of attention. Once learned, essential concepts represented by propositions may be retained even though specific vocabulary terms used to express them are forgotten, as is often found among high school students expected to retain science or foreign language vocabulary terms over a summer.

The second way of storing information in memory, procedural knowledge, concerns what we know "how" to do. This includes both simple and complex physical or mental procedures. Procedural knowledge is stored in memory as *production systems,* which are condition-action sequences that specify what mental action will be taken when a given condition occurs (Carpenter and Just 1989). The condition and action are connected by an IF-THEN sequence, usually with an intermediate "and" clause, which controls whether the action follows from the condition. Production systems can be used to explain a variety of language and other procedural mental processes, including learning strategies and problem solving.

Production systems may be the basis in memory that enables individuals to act on simple language rules such as the rules for pluralization and grammatical construction (Anderson 1983). Production systems may also be the basis for storing more complex skills such as communicative competence. Canale and Swain (1980) define communicative competence as the ability to use grammatical, sociolinguistic, discourse, and strategic skills. An individual who is communicatively competent in a second language might have the following interaction (adapted from O'Malley, Chamot, and Walker 1987):

1. IF my goal is to engage in conversation with Sally,
   and Sally is monolingual in English,
   THEN the subgoal is to use my second language.

2. IF my goal is to use my second language,
   THEN the subgoal is to initiate a conversation.
   (sociolinguistic competence)

3. IF my goal is to initiate a conversation,
   THEN my subgoal is to say a memorized greeting.
   (discourse competence)

4. IF my goal is to say a memorized greeting,
   and the context is an informal one,
   THEN choose the appropriate language style.
   (sociolinguistic competence)

5. IF my goal is to choose an appropriate language style,
   THEN the subgoal is to say, "How's it going Sally?"
   (grammatical and sociolinguistic competence)

This example illustrates four important features of production systems. First, they are oriented toward attaining specific goals, such as interpersonal goals in communication. Second, they are conditional and may proceed in a number of directions depending on the "and" portion of the production. The speaker checks on the identity of the person to be greeted, determines that she is monolingual in English, and then formulates a statement. If the condition specified in the "and" portion is not met, the production could go in an entirely different direction. Third, production systems are sequential. The last clause of each individual production cues the first clause of the next. A fourth feature is their flexibility. At each step, because of the conditionality of the "and" clause, a number of different types of conditions can be accommodated. The example could continue with a series of other exchanges depending on the way in which the person responds to the greeting.

A considerable amount of *metacognitive knowledge* is required in using production systems (Paris and Winograd 1990). At each step in the production system, individuals may reflect on their progress in attaining a goal and take a different path or even change the goal entirely. Furthermore, within each step, the learner makes decisions concerning the conditionality expressed in the "and" statement. Learners also recognize the similarity between new and previous language elements or language-learning opportunities. In this regard, metacognitive knowledge entails (1) matching the pattern of the language elements and context with patterns experienced in the past, and (2) applying strategies that worked in the past to the learning situation at hand. This type of matching requires an interaction between procedural and declarative knowledge, since long-term memory contains experiences with previous language-learning situations that may have similar features.

How Is New Information Learned?

Apart from identifying the ways in which information is stored in memory, why is the distinction between declarative and procedural knowledge important? The major reason is that declarative and procedural knowledge appear to be learned in different ways (Gagné 1985). Furthermore, the information is retrieved from memory in different ways. These differences have implications for what teachers do during instruction and what students should do while learning.

Establishing Links to Long-Term Memory.

Declarative knowledge is learned most effectively by building on previous knowledge represented in existing schemata in long-term memory (Gagné 1985; Stillings et al. 1987). Schemata can be modified by altering an existing concept, linking existing concepts in new ways, adding a new concept to existing schemata, adding new schematic structures, or changing the organizational structure of schemata. To change the structure of existing schemata, the schematic framework for existing concepts can be reorganized or restructured by shifting the basis for the hierarchy or establishing a new foundation altogether for its organization (Rumelhart and Norman 1978). For example, one organizing framework for computer software is the language in which the software is written, while a second is the purposes for which the software was designed. Similarly, literature can be organized in terms of the historical period it represents or recurrent themes developed by the authors.

This theoretical analysis of declarative knowledge has direct implications for instruction and learning. To learn new information through a second language, students should first identify what they already know about the material even if what they know consists of a few target language words or some preliminary concepts in their native language. They can expand on this knowledge by checking what they know against new information being presented, by looking for new concepts that expand on previous concepts, and by looking for the organization of new knowledge to determine if it matches a familiar organization. The least effective way to learn new information would be to construct new schemata out of unfamiliar concepts or language rules (Gagné 1985).

The more ways in which new information is linked to existing information in memory, and the more effectively the information is organized, the stronger the associations become and the easier it should be to remember (Anderson 1983; Stillings et al. 1987). This implies that students should develop images of new words, organize new words into groups, think what they know about the concept the word represents, try to use words in sentences or in meaningful communication, act out sentences, and otherwise build strong associations in multiple ways with existing memory. In contrast, in learning by repetition, students "go over and over" a list of vocabulary or other items, forming only superficial linkages with existing schemata.

There should be little reason to believe that the memory schemata in one language cannot be used to help solve problems or understand similar information in a second language, provided that the concepts in each language are similar. That is, the propositional representations—with their subjects, objects, causal sequences, and hierarchies—can remain the same even though the language used to express them may differ.

Integrative Practice with Procedural Knowledge.

In contrast to declarative knowledge, procedural knowledge is learned most effectively through integrative practice with a complete skill that has meaning and achieves an important goal. There are at least three ways to accomplish this end and avoid the rule-based memorization of which production systems occur in a correct sequence. One method for learning procedural knowledge is to *observe and model complete sequences* of goal-oriented expert performance (Gagné 1985). Provided that the language sequence is not too complex to be retained, the novice learner can repeat the sequence and use it to attain the same goal. A second method is to identify manageable but meaningful and integrated components of the complete skill, *gain partial mastery over the components* by practicing them with feedback, and piece them together to make a complete action sequence that achieves a meaningful goal. The feedback can come either from the teacher or from more skilled peers. Anderson (1983) refers to this process of combining separate productions as *composition.* A third method for learning procedural knowledge is *learning by analogy* (Rumelhart and Norman 1981). For example, a learner can draw a parallel between a familiar and an unfamiliar language in order to facilitate new learning, identifying portions of the familiar language that can be applied to the new task or setting. Individuals can improve execution of a complex skill through practice until it looks like "expert" performance. They can model an ideal performance, seek out feedback, or refer back to the rules only as needed for refinements in the skill performance. Ultimately, the skill will be performed to resemble the speed, accuracy, and flexibility of expert performance. Shiffrin and Schneider (1977) refer to the shift from conscious and controlled processing to fluent processing as *automaticity*.

Application to Second-Language Acquisition

Students in second-language acquisition often strive to improve their skills by modeling expert performance, whether in oral or written language. Students may listen to tapes and imitate model pronunciation or look at written communication or interpersonal exchanges on tape or film for models of communicative competence. As both students and teachers know, achieving expertlike performance in a second language is fraught with difficulties and takes a considerable amount of time. This is consistent with what is known about any complex procedural skill, such as effective reading comprehension, problem-solving, or the effective use of learning strategies in one's first language.

Two additional pieces of information from cognitive theory have a bearing on second-language acquisition. First, procedural skills are difficult to transfer to new complex tasks (Derry and Murphy 1986). For example, effective learning strategies used with reading tasks in a first language do not readily transfer to reading in a second language (McLeod and McLaughlin 1986). Difficulties in transfer may result from the complexity of the new task, lack of similarity between a former task and a new one, inappropriate transfer of interfering skills, or the fact that procedural learning tends to be situationally embedded. Whatever the reason, the difficulty of transferring procedural skills places extra burdens on instructional design (Singley and Anderson 1989). One approach that addresses the difficulty of transferring strategies is to explicitly support the student's metacognitive awareness of the links among the skills, the tasks, and the contexts in which the strategies are used. This "high road" to transfer can be contrasted with a "low road" in which students relearn each new connection between strategies and learning activities (Perkins 1989). A second approach that assists transfer is to have the students apply strategies to learning materials in small groups following guidance from a model provided by the teacher. One highly successful method that supports the transfer of strategies in reading is reciprocal teaching. In small-group instruction, a teacher models aloud how to use strategies such as questioning, summarizing, and predicting with reading materials and asks students to take turns using the same strategies with each new paragraph (Palincsar and Brown 1984).

A second piece of information about procedural skills is that, once learned, they tend to be performed in their original form and are difficult to modify (Gagné 1985). The reason may be that changing a procedural skill requires a considerable amount of metacognitive effort. One example of the persistence of procedural knowledge may be the intransigence of nonstrategic approaches to reading or problem-solving in one's first language. An example in second-language acquisition is the phenomenon of fossilization, in which inaccurate grammatical constructions, pronunciation, or other errors are retained even after the learner has achieved high levels of proficiency in the target language.

We have accumulated anecdotal evidence from a number of accomplished language learners who exhibit flexibility in second-language acquisition and avoid rule-based learning by practicing complete and meaningful components of complex language procedures. In these cases, the students' active mental processes were consistent with what cognitive theory describes as an active and strategic approach. As we have noted elsewhere (Chamot and O'Malley 1993), one second-language student approached reading in the second language by looking through authentic passages for familiar words that would assist her in understanding the purpose and meaning of the passage. She linked this familiar information to what she knew about the topic, even though the text was in an unfamiliar language. She then reread the passage to infer the meaning of unfamiliar words that were needed to construct a more comprehensive understanding of the message, just as she would in English. This strategic approach is in contrast to the approach used by many novices in reading from the first word in the passage, looking up all unfamiliar words, trying to remember the rules for word and sentence formation, etc.

There is little reason to suggest that the basic principles and learner characteristics that are essential to cognitive theory are not important in second-language acquisition. One such learner characteristic is an active and strategic approach to learning. A second is the use of prior memory structures to aid in learning declarative knowledge. A third is the effective use of modeling and integrative construction to build procedural skills. And a fourth is the use of metacognitive knowledge to assist in analyzing and applying strategic mental processes to new learning activities. Although principles and learner characteristics derived from cognitive theory are important, we do not suggest that cognitive theory alone will explain second-language acquisition. We concur with Stillings et al. (1987), who suggest that linguistic analyses of the substance of learning are needed to account for specific language elements such as syntax and phonological representations.

Applications to Learner Characteristics

The cognitive model of learning described above contributes a meaningful perspective on learner characteristics in second-language acquisition because it suggests why some learner characteristics are important in explaining individual differences and others are less so. Learner characteristics that are of most interest are those that are theoretically derived, have an impact on learning, and are responsive to instructional influence. This connection to instruction is important in a chapter purporting to draw instructional implications from learner characteristics. Fixed characteristics such as age and gender are of less interest according to these criteria than learning strategies and motivation. As we shall see in the next section, characteristics discussed previously in the second-language acquisition literature take on a different cast when they are rephrased in terms of cognitive theory.

Theory-Derived Learner Characteristics

The cognitive theory indicated above and extensions of the theory suggest a number of learner characteristics that are related to learning. Two major learner characteristics that have been discussed directly in cognitive theory are learning strategies and motivation.

Learning Strategies.

Throughout the discussion of cognitive theory, we have indicated that learning is strategic and have described a number of highly strategic approaches to learning involving metacognitive awareness, analysis of task demands, and application of various strategic approaches to achieving learning goals. All of these are important learner characteristics in second-language acquisition. Based on various studies in the cognitive literature (Brown and Palincsar 1982; Brown et al. 1983) and on our own work (O'Malley et al. 1985a; O'Malley and Chamot 1990), we classify these strategic approaches into metacognitive strategies, cognitive strategies, and social/affective strategies:

- *Metacognitive strategies*—executive processes used in planning for learning, monitoring one's own comprehension and production, and evaluating how well one has achieved a learning objective
- *Cognitive strategies*—manipulating the material to be learned mentally (as in making images, inferring meaning, or elaborating on previous knowledge) or physically (as in grouping items to be learned or taking notes)
- *Social/affective strategies*—either interacting with another person in order to assist learning, as in cooperative learning and asking questions for clarification, or using affective control to assist in learning tasks

Metacognitive strategies enable one to plan for a task, monitor how well the plan is being executed, and then evaluate one's success at learning after learning activities have been completed. Specific examples of metacognitive strategies include *directed attention,* or focusing attention in order to avoid distractions from the task; *selective attention,* focusing on specific key words, phrases, or types of information; *self-monitoring,* determining whether progress toward the original learning goal is being maintained; and *self-evaluation,* checking on the success of the learning effort relative to the goal once the learning activity is completed.

Cognitive strategies fall into three broad categories: *rehearsal, organization,* and *elaboration* (Weinstein and Mayer 1986). Rehearsal can entail little mental activity, as in repeating a vocabulary list, or it can be quite active and creative, as when learners vary the ways in which they rehearse the list. Organization is a way of reordering new information to be learned so that it is grouped into meaningful categories. Elaboration refers to a strategy in which individuals associate previous knowledge with new knowledge or link together different parts of new knowledge. Elaboration may also be a generic category for other strategies, such as inferencing, imagery, deduction, and summarization.

Social/affective strategies are particularly important in second-language acquisition because so much of learning in this area entails *cooperating* on learning tasks, *asking questions for clarification,* and other communicative exchanges. Students learning specific language functions or structures can practice these in cooperative learning settings and obtain feedback from other students on the effectiveness and coherence of efforts to communicate orally or in writing. Another social/affective strategy is *self-talk,* in which students attempt to alleviate anxiety that detracts from learning through inner speech, assuring themselves that they will be able to perform the task or learning activity at hand. Self-talk is only convincing if the students have had prior success experiences or if they have metacognitive knowledge of success on similar tasks in the past.

Individuals often use a combination of learning strategies to accomplish a task. For example, *elaboration* and *inferencing* may be intertwined so that the learner uses previous knowledge of a topic to infer the meaning of unfamiliar words. In our earlier example of a student making such inferences while reading an authentic text, we noted that she first selectively attended to familiar words in order to build a mental framework for the passage, which she then elaborated with previous knowledge. This combination of a metacognitive with a cognitive strategy could have been paired with a social/affective strategy had she discussed some of the unfamiliar topics or terms in the passage with another learner.

There is extensive evidence for the effectiveness of learning strategies with a variety of first-language tasks and different types of learners (e.g., Palincsar and Brown 1984; Weinstein and Mayer 1986; Pressley and Associates 1990). Furthermore, as described in this literature, learning strategies are more powerful predictors of learning outcomes than other learner characteristics and can be adapted to task and contextual variables. The literature indicates that individuals who take a more strategic approach learn more rapidly and more effectively than individuals who do not take a strategic approach, that strategies can be taught to non-strategy-users, and that such strategy instruction accelerates and facilitates learning. The research on strategy instruction involving first-language tasks is based in part on interventions with experimental studies and in part on correlational studies (e.g., Jones et al. 1987; Pressley and Associates 1990). Strategy instruction has proven effective when presented individually and, more importantly, in regular classroom contexts, provided that certain guidelines for instructional implementation are followed. The tasks used in this research include reading comprehension, writing, and mathematical problem-solving, while the learners include individuals throughout the K–12 years, slow learners, educationally disadvantaged learners, and students with learning disabilities.

Motivation.

Learner motivation has been proposed as one of the major learner characteristics influencing second-language acquisition (Larsen-Freeman and Long 1991). In social-cognitive theory, which posits internal mental processes corresponding to social behavior, motivation can be described in terms of the *value* that learners place on a task, their *expectation for success* in performing the task, and the extent to which they *attribute responsibility* for learning to internal rather than external sources (Bandura 1986). These three elements interact to influence the way in which individuals respond to learning activities and the duration over which they persist in learning. When individuals value the learning task, have a reasonable expectation of success, and attribute learning to their own efforts, they will tend to apply more effort to learning and persist in learning over a longer period of time. The absence of any one of these elements could interfere with or interrupt learning. For example, individuals who fail to see the value in the task, have little reason to anticipate success, and attribute success to luck or an overly generous teacher would be expected to disengage from learning efforts and from learning tasks in shorter periods of time.

An individual's motivation in learning, metacognitive knowledge, and learning strategies are intricately related. Learners with effective metacognitive knowledge will be able to recognize the similarity between tasks they have experienced in the past and their present learning activities (Paris and Winograd 1990). If the learners possess an effective repertoire of strategies for the particular kind of learning activity presented, they will be able to match strategies for learning to the task and successfully pursue learning goals. The combination of metacognitive knowledge and learning strategies suggests that the learners will see the connection between their own strategic efforts and learning outcomes and will attribute responsibility for learning to internal factors. By setting manageable and attainable goals for themselves, students can perceive their learning progress more readily and gain a sense of self-efficacy (Zimmerman 1990). Thus, motivation plays a self-regulatory role in all learning (Jones et al. 1987).

The more traditional view of motivation in the second-language acquisition literature focuses only on the value individuals assign to the purpose of learning. Gardner and Lambert (1972) suggested that individuals may value learning a second language for *integrative* purposes, a personal desire to identify with the culture of the second-language group, or for *instrumental* purposes, deriving advantages from knowing the language in an occupation or to accomplish external goals for learning. Instrumental motivation was hypothesized to be less effective because it is less personalized and more dependent on external motivation, resulting in less sustained effort to learn and use the language. Gardner (1985) later defined motivation as a combination of effort, desire to achieve a goal, and attitudes, and subsequently added the social context to the variables accounting for second-language acquisition. Contexts can be either unicultural, where there are frequent contacts with native speakers of the target language, or multicultural, with varied levels of contact. As Skehan (1989) notes, there could be an interaction between the social context and language group membership, such that groups differ in the type of context in which they would learn more effectively. While these are useful suggestions, they still do not include expectations for success or attribution, components that are important in the social-cognitive model of motivation.

Other Characteristics

A number of learner characteristics discussed in the second-language literature may have an impact on learning and be responsive to instructional influence. A connection will be made in what follows between learner characteristics and cognitive theory to indicate how and why a learner characteristic is expected to influence learning. As will be noted, any of the characteristics may have as much to do with the learner's receptiveness to new learning as it does with their ability to acquire new information.

Aptitude.

Aptitude has been described variously in terms of specific aptitude tests and in terms of characteristics of learners that are not tapped through these instruments but that are expected to influence learning (e.g., Parry and Stansfield 1990; Skehan 1989). One of the reasons aptitude has been of interest is that the selection of individuals with high language-learning aptitude has the potential in some instructional environments to reduce the costs of second-language instruction. Particularly in government settings, individuals are selected for foreign language instruction because they show high potential as second-language learners according to various aptitude measures. Public schools, on the other hand, do not have the latitude to select only the most able learners. They provide foreign language instruction to all who enroll or provide ESL instruction to all students in need of language support. The preselection of individuals based on aptitude has assumed that individuals who are low in aptitude will be less able to profit from instruction. As will be seen, this assumption can be questioned, given that its validity depends on the way in which aptitudes are defined and the way that instruction is presented.

Carroll (1963) proposed a general model of school learning in which individual differences and instructional factors play key roles. The individual differences are general intelligence, aptitude, and motivation, and the instructional factors are time on task and instructional quality. Motivation is of interest here because it may be subject to the influence of instruction, while aptitude is of interest because it may be more adaptable to instruction than was originally anticipated. Carroll (1981) later indicated that aptitude in second-language acquisition has been defined in various ways, including the following:

- Knack for learning a foreign language
- Rate of learning
- Special cognitive talents that are largely independent of intelligence and operate independently of motivation and attitude

None of these definitions suggests that aptitude is anything other than an innate trait or fixed characteristic of learners. There are strong similarities, however, between some of the ways of defining aptitude and ways of defining learning strategies. The four major components of Carroll's operational definition of aptitude have a strong resemblance to learning strategies, as the following examples illustrate (adapted from O'Malley and Chamot 1990):

1. Phonetic coding ability: An ability to identify distinct sounds, to form associations between those sounds and symbols representing them, and to retain these associations (Carroll 1981: 105).

Effective listeners in a second language know how to make use of learning strategies such as directed attention and selective attention to assist in their identification of distinct sounds and segmentation of words in sentences. Furthermore, they will use elaborative processes to build multiple associations between the sounds and the symbols representing them, as when using phonemes in various contexts to achieve meaningful communication goals. These elaborations link to existing memory structures that add to the strength of the associations and aid in later recall.

2. Grammatical sensitivity: The ability to recognize the grammatical functions of words (or other linguistic entities) in sentence structures (Carroll 1981: 105).

Grammatical sensitivity is evidenced in second-language acquisition when structural clues are used to assign meaning to oral or written text. Learners often use structural clues in combination with semantic clues to infer the meaning of unfamiliar words, selectively attending to available clues in order to discern the function of a word in a sentence. Knowledge of the word's function in the sentence along with contextual clues to meaning in the text structure will often suggest a word's meaning. Learners can either discover structural and semantic clues on their own or the clues can be taught, leading to improvements in the ability to infer meaning.

3. Rote learning ability for foreign language materials: The ability to learn associations between sounds and meanings rapidly and efficiently, and to retain these associations (Carroll 1981: 105).

This component of Carroll's model of foreign language aptitude is intended to measure rote learning ability as contrasted with meaningful learning of connected text. While rote learning ability may be correlated with second-language learning, a cognitive theoretical analysis of learning processes suggests that this variable may not be as important as originally suspected. The main purpose of working memory, on which much of comprehension rests, is *not* to store unrelated items (Carpenter and Just 1989). Our analyses of effective second-language learners suggests that they do not learn by rote but by building elaborative associations with prior knowledge and by activating schemata in long-term memory (O'Malley and Chamot 1990).

4. Inductive language learning ability: The ability to infer or induce the rules governing a set of language materials, given samples of language materials that permit such inferences (Carroll 1981: 105).

In using this ability, individuals infer linguistic rules from language examples through inductive reasoning. The heavy reliance on inferencing in this ability is most likely joined with elaboration, or building on one's knowledge of existing linguistic rules, and summarizing, or describing essential information concisely (O'Malley et al. 1985a).

These examples of language aptitude and the accompanying strategies used to describe them suggest that there is a strong link between aptitudes and strategies (McLaughlin 1990; O'Malley and Chamot 1990). What has previously been advanced as fixed aptitudes of learners may be redefined conceptually in terms of the strategies individuals use in learning situations. This redefinition serves to advance a more varied set of learner characteristics that can be linked directly to learning processes, to cognitive theory, and to instruction. Also, rather than preselecting individuals on the basis of fixed aptitudes, this redefinition argues for introducing learning strategies through instruction in order to increase the learning potential of all students. As learning strategies come increasingly under learner control and function independently of instructional supports, instructional designers should be less concerned about matching what are presumed to be the right mix of instructional methods to the proper aptitude profiles of students. It is quite possible that past correlational evidence between aptitude measures and second-language outcomes, while often substantial, will be reduced in instructional settings that emphasize learning strategies. Thus, as Skehan (1989) notes, aptitude tests may be measuring characteristics of learners that have not been emphasized sufficiently in language classrooms.

Measures of student aptitude might focus on the strategies considered most important in second-language acquisition rather than on fixed aptitudes of learners. Skehan (1989) suggests focusing on the student's ability to access relevant schematic knowledge and discourse capacities that facilitate comprehension. He and Oxford (1990) both suggest assessing aptitudes in the components of Canale and Swain's (1980) definition of communicative competence—linguistic, sociolinguistic, discourse, and strategic competence. As we have noted, these types of competence can be described in cognitive theory as procedural knowledge and represented as production systems. We therefore suggest determining the student's ability to make effective use of modeling and integrative construction to build procedural skills in all four areas of communicative competence. In addition, these research efforts could focus on students' use of metacognitive knowledge in analyzing learning tasks.

Learning Style.

Learning style can be defined generally as the way in which an individual prefers to learn or process information. More specifically, Lawrence (1984) indicates that the term *learning style* has been used in four ways: (1) cognitive style, preferred or habitual patterns of mental functioning or information processing; (2) attitudes or interests that influence attention in learning; (3) the tendency to seek learning environments that are consistent with one's cognitive style, attitudes, and interests; and (4) a tendency to use certain learning tools (learning strategies) and to avoid others. Oxford (1990) agrees that cognitive style is a subcategory of and should be differentiated from learning styles, although these concepts tend to overlap in the literature. She cites one review (Shipman and Shipman 1985) that used nineteen variables to represent learning style and adds to this an additional six variables from other studies. Some of these variables are impulsivity-reflectivity, field dependence/independence, and extraversion-introversion. Oxford goes on to discuss seventeen variables under the rubric of cognitive style, about a third of which overlap with the examples she notes illustrating learning style. These variables are a mixed combination of presumably fixed attributes of learners and learned characteristics that could be modifiable in instruction.

There has been no unifying theoretical framework for the variables cited under the rubric of learning style, nor has there been a theoretical argument predicting a link between personality attributes and foreign language proficiency (Gardner 1990). Furthermore, the evidence in support of associations between personality variables and second-language acquisition is inconsistent and weak. Skehan (1989) summarizes the research on cognitive style by noting that "cognitive style and personality variables account for very little of the variance in language achievement tests" (p. 140). The variables included in his review are extroversion-introversion, risk-taking, field independence-dependence, tolerance for ambiguity, and anxiety. This less-than-promising analysis is fairly consistent with conclusions reached by Gardner (1990) and Oxford (1990), although Oxford appears to be more sanguine about what Skehan refers to as correlations of borderline significance.

Skehan cautions that there have been methodological problems in differentiating cognitive style from other variables such as intelligence and the components of language aptitude. For example, variables such as intelligence or aptitude are rarely controlled in these studies. In one exception, Bialystok and Fröhlich (1978) found that neither field independence nor an integrative motivational attitude added to the prediction of reading, listening, writing, or grammar in French beyond what could be accounted for by other variables. A measure of learning strategies, however, contributed significant variance to the prediction of performance on reading, listening, and grammar beyond that provided by learner aptitudes. Gardner (1990) notes that stronger associations between personality variables and language achievement appear to be found when the instruments used to define personality ask questions specifically about language-learning contexts as contrasted with more generic types of learning contexts. Bialystok and Fröhlich, for example, asked students to comment on strategies for language-learning activities related to foreign language classes rather than general learning strategies.

Given these less-than-encouraging results about the relationship between cognitive styles and language-learning outcomes, what can we conclude about the importance of styles and their role in instruction? For that matter, why does interest persist in an area for which there are few unifying constructs, little theoretical support, and only scant empirical evidence? Other than the appearance of an occasional study that gives encouragement to those looking for positive relationships (e.g., Chapelle and Roberts 1986), the answer may lie in part in arguments suggested by Ehrman (1990), who defines aptitude as "the ability to profit from what a training program or teacher has to offer" (p. 127). Ehrman's rationale for a continuing interest in learning styles lies partly in selection, partly in instructional adaptation, and partly in anecdotal reports by teachers. Particularly in government settings, considerable expense can be saved in foreign language training if candidates selected have a known high probability of success, as was noted earlier. In a similar vein, instruction might be more effective if teachers grouped students in terms of instructional methods that are suited to their learning styles. Ehrman reports that teachers of adult foreign language students find psychological types to be "useful in advising students and in designing activities for individual students and for whole classes where there was some homogeneity of personality type" (1990: 154). In other words, Ehrman's claim for the usefulness of cognitive style in instruction seems less based on empirical data than on anecdotal information (except for finding one particular style with a low frequency of occurrence that was somewhat overrepresented among good language learners, based on a small number of cases).

There may be two additional reasons why familiarity with learning or cognitive styles might be advantageous and why interest in this topic could persist. Both reasons assume that the intent of instruction is to produce self-regulated students with metacognitive knowledge of their own styles for studying and learning. They also assume that a student's self-regulation activities interact with the type of learning environment in which they are involved, ranging from the typical public school program to full-day immersion programs, and with the opportunities they have for interaction with native speakers.

The first reason for continuing the analysis of cognitive style is to provide students with more information that will enable them to gain control over their own learning (Ehrman 1990). Ehrman notes that students analyze their own cognitive styles in order to increase their efficiency in studying and working with classmates. From a cognitive-theoretical standpoint, this type of information on self-regulation should be oriented toward enabling students to understand language-learning tasks in terms of their own style preferences. A second reason that familiarity with learning or cognitive styles might be advantageous is that individuals may have different learning strategy preferences depending on their style (Ehrman 1990; Galloway and Labarca 1990; Gardner 1990; Oxford 1990). That is, students who exhibit a style such as field independence are probably using different strategies for identifying and selecting information in learning tasks than students who tend to be field dependent. Learners who are familiar with their personal styles for learning may be able to select from their repertoire of learning strategies the ones that are most personally suitable for particular learning tasks. Both of these reasons suggest that instruction should help learners gain greater metacognitive control over their own learning, whether through an understanding of their cognitive style or other means, while enabling them to develop an increased repertoire of learning strategies.

There are at least two major reasons to raise cautions about the typing of students in terms of their cognitive style: Some of the styles may be situational or unstable. The situational characteristic of cognitive styles might be shown when an individual's preferred style of processing information depends on the type of materials and the context for second-language learning. Students who are field independent with reading materials may be field dependent with other materials, a difference that might not be detected in the typical assessment measures. The situational character of learning styles may be missed, since styles are most often assessed with generic instruments that are independent of specific language-learning contexts. Three notable examples are reflectivity/impulsivity, assessed by the Matching Familiar Figures Test (Kagan 1966); field independence, assessed by the Embedded Figures Test (Witken et al. 1971); and learning styles, assessed with the Myers-Briggs Type Indicator (Myers 1962). Situational variations might lead the student or teacher to erroneous conclusions about appropriate instructional methods. Evidence for the instability of cognitive styles might be seen when individuals seem to prefer one type of processing early in second-language learning but change their preference as they gain proficiency or receive strategy training. Oxford (1990) cites evidence of this type of instability with field independence-dependence (see Berry 1981; Willing 1988). Again, inaccurate judgments could easily be made that lead to erroneous conclusions or the assignment of students to inappropriate instructional methods. Such difficulties are not evident in developing self-regulatory skills and learning strategies among learners because there is no assumption about the permanence of types.

Research Design and Methods

Research designed to investigate individual characteristics of second-language learners has been conducted for two major purposes. The first purpose is to identify relationships between various learner characteristics and achievement, proficiency, or rate of progress in the target language. The bulk of research to date on learner characteristics related to second-language acquisition has been undertaken with this purpose in mind and thus can be classified as descriptive research. The second purpose addressed by research on learner characteristics is to assess the degree to which some learner characteristics can be modified and what effects these modifications may have on second-language learning. This line of inquiry, which can described as intervention research, focuses on those learner characteristics that are amenable to change rather than those considered static and has centered on learning strategies and motivation.

In this section we provide an overview of research design and methods that have been used to address these two main research purposes and provide representative examples of studies illustrating each research purpose that use a variety of research methods. We conclude the section with suggestions for using a cognitive theoretical view of second-language acquisition to design research that can be applied to improving second-language learning.

Descriptive Studies

Research methods to identify and describe learner characteristics include classroom observations, questionnaires and rating scales, and various types of verbal self-reports. Many descriptive studies have used more than one type of instrument to collect data. Instruments have included measures whose validity has been established for native language contexts and speakers (e.g., Myers-Briggs Type Indicator for cognitive style, Embedded Figures Test for field independence/dependence, Matching Familiar Figures Test for reflectivity/impulsivity). Other instruments developed for second- or foreign language learners have been used for data collection to establish construct and/or predictive validity, as in the numerous studies reviewed on the Modern Language Aptitude Test and other similar measures (e.g., see Carroll 1981; Skehan 1989; Larsen-Freeman and Long 1991). While these instruments have proved to be useful in studies of large numbers of language learners, researchers examining learning strategies have tended to develop instruments that relate learner characteristics to specific task demands (e.g., Rubin 1975; Cohen and Aphek 1981; O'Malley et al. 1985a; Wenden 1986; Abraham and Vann 1987). The tendency toward data-collection procedures that are more second-language-specific is of considerable interest and will be given greater attention here than more generic instruments.

Questionnaires and Rating Scales.

Questionnaires have been used extensively to identify motivation, learning strategies, and other learner characteristics that have been related to specific tasks or contexts. A typical questionnaire asks students to identify the frequency (always—usually—sometimes—rarely—never) that corresponds to an attitude, learning strategy, or motivation they have or use in connection with specific language tasks. Rating scales ask students to give a numerical rating or rank ordering for personal characteristics such as preferences for strategies, learning style dimensions, or perceived self-efficacy.

An example of an inventory designed to identify frequency of language-learning strategies for which construct validity has been established is the Strategy Inventory for Language Learning (SILL) developed by Oxford (1986) and used extensively by her and her colleagues in a number of large-scale studies of foreign and second-language learners (e.g., Oxford 1990; Nyikos and Oxford 1993). The SILL is a 121-item Likert-type instrument that lists learning strategies identified in the literature, including cognitive strategies, compensation strategies, metacognitive strategies, social strategies, and affective strategies. In a typical recent study, the SILL was administered to 1200 university students studying various foreign languages (Nyikos and Oxford 1993). A factor analysis of the data indicated that the most frequently reported strategies were associated with formal rule-related processing and bottom-up text analysis. Quite low frequencies were reported for strategies associated with functional practice, such as attempting to use the language in social communicative contexts outside the classroom. A third type of strategies also used infrequently were those associated with independent or self-regulated learning. A medium level of use was reported for a fourth type designated as academic study strategies, which involved self-management, directed attention, and perseverance. A fifth factor involved the elicitation of conversational input, especially within the classroom, and was reported at a medium to high frequency of use by the foreign language students participating in the study. The value of this type of study is in the finding that language students may not use the strategies that research indicates would be most effective, such as strategies that promote self-regulated learning and those that provide meaningful practice in communication. This information is of great utility in designing intervention studies to teach effective strategy use.

Verbal Self-Reports.

Various types of self-reports have been used to gather descriptive information about learner characteristics, in particular learner strategies. These have included a relatively few diary studies of attitudes and learning processes (Schumann and Schumann 1977; Rivers 1981; Chamot and Chamot 1983) and directed diaries of learning strategies (Rubin 1981). More frequent types of self-reports of learning strategies have been classified by Cohen (1987) as self-report, self-observation, and self-revelation. In self-report interviews, learners describe their general approach to completing language-learning tasks. While a great deal of information about student learning strategies can be gathered from these retrospective interviews (see, for example, interviews conducted with ESL and foreign language students reported in O'Malley and Chamot 1990), it appears that a considerable amount of information may be forgotten immediately after the actual learning event (Cohen 1987). In self-observation verbal reports, learners examine their own mental processes while the event is still in short-term memory, or immediately after, whereas in self-revelation, learners engage in a " 'think-aloud' stream-of-consciousness disclosure of thought processes while the information is being attended to" (Cohen 1987: 33).

In think-aloud interviews, students are given a task to work on, such as a cloze passage to complete, a text to read for comprehension, or a taped text to listen to and recall (Faerch and Kasper 1987). Students are asked to describe what they are thinking before, during, and after the task. The interviewer prompts with very general reminders, such as "What are you thinking right now? Tell me what's going through your mind right now." A listening or reading text is either marked for places in which the student is supposed to think aloud, or the student determines a good place to pause and think aloud. The entire interview is audiotaped or videotaped and later transcribed verbatim. The transcript is inspected for evidence of mental processes such as learning strategies, metacognitive or metalinguistic awareness, attitudes toward the task or language, or attitudes toward self. Types and frequency of strategies can be correlated with other measures such as proficiency/achievement, level of language study (first year, second year, etc.), or questionnaire data on strategy use or perceived self-efficacy on tasks like the ones used in the think-aloud session. The advantage of the think-aloud procedure is that it tends to capture students' actual thought processes while engaged in a learning task. A limitation is that in think-aloud sessions students typically have limited opportunities for engaging in planning for learning and reflecting on their degree of success after task completion. This limitation can be easily overcome by providing for planning time before task engagement and for elicitation of self-evaluation through techniques such as stimulated recall, in which students are led through their performance (for example, by viewing a videotape of it) and asked to make judgments about their own level of success.

Think-aloud procedures to probe the language-learning process were first used by Hosenfeld (1976; 1979). Students were asked to report on their thought processes while actually working on various language tasks. Student comments revealed that they approached some tasks in ways designed to get correct answers quickly without attending to meaning. In reading, Hosenfeld (1979; 1984) was able to identify the characteristics of more effective readers through think-aloud procedures. Subsequent research employing think-aloud procedures included a study of high school ESL students (O'Malley, Chamot, and Küpper 1989) and another of foreign language students (Chamot and Küpper 1989). These studies also identified differences in the strategic approaches to various language tasks of more and less effective language learners.

Cohen's (1987) three types of verbal report were used to gather descriptive data in a recent study of high school students of French (Vandergrift 1992). Retrospective structured interviews were first conducted with students to identify types of strategies used and variation by gender and level of study. The results of the retrospective interviews together with teacher judgments were used to select the most and least successful language learners to participate in self-observation and self-revelation verbal reports. Self-observation data were collected through videotaped oral proficiency interviews that were shown to students immediately afterward so that they could comment on their thinking processes at each point of the interviews. Finally, the students participated in think-aloud interviews while listening to a taped listening text interrupted by pauses during which they thought aloud. Differences between beginning and intermediate students were found in strategy use, with higher-level processing strategies replacing less efficient strategies as students became more proficient. Few gender differences were found in strategy use. Students also completed the Learning-Style Inventory (Kolb 1985), and modest differences were found in the listening comprehension strategies displayed by language learners with different learning styles. The Vandergrift (1992) study exemplifies how a variety of instruments and research procedures can provide rich insights into relationships between a number of learner characteristics.

Intervention Studies

In recent years, a number of studies have been conducted for the purpose of modifying less effective learner characteristics in order to improve language learning. This research has centered on strategies instruction for a variety of second- and foreign language tasks. Empirical verification that strategies influence second-language learning has been based on correlational work (Cohen and Aphek 1980; Politzer and McGroarty 1985; Padron and Waxman 1988; Chamot et al. 1993) and experimental interventions (Carrell 1985; O'Malley et al. 1985b; Rubin, Quinn, and Enos 1988). These studies have included both discrete and integrative language tasks.

For example, with discrete language tasks, Cohen and Aphek (1980) trained beginning through advanced students learning Hebrew to use mnemonic associations with vocabulary over a five-week period. Students identified unfamiliar vocabulary words in reading passages, formed their own associations linked to meaning, and then were given various opportunities either to recall the words or use them in sentences. Recall was greater for words with an association than for words where no association was used.

The effectiveness of learning-strategy instruction with integrative language tasks was demonstrated in a study by O'Malley et al. (1985b), who provided high school ESL students at the intermediate level of English proficiency with instruction on the use of metacognitive and organizational strategies in both listening and speaking. Students randomly assigned to control groups received their customary instruction while those assigned to experimental groups received explicit instruction with supported practice on specific strategies that were predicted to be effective with the integrative tasks. Strategy instruction was significantly more effective for listening tasks that were within a manageable level of difficulty as well as for speaking tasks.

A study focusing on integrative language by Carrell (1985) used adult intermediate-level ESL students and reading comprehension tasks. Building on a schema-theoretical view of reading comprehension, Carrell presented students with strategies to identify top-level structure (main ideas, subordinate ideas, details, etc.) in reading prose passages and in organizing written recall of the passage. The strategy instruction involved a number of effective training procedures including explicit instruction on the purpose and use of the strategies, metacognitive awareness of the link between strategy use and learning effectiveness, scaffolding with strong initial instructional support that was gradually shifted to student control, materials that were sequenced in difficulty, individual feedback on strategy use, and practice with various types of materials. A control group, not randomly assigned but comparable to the treatment group on a pretest, was provided with a variety of strategies but was not given the same top-down comprehension strategies. There were significant differences between the treatment and the control group on measures of reading comprehension in an immediate posttest that appeared to be sustained on a delayed posttest (three weeks). Carrell noted that students expressed positive views of the strategy instruction and saw it as beneficial.

What is perhaps most meaningful about the studies by Cohen and Aphek, O'Malley et al., and Carrell is that they included instructional procedures that can be used by most classroom teachers. As noted, the tasks for which strategy instruction has been shown to be effective included vocabulary, listening, reading, and speaking. The strategy training did not take an inordinate amount of time to present and could be accomplished in the context of ordinary instruction, that is, embedded in the materials and methods teachers would typically use. Furthermore, there are indications that the effects of strategy instruction have long-term benefits. As will be seen, these results have important implications for instruction.

Instructional Implications

Language teachers can address the variety of student learning styles in their classrooms by delivering instruction through different modes. Visual, auditory, kinesthetic, and practical application activities can make it possible for students not only to learn through their preferred mode, but also to gain experience in learning through additional modes. Only a few teachers have the option of automatically excluding from their courses students who evince poor aptitude on tests such as the Modern Language Aptitude Test. Certainly public school ESL and foreign language teachers are rarely among them. Instead, most teachers seek ways to compensate for students' low language-learning aptitude. Skehan (1989) suggests that performance on language-aptitude tests relies not only on the capacity to learn language, but also on the ability to learn from decontextualized texts, or language that is not grounded in interpersonal face-to-face interactions. In adapting instruction to meet the needs of low-aptitude students, language teachers might therefore include activities that focus on decontextualized language practice.

One direct implication for instruction from a cognitive-theoretical analysis of learner characteristics in second-language acquisition is that teachers should encourage the development and use of characteristics that support learning. Students provided with strategy instruction should tend to be more regular users of strategies than students not provided with such instruction. A second implication is that students as well as teachers should be aware of the strategies that students use while learning. By gaining greater awareness of initial strategy use by students, teachers and students can expand the repertoire of strategies that students are capable of using with new materials. A third implication is that teachers can play an active role in influencing strategy use and in assisting students in using strategies more effectively. There are specific techniques for teaching procedural knowledge that have direct application to classrooms, as we note below. A fourth implication is that students can take command over their own learning activities and initiate strategic applications that will lead toward more autonomous learning. When students regulate their own learning, they see themselves as more effective and thereby gain confidence with future learning activities. A final implication is that teachers should identify declarative and procedural knowledge in their instructional materials. By capitalizing on ways in which each of these types of information is learned most effectively, teachers will take a major step toward facilitating their students' learning.

Developing Autonomous Learners

Rather than relying solely on instructional modifications adapted to learner characteristics, teachers can provide instruction that shows students how to harness their own metacognition in the service of cognitive, affective, and language development. In this type of instruction, teachers provide for discussions and activities in which students reflect on learning processes, try out new strategies, evaluate their own learning, assess their own attitudes and motivations, and work collaboratively with classmates in order to practice and reflect on their language-learning strategies. These types of activities have been incorporated into an instructional framework that we have used in both ESL and foreign language classrooms to develop learner autonomy.

Instructional Framework for Strategies Instruction

The instructional framework presented in figure 5-1 is based on the instructional sequence in the Cognitive Academic Language Learning Approach (CALLA), which was

Figure 5-1. Framework for Strategies Instruction in CALLA

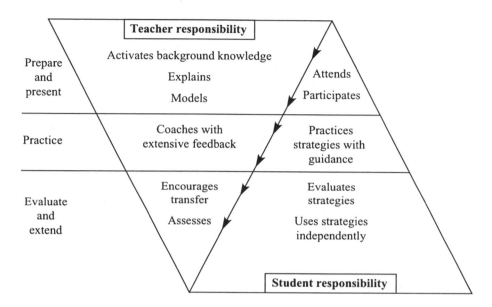

* Adapted by Pamela El-Dinary and Rachel Brown (personal communication, 1992) from:

Bergman, Janet L. 1992. "SAIL—A Way to Success and Independence for Low-Achieving Readers." *The Reading Teacher* 45: 598–602.

Chamot, Anna Uhl, and J. Michael O'Malley. 1993. *The CALLA Handbook: Implementing the Cognitive Academic Language Learning Approach.* Reading, MA: Addison-Wesley.

Pearson, P. David, and Margaret C. Gallagher. 1983. "The Instruction of Reading Comprehension." *Contemporary Educational Psychology* 8: 317–44.

originally developed for intermediate-level upper elementary and secondary ESL students (see Chamot and O'Malley 1987, 1989, 1993). CALLA provides integrated instruction in curriculum content, academic language, and learning strategies. The instructional sequence depicted in figure 5-1 has been used successfully with ESL instruction in selected content areas (Thomas and Collier 1993) but can be adapted for other instruction using learning strategies, as in foreign language instruction.

The instruction is organized into a five-phase sequence as follows:

• *Preparation*: Students' prior knowledge about the lesson topic is elicited through discussion, semantic mapping, and group activities.

- *Presentation*: The teacher presents new content, academic language, and/or learning strategies, using a variety of modes to address students' different learning styles.
- *Practice*: Using cooperative learning techniques, students practice the new content, language, and learning strategy with an academic task.
- *Evaluation*: Students evaluate their own level of achievement and self-confidence through learning logs, questionnaires, think-alouds, and discussion.
- *Extension*: Students reflect on what they have learned, apply it to new situations, and integrate their new learning with their prior knowledge.

This five-phase sequence is helpful in planning and organizing learning-strategy instruction for both ESL and foreign language students. Figure 5-1 illustrates the concept of *scaffolding,* in which the teacher initially provides extensive support for student learning, and then gradually removes the support as students become more adept at independent learning. Teachers have major responsibility during the first two phases of the instructional sequence (*prepare* and *present*) as they activate students' prior knowledge about the strategies they already use, explain the new strategy, and model its application. During the next phase (*practice*), responsibility is shared equally between teacher and students as students engage in guided practice of the strategy. In the last two phases (*evaluate* and *extend*), students assume greater responsibility as they evaluate the effectiveness of the strategy and begin to use it on new tasks without extensive teacher prompting.

In this type of instruction students learn how to expand their own learning approach and overcome language-learning limitations that might be attributed to aptitude, learning style, or motivation.

Conclusion

This paper has encouraged examining learner characteristics in terms of cognitive theory in order to derive an improved understanding of the processes as well as the salient variables that influence second-language acquisition. The theory focuses generally on what and how students learn and identifies specific learner characteristics that may be more powerful in influencing second-language outcomes than some of the aptitudes and personality characteristics traditionally investigated. Some of these characteristics include metacognitive awareness and use of metacognitive, cognitive, and social-affective strategies. One of the arguments advanced here is that relationships between aptitudes and second-language outcomes can be attributed to the strategies used by learners possessing different aptitudes rather than to the aptitudes themselves. A learning-strategies approach is consistent with a social-cognitive view of motivation in which motivation is defined as valuing learning outcomes, expectation for success, and attribution of learning outcomes to one's own efforts. One of the advantages of cognitive theory is that it has direct implications for instruction and leads to instructional procedures that show promise of increasing learner autonomy and self-direction.

A number of changes in research questions and methods taking place over the past decade are implied by this analysis of cognitive theory and learner characteristics. One is that researchers are more interested now in mental processes that support learning and in the learning processes used by effective language students as contrasted with learners' general characteristics, styles, or dispositions. The result is that research is more immediately focused on the content of learners' mental processes during or immediately following specific second-language learning activities. A second change is that there is more interest in characteristics of learners that are amenable to instructional influence than in fixed characteristics of learners. This leads to more direct focus on strategies used by learners, their motivation, and their perceptions or confidence in approaching learning tasks. There is a related interest in learner characteristics that are under the students' own influence so that they can gain increasing control over their learning. And finally, we hope that this use of cognitive theory will encourage others to propose alternative theoretical analyses of learner characteristics so that we all can gain a broader and more complete understanding of individual differences in the rate and level of second-language proficiency.

References

Learner Characteristics in Second-Language Acquisition

Abraham, Roberta G., and Roberta J. Vann. 1987. "Strategies of Two Language Learners: A Case Study," in Anita Wenden and Joan Rubin, eds., *Learner Strategies in Second Language Learning.* Englewood Cliffs, NJ: Prentice-Hall.

Anderson, John R. 1983. *The Architecture of Cognition.* Cambridge, MA: Harvard Univ. Press.

————. 1985. *Cognitive Psychology and Its Implications.* 2nd ed. New York: Freeman.

————. 1989. "The Analogical Origins of Errors in Problem Solving," in David Klahr and Kenneth Kotovsky, eds., *Complex Information Processing.* Hillsdale, NJ: Erlbaum.

————. 1990. *The Adaptive Character of Thought.* Hillsdale, NJ: Erlbaum.

Bandura, Albert. 1986. *Social Foundations of Thought and Action: A Social Cognitive Theory.* Englewood Cliffs, NJ: Prentice-Hall.

Bergman, Janet L. 1992. "SAIL—A Way to Success and Independence for Low-Achieving Readers." *The Reading Teacher* 45: 598–602.

Berry, John W. 1981. "Comparative Studies of Cognitive Styles: Implications for the Education of Immigrant Students." [ERIC ED 215 009].

Bialystok, Ellen, and Maria Fröhlich. 1978. "Variables of Classroom Achievement in Second Language Learning." *Modern Language Journal* 32: 327–36.

Brown, Ann L., John D. Bransford, Robert A. Ferrara, and John C. Campione. 1983. "Learning, Remembering, and Understanding," in John H. Flavell and Ellen M. Markman, eds., *Carmichael's Manual of Child Psychology.* Vol. 3. New York: Wiley.

Brown, Ann L., and Annemarie S. Palincsar. 1982. "Inducing Strategies Learning from Text by Means of Informed, Self-Control Training." *Topics in Learning and Learning Disabilities* 2,1: 1–17.

Canale, Michael, and Merrill Swain. 1980. "Theoretical Bases of Communicative Approaches to Second Language Teaching and Testing." *Applied Linguistics* 1: 1–47.

Carpenter, Patricia A., and Marcel A. Just. 1989. "The Role of Working Memory in Language Comprehension," in David Klahr and Kenneth Kotovsky, eds., *Complex Information Processing.* Hillsdale, NJ: Erlbaum.

Carrell, Patricia L. 1985. "Facilitating ESL Reading by Teaching Text Structure." *TESOL Quarterly* 19: 727–52.

Carroll, John B. 1963. "A Model of School Learning." *Teachers College Record* 64: 723–33.

————. 1981. "Twenty-five Years of Research on Foreign Language Aptitude," in Karl C. Diller, ed., *Individual Differences and Universals in Language Learning Aptitude.* Rowley, MA: Newbury House.

Chamot, G. Alain, and Anna Uhl Chamot. 1983. "Journal of a Ten-Year-Old Second Language Learner," in Ray V. Padilla, ed., *Theory, Technology, and Public Policy on Bilingual Education.* Washington, DC: National Clearinghouse for Bilingual Education.

Chamot, Anna Uhl, Marsha Dale, J. Michael O'Malley, and George A. Spanos. 1993. "Learning and Problem Solving Strategies of ESL Students." *Bilingual Research Journal* 16,3: 1–23.

Chamot, Anna Uhl, and Lisa Küpper. 1989. "Learning Strategies in Foreign Language Instruction." *Foreign Language Annals* 22: 13–24.

Chamot, Anna Uhl, and J. Michael O'Malley. 1987. "The Cognitive Academic Language Learning Approach: A Bridge to the Mainstream." *TESOL Quarterly* 21: 227–49.

Chamot, Anna Uhl, and J. Michael O'Malley. 1989. "The Cognitive Academic Language Learning Approach," in Patricia Rigg and Virginia G. Allen, eds., *When They Don't All Speak English: Integrating the ESL Students into the Regular Classroom.* Urbana, IL: National Council of Teachers of English.

Chamot, Anna Uhl, and J. Michael O'Malley. 1993. *The CALLA Handbook: Implementing the Cognitive Academic Language Learning Approach.* Reading, MA: Addison-Wesley.

Chapelle, Carol, and Cheryl Roberts. 1986. "Ambiguity Tolerance and Field Independence as Predictors of Proficiency in English as a Second Language." *Language Learning* 36: 27–45.

Cohen, Andrew D. 1987. "Studying Learner Strategies: How We Get the Information," in Anita Wenden and Joan Rubin, eds., *Learner Strategies in Language Learning.* Englewood Cliffs, NJ: Prentice-Hall.

————, and Edna Aphek. 1980. "Retention of Second Language Vocabulary over Time: Investigating the Role of Mnemonic Associations." *System* 8: 221–35.

————, and Edna Aphek. 1981. "Easifying Second Language Learning." *Studies in Second Language Acquisition* 3: 221–36.

Derry, Sharon J., and Debra A. Murphy. 1986. "Designing Systems That Train Learning Ability: From Theory to Practice." *Review of Educational Research* 56: 1–39.

Dulay, Heidi, Marina K. Burt, and Stephen Krashen. 1982. *Language Two.* New York: Oxford Univ. Press.

Ehrman, Madeline. 1990. "The Role of Personality Type in Adult Language Learning: An Ongoing Investigation," in Thomas S. Parry and Charles W. Stansfield, eds., *Language Aptitude Reconsidered.* Englewood Cliffs, NJ: Prentice-Hall Regents.

Faerch, Claus, and Gabriele Kasper. 1987. *Introspection in Second Language Research.* Clevedon, Eng.: Multilingual Matters.

Gagné, Ellen D. 1985. *The Cognitive Psychology of School Learning.* Boston: Little, Brown.

Galloway, Vicki, and Angela Labarca. 1990. "From Student to Learner: Style, Process, and Strategy," in Diane W. Birckbichler, ed., *New Perspectives and New Directions in Foreign Language Education.* Lincolnwood, IL: National Textbook.

Gardner, Robert C. 1985. *Social Psychology and Second Language Learning: The Role of Attitudes and Motivation.* London, Eng.: Edward Arnold.

————. 1990. "Attitudes, Motivation, and Personality as Predictors of Success in Foreign Language Learning," in Thomas S. Parry and Charles W. Stansfield, eds., *Language Aptitude Reconsidered.* Englewood Cliffs, NJ: Prentice-Hall Regents.

————, and Wallace E. Lambert. 1972. *Attitudes and Motivation in Second Language Learning.* Rowley, MA: Newbury House.

Hosenfeld, Carol. 1976. "Autonomy as Metacognitive Awareness: Suggestions for Training Self-Monitoring of Listening Comprehension." *Mélanges Pédagogiques:* 69–84.

————. 1979. "Cindy: A Learner in Today's Foreign Language Classroom," in W. Born, ed., *The Foreign Language Learner in Today's Classroom Environment.* Middlebury, VT: Northeast Conference on the Teaching of Foreign Languages.

————. 1984. "Case Studies of Ninth Grade Readers," in J. Charles Alderson and A. H. Urquhart, eds., *Reading in a Foreign Language.* London, Eng.: Longman.

Jones, Beau F., Annemarie S. Palincsar, Donna S. Ogle, and Eileen G. Carr. 1987. *Strategic Teaching and Learning: Cognitive Instruction in the Content Areas.* Alexandria, VA: ASCD.

Kagan, Jerome. 1966. "Reflection-Impulsivity: The Generality and Dynamics of Conceptual Tempo." *Journal of Abnormal Psychology* 71: 17–24.

Kintsch, Walter. 1974. *The Representation of Meaning in Memory.* Hillsdale, NJ: Erlbaum.

Kolb, David A. 1985. *Learning Style Inventory.* Boston: McBer.

Lachman, Roy, Janet L. Lachman, and Earl C. Butterfield. 1979. *Cognitive Psychology and Information Processing.* Hillsdale, NJ: Erlbaum.

Larsen-Freeman, Diane, and Michael H. Long. 1991. *An Introduction to Second Language Acquisition Research.* New York: Longman.

Lawrence, G. 1984. "A Synthesis of Learning Style Research Involving the MBTI." *Journal of Psychological Type.* 8: 2–15.

McLaughlin, Barry. 1987. *Theories of Second Language Learning.* London, Eng.: Edward Arnold.

————. 1990. "The Relationship between First and Second Languages: Language Proficiency and Language Aptitude," in Birgit Harley, Patrick Allen, James Cummins, and Merrill Swain, eds., *The Development of Second Language Proficiency.* Cambridge, Eng.: Cambridge Univ. Press.

McLeod, Beverly, and Barry McLaughlin. 1986. "Restructuring or Automaticity? Reading in a Second Language." *Language Learning* 36: 109–23.

Minsky, Marvin. 1975. "A Framework for the Representation of Knowledge," in Patrick H. Winston, ed., *The Psychology of Computer Vision.* New York: McGraw-Hill.

Myers, Isabel B. 1962. *Manual: The Myers-Briggs Type Indicator.* Princeton, NJ: Educational Testing Service.

Norman, Donald A., David E. Rumelhart, and the LNR Research Group. 1975. *Explorations in Cognition.* New York: Freeman.

Nyikos, Martha N., and Rebecca L. Oxford. 1993. "A Factor Analytic Study of Language-Learning Strategy Use: Interpretations from Information-Processing Theory and Social Psychology." *The Modern Language Journal* 77: 11–22.

O'Malley, J. Michael, and Anna Uhl Chamot. 1990. *Learning Strategies in Second Language Acquisition.* Cambridge, Eng.: Cambridge Univ. Press.

O'Malley, J. Michael, Anna Uhl Chamot, and Lisa Küpper. 1989. "Listening Comprehension Strategies in Second Language Acquisition." *Applied Linguistics* 10: 418–37.

O'Malley, J. Michael, Anna Uhl Chamot, Gloria Stewner-Manzanares, Lisa Küpper, and Rocco Russo. 1985a. "Learning Strategies Used by Beginning and Intermediate ESL Students." *Language Learning* 35: 21–46.

O'Malley, J. Michael, Anna Uhl Chamot, Gloria Stewner-Manzanares, Rocco Russo, and Lisa Küpper. 1985b. "Learning Strategy Applications with Students of English as a Second Language." *TESOL Quarterly* 19: 285–96.

O'Malley, J. Michael, Anna Uhl Chamot, and Carol Walker. 1987. "Some Applications of Cognitive Theory to Second Language Acquisition." *Studies in Second Language Acquisition* 9: 287–306.

Oxford, Rebecca L. 1986. "Development and Psychometric Testing of the Strategy Inventory for Language Learning." ARI Technical Report 728. Alexandria, VA: U.S. Army Research Institute for the Behavioral and Social Sciences.

———. 1990. "Styles, Strategies, and Aptitude: Connections for Language Learning," in Thomas S. Parry and Charles W. Stansfield, eds., *Language Aptitude Reconsidered.* Englewood Cliffs, NJ: Prentice-Hall Regents.

Padron, Yolanda N., and Herschold C. Waxman. 1988. "The Effects of ESL Students' Perceptions of Their Cognitive Strategies on Reading Achievement." *TESOL Quarterly* 22: 146–50.

Palincsar, Annemarie S., and Ann L. Brown. 1984. "Reciprocal Teaching of Comprehension-Fostering and Comprehension-Monitoring Activities." *Cognition and Instruction* 1: 117–75.

Paris, Scott G., and Peter Winograd. 1990. "How Metacognition Can Promote Academic Learning and Instruction," in Beau F. Jones and Lorna Idol, eds., *Dimensions of Thinking and Cognitive Instruction.* Hillsdale, NJ: Erlbaum.

Parry, Thomas S., and Charles W. Stansfield, eds. 1990. *Language Aptitude Reconsidered.* Englewood Cliffs, NJ: Prentice-Hall Regents.

Pearson, P. David, and Margaret C. Gallagher. 1983. "The Instruction of Reading Comprehension." *Contemporary Educational Psychology* 8: 317–44.

Perkins, David N. 1989. "Teaching Meta-Cognitive Strategies." Paper presented at the annual meeting of the American Educational Research Association, San Francisco, CA.

Politzer, Robert L., and Mary McGroarty. 1985. "An Exploratory Study of Learning Behaviors and Their Relationship to Gains in Linguistic and Communicative Competence." *TESOL Quarterly* 19: 103–23.

Pressley, Michael, and Associates. 1990. *Cognitive Strategy Instruction That Really Improves Children's Academic Performance.* Cambridge, MA: Brookline.

Rivers, Wilga M. 1981. "Learning a Sixth Language: An Adult Learner's Daily Diary." Appendix to *Teaching Foreign Language Skills.* 2nd ed. Chicago: Univ. of Chicago Press.

Rubin, Joan. 1975. "What the Good Language Learner Can Teach Us." *TESOL Quarterly* 9: 41–51.

———. 1981. "Study of Cognitive Processes in Second Language Learning." *Applied Linguistics* 11: 117–31.

———, John Quinn, and Joann Enos. 1988. *Improving Foreign Language Listening Comprehension.* Report submitted to the U.S. Department of Education, International Research and Studies Program.

Rumelhart, David E., and Donald A. Norman. 1978. "Accretion, Tuning, and Restructuring: Three Modes of Learning," in John W. Cotton and Roberta L. Klatzky, eds., *Semantic Factors in Cognition.* Hillsdale, NJ: Erlbaum.

———. 1981. "Analogical Processes in Learning," in John R. Anderson, ed., *Cognitive Skills and Their Acquisition.* Hillsdale, NJ: Erlbaum.

Schank, Roger, and Robert Abelson. 1977. *Scripts, Plans, Goals, and Understanding.* Hillsdale, NJ: Erlbaum.

Schumann, Francine M., and John H. Schumann. 1977. "Diary of a Language Learner: An Introspective Study of Second Language Learning," in H. Douglas Brown, Carlos A. Yorio, and Ruth H. Crymes, eds., *Teaching and Learning in English as a Second Language.* Washington, DC: Teachers of English to Speakers of Other Languages.

Shiffrin, Richard M., and W. Schneider. 1977. "Controlled and Automatic Human Information Processing: II. Perceptual Learning, Automatic Attending, and a General Theory." *Psychological Review* 84: 127–90.

Shipman, Stephanie, and Virginia C. Shipman. 1985. "Cognitive Styles: Some Conceptual, Methodological, and Applied Issues," in Edmund W. Gordon, ed., *Review of Research in Education.* Vol. 12. Washington, DC: American Educational Research Assn.

Shuell, Thomas J. 1986. "Cognitive Conceptions of Learning." *Review of Educational Research* 56: 411–36.

Singley, Mark K., and John R. Anderson. 1989. *The Transfer of Cognitive Skill.* Cambridge, MA: Harvard Univ. Press.

Skehan, Peter. 1989. *Individual Differences in Second-Language Learning.* London, Eng.: Edward Arnold.

Stillings, Neil A., Mark H. Feinstein, Jay L. Garfield, Edwina L. Rissland, David A. Rosenbaum, Steven E. Weisler, and Lynne Baker-Ward. 1987. *Cognitive Science.* Cambridge, MA: MIT Press.

Thomas, Wayne P., and Virginia P. Collier. 1993. "Long-Term Academic Achievement of Language Minority Students, K–12." Paper presented at the annual meeting of the American Educational Research Association, Atlanta, GA, April.

Vandergrift, Laurens. 1992. "The Comprehension Strategies of Second Language (French) Listeners." Unpublished Ph.D. diss., Univ. of Alberta, Edmonton.

Weinstein, Claire E., and Richard E. Mayer. 1986. "The Teaching of Learning Strategies," in Merle C. Wittrock, ed., *Handbook of Research on Teaching.* 3rd ed. New York: Macmillan.

Wenden, Anita. 1986. "What Do L2 Learners Know about Their Language Learning? A Second Look at Retrospective Accounts." *Applied Linguistics* 7: 186–201.

Willing, K. 1988. *Learning Styles in Adult Migrant Education.* Adelaide, Australia: NCRC. [Cited in Rebecca L. Oxford. "Styles, Strategies, and Aptitude: Connections for Language Learning," in Thomas S. Parry and Charles W. Stansfield, eds., *Language Aptitude Reconsidered.* Englewood Cliffs, NJ: Prentice-Hall Regents, 1990.]

Witkin, Herman A., Phillip K. Oltman, Evelyn Raskin, and S. A. Karp. 1971. *A Manual for the Embedded Figures Test.* Palo Alto, CA: Consulting Psychologists Press.

Zimmerman, Barry J. 1990. "Self-Regulated Learning and Academic Achievement: An Overview." *Educational Psychologist* 25: 3–17.

6

Reading and Listening Comprehension: *Perspectives on Research and Implications for Practice*

Janet Swaffar
University of Texas at Austin

Susan Bacon
University of Cincinnati

This chapter explores how research design has changed our thinking about language comprehension and discusses the practical impact of research on reading and listening comprehension for the classroom.[1] We first look at tacit assumptions about comprehension processes that currently underlie L1 and L2 research practice. Second, we look at how L2 research assumptions have diverged from those in L1 in order to highlight those issues that are unique to L2 research and that are only beginning to be explored. In addressing these issues, we examine how our definitions of language and language learning are changing, particularly with regard to listening and reading. Third, we suggest premises that need to be foregrounded in future L2 research in order to look at the origin of problems (locating sufficiently inclusive research questions in appropriate terms) rather than their symptoms (deciding how much or whether students learn when given a particular set of questions).

Janet Swaffar (Ph.D., University of Wisconsin) is a professor of German at the University of Texas, where she teaches literary criticism and applied linguistics. Her books include several translations (Raabe, Gustafsson), a handbook on literary magazines (as King), and a coauthored volume entitled *Reading for Meaning* (with Katherine Arens and Heidi Byrnes). Her articles in literary criticism and the role of reading in second-language acquisition focus on how readers interact with the explicit and implicit message systems of texts.

Susan M. Bacon (Ph.D., The Ohio State University), is Associate Professor of Spanish and Undergraduate Director, Supervisor, and Coordinator of Spanish and Italian Programs at the University of Cincinnati. Her research interests include second-language acquisition and learning in children and adults and the use of authentic texts in SL acquisition.

Tacit Assumptions in Current Research

In chapter 1 of this volume, Johnson describes six frameworks for L2 research that currently dominate investigations in FL learning: correlational approaches, case studies, survey research, ethnographic research, experiments, and discourse analysis. While correlational approaches are increasingly evident (e.g., Carson et al. 1990; Lund 1991; Bacon 1992a), experimental studies have dominated L2 listening and reading research to this point in time (Dunkel 1991; Grabe 1991).

Yet, despite increased activity in second-language research in recent years, our experimental research base in L2 listening and reading is relatively small. Bernhardt (1991) documents only 150 second-language studies in reading from the mid-seventies to 1988. In addition, most studies address an L2 (e.g. ESL), not an FL context. Even fewer experimental studies exist in listening comprehension and, until recently, most of these were conducted with L2, not FL, students (Long 1987; Morley 1990).

Thus the reading and listening research base not only is limited in quantity but may also be reductionist in the sense that Johnson (this volume) identifies: viewing issues too narrowly. A research paradigm that narrowly equates FL learners with L2 learners may ask questions that overlook key components in the comprehension process. L2 learners operate in the culture of the language they are learning and can access input outside the classroom with relative ease, whereas FL students cannot. Ethnographically, their cultural and linguistic backgrounds differ. From several research perspectives, then, FL and L2 learning represent two distinct groups involved in second-language acquisition. Given the very few studies comparing performance between these two groups, it is unclear just how applicable L2 research findings are for the FL learner or whether it may be misleading to equate findings (VanPatten 1990; Freed 1991).

Considering the impact of this equation on professional practices, such disparities are cause for concern. First, the number of total studies in either the FL or L2 languages is small. Second, contextual and ethnographic variables are often not monitored. For example, the learner goals and environment of the learning are not factored into conclusions about the learner outcomes. Third, the results of studies we do have are often equated, yet they frequently deal with similar issues in dissimilar ways: dissimilar research foci, treatments, and assessment measures. In other words, the profession may be generalizing about apples and oranges. Thus Larsen-Freeman and Long (1991), among others, caution about the need for follow-up studies to replicate and elaborate on findings among different audiences with different language backgrounds.

That charge, however, is difficult to meet, precisely because of increasing interest in correlational designs that assess multiple factors. Increasingly, even in purely experimental work, researchers are looking for possible interrelationships between such factors as different language skills (Devine 1987), effects of training in particular strategies and comprehension (Barnett 1988a; Carrell, Pharis, and Liberto 1989), and L1 and L2 listening or reading comprehension (e.g., Carrell and Connor 1991; Lund 1991; Murphy 1991). Sometimes learning modalities are compared, as in Herron and Seay's study (1991) assessing students' performance after viewing a video program as opposed to listening to a radio broadcast. Such comparisons also reveal potential effects that may arise from context in largely unpredictable ways.

In other words, even if one planned to replicate L2 or FL data, the difficulty in creating comparable studies remains: Issues addressed in previous experimental designs may not actually be relevant to today's state of the art, especially in correlational designs. Also, the insights gleaned from earlier findings alter research design and interpretation of data. Less than a decade ago, for instance, studies investigating aspects of Krashen's input hypothesis (e.g., Gass and Madden 1985; Faerch and Kasper 1987; Lynch 1988; Pica 1991b) led researchers to conclude that linguistically appropriate input is no guarantee of comprehension. Instead, language-processing factors such as interest and focus of attention often play a major role in determining how input becomes intake (Schmidt 1993). The researcher attempting to recreate results from earlier studies thus is likely to control for processing variables such as these, whereas earlier researchers did not.

A second subtle shift in preferences about study design can alter research as well. Increasingly, researchers today attempt multifaceted designs to uncover learning processes as well as the learned product (Larsen-Freeman 1991). Descriptive, case-study formats are gaining in popularity because they help pinpoint subcomponents in the metaprocess "comprehension" (Scarcella and Perkins 1987). Component processes that researchers frequently try to uncover are reader-based: the comprehenders' strategies (Oxford and Crookall 1989; Oxford and Nyikos 1989), prior knowledge (Carrell 1982; Lee 1986), grasp of text context (Roller and Matambo 1992), linguistic background (Skiba and Dittmar 1992), interest level (Leloup 1993), and the relationship of input to comprehension and output (Tsui Bik-may 1985; Lightbown 1992).

Another set of components involves learner-extrinsic factors that may affect comprehension processes: the text's sociolinguistic context (Pennycook 1989); its rhetorical organization (Chaudron and Richards 1986); its lexicon, style, and morphosyntax (Carrell and Connor 1991); and the effect of instruction in strategy use (Barnett 1988a, 1988b; Kern 1989; Anderson 1991).

Addressing these complex interactions between reader and text-based factors, researchers today are thus increasingly viewing comprehension as several situationally based processes (e.g., recognition, recall, problem-solving) rather than as a single metaprocess. Certainly life was easier for both researchers and teachers prior to the L1 work in psycholinguistics that laid the foundation for our current L2 and FL research designs. Listening and reading were viewed as automatic language recognition "skills" rather than as cognitively controlled and affectively driven abilities. Research assessed a comprehension product without regard to the multiple cognitive, affective, and social variables cited above. Only after research studies were designed to look at such variables did theories about comprehension begin to change. Consequently, the research base of earlier work may not generalize to current strategies of research.

Current Premises about Comprehension Abilities

What follows in this chapter is a discussion of the potential gap between the last generation's work and that which is currently being produced. It will not stress how current research results build on older studies (the more conventional form of a review of the literature); instead, it will concentrate on how that older research has led us to conceptualize our field differently and to operationalize these new ideas in questions of research. This reconceptualization is seen more as a reaction to the older findings than as a development from them. In this section, we will first explore how theory and research about reader processing of texts is expanding the profession's views about how to measure comprehension and how to construct appropriate tasks for readers and listeners. Second, we will look at how this expanded theoretical vision has led to new research designs sensitive to the ways learners construct meaning from texts.

Such initial focus on comprehension models (rather than on results) is uncharacteristic for research summaries. The authors believe, however, that issues in research design must be linked to learning theory in order to identify the fundamental research questions that need to be answered. The key question addressed in this chapter, then, is the following: What are the factors affecting reading and listening comprehension that researchers need to consider when developing their studies and in evaluating their results?

Incidental and Intentional Comprehension

As already noted, the theory underlying most L2 and FL research on comprehension stems largely from first-language work such as that of Ausubel (1963) regarding cognitive scaffolding, Craik and Lockhart (1972) on depth of processing, LaBerge and Samuels (1974) on automatic information processing, Shiffrin and Schneider (1977) on controlled and automatic processing, and Baddeley (1990) on working memory and the storage of information in long-term memory.

Yet, as indicated above, it is not clear how these models transfer to L2 and FL situations. Moreover, the bulk of theories and studies in second-language acquisition stem from L2 (Canadian and American) rather than FL research. Krashen's (e.g., 1985) theories are best known, but they have also posed the most frustrating research issue: What types of studies could be designed to distinguish acquisition from learning, and would those distinctions reveal how language competency develops? Thus, Nagle and Sanders (1986) find that "the notion that learned forms can never be transferred to acquisition is difficult if not impossible to verify" (p. 12). This slippery distinction may not, in fact, be verifiable. However, rather than rejecting explicit instruction, researchers today are looking for a new role for classroom instruction (e.g., VanPatten and Cadierno 1993), one that accommodates both styles of language learning.

In this vein, Bialystok (1990) distinguishes between competence theories that deal with static, presumably complete, knowledge about language rules and processing theories that analyze incomplete knowledge and variability in language use (pp. 637–38). She thus proposes new ways to construe problems in researching comprehension. Conceivably, interaction between incidentally acquired and intentionally learned abilities (unconscious and conscious, implicit and explicit learning) affects both L2 and FL comprehension, notably when students can see that grammar rules can serve as markers for meaning (Doughty 1991).

The Role of Focus in Comprehension

Currently in L1 reading comprehension theory, interactive processes in comprehension (both at the word- and at the global-meaning level) are the most frequently discussed.

Here, again, the transfer to an L2 or FL situation is not immediately evident. Although subject to evolving interpretations, earlier, bottom-up models posited that reading commences with letters and words (e.g., Gough 1984), while top-down theorists suggested that the reader begins with a global concept of text content (e.g., Goodman 1967). Today, interactive models (Rumelhart 1977) assume both processing styles occur simultaneously or in rapid interactional sequence.

LaBerge and Samuels's (1974) automaticity model explains how breakdowns in the interactional comprehension sequence limit automatic processing—having to "stop and think" about the words and structures in a text. Presumably that focus on detail, in turn, interrupts the listener's or reader's chunking of a global story line in long-term memory. (Chunking will be discussed in the next section.) Stanovich's (1980) L1 compensatory model is particularly interesting to researchers attempting to account for what readers do when a particular skill (e.g., word knowledge) is inadequate. Applying these theories, McLaughlin (1987) has investigated how reader and listener focus affects comprehension of an L2 text: the extent to which limited automatic processing inhibits a comprehender's ability to focus attention.

Compensatory theory suggests that listeners and readers lacking automaticity skills rely on other factors, such as their reading goals, background knowledge, metacognitive strategies, or the context in which the text is presented (e.g., as an office memo, an invitation). The classroom consequences of these further interactions have fairly straightforward pedagogical implications. Since misreadings will, in any event, interfere with comprehension processes, teachers assigning reading and listening tasks need to direct student attention toward those textual features that enable accurate global understanding of who and what the text is about before those students are asked to read for detail. Less self-evident are the implications of these interactions for further research.

Problem-Solving as a Means of Activating Reader and Listener Focus

In an effort to identify key factors that account for different kinds of interactive processing, van Dijk and Kintsch (1983) propose that a distinct comprehension mode operates when readers or listeners engage in problem-solving. Unlike a reader's task when he or she engages in recognition (matching concepts) or recall (summarizing concepts), problem-solving tasks require readers to apply textual information to a particular, personal "situation." This model assumes that the comprehender constructs meaning by creating a situation for the text, working through three levels: (1) understanding of verbatim language (detail or microlevel representation); (2) understanding of propositional language (gist or macrolevel); and (3) engaging in performance, operationalizing what is learned from the text.

Yet the situation becomes more complex. Verbatim language is what the listener/reader keeps in immediate or short-term memory, lasting no more than a few seconds. A person is more likely to recognize textual elements that are interrelated either semantically or by means of clear discourse markers (Mohan 1990). Van Dijk and Kintsch compare memory representations of a text to push-down stacks with new elements continuously being added, pushing older elements farther away. Thus the most recent input is that which is most likely to be remembered verbatim, adding a distinct temporal dimension to the interactive model.

Another temporal or ordering subprocess can affect comprehension as well. When the elements are perceived as representing related concepts (a semantic field), they can also be "chunked." Chunking, then, reduces memory load and, because it seems to facilitate depth of processing, enhances it as well. Chunked elements are called propositions. Propositions reduce a text to what the reader or listener grasps as essential information, a stripped-down version of the verbatim statement. Usually only when propositions connect in memory can they be recalled.

Van Dijk and Kintsch illustrate the relationship between verbatim text and propositions with a hypothetical story about Lucy, who overturned her new sailboat on a stormy afternoon. A reader or listener might chunk the extended story by associating the following concepts (the "atomic propositions," capitalized below) to the verbatim language (in lower case) of a spoken or written text:

ACCIDENT overturn (Lucy, sailboat)

    VEHICLE   sailboat

                 new

    PERSON   Lucy

    TIME   on (X, afternoon) - - - - - - - -

                 stormy

    LOCATION outside (X, harbor)

                 just   Sausalito (p. 349)

The resulting propositions (the atomic features chosen) will depend on the comprehender's context and perspective. For instance, assume that someone is listening to this information on a newscast. If Lucy is a personal friend, a proposition like "Lucy had an accident in her boat yesterday" may result. On the other hand, if the listener doesn't know Lucy and wants only to find out whether it is safe to go boating in Sausalito harbor, the chunking will change to a proposition more like "Better check the weather today in view of yesterday's boating accident." Textual propositions, then, are determined, in part, by memory capacity, and in part by the comprehender's point of view (which governs attention and resultant chunking).

As comprehension continues in extensive reading or listening, the situation gets even more complicated. Like point of view, propositions frequently change, as more verbatim text is processed. Assume a listener has chunked "a careless person's sailboat accident" as the foregoing "situation." If the next sentence heard is "On that same afternoon, three other boats sank in the bay," that listener may make a search of episodic text memory to retrieve core concepts like "stormy afternoon." "Careless person" and "sailboat" might now be rechunked as "hazardous conditions" and "boats." In this way individual "atomic propositions" are coalesced into macropropositions as new verbatim language is heard or read. Initial chunking can, in this way, be revised or "rechunked."

As an L2 exploration of the notions about memory and chunking abilities that van Dijk and Kintsch propose, Block's (1986) case studies suggest that students' reading styles may account in part for the propositions they store in memory. Analyzing think-alouds of nine readers, Block found that they tended to read texts in one of two ways: either (1) reacting subjectively to information in the text and *relating it to themselves* (a nonintegrative style) or (2) interacting with the text, monitoring text structure and their own understanding of *what the text says* (an integrative style). For Block's subjects, integrative reading styles were significant predictors of academic success in writing and subject-matter courses. One might hypothesize that nonintegrators would store fewer text-based propositions in memory than would integrators. As a result, they would chunk (and learn) less text-based information.

Propositional chunking styles are also implied in Bernhardt's (1991) analysis of student discourse in recall protocols. For example, her subjects, students of German who were assessed at classroom levels from first to fifth year, tended to coalesce redundant information. When the German language text said both "Reagan" and "U.S. president," student recalls referred to one or the other, not both. While failure to include facts in a recall protocol is not tantamount to forgetting, this analysis suggests that information may actually be lost in memory when it is not necessary for comprehension (Bernhardt 1991: 218). A future correlational study might include discourse analyses of recalls in conjunction with a recognition test, used at intervals to document both short- and long-term memory. Such research might shed light on van Dijk and Kintsch's thinking about how macropropositions develop and what text information is stored in memory and for how long.

Comprehension as an Accretion Process

Case studies and discourse analyses thus seem to uncover what learners chunk from verbatim language. Yet to be comprehensible, a text must also be read or heard as commensurate with the listener's or reader's own experience. It follows, then, that comprehension increases with experience. Analyzing student reports, for example, Bacon (1992b) found that a student listening to a passage about electric converters "saw" a World War II–era refrigerator that had been described to him by his father. This visual situation became a referent for his understanding of the passage dealing with electric currents in other countries.

By analyzing such recalls, student reports, and think-alouds, researchers can trace how readers or listeners create a mental representation of a given text according to their own view of reality—a very particular kind of comprehension that may correlate with learning styles in other dimensions. L1 situation theory assumes that, to extrapolate inferences from texts, readers must create "mental models" (Johnson-Laird 1983). Yet, because they represent a reader's organized view of the text's setting and content, mental models do not necessarily aid in recognition of actual "surface" language. To assess how text language and mental models inform one another, L1 researchers Perrig and Kintsch (1985) looked at how different texts and tasks trigger different situation models. They wanted to investigate how a reader's mental reconstruction of a text affects what is recalled from a text and the way in which it is recalled. This research is beginning to provide answers to the question of how comprehension processes interact.

First, Perrig and Kintsch found that some text factors (e.g., coherence) facilitate recall, but still may fail to facilitate recognition at the microlevel, e.g., the ability to verify on a true/false test which sentences appeared and which did not appear in that text (p. 515). Second, students could recognize and recall high percentages of textual propositions yet be unable to perform tasks based on the information in the text. Such was the case with a description of a drive into a town. Students could recognize and recall information about buildings and where they were located, yet they were unable to draw an accurate map of the town described (a visual model), even after repeated reading of the text (p. 517).

Aspects of the findings cited here are corroborated in other L1 studies (Dellarosa 1983; Marschark 1985; Schmalhofer and Glavanov 1986; Pennington and Hastie 1988.) and in one FL study (Dahl 1991). If further substantiated in L2 and FL research, such findings have important implications for teaching and testing comprehension, particularly in programs involving language for special purposes or content-based instruction, since they suggest that *reading and listening comprehension may be task-specific.*

If so, another dimension in the typical research design or learning model also emerges. Different tasks and different testing modes trigger at least three different reading and listening operations: (1) recognition tests such as true/false, multiple-choice, and multiple-choice cloze seem to assess *the learner's ability to confirm verbatim text-based input;* (2) recall tests, notably recall protocols, apparently assess the learner's ability *to retrieve textual (propositional) information;* (3) inference questions and problem-solving tasks based on oral or written texts assess the learner's ability to create a mental model in order *to apply knowledge gleaned from that text.* In other words, multidimensional comprehension necessitates a multidimensional teaching and testing program.

Synthesizing Text and Reader Perspectives

Recourse to L1 models also highlights another difficulty in L2 research. Central to any mental model is a dimension often missing in L2 and FL programs: the reader's or listener's social context. As Pennycook (1989) and Heap (1991) point out, in theories about cognitive processing, the social role of the comprehender (the reader's context) is usually ignored. Texts are presented to students as a body of information to be acquired, not in terms of the social function they serve. In other words, purely cognitive models assume that the learner's goal will be to acquire text knowledge. In actual practice, readers' and listeners' goals vary. They can range, for example, from "who cares about this, anyway" to "I want to buy this book" to knowing "I need to remember that for my job interview." From a sociolinguistic perspective (Pennycook 1989) purely text-based research inhibits the readers' prerogative to reject, resituate, or assign their own values to the text according to their own belief systems. Increasingly, then, researchers are exploring ways to assess reader and listener perspectives.

In an interactive framework that includes reader perspective and the reader's social context (sometimes characterized as a constructivist approach), researchers look at reader reconstructions of texts and situational readings, not just the reproduction of text information. Hence L2 research designs today must reflect the fact that language behavior will differ with the reader's task. A practical result from preliminary versions of such findings is the current focus on criterion-referenced tests—tests that are sensitive to different comprehension objectives (e.g. Shohamy 1984, 1991). Criterion-referenced tests take into consideration certain identified comprehension goals—recognition, recall, or problem-solving—as well as the information a student can be expected to know prior to reading the text. Yet, to this point in time, most comprehension tests have looked only at recognition ability (e.g., true/false, multiple-choice), cloze, or short-answer recall of isolated facts, reinforcing assumptions of older research studies.

Our emerging research paradigm, then, suggests a need for tests that elicit the comprehender's synthesis of textual information. Proponents of recall protocols point out that this type of instrument has been used extensively and has great reliability and verifiability. Wolf (forthcoming), however, argues that protocols may focus reader attention on details rather than main ideas in a passage. She cites several studies that support this contention (Lee and Ballman 1987; Lee and Wolf 1987; Wolf 1991). Comprehension has many dimensions and must be assessed accordingly. In other words, *because different reading tasks govern how readers reconstruct texts and subsequently convey that reconstruction, we need to assess the listener and reader's ability to comprehend in different ways.*

Yet multiple methods for testing comprehension also complicate assessment. If textual information is to be synthesized, test makers must decide how best to operationalize "effective synthesizing," and how to score information provided by the synthesizer. A "how to" passage about what makes marriages work may be represented propositionally by a list ("monitor emotional outbursts," "don't make unreasonable demands"); but that list may still fail to connect the logic of those propositions ("un-reasonable demands *result* in emotionally charged situations"). Similarly, if a passage deals with a senate debate, and the reader characterizes the debate as between two private individuals (two people mentioned in the text), has the text information been misaligned (Waeltermann 1991)?

As a step toward testing multiple comprehension abilities, Swaffar, Arens, and Byrnes (1991) suggest that a student-generated précis format may integrate retrieval (text-based) and situational (reader-based) features of a comprehender's text reconstruction. Cha (1993) found a significant correlation between the précis and several other measures in a study of ESL students at intermediate and advanced levels.

Since the précis is designed to cross-correlate various comprehension processes, we elaborate upon it here to illustrate current thinking about these interactions. The précis has four stages, designed to suggest how the comprehender moves from preconceived ideas brought to the text, through that person's mental interaction with textual infor-mation, to the modified perspective the reader or listener emerges with after processing the text. In stage 1, students identify the focus or topic of the text and confirm their assumptions using key phrases from initial paragraphs. In stage 2, they specify how that topic is presented (e.g., chronologically, as a contrast with another topic, or in some causal relationship). Once the macropattern is established, students confirm the pattern of information about a topic in stage 3 by selecting text language and sorting it in a matrix. In stage 4, students comment on the implications or significance of the pattern they have recreated. Because of their lexical deficiencies, beginners need some of these pieces provided in the test format. Modified in such a way, the précis would include a statement about how the topic is presented along with some representative answers in the matrix. Since cognitive processes may be more fully accessed in a reader's L1

(Lee 1986) and beginners and intermediate learners can comment more effectively on textual implications in their native language, they should do so if it is feasible for the scorer to correct that language.

To generate a précis, readers might, in stage 1, decide that the passage topic is the beauty myth, and, in stage 2, that the passage reveals a macropattern of causality between media images and unhealthy behaviors such as anorexia. In stage 3, readers will select language from the text describing media images ("Twiggy was the ideal of the fifties") and resultant health fads ("percentage of women on liquid diets," "roller coaster weight gain and loss") and arrange these quotes from the passage in two visually opposing columns.

After selecting two or three micropropositions for each column, readers will comment briefly on what they understand from their reading (e.g., that media images promote destructive images or serve the American diet, clothing, and cosmetic industry). With the précis, students undertake recognition tasks (matching language to categories), synthesis of gist (identifying topic and information pattern), and problem-solving (defined as inferential reasoning about the implications or significance of the information to the reader.)

As the précis example illustrates, there are a variety of skills and processes that interact to contribute to the ultimate comprehension of a text. Researchers are becoming more interested in such interactions and in ways in which various skills inform one another, both within and between modalities. We turn our attention now to the ways in which listening and reading processes might be compared, and how these two modalities might be related.

Listening: To What Extent Are the Comprehension Processes Comparable to Reading Processes?

In our quest for effective instructional modes, we would like to know whether listening and reading activities result in a similar recall of ideas. In their assessment of L1 research, Sticht and James (1984) conclude that age is a key variable in whether reading or listening results in greater recall of texts. Children who are still learning to read recall more information after listening. Literate adults, however, most frequently recall more after reading. Typically, such studies are thus concerned with relationships between modalities such as reading and listening.

Such relationships can further complicate research design. One such complication arises with hidden assumptions about how language learning is sequenced. Many L2 researchers view comprehension practice as the foundation for language learning, the necessary first stage on which acquisition is built. Summing up the research basis for such an assumption, Dunkel (1991) presents four arguments in favor of listening and reading preceding demands for language production:

1. A utilitarian advantage in the classroom: tendency toward better performance (see particularly Thiele and Scheibner-Herzig 1983) and continuation of study (Gary and Gary 1981)

2. A cognitive advantage for the learner: the avoidance of task overload

3. An affective advantage for the learner because comprehension practice lets students wait before producing language on their own. With a structured delay, students can participate more knowledgeably after some weeks of listening and viewing practice than they can when speech is demanded from the outset of instruction

4. A practical postclassroom advantage: Competence in understanding is likely to be of highest use to learners. Reading comprehension is viewed as the most important skill by academic professors. In four out of six disciplines (engineering, psychology, chemistry, and computer science) listening comprehension is ranked second (pp. 436–37)

As a practical rationale for integrating comprehension activities, Dunkel's suggestions synthesize core arguments for earlier and more extensive work in listening and reading and its impact on whole-language learning—and for research that accounts actively for such experience in learners.

Possibly, however, sequencing reading before related listening activities promotes superior language acquisition among adults. Lund (1991) compared recall protocols of adults literate in their native language. In the first part of the experiment, half the subjects read and the other half listened to the same L2 text. In a second exposure to the text, modalities were reversed. Lund found differences in performance that favored those who read the text first. This finding suggests a correlation with Sticht and James's (1984) similar conclusions based on L1 studies.

Two additional findings are noteworthy from the teacher's standpoint. First, both groups in Lund's study heard or read the text only once for their first protocols and then wrote a second protocol after hearing or reading the text a second time. Lund reports that "[t]he second trial benefitted readers and listeners in the same ways, if not to the same degree" (p. 201). In other words, *recursive tasks* (i.e., systematically building repetitions) *significantly expand reading and listening recall.* Lund also emphasizes the importance of the recall task "which encouraged subjects to form an explicit representation of the text" (creating a situation model for the text) and notes that the recall-reprocess combination was less fruitful for the listeners who did not have this task (p. 201).

Lund concludes that listeners concentrated on who the speakers were and the nature of the relationship between those speakers. Possibly the text situation may be more difficult for L2 listeners to establish than for L2 readers. Nonetheless, activities that direct students' attention to the genre, speakers, and situation in the text seem to be even more strongly indicated for listeners than for readers. Visual and written reinforcement in conjunction with a listening task is likely to promote recall among any level of L2 students. Research results can thus also be influenced by the tasks set and by familiarity with the item types used to assess comprehension.

Criteria for Identifying Listening Tasks

In the Lund study, an English-language recall was used to assess listening comprehension. But, as we have seen, no single operation encompasses comprehension. In this respect research of the two modalities of comprehension are similar: Listening research confronts the same theoretical problems as those found in reading research. Should the listener recognize, replicate, or react to a text heard? In other words, as for reading, listening researchers must specify what kind of listening comprehension they are looking for (Glen 1989: 29). The pragmatic approaches in L2 work range from focus on behaviors (e.g., paying attention, deriving meaning—see Underwood 1989) to matrices of tasks and purposes (Lund 1990). Rost (1990) suggests motivational and goal-driven criteria that might apply to the tasks Lund describes: critical, global, intensive, interactional, transactional, recreational, and selective listening.

Dunkel's (1991) review of the literature in the field indicates that failure to agree about listening constituents and how to operationalize listening tasks is a major stumbling block to research. Why should this diffusion characterize listening research more than reading research? Arguably, reading researchers have had a longer period to evolve and modify models in the wake of new information (e.g., Gough 1984). Another less obvious issue may be that in listening comprehension, particularly that involving a video segment, the sociological context (e.g., the social setting, gender, age, dress of speakers) is more evident than in a written text. Thus, as interest in listening comprehension increases, so does interest in how context affects what listeners comprehend. Indeed, there is growing support for an active accounting of the effects of contextual factors on comprehension in research design.

With some exceptions, texts used in most listening research have been relatively short (fewer than 500 words). This brevity puts limits on what authentic or natural texts can be used (e.g., short newscasts, weather reports, announcements). The listeners' focus with short texts is necessarily on propositions mapped to verbatim language rather than on propositions derived from chunking longer segments. Yet researchers who fail to examine comprehension processes accessed in extended listening tasks such as those involved in comprehending lectures or movies are avoiding a wealth of simulated, "real world" options, particularly with regard to chunking processes. Also missing in the research picture emerging when only shorter texts are used are pedagogical implications. What strategies can a teacher suggest to help students become more successful listeners of longer texts, where recall focus is necessarily on linking ideas rather than reiterating them?

To explore what students process when engaged in extended listening, O'Malley, Chamot, and Küpper (1989) investigated the note-taking and comprehension skills of FL learners who listened to science lectures given in English. Analysis of course handouts and students' notes revealed that many students were unaware of lecturers' cues to signal key words. Students had difficulty extracting such key terms from ongoing discourse. In almost half the cases where independent notes were made, layout was poor and relationships between items of information were unclear, leaving an incomplete and misleading summary of the lecture.

In another, shorter listening study, Chaudron and Richards (1986) investigated the impact of various discourse markers: macro markers ("as was mentioned at the outset of this chapter") and micro markers ("earlier"). They found that, when used separately, macro- and micro-styles aided student comprehension. When joined, however, ("earlier, as was mentioned at the outset of this chapter") these cues actually seemed to interfere with comprehension. Aside from issues of language, subject matter, and length, then, such research suggests that the rhetorical devices lecturers use to emphasize central ideas and organize their information will have significant impact on L2 listeners (e.g., Chaudron 1983).

Context: The Marked Sociological Dimension in Listening Comprehension

Context probably influences listening comprehension more directly than it does a particular reading task. This may be true, in part, because print has relatively regular features of typography (e.g., headlines, titles, italics). Consequently, even very different authors use a similar framework. For readers, unless such features are explicitly marked in a text, accent, pitch, speed, gender, register, and inflection remain largely a matter of conjecture and do not function as distractors. This is not so for the listener, whose comprehension tends to be influenced by socially coded acoustic clues about who says what and how (Markham 1988; Bacon 1992a).

Context as a research variable includes the comprehenders' situation (e.g., listening as social interaction or media viewing, reading as entertainment or to prove one's ability to read), the text's situation (e.g., as a newspaper clipping or as a comprehension passage on an SAT test), as well as its distribution (e.g., as a franchised or independent movie, a personal or a commercial videocassette, a desktop publication or a best-seller).

Increasingly, researchers concerned about how texts are understood as cultural documents want research designs to be sensitive to marketing issues. The nineteenth century German sociologist Max Weber identified marketing interests as the social capital in a culture that "determines opinions and attitudes" (1958: 72). As a current example, an Academy Award frequently changes a film's status from that of a trivial to a major statement. If a text's meaning is viewed as originating in its historical-cultural context (just as a film may become significant once it has received an award), comprehension must include awareness of a text's social capital (or perceived value). Studies revealing that, for example, L2 students consistently pay more attention to male than to female voices stating the same information suggest how social capital influences incidental comprehension (Schmidt 1993).

Further complicating the task of situating a listening text within a cultural setting is the fact that listeners must comprehend texts in various stages of completion, extending from polished reading aloud to extemporaneous speech. Yet even extemporaneous speech can vary from the virtually inarticulate to the urbane. Compare, for example, an open debate from the senate floor (often interrupted) with a television interview of those same senators making substantively the same arguments directed by a moderator. The senate debates will probably be harder to process due to interruptions and a probable lack of cohesive statements that sum up and link ideas. Extended rhetorical markers, more usual in a moderated discussion ("In other words, your main concern, senator, is . . ."), apparently aid listener recall (Chaudron and Richards 1986; O'Malley, Chamot, and Küpper 1989).

As a further contrast between reading and listening, the range of speech genres (Bakhtin 1986; Swales 1990) is far greater, and hence less predictable, than that of written texts. Demands on student's acoustic literacy involve a sophisticated awareness of cultural sign systems and how they are coded in spoken contexts. Signs are established by the authority of the speaker (did Madonna or Barbara Bush say that?), the social rules observed (do Jack Palance's one-armed push-ups constitute approved or prohibited behavior when he accepts an Academy Award?), the phonosyntax used (was that a question or a command?), and the vocabulary selected (you say "marvelous," I say

"OK"). Unless listeners can identify and systematize these features, their comprehension will be more difficult and, at best, will only replicate *content* without showing sensitivity to speaker *intentionality*—resulting in comprehension of only half the message. Research about focusing on listening comprehension must provide a means for measurement of students' abilities in these factors, or the results will be uninformative.

Related to acoustic literacy is literacy in visual media. Visual clues via television and microcomputers now augment the formerly heard text (e.g., Herron and Seay 1991). If, as language teachers, we define knowledge in terms of social capital as well as automatic skills in processing words and structures, our instruction must reflect a marriage of formal language features with the semiotic characteristics of those features. As any situation comedy reveals, visual images frequently alter the impact of spoken statements. The statement "Very good, Madam" codes different messages when spoken by a man in a checkered jacket who has just been hit in the face with a lemon pie than when uttered by an impeccably attired butler with an English accent. The systems in spoken and visual messages, whether they contradict or expand the linear text, need to be factored into comprehension. In a period rapidly coming to be designated as the postliterate era, *researching visual literacy becomes a major component alongside the research about "acoustic literacy"* (Kellerman 1990).

For the first time, new technologies now available render such activities a practical reality for researchers and teachers alike. SCOLA with its international newscasts, inexpensive videocassettes of movies, and TV programs are at a classroom's disposal for the price of a VCR. Students, in experiments, classrooms, and on their own, can identify a figure's visual centrality in the scene, whether that person is active or reactive, and his or her characteristic intonational patterns (e.g., loud, fast, cheery) and discourse features (extended sentences, explicatives, words that indicate sequence, etc.).

The question to investigate is how much comprehension learners gain when semiotics are predictable (e.g., viewers see that people being attacked on the street probably call for help or the police, or that speakers addressing an angry crowd use inflammatory language). With authentic materials and instant replay capabilities, students can identify such interactional groups or individuals in a scene and identify macro-features prior to focusing on language. Research can, therefore, now look at whether focus on visual semiotics contributes significantly to language comprehension.

Current Interactions between Listening and Reading Comprehension Research and Practice

Thirty years ago, neither the pragmatics of listening and reading comprehension, such as learner context and goal, nor the holistic possibility of interrelated skills, were part of research design. Carefully standardized in terms of lexical and morphosyntactic features, listening and reading texts in this earlier period were not written or scripted to be read as authentic statements stemming from a culture. Nor were students considered active participants in constructing meaning on the basis of what was read or heard. Such standardized texts were appropriate to use in research if students' comprehension was defined as the ability to register and replicate what was heard or read.

Since that time, as we have outlined, additional factors have become prevalent in research, creating new subfields of the discipline. For both reading and listening comprehension, language is no longer the only basis for text selection. Now researchers also look at how message and reader-based features influence different readings, including factors such as the rhetorical structures of texts (Carrell 1982), reader aims (Oxford and Nyikos 1989), readers' background knowledge (Politzer and McGroarty 1985; Markham and Lathan 1987), and their strategies (Oxford 1993). In short, the idea of a normed reading—one "correct" way to understand what is heard or read—is no longer sought in research (Bernhardt 1991; Dunkel 1991; Swaffar et al. 1991). Investigators consider not only whether learners recognize a text, but how they organize, synthesize, and apply the information they hear or read about. Several new fields of inquiry have been of particular interest.

Student Background

A research area that has had considerable impact on teaching practice in both listening and reading is sometimes referred to as "schema theory" or "background knowledge." Neither of these terms pertains to knowledge acquisition. They merely refer to the fact that human beings organize and store knowledge in systematic ways. Indeed, words such as *schema, background,* and *prior knowledge* have widely different interpretations in research literature. As several authors have pointed out (Alexander, Schallert, and Hare 1991; Swaffar et al. 1991), "background" can refer to cognitive strategy use, prior knowledge of subject matter, or prior familiarity with rhetorical features, to name but a few possibilities. Like recent research in reading, listening comprehension studies assessing the effects of "prior knowledge" consider multiple variables (e.g., length of text, language level, speech modifications) rather than single interactions (e.g., Chiang and Dunkel 1992).

The Impact of Prior Knowledge of Content—Language for Special Purposes

Research suggesting that familiarity with a particular content area eases the comprehension task in the FL has been particularly appealing to program developers, but not yet to researchers in the United States. Initial field reports about cultural learning in secondary programs (Glisan and Fall 1991; Met 1991) and language for special purposes in colleges and universities (Grosse and Voght 1991; Krueger and Ryan 1993) have been enthusiastic, although not without their detractors (Sudermann and Cisar 1992, 1993). As Widdowson (1993) cautions, the profession is ill-advised to assume that the ability to use a foreign language to learn will yield the same results as training in learning a foreign language. In other words, language for special purposes may have utilitarian value for learning and performance in a particular subject field yet fail to enable the student to apply language knowledge in social situations or in an unrelated discipline. Thus, although we have Canadian studies reporting success in their L2 setting (Edwards et al. 1984; Genesee 1987), and while content-based ESL programs appear to be effective in the United States (Snow and Brinton 1988; Crandall 1993), such reports do not provide extensively researched substantiation to support claims about when and how to use content-based instruction to enhance FL acquisition (Leaver and Stryker 1989; Krueger and Ryan 1993).

Strategies: Can They Offset Deficits in Automatic Processing?

As discussed in the section on theory, L1 psycholinguistic studies analyze specific reader and listener interactions with texts that promote recognition and recall, e.g., morphological analysis or word association, gisting, making predictions. Yet can such behaviors be taught and, if so, can strategy training override the effects of language proficiency limitations on either reading or listening comprehension? Heretofore, investigations on this topic have been of three kinds: (1) surveys about how attitudes affect strategy use (e.g., Nyikos and Oxford 1993); (2) comparisons between listening and reading strategies in native and second language (Clarke 1979; Sparks and Ganschow 1993); and (3) studies of pre- and post-training effects in both listening and reading (Barnett 1988a, 1988b; Kern 1989; Anderson 1991).

Several problems exist in applying these findings. First, reviews of the field suggest that there are about two dozen L2 strategy classification systems. Oxford (1993), for example, groups these systems into five major typologies: learner styles (e.g., field dependent, independent), particular language skills (vocabulary, grammar), psychological functions (cognitive, affective, social), linguistically based systems (monitoring, practicing), and success factors such as age, gender, or motivation (p. 183). As Oxford points out, without coherent, shared investigatory premises, studies are difficult to compare. We believe that a second difficulty in comparisons involves the lack of information about how performance corresponds to strategies learners attest to using. Most studies compare strategies of "successful" and "unsuccessful" learners, a status determined by learner-extrinsic factors that are not comparable between studies (e.g., different formats among tests taken, different content of texts read or heard).

Yet a third problem emerges for comparisons among observational studies. Strategies themselves seem to be proliferating. Researchers analyzing the impact of strategy training, for example, will use interviews, group discussions, or think-alouds to determine whether students are listening or looking for particular textual features such as words that signal episodes ("meanwhile, back at the ranch") or contextual factors (such as where a conversation occurs or between whom). As research in the field grows, so do the numbers of strategies being analyzed. Block's (1986) research identified fifteen, Pritchard (1990) found twenty-two, and Anderson (1991), forty-seven strategies. The fact that each study redefines strategies to fit its own purposes makes it even more difficult to generalize about findings on this basis.

The problem for researchers trying to isolate strategies is that, in actual practice, students probably combine or "orchestrate" strategies. Thus, the student who reports "I always listen for nouns," suggests that some learners begin with a metacognitive plan (i.e., the conscious awareness of strategy use) that is also a cognitive strategy (in this case bottom-up focus). Kern's (1989) data suggest, for example, that discourse-level strategies seemed to promote word-recognition skills. Whether gisting is a cognitive or metacognitive strategy seems less important than identifying how gisting directs cognitive focus. Are students focused on bottom-up factors (e.g., words, morphosyntax) or on discourse-level, top-down factors (e.g., referring to a previous sentence or keeping story meaning in mind)?

Studies comparing L1 and L2 reading styles suggest that transfer of strategies does not happen automatically. In other words, good readers in L1 may fail to apply their

L1 resources to L2 reading (e.g., eye movement, Bernhardt 1987; comprehension monitoring, Block 1992; reading strategies, Clarke 1979; background knowledge, Jenkins 1987 and Davis, Cordero-Ponce, and Chandra 1990). These same problems emerge when L1 and L2 listening are compared (Markham 1988; Conrad 1989; Bacon 1992c). Characteristically, L2 listeners are less likely than readers to use advance organizers (e.g., teacher prompts, questions) or contextual clues (e.g., keeping in mind who was speaking to whom, what audience was addressed) to help them understand what they hear (Lund 1991).

Here again, changes in research design are emerging on the basis of findings about students' learning strategies. Two recent studies have looked for possible interactions between strategy training and reading. Barnett (1988b) found significant differences only after two semesters of training in using teacher-directed reading strategies. Kern (1989), examining training in using particular linguistic features rather than general linguistic abilities, found that one semester of explicit training in recognizing features such as cognates and cohesion markers improved the accuracy of word inferencing in his experimental group. Low-, mid-, and high-ability students in the experimental group made gains that were twice as great as those of their counterparts in the control group on a test of word inference (p. 141). Possibly the homily about "time on task" applies in a special way to strategy training: Training in particular linguistic skills may yield demonstrable results in a relatively short period of time. It may be that focused strategy training allows students to monitor one class of problems more rapidly, whereas learning-generalized strategies may only serve to distract readers' attention from the text.

Overall, a considerable body of research establishes that orchestrated strategy use is effective (Chamot and Küpper 1989; see also O'Malley and Chamot, this volume). Yet while the profession assumes that less skilled learners may simply be less skilled strategy users (O'Malley and Chamot 1990), it is possible that strategy use and language acquisition are reciprocal. In other words, successful language acquisition may lead to successful strategy use as well. All indications suggest that teachers enhance language acquisition by using and teaching strategies (Oxford 1990; Wenden 1991), but precisely how, and how effectively, remains unclear.

Comprehension and Skill Acquisition

One teaching strategy that has, as yet, received limited attention in research, is the use of longer listening and reading texts. Certainly L1 research about memory functions suggests that longer text segments are processed differently, possibly at greater depth than passages of fewer than 500 words. Because experiments with longer written texts are difficult to control and administer, little reading research has been undertaken to assess the impact of longer written and oral texts on language learning (Saragi, Nation, and Meister 1978).

As access to video is increasing, however, researchers are investigating the effect of extensive listening comprehension. One such study compared the listening comprehension of second-semester classes exposed daily to ten-minute vignettes from *French in Action* (Capretz and Lydgate 1987) with listening comprehension of classes learning French without these videotapes. Tested with a tape made in Paris for French television, students in the experimental group using *French in Action* demonstrated significantly higher comprehension of both details and main ideas (Secules, Herron, and Tomasello 1992: 483).

In a second experiment, using two first-semester French classes, the authors selected one class to receive explicit classroom training in words and structures used in the *French in Action* videos, followed by teacher-led, contextualized oral drills. The second class saw only the video with training in targeted structures edited out. Both groups received equivalent drill practice in using the targeted words and in all other respects the conditions were equivalent over a ten-week period. On weekly tests that used a selected cloze technique, the class exposed to explicit explanation and drill in targeted structures performed significantly better in vocabulary use, yet on both weekly and immediate posttests using a true/false format, the video-only group performed significantly better on questions about grammatical structures. In view of these unanticipated findings, the authors posit that "listening comprehension can be seen to involve a unique combination of skills, only one of which is knowledge of specific linguistic structures" (p. 487).

More studies that target interactions between comprehension and language acquisition are badly needed—for example, studies of factors that qualify strategies in significant ways, notably field independence or field dependence as relating to specific linguistic tasks (Jamieson 1992).

Memory and Multiple Skills

In view of anomalous findings such as those cited above (Secules, Herron, and Tomasello 1992), another research avenue that is just beginning to influence teaching practice is the study of how comprehension skills are thought to lay foundations for production abilities. Research in comprehension-based learning has resulted in suggestions for programs and materials. Methodologies such as Total Physical Response and the initial stages in the Natural Approach stress the importance of a comprehension phase as the building block to ultimate production. Regrettably, comprehension-based learning has been associated with specific methods rather than with generic suggestions for more effective second-language acquisition. Fortunately, more recent research about authentic texts and strategy practice has avoided the onus of a "method" tag. Hence such materials can be added to textbooks, teacher manuals, and curricular designs regardless of their methodological focus.

Still, if comprehension-based learning is to establish itself as worthwhile in language acquisition, the profession will need more studies about how the manner in which learners process input affects their language production. As a positive case in point, Feyten (1991) looked at the strength of five predictive variables (an L1 listening comprehension test, sex, length of previous language exposure, language exposed to, and the last contact with the language), and reported a positive relationship between listening ability in one's native language and foreign-language acquisition. It may be that training in L1 listening is a useful first stage in preparing students for L2 listening comprehension.

Without additional studies confirming the value of training in listening as well as reading, it will be difficult to alter tacit research and pedagogical assumptions that isolate work in comprehension from work in speaking and writing. Yet, at this point in time, an increasing number of research studies suggest that pragmatic whole-language approaches enhance student learning and are essential for successful applications of FL knowledge in the real world (Shih 1992). The caveat here, however, is that the research clearly indicates that the ability of students to write and speak in the L2 about what they hear and read in that language should not be our sole performance criterion (e.g., Carrell and Connor 1991).

Our Changing Research Assumptions

As illustrated at the outset, and confirmed by the emerging new subfields just outlined, some tacit assumptions that have tended to dominate L1, L2, and FL research in listening and reading are now being called increasingly into question: (1) Can different comprehension tasks and goals yield comparable, mutually informing results, or are we looking at apples and oranges? (2) Should comprehension of normed language (text language organized in idea units) be assessed independently of analysis of situation-specific, contextual use of language (its macropropositions)? (3) If our concern is maximizing language acquisition, is it optimal to view comprehension abilities separately from other language abilities? (4) Is it useful to look at comprehension processes without also assessing listener and reader monitoring of those processes?

While questions such as these interest L1, L2, and FL researchers, FL investigators are also looking for variables unique to their learners' situation, specifically, "a resolution of the question of language-specific processing" (Bernhardt 1991: 225). In other words, in light of the greater focus of attention on interactive processing, failure to distinguish processing differences in foreign language and second-language research may unintentionally blur essential distinctions about the importance of learner factors, such as the role of the students' native language, their cultural background, and the presence or absence of pre-established interlanguage. Perhaps of equal significance, language-specific structures in grammar or discourse patterns may render some tasks easier or harder for learners whose L1 is, for example, an oriental rather than an occidental language.

While descriptive research (ethnography, discourse analysis, case studies) might seem initially to reveal more about individual factors that influence cognitive processes, researchers may ultimately disagree about how well assessment instruments measure cognitive processes. To illustrate the uneven path research findings often take, consider the controversy surrounding the cloze procedure in research design. In the late 1970s and early 1980s, cloze testing was presented as a measure of reading comprehension. Weighed against multiple-choice measures, cloze seemed to yield verifiable results. First-language students who could fill in a blank for every five running words of a text were presumed to have successfully comprehended it.

With increased concerns about discourse features, however, researchers challenged the validity of claims that rational cloze (every nth running word) or multiple-choice cloze measured more than the comprehension of individual sentences (e.g., Shanahan, Kamil, and Tobin 1982). The issue is by no means settled (e.g., Jonz 1990). The ongoing debate illustrates that, ultimately, these researchers are interested in measuring comprehension products. Whether cloze tests measure comprehension within sentences (i.e., reconstructing text elements or comprehension *products*) or between sentences (i.e., chunking concepts, hence implying comprehension *processes*) remains an inference.

Although research findings are, to some extent, always inconclusive, practices unsupported by research are even riskier. The intuitive notion that some text types might be easier to read than others (e.g., instructions about how to plant a garden easier to read than correspondence about the purchasing of garden equipment) was incorporated into the *ACTFL Guidelines* for reading proficiency in the early 1980s. Some practitioners had, in fact, reported anecdotally about success with particular text types, but research confirmation was lacking. In two experimental studies (Allen et al. 1988, Lee and Musumeci 1988), however, text type proved to be an insignificant variable in the assessment of proficiency level for foreign language students at both the high school (years one through four) and the college levels (semesters one through five). When text types suggested for different reading levels by the initial *ACTFL Guidelines* for reading were compared with student performance at various learner levels, no patterns emerged to confirm such presumptions.

A research design that distinguishes between levels of study and proficiency levels might address current ideas about how proficiency relates to comprehension processes. It may well be that, because metacognitive processing plays a significant role in what the comprehender decides the text is about, listening and reading assessment must take processing variables into account (Casanave 1988). Thus, a student with low language proficiency may, nevertheless, due to metacognitive capabilities in evaluating and repairing comprehension, demonstrate listening or reading comprehension that is superior to that of a student with greater L2 proficiency. When Bernhardt (1991) analyzed the quantity of information recalled by readers in her study of students at five levels of instruction, she found that between groups, means were generally (but not consistently) higher for higher language levels. Individual performance profiles, however, revealed an uneven trajectory.

Implications for the Classroom as a Site of Research

As research on interactive procedures in comprehension increases, so does evidence that leads to a more cautious choice of dependent and independent variables in research design. Already mentioned in regard to native language use in testing, Carrell's (1982) study of ESL students suggested that prior knowledge about the text influenced comprehension, but that contextual information such as titles and pictures did not. Would the findings of an FL study designed to look at language-specific processing be different?

Lee (1986) conducted a follow-up investigation of this type in which he changed only one dependent variable. Instead of producing recall statements in the foreign language, Lee's English-speaking learners of Spanish wrote protocols in their native tongue. Under this condition, contextual features (titles and unambiguous cartoon illustrations) enhanced recall significantly in one of the two passages read. He concluded that the use of native-language protocols accounted for the difference in findings.

Inevitably, Lee's study raises new queries. Since he used cartoon pictures to situate the story, the comparable clarity of the pictures, an independent variable, needs to be established. In one case, the illustration failed to clarify the story because the picture displayed "a novel situation" (p. 353). Lee cites an extensive study on the efficacy of pictorial types (Omaggio 1979) in which the results revealed that the best visual was an uncomplicated "pre-thematic" picture from the beginning of the story that contextualized the passage, significantly assisting nonnative readers in both recognition and recall (see also Schallert 1980). But deciding which pictures are uncomplicated could depend on the background of people looking at those pictures.

To avoid misleading analyses, researchers must use consistent procedures in conducting studies and reporting their data—applying standards of conscious control that differ from first-generation studies, allowing for coherent speculation about strategy interaction. Both researchers and readers of studies need to be informed about (1) the native language of learners, (2) whether performance was evaluated based on use of authentic or edited texts, (3) the conditions for collecting data, (4) the measures applied to assess comprehension, (5) all the substeps in all tasks performed and documents about how they were assessed, and (6) the increasingly sophisticated use of statistical tools in methodology and analysis procedures (Bernhardt 1991; Larsen-Freeman and Long 1991). Without such information, the profession lacks a basis for systematic comparison of results, which could lay the foundation for future research conducted on different premises. Without sufficient knowledge about test instruments (e.g., length, basis for validating the scoring measure used), generalizations about comprehension have little meaning (e.g., Shohamy 1984).

Such suggestions have been, and continue to be, made by leading figures in the field. Since a vital profession is one capable of learning from its misfires and blind alleys, research frequently leads to shifts in subsequent research. When multiple findings based on discrete differences in variables start to confirm one another, we can confidently refine practices and teaching techniques to reflect them.

Thus, without the *ACTFL Guidelines,* Allen et al. (1988) and Lee and Musumeci (1988) might never have explored text types as factors in reading comprehension and revealed the extent to which the profession may be underestimating our students' reading comprehension capabilities. Similarly, today's use of the cloze procedure in writing tests emerges after research suggested that the cloze procedure can be used to test comprehension at the sentence level. Furthermore, because studies suggesting that L1 recall protocols yield more information about students' comprehension than a protocol written in a second language, one might argue in favor of English (or possibly Spanish) usage in classroom testing conducted in the United States, at least as a cross-correlation.

In this context, Pica's (1991a) suggestions for making foreign language classrooms "research-ready and research-able" point to action research as an important joint effort that teachers and researchers need to make in order to confirm or disconfirm more strictly controlled findings under real world conditions. The Special Interest Group of the American Educational Research Association (AERA), established in 1985 by Dale Lange, Gil Jarvis, and Elizabeth Bernhardt, has become an important nexus for pragmatically oriented research in both second- and foreign language arenas.[2] Such classroom-related and laboratory studies inform us not only about cognitive processing, but also about how variables such as social roles, awareness of text situation, and students' own performance goals affect comprehension.

At the beginning of this chapter we set out to explore tacit assumptions about reading and listening comprehension and how these assumptions are changing. This chapter has looked at a number of essential shifts in research design:

1. A shift from edited or culturally sanitized texts to authentic materials in assessments
2. A shift from looking at strict skill division to more encompassing formats that enable researchers to compare listening and reading and measure cognitive as well as mutually informing abilities
3. A shift toward including not only recognition, but also recall (measured in protocols, open-ended questions, or diagrams) and performance capabilities (measured by the ability to put a model together based on instructions or draw a map after reading a description) when defining FL comprehension
4. A shift from regarding comprehension skills as isolated learning to considering comprehension as the basis for speaking and writing
5. A shift from one-time listening and reading to scaffolded or recursive tasks *with the same texts* (Grellet 1981; Lund 1990; Swaffar 1993)

From the classroom teacher's perspective, none of these five shifts are major components in most present textbook formats or curricular designs. Although working in the only environment available in which to collect data, the researcher is, then, confronted with a potential research environment that may not be entirely compatible with today's research goals. Current research designs probably do not, in fact, reflect dominant learning practices. It is conceivable that student subjects may not perform informatively on research tasks because item types are so different from those involved in their ordinary language use.

Thus, while many beginning and intermediate textbooks present authentic listening and reading tasks, they frequently appear as isolated components or realia, rather than explicitly structured stages leading to communicative activities (Swaffar 1991). Similarly, differentiated comprehension capabilities (recognition, recall, problem-solving) are rarely reflected in beginning, intermediate, and advanced stages within a given curriculum. Even pedagogical techniques that seem incontrovertibly beneficial, such as rereading or relistening for different linguistic or cognitive goals, are rarely reflected in current textbook practice (Horiba 1993).

The authors of this chapter believe that such anomalies between research, textbook format, and curricular design may arise in part from a misconception that is left over from immersion contexts: namely, that comprehending and producing language involve the same acquisitional approaches (Gary and Gary 1981). Because "input" has been equated with "content," the profession has equated comprehensible input (Krashen's "$i + 1$") with recognition and recall of vocabulary. As we have seen in this chapter, however, research findings suggest that other factors such as topic familiarity, listener or reader focus, and cognitive strategies also play a decisive role in rendering a text comprehensible, e.g., enabling coherent recall.

Issues for Further Research

As we have argued in this chapter by means of example, *researchers need to differentiate between problem-solving, recognition, and recall in order to diagnose comprehension modality and to ascertain how processing rules change with different comprehension goals.* To illustrate, students may be able to answer L2 questions about a film or a TV documentary yet be unable to make coherent L1 statements about how they differ from similar media events in the United States. In other words, they may recognize the language and content accurately but be unable to analyze its underlying cultural and contextual implications.

In a study investigating such abilities, the *context* in which that text was produced becomes critical as a possible variable for which researchers must control. To perform successfully on any evaluation question, the listener or reader must be familiar with the context in which the text would be situated in the target language culture (e.g., Is Betty Friedan or the current Miss America talking about the beauty myth? Is she addressing a television audience or a small group of professional women?). In other words, an FL listener or reader must identify three dimensions of that text: (1) its setting, (2) the speaker/writer and the intended audience, and (3) their shared or antagonistic communicative goal.

These three factors yield a perceptual dialogue between text and reader that governs how language will be perceived. Consider research on incidental vocabulary acquisition through reading (e.g., Hulstijn 1992). The definitions of words—their semiotics—stem not only from the text content but also from the reader's grasp of textual context. Thus, in the election year of 1992, virtually every U.S. voter knew that the contextual connotations for "trust" or "family values" depended on who was talking about whom. Researchers need to describe, in conjunction with their quantitative findings, the way students conceptualize a text's setting and apply their background knowledge to the task at hand. To document these aspects of comprehension, quantitative studies must include qualitative measures such as oral interview techniques and discourse analyses of recall protocols.

Logically, one predictable distinction between the type of language comprehension involved in problem solving and that involved in recall or recognition is the reduced focus on language. In problem-solving, the comprehender's attention is presumably focused on intent and social circumstances (cognitive variables) more than on specific words and phrases in the text (linguistic variables). In recognition and recall, focus of attention may be more on textual language *per se*. As yet, we know of no L2 or FL research exploring these issues.

The second suggestion stemming from the research analysis in this chapter is that comprehensible input needs to be reconsidered with regard to passage or "text" context. When beginning students watch a TV soap opera, listening for content will restrict them to occasional words or phrases. Once, however, they determine where the speakers are (in the living room or the boardroom) and who they are (husband and wife or two executives), intonation patterns will clue any listener to the speech acts involved (e.g., warning, promising, consoling, accepting, or refusing). Framed in this way, the listener's focus can be on words that confirm or disconfirm suppositions about the situation depicted.

Looking for contextual features only (locale, identity of speakers, their speech acts— in short, the genre of the text), listeners could review five-, ten-, or even twenty-minute segments for these global features rather than, as is more common practice, review two- or three-minute segments for language content. As suggested by the *ACTFL Guidelines,* novice students will probably have an inadequate grasp of main ideas, whereas students at the intermediate levels will misunderstand finer points. The difference in extensive reading, as with listening to longer authentic texts, is the focus on speech acts: how settings and social roles define what people can and cannot accomplish with words, not the words themselves.

Our third suggestion is that, in order to inform classroom practice, the profession needs research that compares different comprehension goals under different conditions, such as pragmatic uses of comprehension in content-based instruction. Such research designs could assess performance among students listening to and reading a greater number of more challenging and lengthier texts than those now commonly used, particularly at early stages of instruction. As the work of Allen et al. (1988) demonstrates, there seems little doubt that our students can comprehend more than we give them credit for. Possibly, restrictive materials and tasks may impose early limits on FL comprehension that inhibit performance at advanced levels.

A fourth need we perceive is for a more learner-centered research program—one that would take into consideration our students' comprehension monitoring (Block 1992). As we have indicated, researchers must identify sources of students' errors before they can determine the degree to which mechanisms such as interest, background, or abstract thinking abilities can compensate for deficiencies in L2 language acquisition. The profession's increasing interest in performance factors—how our students improve in academic or other pragmatic settings—has led us to focus increasingly on the type of instruction students need in order to function effectively with the language and to continue to learn a foreign language beyond formal instruction. Research has not, however, specified which comprehension tasks are actually being practiced by our students in and outside the classroom.

Closely linked to the foregoing, but necessitating a distinct research design, is a fifth issue: *the need for research to analyze situations in which students are in charge of their own FL learning.* Such research would investigate, for example, whether text types chosen by students would result in more efficient language acquisition than blanket assignments. Along with established variables (such as students' cognitive maturity or their familiarity with the genre and subject matter presented), student-centered research would consider such issues as the learners' interest level, how students respond to different tasks such as problem-solving or extensive reading or listening, and what they learn, given, for example, such options as viewing media versions or keeping journal accounts.

Sixth, we need to determine whether programs (not just individual classes) encourage developmentally sound approaches to listening and reading. Currently, work on long-term language development has focused on programs involving individual classes or a two-course sequence (Barnett 1988b; Kern 1989). Increasingly, however, the call is being heard for coherent learning sequences that represent longer trajectories, where high schools and universities are accountable to one another (Nunan 1989; Swaffar 1993; White 1993). One longitudinal tool with which to code the achievement results of actual practices is the case study. Monitoring individuals at regular intervals, researchers can trace students' progress through a curricular sequence, and perhaps chart changes in comprehension strategies as well as student progress. Although relatively few students are assessed in case studies, such descriptive projects can investigate issues difficult to ascertain in cross-sectional, experimental research (e.g., how learning changes and what learning processes affect results). Similarly, ethnographic research can examine the way different classes within a program treat and sequence comprehension activities (e.g., as part of a whole-learning process, using comprehension to learn new information, or as isolated activities).

Particularly if considered along with experimental evidence (performance on standardized tests), the case studies and ethnographic approaches could help us establish, for example, whether extensive listening and reading for global comprehension is an efficient way to acquire language detail, or whether there are optimal numbers of repetitions for reading and listening. Research projects might also be designed to determine whether grammar acquisition in a comprehension-based program stressing the monitoring of pragmatic use (grammar as meaning markers) prior to language production compares favorably with acquisition resulting from programs that stress active use in speech and writing from the onset of FL learning.

Seventh, the profession needs studies to identify factors that inhibit and facilitate the way students acquire new information in a foreign language. For instance, studies might look at whether comprehension functions as suggested by the ACTFL scales for reading and listening—whether students' comprehension abilities do indeed develop from a generic grasp of culturally familiar global meaning ("can understand the main ideas and key words in familiar material") to understanding unfamiliar material as well through the use of cognitive strategies. Thus, for more advanced levels, both listeners and readers would have to demonstrate ability to identify FL contexts rather than generic ones familiar to both cultures (i.e., the difference between the comic ploys in a French farce and a Monty Python skit, or between the bargaining rules of a Mexican mercado and an American farmer's market). Here, comparative L1 and L2 studies may help us distinguish between inhibiting and facilitating factors that originate in language deficiencies and those attributable to learning styles (Block 1992).

Studies that investigate such considerations will further redefine comprehension and recontextualize research designs. As currently conceived, comprehension assessment has begun to shift from language performance norms to criterion-based performance— not language use per se, but how task execution reveals how language is used. In the decade to come, researchers must explore what tasks, what monitoring capabilities, what quantities, and what sequences promote optimal language acquisition through both reading and listening, as well as their interactions with whole-language learning.

Notes

1. The authors wish to thank Katherine Arens, Elizabeth Bernhardt, Alice Omaggio Hadley, and three anonymous reviewers for suggestions, many of which were incorporated into the final version.
2. Newsletters and information are currently available from the editor, Professor Leslie Schrier, College of Education, N268 Lindquist Center, Iowa State University, Iowa City, IA 52242.

References

Reading and Listening Comprehension: Perspectives on Research and Implications for Practice

Alexander, P. A., D. L. Schallert, and V. C. Hare. 1991. "Coming to Terms: How Researchers in Learning and Literacy Talk About Knowledge." *Review of Educational Research* 61: 315–43.

Allen, Edward D., Elizabeth B. Bernhardt, Mary Theresa Berry, and Marjorie Demel. 1988. "Comprehension and Text Genre: Analysis of Secondary School Foreign Language Readers." *Modern Language Journal* 72: 163–72.

Anderson, Neil J. 1991. "Individual Differences in Strategy Use in Second Language Reading and Testing." *Modern Language Journal* 75: 460–72.

Ausubel, David Paul. 1963. *The Psychology of Meaningful Verbal Learning.* New York: Grune and Stratton.

Bacon, Susan. 1992a. "The Relationship between Gender, Comprehension, Processing Strategies, and Cognitive and Affective Response in Foreign Language Listening." *Modern Language Journal* 76: 160–78.

———. 1992b. "Phases of Listening to Authentic Input in Spanish: A Descriptive Study." *Foreign Language Annals* 25: 314–34.

———. 1992c. "Authentic Listening in Spanish: How Learners Adjust Their Strategies to the Difficulty of the Input." *Hispania* 75: 398–412.

Baddeley, Alan D. 1990. *Human Memory: Theory and Practice.* Boston: Allyn and Bacon.

Bakhtin, M. M. 1986. *Speech Genres and Other Late Essays.* Transl. V. W. McGee. Austin: Univ. of Texas Press.

Barnett, Marva. 1988a. "Teaching Reading Strategies: How Methodology Affects Language Course Articulation." *Foreign Language Annals* 21: 109–19.

———. 1988b. "Reading through Context: How Real and Perceived Strategy Use Affects L2 Comprehension." *Modern Language Journal* 72: 150–62.

Bernhardt, Elizabeth B. 1987. "Cognitive Processes in L2: An Examination of Reading Behaviors," pp. 35–50 in J. Lantolf and A. Labarca, eds., *Research on Second Language Acquisition in Classroom Settings.* Delaware Symposium No 6. Norwood, NJ: Ablex.

———. 1991. *Reading Development in a Second Language: Theoretical, Empirical, and Classroom Perspectives.* Norwood, NJ: Ablex.

Bialystok, Ellen. 1990. "The Competence of Processing: Classifying Theories of Second Language Acquisition." *TESOL Quarterly* 24: 635–48.

Block, Ellen L. 1986. "The Comprehension Strategies of Second Language Learners." *TESOL Quarterly* 20: 463–94.

———. 1992. "See How They Read. Comprehension Monitoring of L1 and L2 Readers." *TESOL Quarterly* 26: 319–43.

Capretz, Pierre, and Barry Lydgate. 1987. *French in Action.* Videocassettes: Santa Barbara, CA: Intellimation. Print materials: New Haven, CT: Yale Univ. Press.

Carrell, Patricia L. 1982. "Three Components of Background Knowledge in Reading Comprehension." *Language Learning* 33: 183–207.

———, Becky G. Pharis, and Joseph C. Liberto. 1989. "Metacognitive Strategy Training for ESL Reading." *TESOL Quarterly* 23: 647–78.

———, and Ulla Connor. 1991. "Reading and Writing Descriptive and Persuasive Texts." *Modern Language Journal* 75: 314–24.

Carson, Joan Eisterhold, Patricia L. Carrell, Sandra Silberstein, Barbara Kroll, and Phyllis A. Kuehn. 1990. "Reading-Writing Relationships in First and Second Language." *TESOL Quarterly* 24: 245–66.

Casanave, Christine Pearson. 1988. "Comprehension Monitoring in ESL Reading: A Neglected Essential." *TESOL Quarterly* 22: 283–302.

Cha, Khungae. 1993. "Test Tasks and Reading Comprehension of Authentic Texts: The Relationship of Item Constraints to Performance." Unpublished Ph.D. diss., Univ. of Texas at Austin.

Chamot, Anna Uhl, and Lisa Küpper. 1989. "Learning Strategies in Foreign Language Instruction." *Foreign Language Annals* 22: 13–24.

Chaudron, Craig. 1983. "Simplification of Input: Topic Reinstatements and Their Effects on L2 Learners' Recognition and Recall." *TESOL Quarterly* 17: 437–58.

———, and Jack C. Richards. 1986. "The Effect of Discourse Markers on the Comprehension of Lectures." *Applied Linguistics* 7: 113–27.

Chiang, Chung Shing, and Patricia Dunkel. 1992. "The Effect of Speech Modification, Prior Knowledge, and Listening Proficiency on EFL Lecture Learning." *TESOL Quarterly* 26: 345–74.

Clarke, Mark A. 1979. "Reading in Spanish and English: Evidence from Adult ESL Students." *Language Learning* 29: 121–50.

Conrad, L. 1989. "The Effects of Time-Compressed Speech on Native and EFL Listening Comprehension." *Studies in Second Language Acquisition* 11: 1–15.

Craik, Fergus, and Robert S. Lockhart. 1972. "Levels of Processing: A Framework for Memory Research." *Journal of Verbal Learning and Verbal Behavior* 11: 671–84.

Crandall, J. 1993. "Content-Centered Learning in the United States," pp. 111–26 in G. Kasper and S. Blum-Kulka, eds., *Interlanguage Pragmatics*. Oxford, Eng.: Oxford Univ. Press.

Dahl, Tova V. 1991. "The Implication of Language for Theories of Comprehension and the Cognitive Construction of Ideas." Unpublished Ph.D. diss., Univ. of Texas at Austin.

Davis, James, Wanda Cordero-Ponce, and Amitabh Chandra. 1990. "Performance of Expert Non-Native and Non-Expert Native Readers of Scientific French." *Reading Psychology* 11: 22–48.

Dellarosa, Denise. 1983. "The Role of Text Comprehension Processes and Analogical Reasoning in the Development of Problem-Solving Expertise." Unpublished Ph.D. diss., Univ. of Colorado at Boulder.

Devine, Joanne. 1987. "General Language Competence and Adult Second Language Reading," pp. 73–86 in Joanne Devine, Patricia L. Carrell and David Eskey, eds., *Research in Reading in English as a Second Language*. Washington, DC: TESOL.

Doughty, Catherine. 1991. "Second Language Instruction Does Make a Difference: Evidence from an Empirical Study of SL Relativization." *Studies in Second Language Acquisition* 13: 431–69.

Dunkel, Patricia. 1991. "Listening in the Native and Second/Foreign Language: Toward an Integration of Research and Practice." *TESOL Quarterly* 25: 431–57.

Edwards, H. P., M. Wesche, S. Krashen, R. Clement, and B. Kruidenier. 1984. "Second Language Acquisition through Subject Matter Learning: A Study of the Sheltered Psychology Classes at the University of Ottawa." *Canadian Modern Language Review* 41: 268–82.

Faerch, Claus, and Gabriele Kasper. 1987. *Introspection in Second Language Research*. Clevedon, Eng.: Multilingual Matters.

Feyten, Carine. 1991. "The Power of Listening Ability: An Overlooked Dimension in Language Acquisition." *Modern Language Journal* 75: 173–80.

Freed, Barbara F. 1991. "Current Realities and Future Prospects in Foreign Language Acquisition Research," pp. 3–27 in Barbara F. Freed, ed., *Foreign Language Acquisition Research and the Classroom*. Lexington, MA: Heath.

Gary, Judith Olmstead, and Norman Gary. 1981. "Caution: Talking May Be Dangerous to Your Linguistic Health." *IRAL* 19: 1–14.

Gass, Susan M., and Carolyn J. Madden, eds. 1985. *Input in Second Language Acquisition.* Rowley, MA: Newbury House.

Genesee, Fred. 1987. *Learning through Two Languages: Studies of Immersion and Bilingual Education.* Rowley, MA: Newbury House.

Glen, E. 1989. "A Content Analysis of Fifty Definitions of Listening." *Journal of the International Listening Association* 3: 21–31.

Glisan, Eileen, and Thekla F. Fall. 1991. "Adapting an Elementary Immersion Approach to Secondary and Postsecondary Language Teaching: The Methodological Connection," pp. 3–29 in June K. Phillips, ed., *Building Bridges and Making Connections.* Proceedings of the Northeast Conference on the Teaching of Foreign Languages. Lincolnwood, IL: National Textbook.

Goodman, Kenneth. 1967. "Reading: A Psycholinguistic Guessing Game." *Journal of the Reading Specialist* 4: 126–35.

Gough, Philip B. 1984. "Word Recognition," pp. 225–53 in P. D. Pearson, ed., *Handbook of Reading Research.* New York: Longman.

Grabe, William. 1991. "Current Developments in Second Language Reading Research." *TESOL Quarterly* 25: 375–406.

Grellet, Françoise. 1981. *Developing Reading Skills. A Practical Guide to Reading Comprehension Exercises.* New York: Cambridge Univ. Press.

Grosse, Christine Uber, and Geoffrey Voght. 1991. "The Evolution of Languages for Specific Purposes in the United States." *Modern Language Journal* 75: 181–95.

Heap, James. 1991. "A Situated Perspective on What Counts as Reading," pp. 103–39 in C. D. Baker and A. Luke, eds., *Towards a Critical Sociology of Reading Pedagogy.* Amsterdam, Neth.: Benjamins.

Herron, Carol A., and Irene Seay. 1991. "The Effect of Authentic Oral Texts on Student Listening Comprehension in the Foreign Language Classroom." *Foreign Language Annals* 24: 487–95.

Horiba, Yukie. 1993. "The Role of Causal Reasoning and Language Competence in Narrative Comprehension." *Studies in Second Language Acquisition* 15: 49–82.

Hulstijn, Jan H. 1992. "Retention of Inferred and Given Word Meanings: Experiments in Incidental Vocabulary Learning," pp. 113–25 in P. Arnaud and H. Béjoint, eds., *Vocabulary and Applied Linguistics.* London, Eng.: Macmillan.

Jamieson, Joan. 1992. "The Cognitive Styles of Reflection/Impulsivity and Field Independence/Dependence and ESL Success." *Modern Language Journal* 76: 490–501.

Jenkins, Susan Marian. 1987. "The Effect of Language Proficiency and Prior Knowledge on the Reading Comprehension of Graduate Student Native and Non-Native Speakers of English." Unpublished Ph.D. diss., Pennsylvania State Univ., University Park.

Johnson-Laird, Philip Nicholas. 1983. *Mental Models: Towards a Cognitive Science of Language, Inference, and Consciousness.* Cambridge, MA: Harvard Univ. Press.

Jonz, Jon. 1990. "Another Turn in the Conversation: What Does Cloze Measure?" *TESOL Quarterly* 24: 61–83.

Kellerman, Susan. 1990. "Lip Service: The Contribution of the Visual Modality to Speech Perception and Its Relevance to the Teaching and Testing of Foreign Language Listening Comprehension." *Applied Linguistics* 11: 272–80.

Kern, Richard G. 1989. "Second Language Reading Strategy Instruction: Its Effects on Comprehension and Word Inference Ability." *Modern Language Journal* 73: 135–49.

Krashen, Stephen. 1985. *The Input Hypothesis: Issues and Implications.* London, Eng.: Longman.

Krueger, Merle, and Frank Ryan, eds. 1993. *Language and Content: Discipline-Based Approaches to Language Study.* Lexington, MA: Heath.

LaBerge, David, and S. Jay Samuels. 1974. "Toward a Theory of Automatic Information Processing in Reading." *Cognitive Psychology* 6: 293–323.

Larsen-Freeman, Diane. 1991. "Second Language Acquisition Research: Staking Out the Territory." *TESOL Quarterly* 25: 315–50.

———, and Michael H. Long. 1991. *An Introduction to Second Language Acquisition Research.* New York: Longman.

Leaver, Betty Lou, and Stephen B. Stryker. 1989. "Content-Based Instruction in Foreign Language Classrooms." *Foreign Language Annals* 22: 269–75.

Lee, James F. 1986. "Background Knowledge and L2 Reading." *Modern Language Journal* 70: 350–54.

———, and Terry Lynn Ballman. 1987. "FL Learners' Ability to Recall and Rate the Important Ideas of an Expository Text," pp. 108–18 in Bill VanPatten, Trisha Dvorak, and James F. Lee, eds., *Foreign Language Learning: A Research Perspective.* Cambridge, MA: Newbury House.

———, and Diane Musumeci. 1988. "On Hierarchies of Reading Skills and Text Types." *Modern Language Journal* 72: 173–87.

———, and Darlene F. Wolf. 1987. "Accounting for Early Stage Foreign Language Learners' Recall of Passage Information." Paper presented at a meeting of the American Association of Teachers of Spanish and Portuguese (AATSP), Los Angeles, August.

LeLoup, Jean W. 1993. "The Effect of Disposition toward Text Topic on Second Language Reading Comprehension." Paper presented at The Univ. of Texas, Austin, March 10.

Lightbown, Patsy M. 1992. "Getting Quality Input in the Second/Foreign Language Classroom," pp. 187–98 in Claire Kramsch and S. McConnell-Ginet, eds., *Text and Context.* Lexington, MA: Heath.

Long, Donna R. 1987. "Listening Comprehension: Need and Neglect." *Hispania* 70: 921–28.

Lund, Randall J. 1990. "A Taxonomy for Teaching Second Language Listening." *Foreign Language Annals* 23: 105–15.

———. 1991. "A Comparison of Second Language Listening and Reading Comprehension." *Modern Language Journal* 75: 196–204.

Lynch, A. J. 1988. "Speaking Up or Talking Down: Foreign Learners' Reactions to Teacher Talk." *ELT Journal* 42: 109–16.

Markham, Paul L. 1988. "Gender and the Perceived Expertness of the Speaker as Factors in ESL Listening Recall." *TESOL Quarterly* 22: 397–406.

———, and Michael Lathan. 1987. "The Influence of Religion-Specific Background Knowledge on the Listening Comprehension of Adult Second Language Students." *Language Learning* 37: 157–70.

Marschark, Marc. 1985. "Imagery and Organization in the Recall of Prose." *Journal of Memory and Language* 24: 734–45.

McLaughlin, Barry. 1987. *Theories of Second Language Learning.* London, Eng.: Edward Arnold.

Met, Miriam. 1991. "Learning Language through Content: Learning Content through Language." *Foreign Language Annals* 24: 281–95.

Mohan, B. A. 1990. "Integration of Language and Content," pp. 113–60 in C. Simich-Dudgeon, ed., *Proceedings of the First Research Symposium on Limited English Proficient Students' Issues.* Washington, DC: U.S. Department of Education, Office of Bilingual Education and Minority Languages Affairs. [ED 341 260]

Morley, Joan. 1990. "Trends and Development in Listening Comprehension: Theory and Practice," pp. 317–37 in James E. Alatis, ed., *Linguistics, Language Teaching and Language Acquisition: The Interdependence of Theory, Practice and Research.* Georgetown University Round Table on Languages and Linguistics. Washington, DC: Georgetown Univ. Press.

Murphy, John M. 1991. "Oral Communication in TESOL: Integrating Speaking, Listening, and Pronunciation." *TESOL Quarterly* 25: 51–75.

Nagle, Stephen J., and Sara L. Sanders. 1986. "Comprehension Theory and Second Language Pedagogy." *TESOL Quarterly* 20: 9–26.

Nunan, David. 1989. "Toward a Collaborative Approach to Curricular Development: A Case Study." *TESOL Quarterly* 23: 9–26.

Nyikos, Martha, and Rebecca Oxford. 1993. "A Factor Analytic Study of Language-Learning Strategy Use: Interpretations from Information-Processing Theory and Social Psychology." *Modern Language Journal* 77: 11–22.

Omaggio, Alice C. 1979. "Pictures and Second Language Comprehension: Do They Help?" *Foreign Language Annals* 35: 107–16.

O'Malley, J. Michael, and Anna Uhl Chamot. 1990. *Learning Strategies in Second Language Acquisition.* Cambridge, Eng.: Cambridge Univ. Press.

———, and Lisa Küpper. 1989. "Listening Comprehension Strategies in Second Language Acquisition." *Applied Linguistics* 10: 418–37.

Oxford, Rebecca L. 1990. *Language Learning Strategies. What Every Teacher Should Know.* Rowley, MA: Newbury House.

———. 1993. "Research on Second Language Learning Strategies," pp. 175–87 in W. Grabe, ed., *Annual Review of Applied Linguistics,* vol. 13. New York: Cambridge Univ. Press.

———, and David Crookall. 1989. "Research on Language Learning Strategies: Methods, Findings, and Instructional Issues." *Modern Language Journal* 73: 404–19.

———, and Martha Nyikos. 1989. "Variables Affecting Choice of Language Learning Strategies: A Pilot Study." *Modern Language Journal* 73: 291–300.

Pennington, Nancy, and Reid Hastie. 1988. "Explanation Based Decision Making: Effects of Memory Structure on Judgment." *Journal of Experimental Psychology: Learning, Memory and Cognition* 14: 521–33.

Pennycook, Alastair. 1989. "The Concept of Method, Interested Knowledge, and the Politics of Language Teaching." *TESOL Quarterly* 23: 589–618.

Perrig, Walter, and Walter Kintsch. 1985. "Propositional and Situational Representations of Text." *Journal of Memory and Language* 24: 503–18.

Pica, Theresa. 1991a. "Foreign Language Classrooms: Making Them Research-Ready and Research-Able," pp. 393–412 in Barbara F. Freed, ed., *Foreign Language Acquisition Research and the Classroom.* Lexington, MA: Heath.

———. 1991b. "The Selective Impact of Classroom Instruction on Second-Language Acquisition." *Applied Linguistics* 6: 214–22.

Politzer, Robert L., and Mary McGroarty. 1985. "An Exploratory Study of Learning Behaviors and Their Relationship to Gains in Linguistic and Communicative Competence." *TESOL Quarterly* 19: 103–23.

Pritchard, R. 1990. "The Effects of Cultural Schemata on Reading Processing Strategies." *Reading Research Quarterly* 25: 273–95.

Roller, Cathy M., and Alan R. Matambo. 1992. "Bilingual Readers' Use of Background Knowledge in Learning from Text." *TESOL Quarterly* 26: 129–41.

Rost, Michael A. 1990. *Listening to Language Learning.* New York: Longman.

Rumelhart, David E. 1977. "Toward an Interactive Model of Reading," pp. 573–603 in S. Dornic, ed., *Attention and Performance I.* Hillsdale, NJ: Erlbaum.

Saragi, T., S. P. Nation, and G. F. Meister. 1978. "Vocabulary Learning and Reading." *System* 6: 72–78.

Scarcella, Robin, and Leroy Perkins. 1987. "Review Article: Shifting Gears: Krashen's Input Hypothesis." *Studies in Second Language Acquisition* 9: 347–54.

Schallert, Diane L. 1980. "The Role of Illustrations in Reading Comprehension," pp. 503–24 in R. J. Spiro, B. C. Bruce, and W. F. Brewer, eds., *Theoretical Issues in Reading Comprehension: Perspectives from Cognitive Psychology, Linguistics, Artificial Intelligence, and Education.* Hillsdale, NJ: Erlbaum.

Schmalhofer, Franz, and Doris Glavanov. 1986. "Three Components of Understanding a Programmer's Manual: Verbatim, Propositional, and Situational Representations." *Journal of Memory and Language* 25: 279–94.

Schmidt, Richard. 1993. "Consciousness, Learning, and Interlanguage Pragmatics," in G. Kasper and S. Blum-Kulka, eds., *Interlanguage Pragmatics.* Oxford, Eng.: Oxford Univ. Press.

Secules, Teresa, Carol Herron, and Michael Tomasello. 1992. "The Effect of Video Context on Foreign Language Learning." *Modern Language Journal* 76: 480–89.

Shanahan, Timothy, Michael L. Kamil, and Aileen Webb Tobin. 1982. "Cloze as a Measure of Intersentential Comprehension." *Reading Research Quarterly* 17: 229–55.

Shiffrin, Richard, and W. Schneider. 1977. "Controlled and Automatic Human Information Processing: I and II. Perceptual Learning, Automatic Attending, and a General Theory." *Psychological Review* 84: 127–90.

Shih, May. 1992. "Beyond Comprehension Exercises in the ESL Academic Reading Class." *TESOL Quarterly* 26: 289–318.

Shohamy, Elana. 1984. "Does Testing Method Make a Difference?" *Language Testing* 1: 147–70.

———. 1991. "Connecting Testing and Learning in the Classroom and on the Program Level," pp. 154–76 in June K. Phillips, ed., *Building Bridges and Making Connections.* Proceedings of the Northeast Conference on the Teaching of Foreign Languages. Lincolnwood, IL: National Textbook.

Skiba, Romuald, and Norbert Dittmar. 1992. "Pragmatic, Semantic, and Syntactic Constraints and Grammaticalization: A Longitudinal Perspective." *Studies in Second Language Acquisition* 14: 323–49.

Snow, Marguerite Ann, and Donna M. Brinton. 1988. "Content-Based Language Instruction: Investigating the Effectiveness of the Adjunct Model." *TESOL Quarterly* 22: 553–74.

Sparks, Richard L., and Leonore Ganschow. 1993. "The Impact of Native Language Learning Problems on Foreign Language Learning: Case Study Illustrations of the Linguistic Coding Deficit Hypothesis." *Modern Language Journal* 77: 58–73.

Stanovich, Keith E. 1980. "Toward an Interactive-Compensatory Model of Individual Differences in the Development of Reading Fluency." *Reading Research Quarterly* 16: 32–71.

Sticht, Thomas G., and James H. James. 1984. "Listening and Reading," pp. 293–317 in P. D. Pearson, ed., *Handbook of Reading Research.* New York: Longman.

Sudermann, David P., and Mary A. Cisar. 1992. "Foreign Language across the Curriculum: A Critical Appraisal." *Modern Language Journal* 76: 295–308.

———. 1993. "MLJ Forum." *Modern Language Journal* 77: 75–77.

Swaffar, Janet. 1991. "Language Learning Is More Than Learning Language: Rethinking Reading and Writing Tasks in Textbooks for Beginning Language Study," pp. 252–79 in Barbara F. Freed, ed., *Foreign Language Acquisition Research and the Classroom.* Lexington, MA: Heath.

———. 1993. "Using Foreign Languages to Learn. Rethinking the College Foreign Language Curriculum," pp. 55–86 in June K. Phillips, ed., *Reflecting on Proficiency from the Classroom Perspective.* Proceedings of the Northeast Conference on the Teaching of Foreign Languages. Lincolnwood, IL: National Textbook.

———, Katherine Arens, and Heidi Byrnes. 1991. *Reading for Meaning. An Integrated Approach.* Englewood Cliffs, NJ: Prentice-Hall.

Swales, John M. 1990. *Genre Analysis. English in Academic and Research Settings.* New York: Cambridge Univ. Press.

Thiele, Angelika, and Gundrun Scheibner-Herzig. 1983. "Listening Comprehension Training in Teaching English to Beginners." *System* 11: 277–86.

Tsui Bik-may, Amy. 1985. "Analyzing Input and Interaction in Second Language Classrooms." *RELC Journal* 16: 8–32.

Underwood, M. 1989. *Teaching Listening.* New York: Longman.

van Dijk, Teun A., and Walter Kintsch. 1983. *Strategies of Discourse Comprehension.* New York: Academic.

VanPatten, Bill. 1990. "Content, Processes and Products in Second Language Acquisition and Foreign Language Learning," pp. 240–45 in Bill VanPatten and James F. Lee, eds., *Second Language Acquisition—Foreign Language Learning.* Clevedon, Eng.: Multilingual Matters.

———, and Theresa Cadierno. 1993. "Input Processing and Second Language Acquisition: A Role for Instruction." *Modern Language Journal* 77: 45–57.

Waeltermann, Dieter. 1991. "Effects of Discrete Vocabulary Knowledge on Reading Comprehension of Authentic Texts." Unpublished Ph.D. diss., Univ. of Texas at Austin.

Weber, Max. 1958. *The Protestant Ethic and the Spirit of Capitalism.* Trans. Talcott Parsons. New York: Charles Scribner's Sons.

Wenden, Anita. 1991. *Learner Strategies for Learner Autonomy: Planning and Implementing Learner Training for Language Learners.* Englewood Cliffs, NJ: Prentice-Hall.

White, Ron V. 1993. "Innovation in Program Development," pp. 244–75 in William Grabe, ed., *Annual Review of Applied Linguistics,* Vol. 13. New York: Cambridge Univ. Press.

Widdowson, Henry. 1993. "The Relevant Conditions of Language Use and Learning," pp. 27–36 in Merle Kreuger and Frank Ryan, eds., *Language and Content: Discipline-Based Approaches to Language Study.* Lexington, MA: Heath.

Wolf, Darlene F. Forthcoming. "Issues in Reading Comprehension Assessment: Implications for the Development of Research Instruments and Classroom Tests." *Foreign Language Annals.*

———. 1991. "The Effects of Task, Language of Assessment, and Target Language Experience on Foreign Language Learners' Performance on Reading Comprehension Tests." Unpublished Ph.D. diss., Univ. of Illinois at Urbana-Champaign.

7

Second-Language Production: *SLA Research in Speaking and Writing*

Susan M. Gass
Michigan State University
Sally Sieloff Magnan
University of Wisconsin-Madison

Introduction

The field of second-language acquisition (SLA) has taken on new dimensions within the past few decades. It now includes the learning of second languages (L2), typically defined as nonprimary languages learned within the target culture, and foreign languages (FL), typically defined as nonprimary languages learned within the native culture. In reviewing recent SLA research, this article focuses on the productive use of language, that is, on the skills of speaking[1] and writing.

It is clear that the label *productive skill* may be insufficient justification for pairing speaking and writing, for the skills of listening and reading can also be considered productive in the sense of producing meaning. In other words, as someone listens and/ or reads, he or she is also interpreting a text or "producing/creating" meaning from that text. While we acknowledge the imprecise dichotomy we have made, we unite speaking and writing in the traditional sense of translating linguistic knowledge into linguistic form.

Susan Gass (Ph.D., Indiana University) is Professor of English at Michigan State University, where she directs the English Language Center. She has published in many areas of second-language acquisition, including input and interaction, language universals, and language transfer. She has served as President of the American Association for Applied Linguistics and has directed the 1990 TESOL Summer Institute. She is on the editorial board of *TESOL Quarterly* and *Applied Linguistics* and is the associate editor of *Studies in Second Language Acquisition.*

Sally Sieloff Magnan (Ph.D., Indiana University) is Professor of French at the University of Wisconsin–Madison. She has published in the areas of second-language acquisition (primarily writing and error analysis in speech), foreign language instructional methodology, proficiency and achievement testing, and TA development. She has served as President of the American Association of University Supervisors, Coordinators, and Directors of Foreign Language Programs and is currently Series Editor of their annual volume. She is also Editor-Designate of the *Modern Language Journal.*

In considering speaking and writing research together, we also recognize their divergent histories within the context of language learning and language teaching. In earlier traditions of language teaching, such as grammar-translation, the emphasis was not on spoken language, but on written language. As Richards and Rodgers (1986) explain, in a grammar-translation approach "little or no systematic attention is paid to speaking or listening" (p. 3).

> Grammar Translation is a way of studying a language that approaches the language first through detailed analysis of its grammar rules, followed by application of this knowledge to the task of translating sentences and texts into and out of the target language. It hence views language learning as consisting of little more than memorizing rules and facts in order to understand and manipulate the morphology and syntax of the foreign language. (p. 3)

This does not mean to say that the manipulations could not have been done orally. Yet because many of the languages originally taught in this manner were no longer actively spoken (e.g., Latin, Old Irish), teachers used oral activities in class as a way to teach written forms.

There is another aspect to consider when looking at the historical development of research on speaking and writing skills: Even though spoken language was virtually ignored in the days of grammar-translation methodology, writing as a discourse skill was not emphasized. Whatever emphasis there was on the production of written language (as opposed to spoken language), it was placed on writing words on paper as evidence of *grammatical knowledge.* That is, the goal of writing (mostly translation exercises) was to reflect knowledge of grammar, not to reflect evidence of the composing process. Thus, writing was only a medium through which grammatical knowledge, the aim of instruction, could be evaluated (cf. Richards and Rodgers 1986; Stern 1983).

With the change in teaching methodology in the 1940s and 1950s and the advent of audiolingualism with its behavioristic underpinnings, the roles of speaking and writing were reversed: Writing skills came to be seen as having a secondary role to the development of oral skills. The typical behaviorist position was that language is *speech* rather than *writing,* with speech being a precondition for writing. The justification for this position came from two observations: (1) normal children learn to speak before they learn to write and (2) many societies have no written language, but all societies have oral language; there are no attested examples of societies with only written, but no spoken, language systems.[2]

Within a behavioristic tradition, speaking consists of mimicking and analogizing. That is, we say or hear something and analogize from it. Basic to this position is the concept of habits. In acquiring a first language, children establish a set of habits and continue their linguistic growth by mimicking the speech of others and by analogizing from what they already know.

In recent years there has been a dramatic shift in the research traditions that examine both speech and writing. This shift has come about primarily in response to the anti-behaviorist tradition that developed in linguistics and psychology (e.g., Chomsky 1959) as well as an increased interest in the nature of learning for its own sake, and for how it can inform us about language-teaching practices. Current L2 research, in fact, emphasizes the importance of both speaking and writing for their intrinsic value in contributing to acquisition. As pointed out earlier, this view contrasts with earlier research in which skills were seen as only the by-products of acquisition or as the means through which acquisition could be assessed.

Acquisition can also be considered from a broader perspective, namely from the assumption that ability in any one specific skill is related to, and perhaps dependent on, general language proficiency. The nature of the relationship between skills is unclear. Does speaking help writing? Does writing help speaking? (See Lantolf 1988: 938–39.) In considering research on SLA, one needs to understand the extent to which this body of research is based on a solid research foundation or is part of the body of research that is created to formulate theory. A theory of SLA needs to explain what is acquired and what is not acquired of an L2 and how that knowledge (or lack thereof) comes about. This being the case, it is difficult if not impossible to separate language into various skills and make theoretical claims about how those skills result in the acquisition of abstract knowledge.[3]

A related question can be posed concerning the knowledge of the L1. Is the ability to speak and/or write fluently in an L2 related to a similar ability in the L1? It is partly through investigation of the notions of interaction between L1 and L2 that researchers have identified a fairly convincing distinction between speech and writing.

Yet another distinction relates to planned and unplanned discourse. Speaking is for the most part unplanned discourse, whereas writing, at least at the level of composition, is planned discourse (cf. Ellis 1984: 200–201).[4] The distinction between planned and unplanned discourse is basic to theories and research findings about speaking and writing. It is especially important to keep this distinction in mind in order to refrain from automatically generalizing findings from one skill to the other. Still, it is also clear that the planned–unplanned dimension is not categorical, but continuous. As speaking can have formal and highly planned variants, so writing has recently developed a fairly spontaneous, unedited form: electronic mail. According to Garrett (1992), a promising new line of research is concerned with how ideas are expressed in this new medium, which may be viewed as a written version of oral language.

Perhaps, then, it is mostly for expediency that speaking and writing have been combined in one chapter; but their combination can lead readers to ponder broader issues. Such pondering is useful, for at the profession's current stage of theory-building, therein may lie the greatest insights.

The remainder of this chapter focuses on the process of research in the areas of speaking and writing, as well as insights into the nature of acquisition that this research can provide. Such insights can be built on theoretical foundations, in which case research is designed to test predictions stemming from the theory. Conversely, insights may emanate from the data, which then raises questions that can be used to build theories. This chapter thus will investigate areas in which speaking and writing have been used to test or build theories.

Research from both L2 and FL traditions will be discussed for both skills. While there have been differences in the research traditions of L2 and FL acquisition, we do not treat these differences in this chapter. Both research areas consider the same fundamental question: How does nonprimary linguistic knowledge come about? Asking the question in this way enables us to recognize that learning an L2 or an FL is a cognitive act and that what must be investigated are the internal mental activities of learners. These mental activities cannot be assumed to differ according to the learning environment. This is not to say that differences between L2 and FL learning—such as motivation to learn, access to the language, and the need or desire for feedback—are not relevant. Rather, they play a secondary role in the examination of the fundamental cognitive activities involved in L2 and FL acquisition. Thus, in this chapter, the term SLA will refer to the learning of any nonprimary language regardless of the environment or mode of learning.

Speaking Research

Data Collection

As in all areas of SLA, data collection in the area of speaking has not proceeded without difficulty. The major controversy in SLA research is between those who wish to determine a learner's competence and those who argue that we need data that reflect naturalistic speech (performance data). The controversy has been in existence for at least twenty years, perhaps beginning with the work of Selinker (1972: 213–14), who claimed that researchers should "focus . . . analytical attention upon the only observable data to which we can relate theoretical predictions: the utterances which are produced when the learner attempts to say sentences of a TL." While this view (i.e., that spontaneous as opposed to elicited language is preferable) is still maintained by some, it has never been entirely accepted. Corder (1973), for example, argued that forced elicitation data were necessary:

> Elicitation procedures are used to find out something specific about the learner's language, not just to get him to talk freely. To do this, constraints must be placed on the learner so that he is forced to make choices within a severely restricted area of his phonological, lexical or syntactic competence. (p. 41)

The debate is, in a sense, a reflection of arguments relating to the domain of a theory of SLA. If researchers are concerned only with competence, then data that show variability are not interesting. To reflect a learner's internalized knowledge, data such as grammaticality judgments or elicited imitation might be more revealing. On the other hand, for those researchers interested in variation or interaction or input/output relationships (cf. Gass and Lakshmanan 1991), data showing learners in naturalistic settings and/or in a variety of tasks are crucial. Thus, the debate about which research measures to use must be understood within the context of the research questions being asked.

Speaking and Theories of SLA

In this section we discuss ways in which research in speech production has contributed to theoretical issues in SLA. We will look at the role of output and the input/output relationship. In addition, we focus on the issue of variation in SLA, since it has been closely allied with spoken data. It is to be noted that while speaking in and of itself is not a skill around which a theory of acquisition can be developed, it does nevertheless contribute to a theory of acquisition. In particular, we invoke concepts presented initially by Long (1983) in a set of propositions that has come to be known as the interaction hypothesis. Three parts of this hypothesis are important to note: (1) comprehensible input is necessary for acquisition, (2) conversational interactions (negotiation) make the input comprehensible, and (3) comprehensible output aids learners in moving from semantic processing to syntactic processing. The relationship of the first two is as follows:

> Adjustments → Comprehension
>
> Comprehension → Acquisition

Therefore,

> Adjustments → Acquisition

We return to these concepts throughout this section.

What Is the Relationship between Variation and SLA?

Research on SLA has for a long time recognized the fact that there is considerable variation in learner output depending on the context in which language is used and on the tasks that learners perform (Dickerson and Dickerson 1977; Ellis 1985; Sato 1985; Selinker and Douglas 1985; Tarone 1979, 1983, 1985, 1988; Woken and Swales 1989; Zuengler 1989; Crookes and Gass 1993a, 1993b). Thus, the primary research methodology compares data gathered from different settings (linguistic and social) or from different tasks. Tarone, one of the first to point out the variable nature of interlanguages, noted that accuracy depended on the task demands on the learner. Tarone (1985) presented three types of data from learners of English: (1) grammaticality judgments in which learners were asked to judge a set of sentences as grammatical or ungrammatical and then to make appropriate corrections on the sentences that had been judged ungrammatical, (2) free speech in an interview situation, and (3) an oral narrative. Tarone examined the use of obligatory pronoun objects. With the first data set (grammaticality judgments), learners apparently had not recognized the need for an obligatory pronoun object, whereas in the second and the third data sets (face-to-face interviews and an oral narrative, respectively), learners showed increased accuracy. Thus, the use or lack of use of a given linguistic form in these data was dependent on the mode of elicitation.

Type of task is not the only factor that is important in determining the type of linguistic output. Researchers must also consider the degree of formality of the situation, and, crucially from Tarone's perspective, the amount of attention given to speech. Tarone (1983) suggests that accuracy in target language use is a function of the amount of attention given to speech, and that the degree of attention can be determined by the tasks used to elicit speech. Thus, a task that involves a great deal of attention to language is predicted to yield the least targetlike speech. From this, Tarone proposes a continuum of speech styles, with the interlanguage "vernacular" representing that style having the least amount of attention to speech. Central to the recognition of different speech styles is the claim that vernacular style shows the least variability and styles resulting from the most attention paid to speech show the most external influence (i.e., influences from the native language and the target language). It is further hypothesized that when new forms enter the language, they enter into the formal system and spread to the informal system (cf. also Ellis 1985).

While this research was important, it has not been without criticism, both theoretically and empirically. From an empirical point of view, data did not always support the predictions. Tarone herself in a 1985 study considered data from Arabic-speaking and Japanese-speaking adult learners of English based on their performance on three tasks: grammaticality judgment, oral narration, and oral interview. These three tasks were intended to reflect a continuum of attention to language form with the grammaticality-judgment task requiring the most attention and the narrative the least. Both bound morphemes (third singular verb endings and noun plurals) and free morphemes (articles and direct object pronouns) were tested. The results were somewhat complex, but in general it appeared that with the bound morphemes the predicted relationship between task and accurate target language use was not evident; whereas with the free morphemes the opposite of the predicted relationship was noted. These results raised a number of important questions. First, the results called into question the role of attention to form as the unique explanation for interlanguage variation. Second, they suggested an interesting difference between the role of bound and free morphemes in SLA. And third, the results suggested an important role for discourse influences on L2 use. (See also Parrish and Tarone 1986 and Parrish 1987 for issues of methodology in the study of article acquisition.)

Additional empirical evidence against the unique relationship between task and language use is provided by Sato (1984), whose work on the production of consonant clusters by two Vietnamese children learning English showed mixed results. Sampling was done four times over a 10 month period on three tasks (free conversation, oral reading of text, and elicited imitation). In two of the samples, targetlike pronunciation was evident in what Tarone called the vernacular style (free conversation) as opposed to the careful style (oral reading). (See Oyama 1976 for similar results.)

Not only are there empirical difficulties with the "style shifting" paradigm as the unique explanation for L2 use, but there are theoretical difficulties as well. Most notably, the arguments espoused thus far are circular, since there are no *a priori* criteria for determining where a particular task would fall on the continuum. In other words, which is more formal: reading a word list out loud, reading a text, or imitating a speaker? Without explicit criteria, testing the hypothesis is difficult.

Ellis (1985) has also examined variation, claiming that there are essentially two kinds of variation: what he calls *free* variation and *systematic* variation. (See Preston 1989 and 1993 for critiques of Ellis's work.) The first can be exemplified by the following two examples from an eleven-year-old boy who is a native speaker of Portuguese learning English.

No look my card

Don't look my card

During this child's first month in the United Kingdom, he produced 18 negative utterances, 17 using *no* and 1 using *don't*. In the following month, there was an increase in the number of *don't*s although *no*'s were still more frequent. In the sixth month, negatives with *not* were most frequent. Thus, over time the number of *no*'s decreased and the number of *don't*s increased. In the middle of the transition period, there was considerable variation between the two forms.

The second type of variation noted by Ellis is systematic variation. Systematic variation is evidenced when two or more sounds or grammatical forms vary contextually; hence, it might better be termed "context-sensitive" variation. Some variation is linguistically based, while other kinds of variation are sociolinguistically determined. Below we provide an example of linguistically based variation from the acquisition of Swedish as an L2 as it exemplifies important research issues.

Hyltenstam (1977) studied the acquisition of Swedish negation by native speakers of 35 different languages. Data were collected through intuitional judgments of learners, with 24 examples of negation being tested. In Swedish the placement of the negative word *inte* is dependent on whether the negated verb is in a main clause or a subordinate clause as is seen below.

Kalle kommer inte idag

Charlie comes not today

"Charlie isn't coming today"

Det är skönt att Kalle inte kommer idag

It's fine that Charlie not comes today

"It's fine for Charlie not to come today"

The first stage that learners follow in the acquisition of Swedish negation is to uniformly put the negator before the verb, not differentiating between main and subordinate clauses. This is consistent with what we have seen earlier, that learners begin with a simple undifferentiated hypothesis: There is a one-to-one correspondence between form and function. When learners, as a function of greater proficiency, begin to recognize that their own systems do not correspond to the language they are exposed to, there is a need to revise the current hypothesis, in many cases resulting in greater complexity. In the case of Swedish, the change to a target-language system has as intermediate stages the placement of the negative marker after some finite auxiliary verbs and then extending its use to more and more verbs. At this stage, there is variability between placement before and after verbs. The same pattern is repeated with nonauxiliary finite verbs. At this point, learners are still not in conformity with the target system; they must now begin the process of differentiating between main and subordinate clauses. This differentiation takes place in the same gradual way as before, with the learners first placing the negator before main verbs and only later in both main and auxiliary verbs. Throughout this process, there is considerable variability, depending in large part on whether the context is a main verb or an auxiliary verb.

In considering the research process, there are a number of aspects to take into account. Hyltenstam (1977) himself outlines some of them (pp. 384–85):

1. The amount of data must be large enough to display possible regularities in the variation.
2. The variable features should be quantifiable so as to allow comparisons between the behavior of individual learners at different points of time and of individuals and groups at the same point of time.
3. The linguistic environment of the variable feature should also be quantifiable to facilitate the examination of its influence.

4. The data should be such that it shows maximal variation.
5. The data should be valid, i.e., it should tell us something of the linguistic competence of the learner.

Hyltenstam's data illustrate a number of important points about research design and analysis. Although, in general, the research questions dictate the research design, there has been a long dispute in SLA research over the issue of spontaneous speech versus elicited speech. Many have argued that what is needed is spontaneous speech (cf. Selinker 1972; Corder 1973), since it is from spontaneous speech that we are able to determine the vernacular (see above). However, quantity of data is also at issue. Particularly with regard to syntax, spontaneous speech often will not produce sufficient data for analysis, especially for study of a specific grammatical structure . Either the data will be insufficient in quantity (see Hyltenstam's points 1 and 2) or the linguistic environment will not be appropriate to detect variability (Hyltenstam's points 3 and 4 above). Yet another difficulty with spontaneous speech, when considering the variation that Hyltenstam presents, is that we do not always know how to interpret the absence of a form. If learners do not produce form X, does it mean that they don't know form X or does it mean that there was no occasion for X to appear? By specifically probing intuitions, one can determine what a learner does know as well as what he or she does not know. This determination is crucial to an understanding of a learner's knowledge of the second or foreign language.

Research such as Hyltenstam's helps determine the extent of variation. Crookes (1989) and Ellis (1987), however, argue that there is another dimension to be considered with regard to variation: the role of planning in L2 production.

Planning can be conceptualized in the following way:
Sentence production includes the formulation of an idea that initiates an act of speaking and the choice of an appropriate linguistic framework into which to cast it. These, what we might term the "planning" aspects of production, include such things as finding appropriate lexical items to use and arranging them in a suitable semantic and syntactic framework (Hayes-Roth and Hayes-Roth 1979: 170, cited in Crookes 1989).

In studies varying the amount of planning time allowed to subjects, Ellis (1987) and Crookes (1989) found somewhat different results. Ellis, in a study of 17 subjects, examined past tense forms (regular, irregular, and copula) in three conditions: (1) written narrative, (2) oral narrative based on written narrative (planned speech), and (3) oral narrative (unplanned speech). In general, he found that learners supplied the past tense morpheme -ed to a greater extent in those instances in which planning was allowed.

In work by Crookes (1989), each of 40 L2 (Japanese L1) speakers performed two tasks, a Lego-building task and a map task in which learners had to describe how a set of buildings was arranged on a map of a town. Two versions of each task were created with 20 subjects performing each. The two groups of subjects differed in that one was allowed planning time and the other was not. Planning was operationalized as a yes/no phenomenon with the planning group being allowed 10 minutes to plan their words, phrases, and ideas. Members of the nonplanning group began the task as soon as they had understood the instructions. While Crookes's findings on a wide range of language forms (e.g., type/token relations, morphemes, words per utterance, adjective sequences) are not strong in that significance is reached in only some cases, they do provide some initial indication that planning is an important variable in understanding accuracy and complexity issues in speech production. Planning allows L2 learners to produce more "developed speech" (in terms of both overall sophistication and development along an acquisitional sequence).

That learners vary in their production of target-language forms is not in controversy. What is controversial, however, is the appropriate way of representing linguistic knowledge. Researchers whose major interest is in Chomskyan linguistics (see arguments in Gregg 1990) consider the domain of SLA research to be the determination of linguistic competence. Competence, being a representation of abstractions, is not variable. Variability in this view is part of performance, i.e., part of putting language knowledge to use at a given point in time. On the other hand, SLA researchers such as Ellis and Tarone consider L2 knowledge itself as variable. That is, variability is not a matter of performance; it is part of what learners know about their L2. Eckman (in press) argues that the resolution of this issue does not lie in theoretical argumentation over what is and what is not in the domain of a theory of SLA. Rather, it is empirical argumentation that is needed. Those who argue that the appropriate domain for the study of SLA is linguistic competence would want to see a theory that could account for the well-established phenomenon of variation. Those who argue that variation data are crucial to a theory of SLA would want to show that data that are crucial to an understanding of L2 development cannot be incorporated into a competence model of SLA. While this perspective is a valid one, it is also recognized that the field of SLA is not sufficiently developed to provide an all-encompassing theory in the latter instance, nor are variation data sufficiently well understood to allow for an empirical challenge to existing theories.

Input and Interaction

How Does Input Affect Acquisition?

Perhaps the area of research that has had the greatest impact on the development of models of SLA is the work done within the *input* and *interaction* tradition. As we discussed above, earlier conceptualizations of L2 learning were based on a behaviorist view in which the major driving force of language learning (at least for children) was the language to which learners were exposed (the input). Since learning a language involved imitation as its primary mechanism, the language that surrounded learners was of crucial importance. However, as behaviorist theories fell into disfavor in both linguistics and psychology, so did interest in the input.

Inquiry shifted to the internal mechanisms that a learner (child or adult) brings to the language-learning situation, with research focusing on innateness and the nature of the innate system. Learners were viewed as creating language systems; and, at least in the case of children, the input they received was of minor importance. If, as a theory based on Universal Grammar maintains, learners need to discover only which of a limited number of possibilities are represented in their language, then it is possible that only a few instances of exposure are sufficient to trigger the appropriate language forms. Researchers in this tradition minimized the significance of the input to learners.

A research tradition that emphasized the important role of input was greatly influenced by the work of Corder (1967), who distinguished between input and intake. Input refers to what is available to the learner, while intake refers to what is actually internalized (or, in Corder's terms, "taken in") by the learner.

Ferguson (1971), in a study that was designed to look at issues of linguistic simplicity, noted that when speaking to linguistically deficient individuals (young children, nonnative speakers of a language), native speakers made adjustments to their speech in pronunciation, grammar, and lexicon. He called speech directed toward learners *foreigner talk.*

Ferguson's original research was conducted by asking university students what they thought they would say to someone with a low level of language proficiency. Clearly, there is not always a one-to-one match between what one thinks one would say and what one actually does say. In the decade following Ferguson's original work, data were gathered from actual observations. For example, Gaies (1977) tape-recorded classroom sessions of teachers with groups of learners from different proficiency levels; Kleifgen (1985) tape-recorded instances of teacher talk in a kindergarten classroom; Abu-Nahleh et al. (1982) and Tweissi (1987) tape-recorded telephone conversations between randomly selected native speakers of English and Arabic (respectively) and nonnative speakers of those languages who pretended to be conducting a survey on food and nutrition for a university class. The results all point to the notion that native speakers use a linguistically simple version of their language when addressing nonnative speakers.

The literature on foreigner talk has been used for a number of purposes. What is important to note is that there are different kinds and degrees of modifications that can be made when addressing nonnative speakers. For example, using transcripts of the telephone conversations collected by Abu-Nahleh et al. (1982), Gass and Varonis (1985) examined changes in foreigner talk during the course of a conversation. The telephone interview questions on health and nutrition were scripted. Also scripted was a "pardon me?" after the first few questions. In nearly all instances, the native speaker appeared to interpret the "pardon me?" as an indication that the nonnative speaker had not understood due to a language deficit. As a result, there was a change in the way the native speaker addressed the nonnative speaker after the "pardon me?" as opposed to preceding it.

In many instances, when there is a lack of comprehension between speakers, they will stop the flow of conversation to question what is not understood. In discourse where there is not shared background, or in which there is some acknowledged "incompetence" (e.g., incomplete knowledge of the language being spoken, or lack of knowledge of the topic), the conversational flow is marred by numerous interruptions. In other words, the conversation partners will "negotiate the meaning" of an utterance, as in the following example from the food and nutrition survey discussed above:

> NNS: There has been a lot of talk lately about additives and pre-
> servatives in food. How—
> NS: —a a a lot, a lot of talk about what?
> NNS: uh. There has been a lot of talk lately about additives and
> preservatives in food.

NS: Now just a minute. I can hear you—everything except the
       important words. You say there's been a lot of talk lately
       about what [inaudible]
NNS: —additive, additive, and preservative, in food—
NS: Could you spell one of those words for me, please
NNS: A D D I T I V E
NS: Just a minute. This is strange to me
NNS: h h
NS: -uh-
NNS: 'n other word is P R E S E R V A
NS: —oh, preserves
NNS: preservative and additive
NS: -preservatives, yes, okay. And what was that—-what was
       that first word I didn't understand?
NNS: OKAY in—
NS: —additives?
NNS: OKAY.
NS: —additives and preservatives
NNS: yes
NS: ooh right. . .

(Gass and Varonis 1985: 41)

When the flow of conversation is interrupted, participants often compensate by questioning particular utterances (*you say there's been a lot of talk about what?*) and/ or requesting conversational help (*could you spell one of those words for me?*). In other words, they "negotiate" what was not understood. Negotiation allows participants to respond appropriately to one another's utterance and to regain their places in a conversation after one or both have "slipped." In conversations involving nonnative speakers of a language, negotiations of meaning are frequent, at times occupying a major portion of the conversation.

Does Interaction Itself Aid Acquisition?

As we have seen, not only the form of the speech produced by native speakers is modified, but also the structure of the conversation itself. Thus, research in oral language production began to focus attention on discourse phenomena rather than on sentence-level and grammatical phenomena. Long (1980) was the first to point out that conversations involving nonnative speakers exhibited forms that were not generally present when only native speakers were involved. For example, confirmation checks (*Is this what you mean?*), comprehension checks (*Do you understand? Do you follow me?*), and clarification requests (*what, huh?*) are peppered throughout conversations in which there is a nonproficient nonnative speaker participant. While research considering conversational interactions has often used slightly different methodologies for elicitation (e.g., picture-description tasks, object-placement tasks, map-description tasks, describe-and-draw tasks, come-to-a-solution tasks, free-conversation tasks), the findings are consistent enough across studies and with learners of different proficiency levels and language backgrounds to be able to make general statements (cf. Larsen-Freeman and

Long 1991 and Gass and Selinker, in press, about what takes place in nonnative discourse).

The effect of NS and NNS modifications (whether intentional or not) is to help the nonnative speaker understand. This reduces the burden for the nonnative speaker, since he or she is assisted by others in understanding and in producing language appropriate to the situation. It can also be argued, however (as does Aston 1986), that outward signs of negotiation and resolution of that negotiation are only strategies to show solidarity, rather than true indications of meaning negotiation. Hawkins (1985) has shown that this is the case, at least in some instances. In her study, learners and native speakers described objects to a partner so that the partner could guess what the object was. After the description session, she gathered retrospective comments from the participants. In the retrospective session, it became clear that partners often verbally indicated understanding even when they had not understood. They explained this behavior by saying that they didn't think that their partner would be able to understand.

Output: Does Actual Production Contribute to Acquisition?

Up to this point we have discussed the concept of input and interactional modifications. There is another area of research that needs to be considered—*comprehensible output*.

> Being "pushed" in output. . . is a concept parallel to that of the i + 1 of comprehensible input. Indeed, one might call this the "comprehensible output" hypothesis. (Swain 1985: 249)

An early view of the function of output was to generate more input for the learner, but it appears that there is a more central role for output in acquisition. It allows learners to use what they know in a productive way. As with other kinds of learning, one must put one's knowledge to use. Comprehensible output refers to a learner's need to be "pushed toward the delivery of a message that is not only conveyed, but that is conveyed precisely, coherently, and appropriately" (Swain 1985: 249). Output provides learners with a forum for testing hypotheses about the target language and for receiving crucial feedback for the verification of those hypotheses. Input is not sufficient, since when one hears language, one can often interpret its meaning without the use of syntax. For example, if one hears only the words *dog, bit, girl,* regardless of the order in which those words occur, it is likely that the meaning *"The dog bit the girl"* is the one that will be assumed. Little linguistic knowledge, other than knowing the meanings of the words, is needed as long as one knows something about real-world events. This is not the case with production, since one is forced to put the words into some syntactic structure. Production "may force the learner to move from semantic processing to syntactic processing" (Swain 1985: 249). In fact, data from Swain (1985) on children learning French in an immersion context suggest that what is lacking in their development as nativelike speakers of French is the opportunity to use language as opposed to merely comprehending it. She compared results on a number of grammatical, discourse, and sociolinguistic measures of sixth-grade children in a French immersion setting and sixth-grade native French-speaking children. It was the lack of proficiency on the part of the immersion children coupled with their apparent lack of productive use of French that led her to suggest the crucial role for output in the development of an L2.

What Is the Function of Input and Negotiation?

As a first step to learning, a learner must be aware of a need to learn. Negotiation of the sort that takes place in conversation can focus a learner's attention on just those aspects of his or her language that do not "match" with the language being learned.

When we look at the literature on child language acquisition, we find claims that negative evidence (information that a particular utterance is deviant vis-à-vis target language norms) is neither frequent nor necessary for acquisition (e.g., Pinker 1984; Wexler and Cullicover 1980). Since children do not receive much correction (a form of negative evidence), it cannot be a necessary condition for acquisition. In this view, how then does acquisition take place? A set of innate properties that limit the possibilities of grammar formation is posited. The claim is that if grammar formation is limited, the task of language learning is therefore reduced.

What, then, about L2 learning? With regard to the question of negative evidence, or correction, it is undoubtedly true that adults (at least those in formal learning situations) receive more correction than children, and it may also be true that adults need this negative evidence (i.e., that it is a necessary condition) in order to learn an L2 (Gass 1988; Schachter 1988; Birdsong 1989; Bley-Vroman 1989). While this research has been based primarily on theoretical arguments, there is some empirical evidence that negative evidence is, in some instances, necessary for SLA.

White (1991a and b) considered the development of adverb placement by French children learning English. She was interested in the question of how learners learn not to do something that is present in the native language. In particular, French learners of English have to learn that English allows Subject-Adverb-Verb (SAV) order (He always runs) and that it does not allow Subject-Verb-Adverb-Object (SVAO) order (*He drinks always coffee). White's study consisted of five classes of English L2 learners (two at grade five and three at grade six) and one control group of monolingual native speakers of English. One of the grade-five groups and two of the grade-six groups were given explicit instruction on adverb placement including exercises and correction; the other L2 groups were given instruction on questions using the same type of exercises. The classroom treatment lasted two weeks. All the L2 learners were given pretests, posttests immediately following the treatment sessions, a second posttest five weeks later, and a follow-up test a year later. The tests consisted of grammaticality-judgment tasks (with correction), preference tasks, and a sentence-manipulation task. By comparing the groups' performances, White was able to show that negative evidence did indeed promote the learning of adverb placement, but that the effects of the treatment were not as long-lived as anticipated.

While White's study is important in showing that negative evidence may be necessary to trigger a change in a learner's grammar, it does not show that positive evidence alone (i.e., input alone) is insufficient. (In fact, the question-group of White's study received little information about adverbs from the naturalistic classroom data to which they were exposed). Trahey and White (1993) did a follow-up study to determine the effect of positive evidence. Their study consisted of two grade-five classes of French students learning English. Both classes were given an input flood of English adverbs (positive evidence only) over a two-week period. The same timetable as that used in the White study was used with the exception of three-week rather than five-week follow-up testing and no testing one year later. Trahey and White found that input was sufficient for learners to notice that SAV order is possible in English, but that it was not sufficient to detect the ungrammaticality of SVAO sentences. Thus, these two experiments combined show that positive evidence make learners aware of information in the L2 that differs from their L1, but that negative evidence is necessary to reveal what is not possible in the L2 when it is possible in the L1.[5]

It is necessary to examine the function that negative evidence, or error correction, might have. It can be argued that learners who are corrected learn from this feedback that certain utterances are deviant. In an ideal situation, the learner's grammar is then modified. There are obvious limitations to this view. First, corrections cannot occur with all incorrect forms. Secondly, many so-called errors are errors of interpretation for which there may be no evidence that an error has even occurred. In other words, if a learner interprets an utterance with the incorrect syntactic configuration, there is no way of knowing that misinterpretation has occurred and therefore no way of "correcting" the misinterpretation. As an example, consider reflexivization. If a learner of English interprets the sentence "John is afraid that Bill will cut himself" as if the "himself" referred to John (as is possible in some languages), there is no immediate way of disconfirming that hypothesis.

A third and perhaps more important limitation is that error acknowledgment, as in the case of expressions of nonunderstanding (e.g., *huh?*), does not provide information that is sufficiently specific as to inform learners where exactly an error has been made. Is the failure in communication the result of incorrect syntax, phonology, morphology, or vocabulary? Neither does error acknowledgment indicate what would have to be done in order to "correct" the error.

Another account of how L2 grammars develop takes the linguistic input coupled with conversational interaction as the driving force of language development. Wagner-Gough and Hatch (1975) argue that with regard to SLA, conversational interaction forms the *basis* for the development of syntax rather than being only a forum for practice of grammatical structures. Syntax, they claim, develops out of conversation rather than the reverse. The example below illustrates the way learning can take place within a conversational setting, as the learner in this case uses the conversation to further her syntactic development. The example is an excerpt from a conversation in which a teacher, a native speaker of English, is conversing with a child whose native language is Punjabi.

> NS: I want you to tell me what you can see in the picture or what's wrong with the picture.
> NNS: A /paik/ (= bike)
> NS: A cycle, yes. But what's wrong.
> NNS: /ret/ (= red)
> NS: It's red yes. What's wrong with it?
> NNS: Black
> NS: Black. Good. Black what?
> NNS: Black /taes/ (= tires)

(Ellis 1985: 79)

Prior to this point in time there were no examples of two-constituent utterances in this child's L2 discourse. As can be seen, the conversation itself provides the framework, or as Ellis states, "the break through points," for a two-constituent utterance to develop. The teacher broke the task into parts and helped with the crucial vocabulary that appears to have enabled the child to juxtapose *black* and *tires,* as can be seen in her final utterance. From this time on there were frequent examples of two-constituent utterances in this child's speech.

According to Ellis (1984: 95) "interaction contributes to development because it is the means by which the learner is able to crack the code. This takes place when the learner can infer what is said even though the message contains linguistic items that are not yet part of his competence and when the learner can use the discourse to help him modify or supplement the linguistic knowledge already used in production."

But what evidence is there that interaction indeed drives language development? Consider the conversation below involving two adult learners of English. These data were collected as one person was describing a picture while her partner was drawing it.

Hiroko:	A man is uh drinking c-coffee or tea uh with the saucer of the uh uh coffee set is uh in his uh knee
Izumi:	in him knee
Hiroko:	uh on his knee
Izumi:	yeah
Hiroko:	on his knee
Izumi:	so sorry. On his knee

(Gass and Varonis 1989: 81)

In this example Hiroko said "in his knee" and Izumi responded with an incorrect form, "in him knee." Hiroko maintains the original pronominal case form, although she changed the preposition from the original "in" to the correct "on." Both participants, as a result of the negotiation, ended up using the same correct form. It is through such negotiation that learners modify their speech to incorporate correct target-language forms.

More direct evidence of the importance of negotiated interaction comes from three recent studies. In one study (Pica, Young, and Doughty 1987), the researchers showed that there was better comprehension by a group of L2 learners who were allowed to interact while doing an object-placement task (based on input from a native speaker) than by those who were not allowed to interact, but who were provided with modified input from a native speaker. The second study (Gass and Varonis, in press) reports similar results, although in that study there was evidence that the interaction affected not only immediate comprehension but also a follow-up activity that required productive language use. In that study the learners were given modified input and either were allowed to negotiate or were not allowed to negotiate. In the first part of the task native speakers told nonnative speakers where to place objects on a board. There were four conditions: (1) modified input, (2) nonmodified input, (3) negotiated interaction, and (4) nonnegotiated interaction. In the second part of the task, nonnative speakers described to native speakers where to place objects on a different board. In this part, there were two conditions: (1) negotiated interaction and (2) nonnegotiated interaction. The best performance (measured in terms of ability to give accurate instructions on the second part of the task) was obtained in that treatment condition in which learners were allowed to negotiate on the first part of the task. This suggests that interaction is indeed beneficial, and not just for the immediate present. This, of course, says little, if anything, about retention over the long run.

The third study (Loschky 1989) was similar in that the experimental conditions included modified input and negotiated interaction. Findings differed in that negotiated interaction affected only immediate comprehension. There was no positive effect found for syntactic development or vocabulary retention.

Even though the tasks used for data collection were not identical, these three studies produced comparable results. We can conclude that negotiated interaction has a positive, although at this point unspecified, effect. The effect may be different at different levels of proficiency (Pica 1989) or for child versus adult learners (cf. Scarcella and Higa 1981). Future research might examine this possibility by considering the long-term effects of negotiated interaction and by comparing those effects across proficiency levels and perhaps across native language groups.

A more specific study on the effect of corrective feedback on grammatical reorganization was carried out by Carroll, Roberge, and Swain (1992). Seventy-nine native speakers of English learning French as an L2 were first trained on two word-formation rules. Following the training session, the testing session began. All subjects were tested individually. The subjects were divided into experimental and control groups. In the first part of the test, subjects were asked to form nouns from verbs presented in sentences on a card. The experimental group received corrective feedback; the control group did not. In the second part, neither group received feedback. This procedure was repeated three times with different verb types. There were also two recall tests for both groups, one immediately after the session and another one week later. Comparisons were made between the group with corrective feedback and the group with no corrective feedback. As the following example shows, the linguistic focus of this study was on word formation.

> In French, one can say *Marie a bien attelé les chevaux* ("Marie harnessed the horses well"). Once again, *Marie a bien attelé les chevaux.* One can also say *Marie a fait un bon attelage des chevaux.* ("Marie did a good harnessing of the horses"). Once again, *Marie a fait un bon attelage des chevaux.* The word *attelé* resembles the word *attelage,* and they have a similar meaning. (p. 180)

The results showed that corrective feedback was important in the learning of individual items, but that it had little effect on a learner's ability to generalize this information to new items.

A set of studies by Tomasello and Herron (Tomasello and Herron 1988, 1989; Herron and Tomasello 1988, 1992; and Herron 1991), known as the Garden Path Studies, also provide some evidence on the role of corrective feedback in the context of FL learning. While space limitations preclude an exhaustive accounting of their findings, in general, it appears that feedback produces more accurate target-language forms than does pure modeling (i.e., input) and that correction is more beneficial when learners are led down the "garden path" and are induced to make errors (with follow-up feedback) than when they are instructed on correct forms before making errors.[6]

What, then, is the role of negotiated interaction in the development of L2 knowledge? We support the common belief that negotiation is what leads learners to notice that there is a mismatch between what they are producing and what native speakers of the target language produce. In other words, negotiation leads learners to a type of metalinguistic awareness.

Much classroom activity in earlier language-teaching methodologies engaged learners in a type of "consciousness raising" (e.g., focused grammar instruction). These methodologies provided direct means of making learners aware of the language at the expense of spending classroom time in "practice" activities. However, there are other ways in which increased metalinguistic awareness can take place. As shown in the earlier discussion of negotiation, learners can be made aware of errors in their speech (whether in grammar, pronunciation, content, or discourse) and of the incongruity between their own and native speech through the questioning and clarification that is part of negotiation.

In order for negotiation to begin, someone must become aware of a problem and there must be an attempt to resolve it. Awareness of a problem may come through an inquiry of nonunderstanding or through an explicit explanation. Once learners recognize the problem, they must modify their output. Hence, the more learners are made aware of unacceptable speech, the greater the opportunity for them to make appropriate modifications.

In an L2 context, learners encounter native speakers outside the classroom and thus may have more opportunity for negotiation and subsequent modification of their deviant speech than do FL learners, who interact mainly, if not exclusively, with their teacher and other learners. Data such as the "on the knee" example discussed earlier (Gass and Varonis 1989) are thus particularly important because they show how learners can benefit from negotiation with each other. If replicated in FL contexts, such studies would suggest further links between L2 and FL learning that could help develop a more unified theory of SLA.

Before leaving this topic, it should be pointed out that as yet the evidence is limited about the long-range effects of modifications resulting from negotiation. It can be hypothesized, however, that because negotiation leads to heightened awareness, it ultimately leads to increased knowledge of the L2.

Writing Research

In focusing on writing, we consider many of the research issues already discussed with regard to speaking, while also considering new matters unique to research on writing.

Teachers and researchers often differentiate between writing as a support skill and writing as a communicative skill (Magnan 1985; Omaggio 1986; Omaggio Hadley 1993). Writing as a support skill usually involves word-level or sentence-level practice of target-language forms. Writing as a communicative skill involves composition of discourse-level texts that share information with a reader. While both types of writing contribute to learning an L2, research on learner writing is typically concerned with students' attempts to produce discourse-level language, that is, chunks of language with a coherent structure and unified message. It is in this communicative sense that we will discuss writing research. We will look at studies that examine the structure, cohesion, and accuracy of learner writing in a global sense. Due to space constraints, we will not discuss studies that focus on the acquisition of specific grammatical forms.

The past decade has witnessed an increase in research on communicative writing in SLA to produce a field that is "not especially cohesive" (Schecter and Harklau 1992: iii). For discussion purposes, we divide this research into two general areas: research on how learners compose and research on how instructor intervention affects the quality of learner composition. While both L2 and FL researchers have worked in both areas, L2 research offers more studies of the composing process and FL research is particularly concerned with the effects of instructor feedback. We will first consider studies about the composing process and then examine studies on instructional intervention.

Most studies of the L2 writing process are qualitative in nature. L2 researchers, often adopting research designs used in L1 composition research (Krapels 1990), have primarily used case studies built on direct observations, think-aloud protocols, interviews, or questionnaires and retrospective surveys. Emig's (1971) case study of the L1 writing of eight high school seniors is generally considered the first major study to focus on the writing process (Krapels 1990: 38). To gain insights on what students do as they compose, Emig had her subjects compose aloud on audiotapes as they wrote. She also observed her subjects writing and took notes, interviewed each subject to elicit a "writing autobiography," and collected her subjects' notes and outlines as well as their final pieces of writing. As a survey by Krapels shows, these techniques first developed for L1 have subsequently been widely used in L2 research, with similar findings.

Qualitative in nature, case studies look first at what data reveal descriptively and then move toward theoretical claims. In this sense, they fit McLaughlin's (1987: 158) definition of "research-then-theory" strategies, contributing more to identifying variables and developing theories than to testing theories.

Some case studies add a quantitative dimension, often by using a coding system patterned after Perl's (1978) schema, developed and first used for L1 writing.[7] Perl's system codes writing behaviors according to three major categories: (1) what students say as they write, (2) the type of writing and rewriting activities students perform as they compose, and (3) how students read and reread their compositions during the writing process. Within these major categories, Perl identifies sixteen behaviors, some broken down into more precise behaviors, and charts each one on a time-line to show when each behavior occurred during the writing process. The finished code is a concise representation of the frequency, relative importance, and place of behaviors exhibited by a particular writer while doing a writing task.

Using a coding system such as Perl's provides a visual description of what happens during the writing process. It also allows the researcher to count and compare data in a way not possible with a narrative description. As many of the studies discussed here illustrate, SLA research is becoming more multidimensional in nature, often using both qualitative and quantitative approaches to allow researchers to look at data in different ways. In fact, with multimethod inquiry it becomes difficult to speak of "process studies" and "product studies," for some studies look at both, or to classify studies as solely theory building or theory testing in nature. For indeed, theory building and theory testing exist in a cyclic relationship: As variables are identified, it becomes possible to develop and test theories; and when theories are tested, new variables are often identified.

Research on the L2 Composing Process

Perhaps the most basic question about the process of L1 and L2 writing concerns its nature: Is writing essentially linear or recursive? According to the linear model, writing relies on a hierarchy of separate skills. The model assumes that good writers plan their compositions first and then move through the discrete stages of prewriting, writing, rewriting, and editing (Rohman and Wlecke n.d.; Britton et al. 1975). Flower and Hayes (1981) challenged this model with their work using protocol analysis. They believe that writing is an act of discovery and that it is the act of writing itself that drives the highly recursive composition processes. This is similar to what we discussed previously in the section on speaking: Learner production can itself drive acquisition.

As Sommers (1980: 378) points out, the difference between the linear and cognitive/recursive models relates to the basic difference between speech and writing. The linear model is based on traditional rhetorical models of oratory and on the irreversibility of speech. Revision in the linear model, then, is an afterthought, a repetition or second act of writing. In contrast, the recursive model views revision as the motivating force of writing, a creative process through which writers discover the shape and message of their written texts.

Sommers worked with experienced and student native English writers to investigate whether good writing is essentially linear or recursive. Each of her subjects wrote three essays (expressive, explanatory, and persuasive) with three drafts each and suggested revisions for a composition written by an anonymous author. Sommers interviewed the writers after each draft and counted and analyzed the types of changes made from draft to draft. Her work revealed basic differences between the two groups: Students viewed revision as an option in a linear process; experienced writers saw revision as a mandatory recursive process with a different agenda for each cycle. Sommers's findings can be compared with findings of L2 research to help answer the question: Do good L2 writers, like good L1 writers, favor recursive processes over linear ones?

To answer this question, it is, of course, necessary to define the notion of a "good" writer. L2 researchers tend to speak of writers as "skilled" and "unskilled." The term *skilled writer* is perhaps best known with regard to a distinction for native writers: basic (remedial) writer, traditional/freshman writer, and skilled writer. Generally following this distinction, L2 research often uses the term *unskilled writers* to refer to those below the traditional freshman level. Sometimes, however, the terms *skilled* and *unskilled* relate to the levels of courses in which students are enrolled or to how well students perform on researcher-designed measures of writing proficiency. Thus the terms *skilled* and *unskilled* often do not define proficiency levels absolutely. Rather, their use allows readers to contrast stronger and weaker groups in relative terms.

It is often difficult to define skill even relatively in a way that will clearly differentiate groups of writers. Raimes (1985) compared different types of data for the same student to find that, indeed, assessing level of writing proficiency is not straightforward. In her study, students' language proficiency scores did not match the level of courses in which they were placed, the holistic assessment of their writing ability, or their length of exposure to English. The fact that the operational definitions of skilled and unskilled writers differ across studies makes it difficult to compare findings precisely.

The question of how to compare what good writers do with what weak writers do is thus a question of how to compare two continua that may be distinct or may be interrelated: level of writing proficiency, from weak to strong; and preferred approach to writing, from linear to recursive. Researchers can then ask "What are the trends?" not "What is the difference?"

In her widely quoted study, Zamel (1983) investigated trends in L2 writing to see how they would correspond to observed trends in L1 writing. Using Flower and Hayes's (1981) framework and a case-study approach, she analyzed the writing of six students in an L2 composition course considered to be at about the same level as a first-year composition course for native English speakers. Related perhaps to the fact that these L2 writers were approaching a writing level equivalent to that of some native writers, Zamel's findings for L2 writers were similar to Sommers's (1980) findings for L1 writers: Students' writing behaviors did not break down neatly into the linear categories of prewriting, writing, and revising, regardless of level of writing ability.

Because her focus was L2 writing, Zamel was particularly interested in how L2 writers dealt with language difficulties during the composing process. Whereas her four strongest writers did not allow their language difficulties to distract them from expressing and revising their message, her weakest writer was driven by a constant concern for language that appeared to block global attempts at revision and thus interfere with the recursive process.

From a methodological point of view, Zamel's study exemplifies early qualitative research in the L2 composing process. She determined quality of the written product through holistic assessment done by L2 instructors, a procedure whose subjectivity is questioned by Raimes (1985: 232). To examine the writing process, she interviewed and observed students while they composed, recording her impressions and noting impromptu comments that students made during and after writing. Zamel's methods differed in one important respect from those used in most composing studies: She did not use the popular think-aloud procedure, fearing, as did Perl (1980) and Faigley and Witte (1981), that having students verbalize their thoughts while writing would alter the composing process. Like most L2 qualitative writing-process studies of the 1980s, Zamel's report is a rather free-flowing collection of observations, quotes, and comments. Given the obvious limitations of her sample of only six students, her findings serve primarily to describe potential differences among L2 writers. Writers toward the skilled end of the continuum "consider how to make meaning first, then how to order it, and finally how it can best be expressed," whereas writers toward the unskilled end of the continuum seem "to view writing as a static transcription of 'a series of parts—words, sentences, paragraphs,' rather than the creation of a 'whole discourse' " (p. 180, including phrases in single quotes from Sommers 1982: 151).

Raimes (1985) builds on Zamel's work to suggest that skilled and unskilled L2 writers may not always approach writing in fundamentally different ways. She worked with 8 L2 students in a course that was a prerequisite to freshman composition, and, following the tradition of categorizing L1 writers, considered all her subjects to be unskilled writers. From these students, she gathered four types of data: (1) their scores on the grammar, vocabulary, and reading sections of the multiple-choice 1962 Michigan

Test of English Language Proficiency; (2) holistic evaluation of their essays; (3) their responses to a background questionnaire about their experience with and attitude toward English and writing; and (4) their think-aloud protocols, recorded in a language laboratory and analyzed using a slight modification of Perl's 1981 coding scheme.

Unlike Perl and Zamel, Raimes did not arrive at a discouraging profile of the unskilled writer. Her unskilled writers produced a lot of text, worked through their essays in a recursive rather than linear manner, and were generally able to separate focus on meaning from focus on form. Her observations suggest that the continua of level of writing proficiency and preferred approach to writing may indeed overlap and intertwine.

Raimes's research also demonstrated the value of the think-aloud procedure, especially when used with a coding system. To arrive at the total time spent prewriting and writing, she coded the occurrences of rereading the topic, planning, repeating words or phrases, reading sentences or parts of sentences, reading the whole draft, and rehearsing. Because of the time required to transcribe think-aloud protocols and to identify and count instances of behaviors, researchers have often restricted their case studies to a small number of learners. Krapels (1990) estimates that in all the L2 case studies she reviewed, there was a total of only about 100 subjects. She points out further that most of these subjects were not randomly selected and they did not equally represent students of both sexes and of different national backgrounds, ages, and proficiency levels. Compared with the world's general population, a disproportionate number of these subjects were female, native speakers of Spanish or Chinese, and advanced L2 learners of English in college (pp. 48–50).

One way to apply the case-study approach to more subjects and types of behavior is to use computers to track how students compose at the keyboard. Poulsen's (1991) research is a step in this direction, although he uses the computer more as a pedagogical implement and counting tool than as a research instrument. Poulsen gathered data over three years for a qualitative study of how Danish students use word processors to write compositions in an intermediate course of English as an FL. He gathered data in a pyramid-structure design, collecting at the top the most specific data from the fewest subjects, and at the base the most general data from the greatest number of subjects. Poulsen advocates this pyramid design as a way to give research "a degree of breadth as well as depth in the sense that the various layers can supplement and elucidate one another" (p. 78). His pyramid has four layers: from top to bottom, the types of errors identified by students using a spell-checker and the degree of success students had in correcting these errors, video-recorded observations of students as they compose, scores of student performance on the National Examination in Written English, and classroom observation of students planning and writing successive drafts of essays.

Preliminary findings suggest that students plan little, focus on the first draft, revise mostly at the sentence level, and are only partially successful with the spell-checker. No preliminary results on the National Examination are reported. In terms of methodology, the Poulsen study suggests an effective and efficient means of gathering data for either qualitative or quantitative analysis. As Garrett (1992) and others have pointed out, computer-tracking possibilities could greatly facilitate data collection and analysis by quantifying observations that researchers have generally only described. Programs are needed to manage the large sets of data that would come from large numbers of subjects. If researchers could randomly select these subjects and manipulate variables, it would open the door for statistical analysis from which generalizations could be made.

Research on Factors Associated with How Well L2 Learners Write

Beyond writing processes, what other factors differentiate strong and weak writers? To answer this question, research on L2 composing explores many possible relationships: proficiency in L2 writing with general L2 proficiency; L2 writing ability with L2 reading ability; L2 speaking ability with L2 writing ability; writing ability in L1 with writing ability in L2, giving some attention to cultural variables; types of instructional intervention with quality of student composition; and learner reactions to the type of instructional feedback they receive. We will consider only the last three relationships. According to our analysis of the Schecter and Harklau bibliography (1992) and our extensive bibliographic search for this chapter, these areas include the largest number of recent studies found in L2 and FL literatures on composition research.

Does Writing Ability in L2 Relate to Writing Ability in L1?

If writing is a cognitive process that is not language-dependent, good writers in L1 might be expected to write well in L2. Writers in L1 and L2 might also be expected to follow similar developmental patterns. In a descriptive study, Kern and Schultz (1992) used holistic scoring and T-unit analysis to study the writing development of 73 second-year FL students of French over an academic year. They divided the students into three groups according to how well they wrote an initial essay in French as compared with their classmates: Those who produced the weakest essays were grouped as "low ability"; those who produced average essays were grouped as "mid ability"; and those who produced the best essays were grouped as "high ability." Over the year of instruction, they found that the low and mid ability writers progressed steadily in a similar pattern, while the high ability writers did well initially, produced poorer writing subsequently, and then improved slightly beyond their beginning level at the end of the year. Yet even with this dip in performance, the high ability writers consistently wrote better essays than did students in either the low or mid ability groups. Over the semester then all three groups improved in their ability to write French and the distinctions among the three groups did not change. The authors conclude that the differences in performance by ability group "suggest that writing skill in a foreign language may in fact be more closely tied to one's ability to write in the native language than to general level of linguistic competence in foreign language" (p. 6). They interpret their conclusions as being in support of Cummins's (1981, 1987) Underlying Proficiency Hypothesis, which posits a high degree of skill interdependence between L1 and L2 for the thinking skills used in understanding and producing extended discourse.

All groups in the Kern and Schulz study progressed in their L2 writing from using coordination to using subordination and finally to clause reduction. Because they did not have a control group for the type of teaching intervention, Kern and Schultz could not determine specifically what factors influenced their students' writing development. Yet they note that their results supported Monroe's (1975) hypothesis that L2 French students go through a developmental sequence similar to that of students learning to write in English as their native language. Stalker and Stalker (1988) provide supporting evidence, showing that native English-speaking students at a large Midwestern university and their international classmates, who are novice, nonproficient writers of English, make the same kinds of sentence-level errors in morphology, syntax, lexicon, spelling, and punctuation on their English compositions.

Case studies in a bilingual setting have also served to investigate the developing theory that L1 writing processes influence L2 writing. For example, Fagan and Hayden (1988) studied native English-speaking fifth-graders in a French immersion school and Edelsky (1982) worked with first-, second-, and third-graders in a Spanish-English program to investigate the relationship between writing in L1 and writing in L2. Both studies looked at both the writing process and the written product.

Fagan and Hayden observed or talked with 10 fifth-grade students to investigate what they did as they wrote in English and in French and to compare the compositions they produced in the two languages. Although no statistical tests were done, the authors estimated that differences across languages occurred in the following features: the degree of pausing and rereading, the number and variety of content words used, the syntactic density or complexity, the number of cross-outs or rewrites, and the appropriateness of the mechanics. Similarities across languages were found in the following features: selection time for the topic, prior awareness of the text ending and amount of text to be written, use of title, choice of genre, awareness of audience, length of text, composing time, and reasons for pausing and rereading. Overall, the quality of the compositions was judged to be similar in the two languages, indicating that the students performed at about the same level in both languages.

Edelsky analyzed 477 examples of Spanish writing and 49 examples of English writing by first-, second-, and third-grade students in a Spanish-English bilingual program. She considered the following features: code switching; spelling invention; nonspelling conventions, such as segmentation and punctuation; structural features, such as beginnings, endings, and links between propositions; and content features, such as stylistic devices, characters, and settings. In addition, Edelsky solicited the impression of adult raters on the quality of the content. Unfortunately, neither Fagan and Hayden's nor Edelsky's report offers detailed behavioral data or evaluative information or provides statistical tests for comparison. Although both studies claim attempts at quantifying data, the reports are primarily descriptions of what might be considered raw information.

Given the leap from observations about limited data to conclusions without the benefit of statistically based comparison, these studies, and others that rely heavily on descriptive information in a nearly anecdotal fashion, may not individually be convincing. Nevertheless, it should be noted that they do reach similar conclusions: Much of the writing process appears to transfer across languages.

In a particularly well conceived study, Hansen-Strain (1989) extends the question of L1 influence on L2 to cultural traditions. Is there a cultural discourse that L2 learners bring to the new language from their L1? To answer this question, Hansen-Strain considered whether L2 learners from traditional oral cultures have more interpersonal involvement in their English writing and speaking than do students from more literate cultural traditions. She worked with 75 L2 English students from three national backgrounds: Samoan and Tongan (representing predominantly oral cultures) and Japanese, Chinese, and Korean (representing predominantly literate cultures). A one-way ANOVA by culture for the five groups indicated no significant difference in their English proficiency level.

Hansen-Strain had her learners retell stories orally and in writing and analyzed four measures of the speaker's or writer's involvement with the audience: reference to self, references to addressee, references to one's own mental processes, and monitoring of information flow. To control for the varying length of learner's stories, she used ratios of the occurrence of each involvement measure to the total words in the learner's text.

As hypothesized, Hansen-Strain found that the learners from traditional oral cultures showed significantly more involvement with the audience in all four measures for the oral mode and in first-person reference and reference to personal mental processes for the written mode. There were too few occurrences of second-person reference and monitoring of information flow to yield significant differences in these measures for the written mode.

As Hansen-Strain states, "these findings contribute to our understanding of task variability in interlanguage performance." It appears that "the particular configuration of the variability may be influenced by discourse patterns of the native language and culture" (p. 489). The influence that L1 exerts on L2 in both writing and speaking can thus be described, at least partially, in terms of cultural patterns of discourse. On the basis of her findings, Hansen-Strain proposes a model of discourse variability with two axes: a continuum based on Ellis's (1984) notion of planned versus unplanned, and a continuum ranging from personal involvement with audience to focus on message content.

This model offers yet another theoretical framework for studying L1 and L2 relationships and similarities and differences between the language that learners produce in speech and in writing.

How Does Instructional Intervention Relate to Quality of L2 Writing?

It is only natural that teachers assume, or at least hope, that their instruction helps students acquire the L2. In the case of writing, research on instructional intervention looks at the effects of both teaching techniques—usually activities such as brainstorming that can be associated with the writing process—and teacher feedback, including both positive comment and correction. The study of correction for composition parallels the study of negative evidence for speech. Similar questions can be asked for both skills. Do learners apply corrections only to specific items or instances, or can they generalize them to new situations? Do learners need to negotiate an understanding of correction? Do learners expect, desire, and benefit from both positive and negative appraisal of their attempts to communicate?

In the first area of teaching techniques, there are many personal accounts, such as those of Barnett (1989) and Hall (1993), that use findings from composition research to offer suggestions for L2 teaching. An example of how research applications can generate new classroom or "action" studies is offered by Liebman-Kleine (1987). She compares the effectiveness of prewriting techniques for L2 students of English from different cultural backgrounds (predominantly from the Middle East and Malaysia, with some students from Venezuela, Cuba, and Portugal). She examined her students' papers and notebooks, discussed with them their teaching preferences, and had each student take the Myers-Briggs psychological personality preference test. She noted that the Malaysians and Saudis in her class tended to prefer to map out ideas for their writing in "hierarchical trees" while the students from Venezuela, Portugal, and Cuba did not like and sometimes could not do "treeing." This latter group tended to prefer more open-ended prewriting activities such as brainstorming, rushwriting or freewriting, and listing. Based on her observations, she concluded that cultural background and personality underlie preferences for instructional techniques.[8]

Might not these preferences for teaching techniques relate to learners' perceptions of the nature of writing: a linear process of writing and its dependence on preplanning or a recursive process that finds meanings in the act of writing itself? In studying teaching techniques, then, we return to notions discussed earlier: the nature of the composition process and the influence of L1 writing and its cultural frame on L2 writing.

In comparison with intervention through teaching techniques, a substantial amount of research has been conducted on teacher feedback in both L2 and FL writing. This research stems primarily from teaching practice. Guberman (1988: 704) states that traditional correction is not based on any explicit or coherent theory of correction; it is simply common practice related to the need to justify a grade. It is also related to a traditional assumption that correction will help students write better. Findings challenge this assumption, and in so doing, offer insights toward developing theories about why certain types of negative evidence are more useful than others at different points in the acquisition process. Working toward a unified theory of SLA, then, it might be hypothesized that teacher feedback and student response to it affect FL learning in ways that are similar to how negative evidence and negotiation between native and nonnative speakers affect L2 learning.

The basic research questions have been the following: Does correction improve writing? If so, what type of correction helps learners most? According to Kepner (1991: 305–6), the issue of instructor feedback relates to the current theoretical debate between advocates of "traditional, deductive formal-grammar L2 learning" and advocates of "communicative, inductive, 'natural'/ whole-language L2 acquisition." Thus, how teachers choose to respond to student writing reflects their views on how language is learned, and data on the effects of instructor feedback contribute to developing theories of SLA.

Research on instructor feedback is more often quantitative in nature than is research on the composing process. There are generally control and experimental groups that use different types of correction. Statistical tests are used with caveats against generalizing results when subjects could not be selected randomly. Not all studies are exclusively quantitative, however. Since the manipulated variable is often the instance of error or the correction of it, the n (number of cases measured) is often large. Some studies blend quantitative and qualitative methods. To provide the qualitative dimension, interviews, protocols, and questionnaires are frequently used techniques.

The major research questions in L2 research on instructor feedback echo those asked for L1 (Radecki and Swales 1986). Do the markings instructors put on student papers lead students to revise successfully the content or macrostructure of their writing? What type of comments are more helpful: those referring to the meaning of the text or those focusing on grammatical or mechanical errors? And most recently, what are students' attitudes toward the instructor feedback they receive? In their review of English L2 research, Radecki and Swales note that research in L1 and L2 has often found similar answers to these questions. In many cases—but not all—research in both fields casts doubt on the value of extensive instructor feedback on all students attempts at writing.

Examining the conditions under which writing occurs, Chastain (1990) compared graded and ungraded writing in a Spanish FL classroom. With his small sample of 14 students in third- and fourth-year classes, he found no significant difference in ratios of syntactic and morphological errors to total words or in content and organization, although he did note that students writing for a grade tended to produce longer essays with longer and more complex sentences than students whose assignments were not going to be graded.[9]

Chastain's research also highlighted a question not yet widely researched: Does type of essay (such as narrative vs. descriptive vs. argumentative) influence discourse fluency or mechanical accuracy? Chastain used argumentative and comparison/contrast essays, which he believed placed equivalent demands on the writer. Most other studies reviewed in this chapter used narrative essays. As Chastain points out, however, it may be wrong to assume that different types of writing present students with tasks of similar difficulty. Indeed, Bridgemen and Carlson (1983) found that descriptive and persuasive modes were the most different from each other on a multidimensional scaling analysis of several essay topics. Carrell and Connor (1991: 323) provide some evidence that descriptive texts may be "easier" than persuasive texts, for in their research descriptive writing produced higher qualitative scores than did persuasive writing. This difference disappeared, however, when written genre was considered in combination with language proficiency. Furthermore, other aspects of Carrell and Connor's study showed descriptive texts to be "easier" primarily in reading and not in writing. Type of essay, precise topic, and the student's role in choosing it could, therefore, be potent variables for future investigation.

Focusing on the nature of instructor comments, Applebee (1981) found that 80 percent of L1 English teachers ranked mechanical errors as the most important criterion in their feedback. Zamel (1985) compared the feedback of L2 teachers with what she considered typical feedback of L1 writing teachers. She concluded that L2 teachers are very concerned with language-specific errors and problems, that their feedback is often confusing, arbitrary, and inaccessible, and that, like their L1 counterparts, they rarely seem to expect students to revise their writing beyond the surface level. Zamel's findings support those of Applebee: L2 teachers, like their L1 counterparts, focus more on sentence-level mechanics than on content issues.

It is thus not surprising that SLA research has recently given considerable attention to the effectiveness of correcting mechanical errors in composition. Discussing learner errors in Spanish as an FL, Hendrickson (1978) emphasized the need to control for error gravity, with a modified version of Burt and Kiparsky's (1972) local and global error taxonomy, and used a combination of direct and indirect techniques for error correction. From Hendrickson's work and that of other researchers after him there emerges a continuum of possibilities for correction, often used as the manipulated variable: no feedback (Graham 1983; Fathman and Whalley 1990); no correction, but comments and questions (Semke 1984; Kepner 1991); positive comments and suggestions for improving content (Fathman and Whalley 1990); positive comments and suggestions for improving content and grammar (Fathman and Whalley 1990); identification of form errors without help toward correction (Fathman and Whalley 1990); indirect error marking using a coding system for student self-correction (Lalande 1982; Semke 1984); direct correction of form errors and positive comments (Semke 1984); direct correction of form errors (Semke 1984; Lalande 1982; Kepner 1991).

Studies have contrasted these correction types in various combinations. While L1 research, according to Hillocks (1986) and Herrington (1989), shows feedback to have little effect, L2 studies are less conclusive (Fathman and Whalley 1990). Graham (1983) found that students who received feedback on every assignment did not make fewer errors than students who received feedback on every third assignment. Comparing correction of surface errors with comments on content, Kepner (1991) found no difference in accuracy between the two feedback modes and a greater number of higher-level propositions with comments on content. Similarly, Semke (1984) found that different forms of feedback did not yield significant differences in accuracy, while feedback with comments improved only fluency. Hendrickson (1978) found that direct correction of deviant forms had no statistically significant effect on students' writing proficiency. Fathman and Whalley (1990) found that student revisions benefited from both correction of grammar errors and feedback on content, yet students who received no feedback still made useful revisions. In fact, they generated more new language during the rewrite phase than students who received either form or content feedback. Lalande's (1982) research makes a clear statement about which type of form-based feedback is the most useful: error marking using a coding system for student self-correction. Recalling Corder's (1967) argument, Lalande's findings might suggest that involving students in the revision process is the key to making feedback more effective. Indeed, Vandergrift (1986: 660) suggests that the students in Semke's correction groups might not have improved their writing because they were not required to refer to their previous errors when doing subsequent assignments. But the students in one of Semke's feedback groups did use a correction code and rewrite their essays, and yet results showed this treatment to be the least effective in terms of both achievement and attitudes.

The difference in Semke's and Lalande's results might be related as much to research design as to instructional technique. As Semke points out, different treatment groups were required to write different numbers of essays. Furthermore, in Semke's study, students were graded differently in different treatment groups: The essays of students who received feedback on errors were graded on the basis of ratios of the number of mistakes made to the number of words written; students who did not receive any feedback on errors were graded solely on the amount of information they conveyed. Grading practices may thus have had a confounding effect on Semke's results, even though Chastain's (1990) study did not reveal significant differences in the number of errors that students made in graded and ungraded assignments.

It is not the purpose of this chapter to criticize individual studies in order to find weaknesses in their research design. For there are indeed many weaknesses. Given the fact that L2 inquiry, as we know it, is a young discipline and given the complexity of human research, especially within the constraints of the classroom setting, such weaknesses are perhaps inevitable. Still, if Hillocks (1986) is justified in not including over 80 percent of the writing studies he reviewed in his meta-analysis because of design flaws, the profession needs to view its research findings with a certain degree of caution and to work toward carefully controlled research in the future.

One route toward improving language acquisition research is to begin systematically to replicate studies in both the same and different contexts. Robb, Ross, and Shortreed (1986) attempted to verify, in the context of teaching English in Japan, the findings of Lalande, Hendrickson, and Semke, who worked with different FLs taught in the United States. Working with 134 elementary-level writers enrolled in college English FL composition courses, Robb, Ross, and Shortreed developed an experimental design using four treatment groups: (1) instructor corrects all errors of word choice, syntax, and level of style; (2) instructor codes errors for student correction; (3) instructor identifies errors but offers no indication for correction; (4) instructor indicates in the margin the number of errors in each line but not precisely where errors occur or how to correct them. In the four treatment groups students did identical classroom activities and wrote identical composition assignments, which they were all required to revise. Therefore the amount and the type of writing practice were held constant; the manipulated variable was the type of instructor feedback. Robb, Ross, and Shortreed found no improvement in any group that could clearly be attributed to type of feedback. This finding led them to conclude that improvement in writing related mainly to the practice of writing itself (p. 89).

Since the students in all four treatment groups improved, without a significant difference being found among them, Robb, Ross, and Shortreed suggested that if any of the correction techniques had negative effects, they seemed to be offset by the positive effect of weekly writing practice. This observation runs counter to the claim that negative feedback may make L2 writers concerned with accuracy to the detriment of fluency or may decrease their motivation to write (Sommers 1982). As Radecki and Swales (1986: 71) point out, Robb, Ross, and Shortreed's findings corroborate, for an EFL context, a popular "view of many L1 composition theorists such as Knoblauch and Brannon (1984), who maintain [that] 'composing is a competence which develops through use, not a system of skills to be serially introduced . . . and then practiced' (p. 104)." Such corroboration of findings is needed before beliefs and conclusions from L1 can be applied to an L2 context. For these two groups of learners and these two learning contexts are clearly different, to the point that conclusions reached for one group cannot be automatically taken as applicable to the other. However, when we find general trends and parallel results that apply across these two distinct, yet related disciplines, we move toward a broader definition of what it means to work through the writing process and to be able to write well.

Information on feedback is already available on a large number of students at different levels of study in several languages. From the main studies discussed here alone, subjects in FL courses at the college level include 134 elementary-level students of English (Robb, Ross, and Shortreed 1986), 141 third-quarter students of German (Semke 1984), 60 students of intermediate-level German (Lalande 1982), and 60 intermediate Spanish students (Kepner 1991), plus 72 L2 students in intermediate English composition (Fathman and Whalley 1990). Several national backgrounds are also represented: Japanese (Robb, Ross, and Shortreed), American (Semke; Lalande; Kepner), and Asians and Hispanics (Fathman and Whalley).

The studies sampled here for review used a variety of means to assess quality of writing: holistic subjective evaluation and objective measures relying on amount written and T-unit analysis (Robb, Ross, and Shortreed); a multiple-choice cloze test, word counts for fluency and ratios of errors to correct words for accuracy, and background and attitude questionnaires (Semke); pretest assessment of grade-point, scores on initial essays and posttest counts of grammatical and spelling errors (Lalande); number of higher-level propositions and surface-level errors (Kepner); and number of grammar errors and holistic ratings for organization, description, coherence, and creativity (Fathman and Whalley). Researchers can, of course, question the appropriateness of these individual measures. What is interesting here are the trends that appear across studies. Looking at these studies together, researchers can be more confident that their findings reflect the feedback variable more than they reflect different views of what makes good writing.

Do Learners Perceive Feedback as Useful?

While SLA research is developing a picture of what types of instructor feedback correspond to improved writing, this line of inquiry reveals only through anecdotal remarks what students themselves perceive as helpful. In 1981 Krashen pointed out that, even if research shows little value in correction, adult students want to be corrected, presumably because their cognitive abilities are fully developed (p. 7). An area of inquiry is now developing around how students perceive and use feedback. Whereas the feedback studies discussed earlier considered how writing improved as a result of correction and comments, this line of research looks at what students do as they consider instructor feedback on their written work and what value they place on these corrections and suggestions.

Data come from four main sources: supplementary, sometimes anecdotal, information from studies on the effect of feedback on writing quality, questionnaire research, interview studies, and protocol analysis. As an example of the first type, Lalande (1982) asked his students if they felt their writing improved during the course. Both students receiving direct correction and students using codes for self-correction felt that their writing improved considerably, although the writing of the direct correction group actually deteriorated in some areas.

Cohen (1987) developed a questionnaire to elicit perceptions from 217 L2 and FL students at New York State University at Binghamton. The students were enrolled in freshman English rhetoric courses, beginning and intermediate English classes, beginning and intermediate French classes, an intermediate German class, and an advanced Hebrew course.

The questionnaire considered the following: which aspects of their writing students believed received feedback, whether they read over comments and gave them thoughtful attention, how they used comments, how often they did not understand comments, and how they rated themselves as language learners in general and in each of the four skills. Cohen found that most comments were in the form of single words, focused on mechanics and grammar, and—perhaps due to their brevity—were sometimes unclear to students. Most students read the comments, but students who considered themselves good learners were more likely to do so than students who considered themselves poor learners. Self-assessed good learners also reported paying more attention to comments on vocabulary, grammar, and mechanics than did self-assessed poorer learners. The most popular learner strategy by far was simply making a mental note of the teacher's comment.

Students reported doing only limited revision of their papers. It is important to note that only the English students were required to rewrite their papers. Even among this group, however, few students reported consistently incorporating teacher comments in their revisions. Contrary to what we might expect, revision was most prevalent among the self-assessed poor learners; the self-assessed good writers often relied exclusively on making a mental note of their teacher's comments (p. 64).

The format for student perception questionnaires was further developed by Leki (1991), whose survey had four parts: a 7-point Likert scale about the perceived importance of accuracy, a 5-point Likert scale about responses to a marked paper, a multiple-choice section in which students indicated their preference for how teachers mark compositions, and a 5-point Likert scale on which students assessed the quality of example sentence-length corrections. Leki surveyed 100 students from 37 countries enrolled in first-year English L2 composition classes to find that they equated good writing with error-free writing and, therefore, that they wanted and expected their composition teachers to correct all their errors.

Leki stressed that questionnaires administered outside the context of a specific writing task have two weaknesses: They do not usually control whether students interpret questions as pertaining to rough drafts or final products and their focus on errors directs the students' attention to accuracy and away from organization and content.

Radecki and Swales (1986) offer a check on such confounding variables by using interviews of selected students to substantiate the validity of questionnaire responses. As Radecki and Swales and Leki point out, questionnaires assess only perceptions of behavior as they are remembered later. To assess actual behavior, protocols or video-tapes might be more appropriate. With protocols, however, there is the danger that the intervention itself—having writers comment on what they are doing—may influence how the writing behavior evolves. Such influence seems especially likely if the writers are trained in how to do protocols (Cohen 1991). The choice, then, of whether to use the protocol technique or not presents the researcher with a paradox. If writers are not trained in doing protocols, they may not attend to the information needed by the researcher. If they are directed to do protocols in specific ways, this direction may well influence the protocols and ultimately the writing they produce. If writers do not do protocols, researchers may miss insights into their behaviors as they develop. If they do protocols, the act of doing the protocol may influence the behavior that the researcher wishes to observe.

Radecki and Swales chose not to use protocols, relying on information gathered with questionnaires and substantiated through interviews. This data led them to divide their respondents into three groups, based on their attitude toward types of feedback and revision and their sensitivity to instructors' expectations: receptors (46 percent), semi-resistors (41 percent), and resistors (13 percent). Grouping students by preferred and accepted feedback style is a first step toward considering learner traits that go beyond level of study and nationality.

Most recently, Cohen (1991) used think-aloud protocols done by teachers as they marked compositions and student protocols done as they read the comments. As in the protocol studies of the process of writing, Cohen's research involved a very small sample: two teachers, one English as an FL and one Portuguese L1, with three students each. The students were chosen to include, in each language, one student of "high ability," one student of "intermediate ability," and one student of "low ability," as determined by their respective teachers, who based their judgments primarily on the students' ability to write argumentative discourse (p. 139). In addition, Cohen used questionnaires and checklists with two teachers and 13 FL English students and 19 Portuguese L1 students to identify further what both groups believed important in the feedback process. Results showed a good fit in both groups between the feedback the teachers reported giving and what their students believed they received. Replicating the findings of his 1987 report, Cohen found that students' most common strategy for benefiting from feedback was to make a mental note of it, rather than recording the feedback systematically. This finding led Cohen to suggest that teachers require students to attend to feedback by rewriting their compositions, a requirement not always imposed by the teachers in his study.

Research on learners' perceptions of feedback and its use illustrates how SLA writing research is rapidly developing multimethod approaches. Indeed, researchers (Chaudron 1986; Lightbown 1986) have advocated the need to view the same question from different perspectives in order to identify and study more variables. The individual and in-depth nature of case studies reveals possible confounding variables, such as how different understandings of what constitutes "grammar," "vocabulary," "organization," or "content" can underlie lack of consensus in teachers' responses to surveys (Cohen 1991). Ideally, these variables can then be controlled in larger experimental studies with random samples and statistical tests to build toward conclusive findings and meaningful generalizations.

Through replication of studies in different instructional situations with different types of students, SLA research is beginning to develop a picture of how learners develop their writing skills and the role of instruction in this process. We now see writing as mainly a recursive process with positive links to ability to write in L1. We see instruction as most beneficial when it helps students understand and become fully involved in the recursive process of writing. The value of instructor feedback is still undetermined, with indications that important factors are the amount students write and the degree of their involvement in the revision process.

Questions for Future Research

Research on speaking and research on writing have generally (and unfortunately) been conducted independently of one another. While we have attempted in this chapter to maintain the position that the process of acquisition is fundamentally the same regardless of the learning environment, we also acknowledge that this position is not recognized by everyone. Research on these two skill areas is being carried out on two fronts: one by those concerned with broader issues of SLA and the other by those interested primarily in foreign language teaching. Recent conferences such as SLA-FLL[10] are devoted to bringing the two areas together, as is this ACTFL volume.

In the early stages of SLA research, separation of speaking and writing were perhaps necessary as each area attempted to determine its own research agenda. As we have seen in this chapter, however, there are many areas of common concern, as well as areas where the research agendas are indeed separate.

The most striking observation to be gleaned from comparing speaking and writing research in an L2 context is the similarity between these two fields. They have often asked the same questions, used the same or related methods of inquiry to research them, found similar results, and come to comparable conclusions.

In the hopes of stimulating collaborative inquiry, we suggest some research questions that reflect a common agenda, as well as some that reflect, at least for the time being, separate agendas.

1. Does variation in the language produced have an impact on acquisition? That is, can variation in speech production be an impetus for acquisition of forms? Does exposure to different writing styles help learners develop more fluent written expression? Does deviant speech or writing that is uncorrected serve as a negative input model for future speech or writing?

2. How does type of classwork relate to how students develop speaking and writing ability? Are certain tasks more conducive to certain kinds of processing phenomena? (See Chastain 1990; Carrell and Connor 1991; Loschky and Bley-Vroman 1993). Does the method by which speaking and writing are taught relate to how students respond to different types of feedback?

3. How are student speech and writing influenced by how teachers exercise their social power, their dual roles as both evaluators of writing and its audience? This question has both pedagogical and sociolinguistic consequences. From a pedagogical point of view, L2 research is investigating how positive and negative feedback affects student motivation to write. Zellermayer (1989) points out that little has been done in L1 from the sociolinguistic point of view. For L2, this perspective might be even more crucial. How well can teachers replicate a real communicative audience so that a teacher's intentions for that audience match students' expectations of it? Especially in the FL context, the student is highly dependent upon the teacher to provide models of interaction with the target community. Both speech and writing become communicative skills only to the degree to which students attempt to communicate real information to an authentic audience.

4. What factors influence the teacher's choice of feedback model for writing and for speech: the teacher's experience? training? educational attitudes? language taught? Current findings suggest that past differences found in L2 and FL are becoming less acute as the two fields interact and learn from each other.

5. How do cultural factors inherent in the instructional setting interact with expectations for oral or written discourse that come from the native and target cultures? Do cultural expectations about when to speak and how accurately to speak play a role in what happens in the L2 or FL class? What happens when cultural notions clash about how writing should be done (with outlines and drafts, with what type of revision) and how it should be evaluated? Do students develop speech and writing best when lessons are built on expectations and strategies found in their native language(s) and culture(s)? Or should strategies and expectations come from target-language groups?

6. What role do students' individual cognitive and affective profiles play in how they develop speaking and writing? Most SLA research has relied on groups of students found in existing classrooms, sometimes with controls for language background and ability. Such studies do not consider individual learner variables in any systematic way.[11] Case studies come closer to examining individual learner profiles, but they still do not make extensive, focused use of learner variables. For the studies reviewed here for both speaking and writing, the lack of systematic attention to individual learner difference increases greatly the risk of inappropriate overgeneralization of their findings.

7. Are there universal notions of speaking or composing that go beyond L1 and L2? According to Krapels (1990: 53) the field of universal notions for writing remains "yet untouched." To investigate this question, collaboration among SLA and L1 researchers would clearly be needed.

Pedagogical Implications

In drawing pedagogical implications from research, similar conclusions have often been reached by both L2 and FL instructors. This should not be taken to mean that research tells us how to teach. As Silva (1988: 6) points out, the pedagogical interpretations of language acquisition research are still highly problematic. Based on his review of research in college-level English L2 writing, Silva states:

> While some researchers were very careful, modest, tentative, and reasonable, just as many were not. There seem to be more than a few instances of over- and misinterpretation of evidence here; these include unjustified cause and effect inferences—both implicit and explicit; unjustified generalization from very small samples to large sub-groups or the entire population of ESL writers; suggested implications for the classroom not well supported by the evidence provided; and sweeping claims that go way beyond findings in support of a particular popular approach or orientation to writing instruction (cited in Krapels 1990: 50).

Although most researchers recognize the limitations of their studies, some do not find it premature to make concrete teaching suggestions based on their results.

To Silva's warning that research findings are often inappropriately applied to teaching, we add an additional note of caution by reminding readers of the commonly held position articulated by Lightbown (1985):

> I am convinced that second-language research does have much to contribute to teaching practice in the long run. However, I believe that at present its contribution lies not so much in what it has to say regarding the development of syllabus content or specific teaching methods as in what it has to say regarding the development of expectations on the part of teachers for what they and their students can accomplish (p. 173).

While we discuss some specific suggestions regarding teaching practices, we also note that these are intended only as suggestions and must be followed up by specific research projects designed to investigate their pedagogical value and implementation.

Given the consistent findings that students develop writing skills through extensive practice and the inconclusive findings about the value of correction in that development process, many SLA researchers suggest that teachers devote their time to developing writing activities or responding to global aspects of student work rather than primarily correcting sentence-level mechanical errors (Semke 1984; Raimes 1985; Robb, Ross, and Shortreed 1986; Fathman and Whalley 1990). Others are more hesitant to move away from systematic correction, recognizing that some students desire correction (Krashen 1981; Leki 1991) and suggesting that students analyze and record their errors (Lalande 1982; Vandergrift 1986) and be required to revise their compositions (Cohen 1991).

Furthermore, given the relationship among general language skills within the L2 and from the L1 to the L2, it is not surprising that researchers and teachers advocate increased language practice in all skills, and particularly instruction and practice in the composing process as well as attention to the written product (Raimes 1985). It is also not surprising to find justification in SLA research for certain types of pedagogical activities that require information exchange and negotiation in the classroom.

An interesting proposal is made by Loschky and Bley-Vroman (1993). They attempt to position different language tasks in the classroom along a continuum that reflects the processing mechanisms of L2 learners. For the FL classroom, Omaggio Hadley (1993) does something similar in suggesting how to sequence written and oral activities on a continuum of task demands.[12] If these continua are found to portray task types accurately (cf. Delk, Evart, and Helling 1993), we will be provided with a rationale for using particular tasks at particular times in the classroom.

Perhaps most useful is the suggestion that research tools, such as the think-aloud procedure, can be used as pedagogical techniques (Raimes 1985: 251). Might not questionnaires soliciting student attitudes about instructors' feedback be useful as classroom tools to help students become aware of and expand their learning strategies? As classroom "action" research continues to influence classroom practice, it may become increasingly common to find "research" tools used as pedagogical techniques. (See also Loschky and Bley-Vroman 1993 for elaboration of this issue.)

Conclusion

In the past decade, there has been much investigation about how students produce language, be it through speaking or through writing. Although theories and models are being tested, such as the linear vs. discourse model for writing, we are still very much in the theory-building stage. The basic problem is establishing the number of variables and determining the degree to which they are interrelated. Independent of classroom instruction, we must consider the learner, the skill, the task, and the cultural conventions associated with each form of communication. In a school situation, we add instructional variables such as the physical classroom, the teacher, the materials, the other students, the learning activities, and the feedback system, as well as how these variables interact.[13] A large part of SLA research to date has been concerned with identifying more precise variables in these already diverse categories. From a better understanding of these variables and how they interact, we can only hope that a comprehensive, testable theory will emerge.

How learners produce language has always been a basic concern of SLA. What is new is the broadening of the domain of SLA itself to include the acquisition of both second- and foreign languages. Research in these two once fairly separate disciplines is beginning to take parallel paths. Researchers are working in collaborative ways. Teachers are sharing interpretations of research findings and thus opening the door to more intensive collaboration in the future. This trend is significant, for clearly we need to look beyond single languages and beyond specific learning contexts in order to understand the complex processes of second-language acquisition.

Notes

1. For an excellent review of the acquisition of phonological features (perception and production), see Leather and James 1991.
2. Those working on linguistic analysis at that time (e.g., Bloomfield 1933; Sapir 1921) were primarily involved with languages for which there was no writing system. This may have influenced their views on the primacy of speech over writing. Writing in this earlier view was seen as a means of transcribing oral language. "Writing is not language, but merely a way of recording language by means of visible marks" (Bloomfield 1933: 21).
3. Of course, similar questions could be asked about the two remaining skills, listening and reading. While an understanding of the relationship between reading and writing is a growing field in and of itself, a discussion of this relationship is beyond the scope of this chapter.
4. See Crookes (1991) for a distinction between planned and unplanned discourse within the area of speech production.
5. It must be recognized that these studies were done with children. One does not know to what extent the same results would obtain with adult learners.
6. These results are in need of cautious interpretation given the numerous methodological difficulties (Beck and Eubank 1991) and the difficulties of replication (Valdman 1993).
7. The most common reference given for Perl's coding system is her doctoral thesis (Perl 1978). Since it was not available to us, however, we based our report on information from an ERIC article (Perl 1979). In the introduction to this article, Perl writes that the material presented is from her thesis.
8. This report offers little detail on research procedures or data and no statistical tests. It should be considered as a report of informed observations: the "action research" of one teacher in her class. Such studies can help us identify research variables, but it is not appropriate to generalize their findings beyond the classroom in which they were observed.
9. In this study, Chastain (1990) noted that most students were quite accurate in their writing, making few errors: of total words 4.65 percent were faulty in graded papers and 4.72 percent were faulty in ungraded papers (p. 12). He notes further that the students had received formal grammar instruction prior to the classes or during the class in which the study was conducted (p. 11).
10. SLA-FLL stands for Second Language Acquisition and Foreign Language Learning.
11. Rieken (1991) compared how field-independent and field-dependent students of beginning French benefited from different types of feedback in terms of how often and how accurately they used the *passé composé*. Since this study looked at how students used a grammatical form, rather than how they produced chunks of discourse, it is not discussed in this chapter. Rieken's findings are nonetheless worthy of note, as they may encourage researchers working in a discourse context to examine the field independent/field dependent variable.

Rieken's study used three feedback groups: no corrective feedback, implicit corrective feedback, and explicit corrective feedback. For frequency or breadth of use of the *passé composé*, no significant differences were found among the feedback groups or between students considered field independent or field dependent. In the measure of accuracy, however, students of low field independence in the explicit feedback group achieved a higher accuracy score on a cloze test than did students of low field independence in the other feedback groups.

12. See also Pica, Kanagy, and Falodun (1993) on the classification of task types.

13. For example, Rieken (1991) points out how few studies investigate the teacher variable. In her study about students' use of the *passé composé,* she found a significant teacher effect in terms of how much students benefited from direct correction techniques.

References

Second-Language Production: SLA Research in Speaking and Writing

Abu-Nahleh, Lamice, Shelton Allen, Bradford Arthur, Sandra Beals, Martha Butler, Barbara Drezner, Gro Frydenburg, Maha Galal, Susan Gass, Kim Hildebrandt, Evangeline Marlos, and Terry Ostrander. 1982. "The Scope and Function of Language Repair in Foreigner Discourse." *Interlanguage Studies Bulletin* 6,1: 112–20.

Applebee, Arthur N. 1981. *Writing in the Secondary School.* NCTE Research Report No. 21. Urbana, IL: National Council of Teachers of English.

Aston, Guy. 1986. "Trouble-Shooting in Interaction with Learners: The More the Merrier?" *Applied Linguistics* 7,2: 128–43.

Barnett, Marva A. 1989. "Writing as a Process." *French Review* 63: 31–44.

Beck, Maria, and Lynn Eubank. 1991. "Acquisition Theory and Experimental Design: A Critique of Tomasello and Herron." *Studies in Second Language Acquisition* 13: 73–76.

Birdsong, David. 1989. *Metalinguistic Performance and Interlinguistic Competence.* New York: Springer.

Bley-Vroman, Robert. 1989. "What Is the Logical Problem of Foreign Language Learning?" in Susan Gass and Jacquelyn Schachter, eds., *Linguistic Perspectives on Second Language Acquisition.* Cambridge, Eng.: Cambridge Univ. Press.

Bloomfield, Leonard. 1933. *Language.* New York: Holt, Rinehart and Winston.

Bridgemen, Brent, and Sybil Carlson. 1983. *Survey of Academic Writing Tasks Required of Graduate and Undergraduate Foreign Students.* TOEFL Research Report 15. ETS Research Report 83–118. Princeton, NJ: Educational Testing Service.

Britton, James, Anthony Burgess, Nancy Martin, Alex McLeod, and Harold Rosen. 1975. *The Development of Writing Abilities.* London, Eng.: Macmillan.

Burt, Marina K., and Carol Kiparsky. 1972. *The Gooficon: A Repair Manual for English.* Rowley, MA: Newbury House.

Carrell, Patricia L., and Ulla Connor. 1991. "Reading and Writing Persuasive Texts." *Modern Language Journal* 75: 314–24.

Carroll, Suzanne, Yves Roberge, and Merrill Swain. 1992. "The Role of Feedback in Adult Second Language Acquisition, Error Correction, and Morphological Generalizations." *Applied Psycholinguistics* 13,2: 173–98.

Chastain, Kenneth. 1990. "Characteristics of Graded and Ungraded Compositions." *Modern Language Journal* 74: 10–14.

Chaudron, Craig. 1986. "The Interaction of Quantitative and Qualitative Approaches to Research: A View of the Second Language Classroom." *TESOL Quarterly* 20: 709–17.

Chomsky, Noam. 1959. "Review of *Verbal Behavior* by B. F. Skinner." *Language* 35: 26–58.

Cohen, Andrew D. 1987. "Student Processing of Feedback on Their Compositions," in Anita Wenden and Joan Rubin, eds., *Learner Strategies in Language Learning*. Englewood Cliffs, NJ: Prentice-Hall.

———. 1991. "Feedback on Writing." *Studies in Second Language Acquisition* 13: 133–59.

Corder, S. Pit. 1967. "The Significance of Learner's Errors." *International Review of Applied Linguistics* 5: 161–70.

———. 1973. "The Elicitation of Interlanguage," in J. Svartvik, ed., *Errata: Papers in Error Analysis*. Lund, Sweden: CKW Geerup.

Crookes, Graham. 1989. "Planning and Interlanguage Variation." *Studies in Second Language Acquisition* 11,4: 367–83.

———. 1991. "Second Language Speech Production Research: A Methodologically Oriented Review." *Studies in Second Language Acquisition* 13,2: 113–32.

———, and Susan Gass, eds. 1993a. *Tasks and Language Learning: Integrating Theory and Practice*. Clevedon, Eng.: Multilingual Matters.

———, and Susan Gass, eds. 1993b. *Tasks in a Pedagogical Context: Integrating Theory and Practice*. Clevedon, Eng.: Multilingual Matters.

Cummins, James. 1981. "The Role of Primary Language Development in Promoting Educational Success for Language Minority Students," in *Schooling and Language Minority Students: A Theoretical Framework*. Los Angeles: California State Univ., Evaluation, Dissemination and Assessment Center.

———. 1987. "Second Language Acquisition within Bilingual Education Programs," in Leslie M. Beebe, ed., *Issues in Second Language Acquisition: Multiple Perspectives*. New York: Newbury House.

Delk, Cheryl, Kevin Evart, and Sabine Helling. 1993. "An Investigation of Task-Types as a Reflection of Processing Demands." Unpublished ms., Michigan State Univ.

Dickerson, Lonna, and Wayne Dickerson. 1977. "Interlanguage Phonology: Current Research and Future Directions," in S. Pit Corder and Eddy Roulet, eds., *The Notions of Simplification, Interlanguages and Pidgins and Their Relation to Second Language Learning*. Actes du 5ème Colloque de Linguistique Appliquée de Neufchâtel. Paris, Fr.: AIMAV/Didier.

Eckman, Fred. In press. "The Competence-Performance Issue in Second-Language Acquisition Theory: A Debate," in Elaine Tarone, Susan Gass, and Andrew Cohen, eds., *Research Methodology in Second Language Acquisition*. Hillsdale, NJ: Erlbaum.

Edelsky, Carole. 1982. "Writing in a Bilingual Program: The Relation of L1 and L2 Texts." *TESOL Quarterly* 16: 211–28.

Ellis, Rod. 1984. *Classroom Second Language Development: A Study of Classroom Interaction and Language Acquisition*. New York: Pergamon.

———. 1985. *Understanding Second Language Acquisition*. Oxford, Eng.: Oxford Univ. Press.

———. 1987. "Interlanguage Variability in Narrative Discourse: Style Shifting in the Use of the Past Tense." *Studies in Second Language Acquisition* 9,1: 1–20.

Emig, Janet. 1971. *The Composing Process of Twelfth Graders*. Urbana, IL: National Council of Teachers of English.

Fagan, William T., and Helen Mary (Ruth) Hayden. 1988. "Writing Processes in French and English of Fifth Grade French Immersion Students." *Canadian Modern Language Review* 44: 653–68.

Faigley, Lester, and Stephen Witte. 1981. "Analyzing Revision." *College Composition and Communication* 32,4: 400–14.

Fathman, Ann K., and Elizabeth Whalley. 1990. "Teacher Response to Student Writing," in Barbara Kroll, ed., *Second Language Writing: Research Insights for the Classroom.* New York: Cambridge Univ. Press.

Ferguson, Charles. 1971. "Absence of Copula and the Notion of Simplicity: A Study of Normal Speech, Baby Talk, Foreigner Talk and Pidgins," in Dell Hymes, ed., *Pidginization and Creolization of Languages.* Cambridge, Eng.: Cambridge Univ. Press.

Flower, Linda, and John R. Hayes. 1981. "A Cognitive Process Theory of Writing." *College Composition and Communication* 32: 366–87.

Gaies, Steven. 1977. "The Nature of Linguistic Input in Formal Second Language Learning," in H. Doug Brown, Carlos Yorio, and Ruth Crymes, eds., *On TESOL '77.* Washington, DC: TESOL.

Garrett, Nina. 1992. "Technology as a Medium for SLA Research." Paper presented at the ACTFL Annual Meeting, Chicago, IL.

Gass, Susan. 1988. "Integrating Research Areas: A Framework for Second Language Studies." *Applied Linguistics* 9,2: 198–217.

———, and Usha Lakshmanan. 1991. "Accounting for Interlanguage Subject Pronouns." *Second Language Research* 7,3: 181–203.

———, and Larry Selinker. In press. *Second Language Acquisition: An Introductory Course.* Hillsdale, NJ: Erlbaum.

———, and Evangeline Varonis. 1985. "Variation in Native Speaker Speech Modification to Non-Native Speakers." *Studies in Second Language Acquisition* 7,1: 37–57.

———, and Evangeline Varonis. 1989. "Incorporated Repairs in NNS Discourse," in Miriam Eisenstein, ed., *Variation and Second Language Acquisition.* New York: Plenum.

———, and Evangeline Varonis. In press. "Conversational Interactions and Subsequent L2 Use." *Studies in Second Language Acquisition.*

Graham, Macy S. 1983. "The Effect of Teacher Feedback on the Reduction of Usage Errors in Junior College Freshman's Writing." Unpublished Ph.D. diss., Univ. of Southern Mississippi. [Cited in Ann K. Fathman and Elizabeth Whalley. "Teacher Response to Student Writing," in Barbara Kroll, ed., *Second Language Writing: Research Insights for the Classroom.* New York: Cambridge Univ. Press, 1990.]

Gregg, Kevin. 1990. "The Variable Competence Model of Second Language Acquisition and Why It Isn't." *Applied Linguistics* 11,4: 364–83.

Guberman, Solange. 1988. "Étude comparée de trois approches: la correction des erreurs dans les compositions écrites." *Canadian Modern Language Review* 44: 702–14.

Hall, Katrina. 1993. "Process Writing in French Immersion." *Canadian Modern Language Review* 49: 255–74.

Hansen-Strain, Lynne. 1989. "Orality/Literacy and Group Differences in Second-Language Acquisition." *Language Learning* 39,4: 469–96.

Hawkins, Barbara. 1985. "Is an 'Appropriate Response' Always So Appropriate?" in Susan Gass and Carolyn Madden, eds., *Input in Second Language Acquisition.* Rowley, MA: Newbury House.

Hayes-Roth, Barbara, and Frederick Hayes-Roth. 1979. "A Cognitive Model of Planning." *Cognitive Science* 3: 275–310.

Hendrickson, James M. 1978. "Error Correction in Foreign Language Teaching: Recent Theory, Research, and Practice." *Modern Language Journal* 62: 387–425.

Herrington, Anne. 1989. "The First Twenty Years of Research in the Teaching of English and the Growth of a Research Community in Composition Studies." *Research in the Teaching of English* 23: 117–38.

Herron, Carol. 1991. "The Garden Path Correction Strategy in the Foreign Language Classroom." *French Review* 64: 966–77.

———, and Michael Tomasello. 1988. Learning Grammatical Structures in a Foreign Language: Modelling versus Feedback." *French Review* 61: 910–22.

———. 1992. "Acquiring Grammatical Structures by Guided Induction." *French Review* 65: 708–18.

Hillocks, George, Jr. 1986. "Research on Written Composition: New Direction for Teaching." Urbana, IL: ERIC Clearinghouse on Reading and Communication Skills and the National Conference on Research in English. [ED 265 552]

Hyltenstam, Kenneth. 1977. "Implicational Patterns in Interlanguage Syntax Variation." *Language Learning* 27,2: 383–411.

Kepner, Christine Goring. 1991. "An Experiment in the Relationship of Types of Written Feedback to the Development of Second-Language Writing Skills." *Modern Language Journal* 75: 305–13.

Kern, Richard G., and Jean Marie Schultz. 1992. "The Effects of Composition Instruction on Intermediate Level French Students' Writing Performance: Some Preliminary Findings." *Modern Language Journal* 76: 1–13.

Kleifgen, Jo Anne. 1985. "Skilled Variation in a Kindergarten Teacher's Use of Foreigner Talk," in Susan Gass and Carolyn Madden, eds., *Input in Second Language Acquisition.* Rowley, MA: Newbury House.

Knoblauch, C. H., and Lil Brannon. 1984. *Rhetorical Traditions and the Teaching of Writing.* Upper Montclair, NJ: Boynton/Cook.

Krapels, Alexandra Rowe. 1990. "An Overview of Second Language Writing Process Research," in Barbara Kroll, ed., *Second Language Writing: Research Insights for the Classroom.* New York: Cambridge Univ. Press.

Krashen, Stephen. 1981. *Second Language Acquisition and Second Language Learning.* Oxford, Eng.: Pergamon.

Lalande, John F. 1982. "Reducing Composition Errors: An Experiment." *Modern Language Journal* 66: 140–49.

Lantolf, James P. 1988. "The Syntactic Complexity of Written Texts in Spanish as a Foreign Language: A Markedness Perspective." *Hispania* 71: 933–40.

Larsen-Freeman, Diane, and Michael Long. 1991. *An Introduction to Second Language Acquisition.* London, Eng.: Longman.

Leather, James, and Alan James. 1991. "The Acquisition of Second Language Speech." *Studies in Second Language Acquisition* 13,3: 305–41.

Leki, Ilona. 1991. "The Preferences of ESL Students for Error Correction in College-Level Writing Classes." *Foreign Language Annals* 24: 203–18.

Liebman-Kleine, JoAnne. 1987. "Teaching and Researching Invention: Using Ethnography in ESL Writing Classes." *ELT Journal* 41: 104–11.

Lightbown, Patsy M. 1985. "Great Expectations: Second-Language Acquisition Research and Classroom Teaching." *Applied Linguistics* 6: 173–89.

———. 1986. "The Influence of Linguistic Theory on Language Acquisition Research: Now You See It, Now You Don't," in James E. Alatis, ed. Georgetown University Round Table on Languages and Linguistics. Washington, DC: Georgetown Univ. Press.

Long, Michael. 1980. "Input, Interaction and Second Language Acquisition." Unpublished Ph.D. diss., Univ. of California–Los Angeles.

———. 1983. "Linguistic and Conversational Adjustments to Non-Native Speakers." *Studies in Second Language Acquisition* 5,2: 177–93.

Loschky, Lester C. 1989. *The Effects of Negotiated Interaction and Premodified Input on Second Language Comprehension and Retention.* Occasional Paper No. 16. Manoa: Univ. of Hawaii.

———, and Robert Bley-Vroman. 1993. "Grammar and Task-Based Methodology," in Graham Crookes and Susan Gass, eds., *Tasks and Language Learning: Integrating Theory and Practice.* Clevedon, Eng.: Multilingual Matters.

Magnan, Sally S. 1985. "Teaching and Testing Proficiency in Writing: Skills to Transcend the Second-Language Classroom," in Alice C. Omaggio, ed., *Proficiency, Curriculum, Articulation: The Ties That Bind.* Middlebury, VT: Northeast Conference on the Teaching of Foreign Languages.

McLaughlin, Barry. 1987. *Theories of Second-Language Learning.* Baltimore, MD: Edward Arnold.

Monroe, James H. 1975. "Measuring and Enhancing Syntactic Fluency in French." *French Review* 48: 1023–31.

Omaggio, Alice C. 1986. *Teaching Language in Context: Proficiency-Oriented Instruction.* Boston: Heinle and Heinle.

Omaggio Hadley, Alice C. 1993. *Teaching Language in Context.* 2nd ed. Boston: Heinle and Heinle.

Oyama, Susan. 1976. "A Sensitive Period in the Acquisition of a Non-Native Phonological System." *Journal of Psycholinguistic Research* 5: 261–85.

Parrish, Betsy. 1987. "A New Look at Methodologies in the Study of Article Acquisition for Learners of ESL." *Language Learning* 37,3: 361–84.

———, and Elaine Tarone. 1986. "Article Use in Interlanguage: A Study in Task-Related Variability." Paper presented at the TESOL Convention, Anaheim, California.

Perl, Sondra. 1978. "Five Writers Writing: Case Studies of the Composing Process of Unskilled College Writers." Unpublished Ph.D. diss., New York Univ.

———. 1979. "The Composing Process of Unskilled College Writers." Paper presented at the Annual Meeting of the American Educational Research Association, San Francisco, April. [ED 170 764]

———. 1980. "A Look at Basic Writers in the Process of Composing," in N. Kasden and D. R. Hoeber, eds., *Basic Writing.* Urbana, IL: National Council of Teachers of English.

Pica, Teresa. 1989. "Classroom Interaction, Participation and Comprehension: Redefining Relationships." *Papers in Applied Linguistics* 1: 1–36 (Univ. of Alabama).

———, Richard Young, and Catherine Doughty. 1987. "The Impact of Interaction on Comprehension." *TESOL Quarterly* 21,4: 737–58.

———, Ruth Kanagy, and Joseph Falodun. 1993. "Choosing and Using Communication Tasks for Second Language Instruction and Research," in Graham Crookes and Susan Gass, eds., *Tasks and Language Learning: Integrating Theory and Practice.* Clevedon, Eng.: Multilingual Matters.

Pinker, Steven. 1984. *Language Learnability and Language Development.* Cambridge, MA: Harvard Univ. Press.

Poulsen, Erik. 1991. "Writing Processes with Word Processing in Teaching English as a Foreign Language." *Computers and Education* 16: 77–81.

Preston, Dennis. 1989. *Sociolinguistics and Second Language Acquisition.* Oxford, Eng.: Basil Blackwell.

———. 1993. "Variation Linguistics and SLA." *Second Language Research* 9,2: 153–72.

Radecki, Patricia, and John Swales. 1986. "ESL Students' Reaction and Response to Feedback." *Papers in Applied Linguistics* 1: 69–86 (Univ. of Michigan).

Raimes, Ann. 1985. "What Unskilled ESL Students Do As They Write: A Classroom Study of Composing." *TESOL Quarterly* 19: 229–58.

Richards, Jack, and Theodore Rodgers. 1986. *Approaches and Methods in Language Teaching.* Cambridge, Eng.: Cambridge Univ. Press.

Rieken, Elizabeth Grace. 1991. "The Effect of Feedback on the Frequency and Accuracy of Use of the Passé Composé by Field-Independent and Field-Dependent Students of Beginning French." Unpublished Ph.D. diss., Univ. of Illinois at Urbana–Champaign.

Robb, Thomas, Steven Ross, and Ian Shortreed. 1986. "Salience of Feedback on Error and Its Effect on EFL Writing Quality." *TESOL Quarterly* 20: 83–93.

Rohman, D. Gordon, and Albert O. Wlecke. n.d. "Pre-Writing: The Construction and Application of Models for Concept Formation in Writing." Cooperative Research Project No. 2174. Washington, DC: U.S. Office of Education. [Cited in Nancy Sommers. "Revision Strategies of Student Writers and Experienced Adult Writers." *College Composition and Communication* 31 (1980): 378–88.]

Sapir, Edward. 1921. *Language.* New York: Harcourt, Brace.

Sato, Charlene. 1984. "Phonological Processes in Second Language Acquisition: Another Look at Interlanguage Syllable Structure." *Language Learning* 34,4: 43–57.

———. 1985. "Task Variation in Interlanguage Phonology," in Susan Gass and Carolyn Madden, eds., *Input in Second Language Acquisition.* Rowley, MA: Newbury House.

Scarcella, Robin, and Corrine Higa. 1981. "Input, Negotiation and Age Differences in Second Language Acquisition." *Language Learning* 31: 409–38.

Schachter, Jacquelyn. 1988. "Second Language Acquisition and Its Relationship to Universal Grammar." *Applied Linguistics* 9: 219-35.

Schecter, Sandra R., and Linda A. Harklau. 1992. *Annotated Bibliography of Research on Writing in a Non-Native Language.* National Center for the Study of Writing and Literacy Technical Report No. 51. Rev. Berkeley, CA: Univ. of California; Pittsburgh, PA: Carnegie-Mellon Univ.

Selinker, Larry. 1972. "Interlanguage." *International Review of Applied Linguistics* 10: 209–31.

———, and Dan Douglas. 1985. "Wrestling with 'Context' in Interlanguage Theory." *Applied Linguistics* 6,2: 190–204.

Semke, Harriet D. 1984. "Effects of the Red Pen." *Foreign Language Annals* 17: 195–202.

Silva, Tony. 1988. "Research on the Composing Process of College-Level ESL Writers: A Critical Review." Unpublished ms. of paper presented at the 39th Annual CCCC Convention, St. Louis, March. [Cited in Alexandra Rowe Krapels. "An Overview of Second Language Writing Process Research," in Barbara Kroll, ed., *Second Language Writing: Research Insights for the Classroom.* New York: Cambridge Univ. Press, 1990.]

Sommers, Nancy. 1980. "Revision Strategies of Student Writers and Experienced Adult Writers." *College Composition and Communication* 31: 378–88.

———. 1982. "Responding to Student Writing." *College Communication and Composition* 33: 148–56.

Stalker, Jacqueline, and James Stalker. 1988. "A Comparison of Pragmatic Accommodation of Nonnative and Native Speakers in Written English." *World Englishes* 7: 119–28.

Stern, Hans Heinrich. 1983. *Fundamental Concepts of Language Teaching.* Oxford, Eng.: Oxford Univ. Press.

Swain, Merrill. 1985. "Communicative Competence: Some Roles of Comprehensible Input and Comprehensible Output in Its Development," in Susan Gass and Carolyn Madden, eds., *Input in Second Language Acquisition.* Rowley, MA: Newbury House.

Tarone, Elaine. 1979. "Interlanguage as Chameleon." *Language Learning* 29: 181–91.

———. 1983. "On the Variability of Interlanguage Systems." *Applied Linguistics* 4: 142–63.

———. 1985. "Variability in Interlanguage Use: A Study of Style-Shifting in Morphology and Syntax." *Language Learning* 35: 373–404.

———. 1988. *Variation in Interlanguage.* London, Eng.: Edward Arnold.

Tomasello, Michael, and Carol Herron. 1988. "Down the Garden Path: Inducing and Correcting Overgeneralization Errors in the Foreign Language Classroom." *Applied Psycholinguistics* 9: 237–46.

———. 1989. "Feedback for Language Transfer Errors: The Garden Path Technique." *Studies in Second Language Acquisition* 11: 385–95.

Trahey, Martha, and Lydia White. 1993. "Positive Evidence and Preemption." *Studies in Second Language Acquisition* 15,2: 181–204.

Tweissi, Adel. 1987. "Language Simplification in Foreigner Talk and Second Language Development." Unpublished Ph.D. diss., Univ. of Michigan.

Valdman, Albert. 1993. "Classroom Language Learning Research: Reliability and Applicability." Paper presented at SLA-FLL, Purdue Univ., February.

Vandergrift, Laurens. 1986. "Second Language Writing and Correction: Toward an Improved Model for Composition Correction." *Canadian Modern Language Review* 42: 658–67.

Wagner-Gough, Judy, and Evelyn Hatch. 1975. "The Importance of Input in Second Language Acquisition Studies." *Language Learning* 25: 297–308.

Wexler, Kenneth, and Peter Cullicover. 1980. *Formal Principles of Language Acquisition.* Cambridge, MA: MIT Press.

White, Lydia. 1991a. "Adverb Placement in Second Language Acquisition: Some Effects of Positive and Negative Evidence in the Classroom." *Second Language Research* 7: 133–61.

———. 1991b. "The Verb-Movement Parameter in Second Language Acquisition." *Language Acquisition* 1: 337–60.

Woken, Miles, and John Swales. 1989. "Expertise and Authority in Native–Non-Native Conversations: The Need for a Variable Account," in Susan Gass et al., eds., *Variation in Second Language Acquisition: Discourse and Pragmatics.* Clevedon, Eng.: Multilingual Matters.

Zamel, Vivian. 1983. "The Composing Process of Advanced ESL Students: Six Case Studies." *TESOL Quarterly* 17: 165–87.

———. 1985. "Responding to Student Writing." *TESOL Quarterly* 19: 79–101.

Zellermayer, Michael. 1989. "The Study of Teachers' Written Feedback to Students' Writing: Changes in Theoretical Considerations and the Expansion of Research Contexts." *Instructional Science* 18: 145–65.

Zuengler, Jane. 1989. "Performance Variation in NS–NNS Interactions: Ethnolinguistic Difference, or Discourse Domain?" in Susan Gass et al., eds., *Variation in Second Language Acquisition: Discourse and Pragmatics.* Clevedon, Eng.: Multilingual Matters.

8

Research in the Less Commonly Taught Languages

Michael E. Everson

U.S. Air Force Academy

Introduction

One of the more noteworthy developments in foreign language education is the recent attention paid to issues concerning the so-called "less commonly taught" languages, or LCTs. Walton (1992) defines the LCTs from the perspective of foreign language education as "all languages other than French, German, and Spanish" (p. 1), then goes on to suggest three subgroups that organize the LCTs more concisely: (1) LCT European languages such as Russian, Italian, Portuguese, and Swedish; (2) higher enrollment non-Indo-European languages, such as Arabic, Chinese, and Japanese; and (3) lower-enrollment non-Indo-European languages such as Burmese, Indonesian, and Swahili. For the purposes of this chapter, the term LCT will include the languages of Arabic, Chinese, Japanese, and Russian—languages that have demonstrated stabilized or growing enrollments in the past few years, and languages that researchers are investigating with increased fervor.

Despite the encouraging enrollment figures indicating increased interest in these languages (Dandonoli 1987; Draper 1991; Brod and Huber 1992), advocates of the LCTs still foresee an uphill battle if the LCTs are to make strides in such critical areas as curricular development and teacher training (Walker 1989). Walton (1989) believes we are still at the point where the enormity of the task of teaching these languages is greatly underestimated and generally misunderstood by those who approach it. Still, on examination of edited collections, mainstream foreign language journals, and journals specific to the individual LCTs, there seems to be a growing interest among members of the LCT teaching community in such topics as classroom methodology, language testing, and curriculum development.

Michael E. Everson (Ph.D., The Ohio State University) is a Tenure Associate Professor of Chinese at the United States Air Force Academy, where he is Deputy for Academics for the Department of Foreign Languages. He researches and writes on a variety of topics dealing with reading in languages employing non-Roman orthographies. He is a member of the ACTFL SIG on research, and member of the executive board of the AERA SIG on Second Language Acquisition. His professional affiliations include ACTFL, AERA, and CLTA.

While topics specific to language instruction (generally subsumed under the seemingly all-encompassing rubric "pedagogy") are gaining acceptance, there still has been relatively little research produced involving Western learners as subjects for experimentation or observation in second-language (L2) LCT learning environments. This should not be surprising, given the number of factors that need to be in place for research to be conducted: competent researchers with expertise in the language under investigation, as well as teachers and administrators of established LCT language courses who are supportive of such research in their learning setting. Still, spokespersons for a more enlightened approach to the teaching of the LCTs agree that research is essential but decry the lack of focus among professional members about what should be investigated (Walton 1989: 25). They are also concerned because research findings are rarely translated into practice to improve classroom learning (Walker 1991: 147). Despite these criticisms, initial research has been undertaken by investigators who are attracted by the seemingly endless questions that the unique features of these languages can offer.

General Characteristics of LCT Research

A review of the literature suggests that research centering upon the LCTs falls into a limited number of categories. Moreover, at this point in the evolution of LCT research, investigators are focused not only on specific research topics, but also on similar research paradigms and data analysis procedures. To use Johnson's (this volume) six approaches to conducting research as a means of categorization, LCT research is highly experimental or quasi-experimental in nature. That is, researchers select certain variables of interest for exploration and manipulation, and then obtain measures of performance from experimental subjects to assess the effect of manipulating these variables. Researchers have concentrated their experimental efforts on the LCT reading process, as well as on classroom-based, methodological comparison studies. Correlational studies (to include more sophisticated techniques such as regression and discriminant analysis) have also been conducted to determine the power of learner variables in predicting success in selected language activities or in large-scale programs. Lastly, survey research of selected Chinese and Japanese academic programs has investigated issues germane to both teachers and learners of these languages.

The purpose of this chapter is to highlight specifically the questions asked by LCT researchers and to describe the research processes and methodologies employed to answer these questions. In addition, the more substantive findings of researchers involved in studying the LCTs are summarized. This chapter provides a comprehensive synthesis of LCT research for anyone interested in language learning and teaching and is also designed to serve as a point of departure for researchers who have experienced difficulty and frustration locating studies dealing with LCTs. To highlight the various research perspectives, Johnson's (this volume) six approaches to research serve to organize the studies. The studies are also organized topically so that common themes and questions can be explored. Lastly, the chapter proposes a general research agenda that underscores the need for better communication and collaboration among those interested in LCT research.

Common Areas of Inquiry in the LCTs: Perspectives on Reading

Before discussing the main approaches to LCT research, it might be useful to consider first what general questions have preoccupied researchers in the LCTs in the past few years. For anyone reviewing the LCT research in the more prominent foreign language journals, it becomes apparent that the lion's share of the research centers on some aspect of the reading process. Perhaps this is due to a parallel research interest in the field of ESL (Mackay, Barkman, and Jordan 1979; Alderson and Urquhart 1984) and foreign language education (Swaffar 1988; Barnett 1989; Bernhardt 1991; Swaffar, Arens, and Byrnes 1991; Swaffar and Bacon, this volume). Following the lead of L1 reading researchers, philosophers, and cognitive psychologists who broadly conceptualize the act of reading as involving both the printed page and the reader's own background knowledge, L2 researchers have long been conducting second-language studies to validate the contribution of the reader's schema in the L2 reading experience (Omaggio 1979; Adams 1982; Levine and Haus 1985; Bernhardt 1986b; among others).

While this deemphasis on text-related or "bottom-up" factors has led to more enlightened classroom teaching methodologies for L2 reading instruction, wholesale transfer of these methodologies to the LCTs is not as immediately feasible due to the difficulty learners encounter when working with new orthographic systems. According to Tzeng and Hung (1981), the significance of orthography lies in the fact that different writing systems have different script-speech relationships. Thus the acquisition of reading skills may in fact be hindered by the printed representation of the spoken language. Tzeng and Hung's (1981) view of the problems inherent in learning different orthographies seems particularly germane:

> sometimes our thinking is blocked not because we lack the necessary mental power, but because the graphemic symbols used to represent certain concepts happen to be clumsy and thus require a great deal of mental resource (central-processing capacity) in order to hold them in our working memory, let alone to further operate on them. (p. 238)

Bernhardt (1986a), in discussing the L2 reading process, hypothesizes that the "clumsiness" students experience when learning to read in non-Roman orthographies "may be due partially to a set of developmental, perceptual stages through which readers must progress in order to reach a level of preparation for comprehension" (p. 97).

The Beginnings of Cross-Orthographic Processing.

One of the first tasks the student of an LCT language must face is learning the orthography, defined as "the graphemic patterns of a written language and their mapping onto phonology, morphology, and meaning" (Henderson 1984: 1). While difficulties certainly arise for learners adjusting to languages using different alphabets, such as Russian (Leaver 1984), languages such as Arabic with its diglossia (Alosh 1991) and general lack of graphemic representation for short vowels (Robertson 1990) present curriculum designers with very special challenges. Furthermore, languages such as Chinese and Japanese offer perhaps the greatest challenges to L2 learners and the instructional process because of the radically different nature of their orthographies. Chinese, for instance, is termed a logography, where "one grapheme represents primarily the meaning (and sometimes secondarily the sound) of one word or morpheme" (Taylor and Taylor 1983: 20), and is therefore considered a more meaning-based system. The Japanese language also uses Chinese characters (known as kanji), as well as two syllabary systems (hiragana and katakana) known collectively as kana. Syllabaries are phonetic systems of writing in which each symbol represents a syllable. From a learner's standpoint, these orthographies are problematic because the spoken language maps onto print with varying degrees of regularity and systematization.

To begin the process of reading instruction, learners are generally introduced to a "helping" system whereby Arabic, Japanese, or Chinese sounds are written using the Roman alphabet. These romanization systems aid the language-learning process by providing a means by which students can rapidly acquire vocabulary and begin to use the spoken language immediately. After learners attain a limited amount of spoken proficiency, they begin learning the target language orthography and are eventually "weaned off" of the romanization. When this time comes is language dependent: If the language employs an alphabet or syllabary system, students can begin using the target-language orthography quite early in their language-learning experience. In the case of Chinese characters for which there are few clues to indicate how a character is pronounced, learners will use romanization or some other system as a working aid throughout their language-learning experience. One of the more controversial curricular issues among LCT language teachers centers on the question of when the target language writing system should be introduced to the learner (Mickel 1980; Liu 1983; Walker 1984; Hatasa 1989). Researchers in Japanese (Koda 1992; Saito 1992) seem to be more predisposed to introduce the Japanese scripts, especially the syllabaries, early on in the curriculum, given the recent emphasis on the use of authentic materials in the classroom by the L2 community in general. While the use of authentic materials has also been encouraged in Chinese, the nature of the orthography is so memory-intensive for Western learners that educators in theory and in practice are still divided on this issue.

Developing Lower-Level Processing Skills.

Perhaps the most basic question asked among researchers of the LCTs is how learners process smaller orthographic units, such as words or sentences composed in Chinese characters or Arabic script. How are these units processed and stored in memory? Do learners rely on the shape and visual characteristics of these writing systems to hold them in memory, or do they rely on the phonetic aspects of the orthography to facilitate recognition through sound mediation? Are there any aspects of the orthography itself that help or hinder word recognition? These are some of the questions asked by researchers whose work has clear antecedents in experimental verbal-learning research.

Experimental Studies

The most widely used approach to conducting research in the LCT reading process is the use of experiments. In experimental research, the investigator carefully controls and manipulates specific conditions (independent variables) and then assesses the effect of these manipulations on one or more stated outcomes (dependent variables). Perhaps the greatest advantage of this type of inquiry is that the researcher can claim a cause-and-effect relationship between the manipulated variables and their effect upon the observed behavioral measures obtained from the experimental subjects.

One of the hallmarks of true experimental design is the randomization of subjects to treatment conditions, a procedure that attempts to distribute evenly any contaminating variables that may exist within the subject population. When this is not possible due to factors beyond the control of the investigator, the experiments are termed "quasi-experimental." In many of the LCT experiments reviewed in this chapter, the necessity of using intact classes or only select members of the population under investigation dictates that many of these experiments be termed "quasi-experimental." The inability to randomize subjects tends to limit the study's external validity, the ability to generalize results to larger populations from which the subjects were drawn.

The LCT experiments also share common research designs and statistical analysis procedures. Because of the importance of comparing the performance of native-language learners with that of nonnative learners of the language, researchers often include an independent variable for language proficiency that is stratified into levels of native and nonnative subjects. Because a subject can be assigned to only one level of this variable (i.e., one cannot be a native speaker and an advanced L2 learner at the same time), these variables are known as "between-subjects" variables. On the other hand, when subjects participate in an experiment in which they will be exposed to all levels of an independent variable, the variable is termed a "within-subjects" variable, also known as a "repeated measurements" or "repeated measures" variable. Repeated measures designs are often used when, as in LCT research, the available subject pool is extremely limited. When between- and within-subject variables are analyzed within the same design, they are known as "mixed designs." When the experiment is completed, many of the researchers analyze their data through a procedure known as "analysis of variance" or ANOVA. Simply stated, ANOVA is a family of statistical procedures that evaluates whether the difference between two or more mean scores on a dependent variable occurred by chance or was indeed influenced by the experimenter's manipulation of the independent variable(s).

Developing Basic Recognition Skills

Decision Tasks.

Researchers of the LCTs have used a variety of tasks for subjects to perform so as to infer the subjects' language-processing capabilities and strategies. A common methodology used in verbal-learning experiments is to have subjects make decisions on the correctness of words or sentences shown to them by means of slide projection or computer display. Subjects, for example, might be asked to judge the correctness of the sentence "A pair is a fruit" to infer by their response whether they have visually analyzed the spelling of the word or have relied more heavily on the sound of the word to interpret the correctness of the sentence. In addition, to assess the strategies used by subjects to hold words in short-term memory, investigators project a series of words and ask the subjects to remember them. After the experimenter has removed the words from the screen, the subjects are given a list of words on a separate piece of paper and asked to circle the words they have just seen. In addition to the target words, the list contains words that look or sound like, or have similar meanings to, the target words. Through an analysis of the subjects' errors, researchers believe they can infer strategies for holding words in short-term memory.

An example of this type of study was conducted by Hayes (1988) who investigated the strategies used by native Chinese and L2 learners of Chinese to hold characters in short-term memory. Although researchers place a great deal of emphasis on the pictorial nature of the Chinese character, both researchers (Chu-chang and Loritz 1977; Treiman, Baron, and Luk 1981; Tzeng and Hung 1981) and theorists (DeFrancis 1984) maintain that Chinese characters may be processed in a more phonetic manner than had previously been thought. Hayes's line of inquiry parallels that of researchers who strive to understand the nature and extent of both visual processing and phonological encoding, which consists of "converting a printed word into a phonetic internal representation" (Taylor and Taylor 1983: 214). One of Hayes's research questions was to test whether native Chinese and L2 learners of Chinese would use different strategies for remembering Chinese characters. Designating one of his independent variables as "language level," he employed a stratified sample of native and proficient L2 readers of Chinese. To carry out his experiment, Hayes showed students a set of slides that contained a series of Chinese characters. After viewing each slide, the subjects were asked to open a booklet and circle from a series of characters any that they had seen on the slide. The target characters were embedded among other characters that either looked like, sounded like, or had the same meaning as the target characters. That is, the distractor characters were either graphically, phonetically, or semantically similar to those the students had seen on the slides. Forming the second independent variable, error type, Hayes counted the number of errors for each subject and scored whether the error was graphic, phonetic, or semantic in nature. Hayes's analysis revealed that the natives made more phonological errors than the nonnatives, indicating an acoustically oriented strategy for holding the characters in short-term memory. Nonnatives, on the other hand, used a mixed strategy of phonological and graphic processing, suggesting that their lack of a consistent, clear-cut strategy indicated a good deal of uncertainty about how to remember the characters.

Hayes also ran an experiment in which subjects read sentences that they had to judge as true or false, some of which contained semantic, phonetic, or graphic distractor characters that would invalidate the sentence. Hayes's analysis indicated that the L2 subjects made more graphic errors at the sentence level, while the errors committed by the native subjects indicated that they were using a mix of graphic and semantic strategies. Hayes hypothesized that these patterns indicated that the L2 subjects were still attending to the graphic nature of the characters, while the native subjects were processing the text for meaning.

Khaldieh (1990) used a similar methodology to investigate the strategies used by native and L2 learners in recognizing Arabic words. Khaldieh's error analysis indicated a predominantly phonological strategy on the part of the subjects, a strategy that was often faulty due to the subjects' incomplete mastery of Arabic phonology. The difficulty of mastering the Arabic script for the advanced L2 learners of Arabic was underscored by the fact that they still made a substantial number of phonological errors. Even at the advanced level of L2 learning, it appeared that learners still relied heavily on phonological strategies and had not yet attained automaticity in reading. In contrast to the L2 learners, the native subjects in the study made virtually no phonological errors in the identification task.

While Hayes's and Khaldieh's studies are useful in generating hypotheses concerning the strategies used by L2 learners to process small units of Chinese and Arabic, other studies using different response measures have focused on how characteristics of the orthography itself may influence processing.

Recall Tasks.

In modern Chinese, nouns are often composed of two-, three-, or sometimes even four-character combinations to form "words." Words composed of two characters are most prevalent in the modern language (Taylor and Taylor 1983). While some methodologists espouse the notion of learning characters individually, most textbooks arrange vocabulary into multicharacter compounds that correspond to equivalent words in English so that they may be learned in a more meaningful context. Because of the authenticity of multicharacter compounds and the fact that they more accurately reflect the structure of the modern language, Hayes (1990) attempted to determine whether "words" with increasing numbers of characters in them were more memorable for native Chinese and L2 learners. Employing a stratified sample of native Chinese and advanced L2 learners of Chinese for subjects, Hayes projected several overhead transparencies containing sentences written in Chinese characters. Each sentence contained a noun of either one, two, three, or four characters. After viewing the transparency, the subjects were instructed to write in their native language everything they remembered. His analysis indicated that while the native Chinese remembered more words overall, they remembered more one-character and four-character nouns than two-character nouns; there was no significant difference between their recall of two- and three-character words. With the L2 subjects, there was a significant difference in their remembrance of four- and two-character nouns. Hayes concluded that the L2 learners' relative familiarity with the more common two-character combinations made them less memorable while the rarity and enhanced context of the three- and four-character combinations helped make them more memorable.

Voice Latency Experiments.

Because the research suggests that L2 learners of Chinese employ visual processing strategies for certain memory tasks, researchers have also taken an interest in whether the actual stroke composition of a character in some way affects visual processing. In a post-hoc data analysis from his short-term memory experiments, Hayes (1987) determined that the correct recognition of the characters was not influenced by the number of strokes present in the characters.

Sergent and Everson (1992) revisited the issue of character complexity using a different experimental methodology. While Hayes (1987) found that in a short-term-memory recognition task, there was no effect for character complexity, Sergent and

Everson wondered whether the density of a character would affect how quickly and accurately it would be named by L2 learners of Chinese possessing different levels of proficiency. In addition, the researchers tested whether the frequency with which the characters appeared in the subjects' text would have an effect upon recognition speed and accuracy. In a character-naming experiment, one group of beginning learners and one group of advanced learners were asked to name as quickly and as accurately as possible characters that were shown to them via a 35-mm slide viewer. The stimulus characters were of either high or low density, defined by the number of strokes in each, and of either high or low frequency, defined by their frequency of occurrence in the textbook. The dependent measures were (1) the amount of time subjects took to name the character, measured by a voice-activated reaction timer, and (2) the number of correct namings, as judged by the two investigators.

In order to test how speed and accuracy were interrelated, the researchers used a mixed-design multivariate analysis of variance (MANOVA). A MANOVA is used when the researcher wishes to investigate two or more dependent variables in the same analysis. Researchers also prefer to use MANOVA over a series of univariate ANOVA's to protect against inflated Type 1 error, or finding a significant difference between groups by chance. In this study, the multivariate analysis indicated that the more proficient L2 learners named all characters faster and more accurately. Accuracy seemed to be related to the frequency with which a character appeared in the text, as the more frequently appearing characters were named more accurately. There was a less striking effect for the speed with which such characters were named, however. Unlike Hayes's (1987) post-hoc analysis, the effect of the density of the character manifested itself quite clearly on both measures and for both levels of subjects. In this case, the denser the character, the less rapidly and the less correctly characters were named, suggesting a relationship between the processing time and accuracy and the number of visual elements in the character itself.

A summary of research studies discussed in this section is given in figure 8-1.

Processing Larger Units of Text

While the individual word or character has received a significant amount of attention in the LCT research literature, investigators have also been interested in the ways in which learners process progressively larger units of text. Research questions in this area are diverse. Will learners of Chinese, for instance, read more efficiently if word boundaries are demarcated in their text? Are the two Japanese orthographies of kanji and kana processed differently by learners of Japanese? Are there patterns of oral reading errors among learners of Chinese that lend insight into their processing strategies? To investigate these questions, researchers have employed more varied research methodologies such as eye-tracking, error correction, and miscue analysis. As with the research investigating word recognition and sentence-level processing, experimental research predominates, though researchers have expanded their dependent measures to include measures involving qualitative observation.

Figure 8-1. Developing Basic Recognition Skills (A: Arabic; C: Chinese)

Study	Language	Research Question	Sample	Dependent Measure	Design & Analysis
Hayes (1988)	C	Strategies for remembering Chinese characters	17 natives, 17 L2 learners	Decision task	One between, one within ANOVA
Results: Strategies differed between natives and L2 learners; strategies also differed between character and sentence level.					
Khaldieh (1990)	A	Strategies for remembering Arabic words	9 natives, 9 beginning, 9 intermediate, 9 advanced L2 learners	Decision task	One between, one within ANOVA
Results: Groups used predominantly phonological processing strategies.					
Sergent & Everson (1992)	C	Character frequency and density	17 L2 beginners & 5 advanced L2 learners	Naming task	One between, two within MANOVA
Results: Density of character related to speed and accuracy of naming; frequency less so.					
Hayes (1990)	C	Memorability of Chinese compounds	13 natives, 13 advanced L2 learners	Recall task	One between, one within ANOVA
Results: Three- and four-character combinations are more memorable for L2 subjects.					

Eye-Tracking Experiments and the Use of Recall Protocols.

Researchers interested in quantifying the effort needed to process Chinese and Japanese have employed the use of eye-tracking as their investigative methodology. With a long tradition going back in L1 (Buswell 1922; Just and Carpenter 1980; Rayner 1983) as well as L2 reading research (Buswell 1927; Oller and Tullius 1973; Bernhardt 1985; Berkemeyer 1991), eye-tracking has been considered to be a valid measure of reading performance because of the on-line data that can be quantified and analyzed. Called "an old and enduring line of research" (Kamil 1984: 51), eye-tracking measures the duration of the eye fixation (generally agreed to be the only time the eye can acquire information for reading), the length of the jump, or saccade, between fixations (which generally correlates to a reader's experience and proficiency), and the number of backward jumps, or regressive fixations, that a reader performs to rescan parts of the text.

Recall protocols refer to a reading comprehension assessment measure wherein the subjects write in their native language everything they can remember about the passage they have just read. Both L1 and L2 reading researchers consider the recall protocol to be a valid assessment of reading comprehension, and one that does not give clues or information about the reading passage as do other, more commonly used, measures. Moreover, recall protocols provide descriptive data that elucidate the processing strategies used by the reader and potentially reveal gaps in the reader's comprehension (Aweiss 1993).

Recent L2 studies in German have yielded interesting results that only the precise measurement of eye-tracking technology can provide. Bernhardt (1986b), for instance, found that native German and experienced L2 readers of German expended more processing time on function words than on content words, a strategy that was not demonstrated by the inexperienced L2 readers used in her sample. Presumably, native and experienced L2 readers are finding cues in these function words that enhance their ability to construct meaning from the entire text, cues that have not yet been acquired by the beginning reader. Berkemeyer (1991) investigated whether learners of German would apply first-language reading skills to reading German texts. More specifically, she investigated whether manipulating a text by replacing anaphoric (pronoun) references with repeated nouns and noun phrases would aid in comprehension and processing, since gendered pronouns and their referents are sometimes confused by L2 learners. The results of her subjects' reading this altered version and the authentic version of the text indicated that there was no difference in the subjects' performance regardless of which text they read.

Assessing the effects of reading altered text has also been of interest to researchers in the LCTs. Everson (1986) used eye-tracking to investigate the effects of artificially spacing a Chinese text so that the boundaries between words were demarcated. This demarcation is not done in authentic Chinese texts except when punctuation is used; that is, there are no spaces in Chinese texts to show boundaries between words. Everson's native Chinese and L2 subjects read an artificially spaced text and the same text spaced normally while a special computer program monitored and recorded their eye movements. After the reading, the subjects wrote recall protocols in their native language so that their comprehension could be evaluated. His findings indicated that the manipulated text had more of a disruptive influence on the advanced L2 subjects, but not on the beginners or the Chinese natives. He hypothesized that the beginners were at such an initial level of reading Chinese that the spatial manipulation had no effect, while the native readers had such robust strategies that they could process the manipulated text with ease. The advanced L2 learners, on the other hand, while familiar with Chinese orthography, may not have had strategies that were sufficiently robust to allow them to ignore the manipulation. Consequently, the manipulated text seemed to disrupt their reading. Everson also found that unlike the other eye-tracking measures, fixation duration did not differ significantly between the two L2 learner groups. He concluded that this variable demonstrates the processing demands put on L2 learners of Chinese regardless of proficiency level and may be symptomatic of a processing plateau that is difficult to exceed.

While Chinese offers limitless research possibilities due to the difficulty of phonetic processing for L2 learners, Japanese orthography is intriguing because it contains the multiple writing systems of kanji (Chinese characters) and the syllabary systems of kana. To acquire data on how readers process these different systems, Harada (1988) conducted a similar study in which native Japanese and L2 subjects read a Japanese text printed (1) normally (with kana and kanji), (2) in kana only, and (3) in hiragana and katakana with spaces to denote word separation. An analysis of the subjects' eye-tracking and recall-protocol data led Harada to conclude that Chinese characters in the Japanese text served to demarcate boundaries in the text and served primarily as meaning carriers. Harada was also able to document a gradual decrease in fixation duration among the L2 subjects when reading the texts that did not contain kanji. This was most probably due to the decrease in processing demands provided by the all-kana texts. Across the board, readers required less fixation time to process kana, indicating qualitatively different processing demands associated with logographies and syllabaries.

Measures of Speed and Accuracy.

While eye-tracking technology can quantify many of the physical manifestations of microprocessing during the act of reading, researchers have used reading time as an indicator of reading proficiency because faster reading speed suggests the presence of automatic processing (LaBerge and Samuels 1974). This variable is often compared with some measure of reading comprehension or error analysis to determine correlations between speed and accuracy.

Saito (1992), for example, compared the speed and accuracy demonstrated by native Japanese and L2 learners of Japanese reading (1) a normal text and (2) the same text written in hiragana only. She further added (3) a normal version of the text from which the (kana) relational particles were deleted—particles that in Japanese serve as case markers for nouns. The dependent measures in the study were reading time, comprehension as derived from subjects' reading protocols, and the rate at which subjects were able to supply the missing relationals in the text. To supplement her quantitative findings, Saito also conducted interviews after the experiment to assess the effects of omitting the relationals. Her qualitative interview data indicated that the Japanese readers found it difficult to read the manipulated texts but were still able to supply enough information from other knowledge sources so that comprehension did not suffer. The more inexperienced readers of Japanese were not as sensitive to the relational deletion, relying more on vocabulary knowledge than on grammatical cuing to build meaning. Furthermore, the qualitative interviews indicated that both intermediate and advanced L2 readers were comfortable with the mixture of kanji and kana in the normal text; however, when the text was transformed primarily into kanji due to relational deletion, or when the kanji in the text were deleted and replaced totally by kana, both groups found the processing difficult. It is possible that L2 learners of Japanese find the two writing systems to be complementary; that is, the syllabary systems of hiragana and katakana provide "processing relief" from the memory-intensive kanji. Kanji, on the other hand, may provide visual demarcation of word units in text, as well as give stronger semantic cues than the phonologically based kana.

Another study employing speed and accuracy of reading was conducted by Everson (1988), who investigated whether beginning learners of Chinese could read a short passage of Chinese characters faster and more accurately than the same passage in romanization. He further blocked the sample into three levels of reading proficiency to test for any interaction between the proficiency and orthography variables. The subjects were timed during the reading task; to assess comprehension, the subjects wrote recall protocols in English describing what they had read. Everson's analysis indicated that across all proficiency levels, readers took much longer to read characters than romanization and also scored much higher on the recall protocol measure for the passage written in romanization.

Miscue Analysis.

While miscue analysis has stimulated a great deal of interest among L1 researchers, it has found only limited acceptance in foreign language reading research (Allen 1976; Honeycutt 1982). This may be due to the difficulties researchers have encountered in demonstrating a relationship between miscues and comprehension; moreover, research suggests that oral reading actually impedes comprehension (Bernhardt 1983, 1986a). Yet, due to the nonalphabetic nature of Chinese orthography, Sergent (1990) used miscue analysis as his primary methodology for assessing oral reading errors. Sergent's primary research question was whether the types of miscues generated by L2 readers of Chinese would differ between advanced and highly advanced Chinese learners. His analysis indicated that for both levels of learners, there was a significantly higher proportion of graphically constrained miscues, errors that occurred when the subject mistook the reading of a character for one that was visually similar to it. Also noticeable from the data was a general lack of contextually constrained miscues, or errors syntactically and semantically consistent with context prior to the miscue. Sergent hypothesized that while these readers were advanced in the sense that they had taken Chinese for some time, they were as yet not proficient readers of Chinese and therefore did not demonstrate the characteristics of good readers through their miscues. Thus it appears that the predominant use of graphically constrained miscues may suggest a deficit in rapid recognition skills among these learners.

The Use of Think-Aloud Protocols.

Think-aloud protocols require readers to actually talk out loud about their reading processes and strategies during the act of silent reading, thus giving the researcher a mentalistic measure from which to draw conclusions about the metacognitive strategies employed by the reader. In a study designed to investigate how readers generate causal links in the construction of meaning, Horiba (1990) analyzed the think-aloud protocols of native readers and advanced learners of Japanese. She also used recall protocols to investigate the type of information that was recalled by both groups. Horiba also investigated the effect of repeated readings on the reading strategies of these two groups. To analyze the data, she scored the think-aloud protocols and the recall protocols for propositional analysis and causal structure and then subjected the means to statistical analysis. The think-aloud protocols indicated that the L2 readers were heavily involved in self-monitoring of vocabulary comprehension; additionally, significant attention was being paid to language mechanics. The L1 readers, on the other hand, made frequent inferences and elaborations from background knowledge, indicating more detailed schematization and attention to conceptualizing the story. Moreover, the L1 readers' performance was more causally coherent than that of the L2 readers. With regard to the repeated reading variable, the second reading was beneficial to the L2 group, as it generally improved their recall and increased the number of causal structure units, while the questions learners asked decreased from their first reading. This increase in comprehension from one reading to the next has also been empirically demonstrated with L2 readers of German (Bernhardt 1983).

Zamojska-Hutchins (1986) also employed a combination of think-aloud protocols and quantitative measures to determine the reading strategies used by beginning and intermediate students of Russian. The study specifically investigated the impact of providing the title of a passage, cultural elements, and verb modules that supplied morphological information to enhance comprehension. Zamojska-Hutchins observed the students while they were reading, tape-recorded the students' perceived strategies during the reading (Hosenfeld 1977), and had test administrators document the reading strategies of the readers. She also administered reading tests to analyze the subjects' reading performance. After an analysis of the qualitative data, Zamojska-Hutchins felt that Hosenfeld's list of reading strategies could be expanded to include strategies such as the use of verb morphology to derive meaning, reviewing the text more than once to verify assumptions about the meaning, and devoting maximum attention to the task. She also found that supplying a combination of title, culture, and verb-module information led to the greatest improvement in the readers' comprehension. Of these three factors, supplying the verb module seemed to be the factor most responsible for increasing comprehension.

A summary of research studies reviewed in this section is provided in figure 8-2.

Critique of the LCT Reading Studies

While researchers have made promising beginnings in the area of LCT reading research, there are issues that researchers need to consider for the future. First, much of the research conducted in LCT reading lacks overall context. In other words, researchers have their subjects perform selected tasks, then report the results without describing the language-learning setting in which their subjects acquired their language ability. In a sense, the research has focused so finely on "bits" of reading that an overall grasp of the more holistic process of reading remains elusive. Thus, we are left with intriguing results that are often difficult to link to an overall framework.

Another contextual problem lies in the very general nature of the description of the subjects. Subjects are often blocked in the research design according to the number of contact hours they have had in the language, or according to their performance on a language proficiency test. If investigators do not exercise greater precision in assigning subjects to groups, the unchecked variability tends to mask effects that might have been detected if more rigorous design procedures had been employed. Again, more descriptive data is needed to operationalize more accurately what is really meant, for example, by the term "intermediate level learner of Chinese."

Lastly, LCT reading research needs to be guided and organized by better theory. At present, much of the theoretical base used by LCT researchers is borrowed from either L1 research or L2 research involving the more commonly taught languages. Perhaps it is time for researchers to collaborate on a model of reading that seems particular to an LCT language and then proceed with the age-old process of verifying or rejecting hypotheses so as to define the model further. Researchers have certainly provided a promising start in quantitatively documenting reading performance through a variety of methodologies. What remains now is for them to apply these data in the productive process of theory and model building so as to eventually inform classroom teaching and learning.

Figure 8-2. Processing Larger Units of Text (C: Chinese; J: Japanese; R: Russian)

Study	Language	Research Question	Sample	Dependent Measure	Design & Analysis
Everson (1986)	C	Effect of manipulating Chinese text	6 native, 6 beginning L2 learners, 6 advanced L2 learners	Eye-tracking measures; recall protocols	One between, one within ANOVA
Results: Advanced L2 learners found artificially spaced text disruptive.					
Harada (1988)	J	Effect of manipulating orthographic presentation	8 native, 6 intermediate, 6 beginning L2 learners	Eye-tracking measures; recall protocols	One between, one within MANOVA
Results: Hiragana easier to process than kanji.					
Saito (1992)	J	Effect of manipulating orthographic and grammatical presentation	22 native, 36 advanced, 41 intermediate, L2 learners	Recall protocols: correction task; interviews	3 × 3 factorial ANOVA
Results: Manipulated text more difficult to process.					
Everson (1988)	C	Effect of reading in romanization vs. characters	60 beginning L2 learners	Recall protocols	2 × 3 factorial MANOVA
Results: L2 subjects at this stage read faster and comprehend more in romanization.					
Sergent (1990)	C	Relationship between error types and proficiency	10 advanced, 10 highly advanced L2 learners	Miscue analysis	One between, one within ANOVA
Results: Tendency for L2 readers to rely on visual strategies for processing the characters.					
Horiba (1990)	J	Relationship between reader-generated causal links and reading comprehension	9 native, 11 advanced learners	Think aloud protocols; recall protocols	T-tests; qualitative analysis
Results: Native readers recalled greater number of causal links; L2 readers' recall of causal links improved when text was reread.					
Zamojska-Hutchins (1986)	R	Effect of providing title, cultural, and verb information	13 beginning, 11 intermediate L2 learners	Observation; comprehension measures; tape recording of think-aloud protocols	ANOVA; analysis of think-aloud protocols
Results: Readers' comprehension is influenced by availability of background information.					

The Perception and Acquisition of the Spoken Language

We have seen the overwhelming interest researchers have demonstrated in investigating how learners of the LCTs acquire basic and, to a certain extent, advanced reading skills. But characteristics of the spoken language have been attractive for researchers as well. What strategies, for example, do learners employ when the sound system of their L2 is different from that of their native language?

Perceptual Data Measures and Error Analysis.

Alosh (1987), for example, investigated the perceptual strategies used by L2 learners of Arabic when aurally perceiving pharyngealized consonants. Alosh employed native Arabic speakers and beginning, intermediate, and advanced learners of Arabic in an experiment designed to test the subjects' ability to perceive pharyngealization. His analysis revealed that natives generally ascribed pharyngealization to the consonant while most of the L2 learners ascribed it to the contiguous vowel, indicating that the vowel is a more powerful cue in aiding phonetic perception for L2 learners. Alosh's data also indicated that the L2 subjects' level of proficiency was a crucial factor in their ability to perceive pharyngealization of the consonant, suggesting the critical role of exposure in aiding correct sound perception among L2 learners of Arabic.

Shen (1989) investigated the difficulty L2 learners experience in acquiring the tonal system of Mandarin Chinese. She began with the hypothesis that in L1 child acquisition, the first and fourth tones are easiest to acquire and the contoured tones (second and third) more difficult. She also investigated whether Americans make errors of register through using a low voice register to articulate high tones, and vice versa. Shen recorded beginning learners reading texts printed in romanization, which were subsequently scored for accuracy by four Chinese evaluators. She then subjected the recordings to acoustical analysis whereby the subjects' pitch range could be established. Shen's findings indicated a great amount of variability, with the subjects clearly dividing themselves into two groups of proficient and less proficient learners. When Shen analyzed the data generated by the more proficient group in isolation, there were no differences in errors according to tone, but when the analysis included the whole sample, tones one and four accounted for the most errors. In addition, both groups seemed to experience problems using appropriate tonal register.

Because the normal pitch range of American English speakers is smaller than that of native Chinese speakers, Miracle (1989) hypothesized that the English intonational system could affect the acquisition of the Mandarin Chinese tones. To test his hypothesis, Miracle had intermediate L2 learners of Chinese read a variety of sentences printed in romanization. Using equipment that graphically represented the speech spectrum, Miracle classified errors as either tonal register errors (pronouncing the tone in too high or low a register, based on the individual subject's tone register) or tonal contour errors (based on native-speaker models of tone production). He then compared the expected rate of errors with the observed error rate. His analysis, unlike Shen's, revealed that the error rate was divided evenly over register and contour errors, and that all tones were equally affected; it seems, however, that the rising tone was potentially more difficult for students to acquire. Miracle also found that there were significantly more errors made in the initial syllables than in the finals. The difference in the results of these studies might be due to the fact that Shen's students, who had just begun to study Chinese, found the first and fourth tones more difficult to produce. Miracle's findings revealed that these differences might indeed regularize over time. Furthermore, Shen's subjects read a paragraph in Chinese while Miracle's read a series of sentences, a difference that might have affected the experimental results.

Research has also been done in the LCTs investigating the relationship between spoken and written proficiency. Rosengrant (1987) investigated whether writing ability could be predicted on the basis of oral proficiency. This study also investigated the notion that students are more sensitive to grammatical accuracy when they write than when they speak, and that at lower levels of proficiency, a larger vocabulary may compensate for incomplete control of grammar. Rosengrant hoped to determine the extent to which the Intermediate–Mid writing description of the ACTFL Russian guidelines characterized subjects who were rated Intermediate–Mid in speaking. This was done by interviewing seven students of a third-year Russian class who, after an oral interview, wrote compositions, which allowed the researcher to compare their spoken and written proficiency. The error analysis revealed that a relationship indeed existed between the students' speaking and writing skills but unexpectedly revealed patterns of errors in the written work that were clearly tied to the students' level of oral proficiency. The analysis revealed, for instance, that when students were assigned functions appropriate to higher levels of proficiency, both the number and types of errors increased. Case, spelling, and word order errors were detected when students approached levels that were just slightly higher than their own, though when subjects were required to perform at levels much higher than their own, mistakes increased and were noticed in other grammatical areas.

A summary of studies on the perception and acquisition of spoken language reviewed in this section can be found in figure 8-3.

Critique of the Spoken Language Studies

Like many of the reading studies already discussed, research into the spoken language has largely focused upon the micro level of perception—in this case, the perception of certain sounds or tones. Miracle (1989) and Shen (1989) have provided valuable studies that have yielded some conflicting findings, perhaps due to the different tasks and subjects used in the experiments. Expanding the research into other learning contexts may provide more information to resolve these conflicts. Are there, for instance, more clear-cut patterns of tonal acquisition for learners studying Chinese in a Chinese-speaking environment overseas? How about for those learning Chinese in an immersion program in the United States?

In addition, all the spoken language studies employed relatively small sample sizes, a factor that will perhaps always plague LCT classroom-based research. To compensate for this problem, researchers might well consider a case-study approach to their research whereby the unit of analysis is an individual learner or even a class of learners observed in their language-learning environment. In this way, more descriptive data might be generated so as to account for the conflicting findings generated by our quantitative studies.

Figure 8-3. Perception and Acquisition of the Spoken Language (A: Arabic; C: Chinese; R: Russian)

Study	Language	Research Question	Sample	Dependent Measure	Design & Analysis
Alosh (1987)	A	Perceptual strategies for perceiving selected phonemes	10 native, 10 beginning, 11 intermediate, 15 advanced L2 learners	Judgment task	One between, one within ANOVA

Results: Natives ascribed pharyngealization to the consonant while most L2 subjects ascribed it to the contiguous vowel.

Study	Language	Research Question	Sample	Dependent Measure	Design & Analysis
Shen (1989)	C	Investigation of tonal acquisition	8 beginning L2 learners	Oral reading task	Error analysis

Results: Production of first and fourth tones seemed to be the most problematic.

Study	Language	Research Question	Sample	Dependent Measure	Design & Analysis
Miracle (1989)	C	Investigation of tonal acquisition	3 native, 10 intermediate L2 learners	Oral reading task	Error analysis

Results: Errors evenly divided between register and contour errors. Production of second tone problematic.

Study	Language	Research Question	Sample	Dependent Measure	Design & Analysis
Rosegrant (1987)	R	Relationship between oral proficiency and writing ability	7 intermediate L2 learners	Interview; written composition	Data comparison

Results: Relationship exists between speaking and writing skills. Patterns of errors seemed related to students' level of oral proficiency.

Methodological Comparison Research

Finding "the method" of foreign language instruction that results in the most learning for the most students has always been a subject of controversy among foreign language educators. The same is true for researchers of the LCTs, who have conducted studies that test the effects of teaching one methodology in comparison with another. The studies in this section share certain characteristics. First, while some of these questions are of interest to all language researchers, the majority of them are language-specific and represent important questions raised by researchers and practitioners within the teaching profession of a particular language. Investigating the optimum time to introduce characters into the beginning Chinese language curriculum and whether word recognition in Arabic is facilitated by adding diacritical vowel markings to introductory reading texts are examples of the language-specific nature of these questions. Second, the questions are very pedagogically driven so that if clear-cut answers are obtained, implications for curricular design, materials development, or classroom methodology seem readily apparent. Third, all the studies were conducted during an actual LCT language course, thus providing curricular context for the study. In this way, they differ from studies in which the independent variables were not specifically tied to the actual teaching of a course. Finally, all the studies use the experimental or quasi-experimental approach to research.

The question of how best to teach reading in the LCTs has always been controversial among teachers of Chinese, Japanese, and Arabic. Hatasa (1989), for example, investigated the effectiveness of pretraining sessions that were designed to explain the structural makeup of Chinese characters to learners. He also tested whether it was more beneficial to learn pictographic characters first or to learn characters of all types in the order in which they were presented in the textbook. Hatasa divided first-year Japanese students into groups, randomly determining which group would receive (1) training to introduce subjects to the structural makeup of characters, (2) a training strategy stressing the pictographic nature of characters, or (3) a presentation of the characters in the order presented in the textbook. Hatasa's analysis of the groups' performance on measures of kanji recall and production did not indicate that one method was more effective than another. This may have been due to the fact that the experimental period was too short for the differences in methodological approaches to be detected. Also, students at this level may not have needed to use strong organizational strategies, strategies that might be necessary later when the students began to learn larger amounts of kanji.

In an attempt to answer one of the more controversial questions put forth by Chinese language educators, Packard (1990) used a methodological comparison approach to investigate whether there is an optimum time to introduce characters into the beginning Chinese language curriculum. More specifically, learners from two sections of a beginning Chinese course served as subjects to investigate the effects of delaying the time when characters were introduced into the curriculum. One class learned characters immediately (the "no-lag" group), while the other class (the "lag" group) began the study of characters after a three-week time lag. Multiple measures of Chinese language performance over all four modalities were taken over the following two semesters. Over the first semester, while most tests showed no significant difference between groups, there was a significant difference between groups in a test of phonetic discrimination, with the lag group scoring higher than the no-lag group. At the end of the year, oral tests revealed that the lag group had reached a significantly higher level of oral production than the no-lag group.

In a related experiment testing the effects of teaching methodologies, Packard (1989) compared the effects of "high-pressure" instruction versus "low-pressure" instruction. He arranged for one section of Chinese to be taught using a high-pressure method in the fall semester, followed by a low-pressure method in the spring semester. Packard described the characteristics of the high-pressure method as follows: moderate-to-high tension, rapid pace, high student readiness, fast response, more emphasis on correction, and little interaction. The low-pressure method used in the spring emphasized a more relaxed classroom atmosphere, a slower pace, lower but adequate readiness, relaxed response time, less emphasis on correction, less reliance on memory tasks per se, and more student–teacher interaction. The subjects were assessed on measures of listening comprehension, grammar, and character reading and writing. The group means from the performances over the first and second semester were compared and analyzed, yielding a significant positive effect for grammar ability in the fall semester. Packard interpreted this finding to mean that the high-pressure method was beneficial for the grammar skills of students who had had no previous exposure to the Chinese language while the low-pressure method seemed to be beneficial for the auditory comprehension skills of students who had already had some experience with the language.

Comparative methodology studies have also been done in Japanese to test the difference between methods more specifically associated with foreign language learning. Samimy (1989) investigated the differences between a modified version of the audiolingual method and the Counseling-Learning approach. Samimy divided students in a Japanese class into groups and taught them Japanese by one of these two methodologies. Throughout the course, the subjects were assessed on measures of motivation, anxiety, and self-esteem, as well as on measures of communicative competence. The subsequent statistical analysis revealed no significant difference between groups on measures of desire to learn Japanese, motivational intensity, or on measures of communicative competence. There was also no significant difference between groups in terms of final course grade.

Methodological studies have also been conducted to test the effect of altering study materials. In a first-year Arabic course, Robertson (1990) tested whether the inclusion of short-vowel markings in the students' reading materials would affect the speed and accuracy with which learners recognized Arabic words. In Arabic, the diacritical markings used to indicate short-vowel phonemes are normally not used, except for instances where the oral reading of the text takes on particular importance, as in the case of the Koran. After the students were introduced to the Arabic script, one group was gradually taught Arabic words without vowel markings, while another was taught using the diacritics to represent the short vowels. At the end of the semester, the students were shown a series of Arabic words in vowelled and unvowelled format and measured on how quickly and accurately they named the words. Robertson's analysis revealed that both groups named vowelled words more slowly than unvowelled words but also pronounced vowelled words more accurately than unvowelled words. The longer reaction times suggest that learners process Arabic words letter by letter. However, the inclusion of diacritics facilitates the phonological recoding process for beginning learners.

The methodological comparison studies reviewed in this section are summarized in figure 8-4.

Critique of Methodological Comparison Research

While it is important to conduct studies that focus on language learning in the classroom environment, long-term methodological studies have certain drawbacks (Reeves 1986; Pederson 1988). First, there is an assumption implicit in conducting comparative methodological studies that the two methods are indeed different. All too often, however, there is so much overlap between the methods that any uniqueness is washed out in a sea of shared methodological characteristics. Given this situation, it is no wonder that the subsequent analysis of the dependent measures fails to detect a significant difference between groups. Second, even if the methodologies are in fact so different as to affect instructional outcomes, it is difficult to ensure that teachers provide consistent, systematic instruction according to the methodology in question. Termed "procedural slippage"

Figure 8-4. Methodological Comparison Research (A: Arabic; C: Chinese; J: Japanese)

Study	Language	Research Question	Sample	Dependent Measure	Design & Analysis
Hatasa (1989)	J	Effectiveness of pretraining session and character presentation order	110 beginning L2 learners	Kanji recognition and production	Two-way factorial ANOVA

Results: Neither training sessions nor order of kanji presentation improved subjects' kanji recognition or production.

| Packard (1989) | C | Effect of "high-pressure" vs. "low-pressure" method | 12 beginning L2 learners | Multiple proficiency measures | T-test |

Results: Most measures showed NSD between groups except when groups were broken down into language background. High-pressure method seemed beneficial for grammar skills of students with no previous background in Chinese. Low-pressure beneficial for auditory comprehension skills of students with some background in Chinese.

| Packard (1990) | C | Effect of introducing Chinese characters into curriculum at different times | 23 beginning L2 learners | Multiple proficiency measures | ANOVA |

Results: Most measures showed NSD between groups. Over first semester, lag group scored higher in phonetic transcription task, though this effect was not significant over the entire year. Oral testing indicated lag group to be more fluent in oral production.

| Samimy (1989) | J | Effect of modified audiolingual method vs. Counseling-Learning method | 29 beginning L2 learners | Multiple attitudinal and language proficiency measures | ANOVA; correlations; discriminant analysis |

Results: Most measures showed NSD between groups. Linguistic competence seemed a good predictor of communicative competence.

| Robertson (1990) | A | Effect of adding vowel markings to beginning reading texts | 48 beginning L2 learners | Speed and accuracy of word naming | ANOVA |

Results: Words with vowel markings named less quickly but more accurately than unvowelled words. Inclusion of vowel markings seems to facilitate phonological recoding process for beginning L2 learners.

by Kennedy (1978), this becomes another source of variability that will contribute to the masking of significant effects. Lastly, when researchers take multiple measures from subjects over long periods of time, they run the risk of detecting a significant difference by chance. The best guard against the wholesale acceptance of significant effects is for the study to have a strong theoretical base so that the results can be evaluated and explained within the predictive parameters laid down by theory.

Correlational Studies

What are the characteristics possessed by language learners that seem to predict success in certain language-learning settings and with certain language tasks? Do learners from language backgrounds that have orthographical characteristics similar to Japanese, for example, have an advantage over American students studying this language? Is there a relationship between selected affective variables and performance in Japanese?

To answer these questions, researchers collect data on student attitudes, personality, and language performance and use correlational methods to assess the strength of the relationship between the variables of interest. One drawback of correlational research is that the variables of interest cannot in most cases be directly manipulated, and so the researcher cannot claim a causal relationship between them. While correlation is generally used to measure the degree of association between variables, researchers prefer statistical techniques such as multiple regression when their goal is to predict the effect of multiple independent variables on a dependent variable. Other techniques such as discriminant analysis are used to predict group membership on the basis of a set of predictor variables.

Predicting Success in Language Learning

An example of a study using correlation and discriminant analysis was conducted by Koda (1989). She investigated whether learners of Japanese who came from language backgrounds with similar orthographic systems transfer these skills to the learning of Japanese and therefore outperform American students. Koda divided members of a first year Japanese class into two groups: One group consisted of students with Korean and Chinese backgrounds (the kanji group) and one group consisted of American learners (the nonkanji group). Several Japanese language proficiency measures were used to investigate which variables separated the two groups. Koda's correlational and discriminant analysis revealed that the kanji group performed better in all test batteries and across time, and that vocabulary knowledge was the single most significant factor distinguishing the two groups. Vocabulary knowledge correlated the most highly with reading comprehension, indicating that the advantage in vocabulary knowledge among members of the kanji group benefited them as the task complexity increased.

Koda (1992) also investigated the relationship between lower-level processing skills (defined as extracting visual information from print, such as letter identification and word recognition) and L2 reading comprehension in Japanese. She collected reading-comprehension and verbal-processing data from students enrolled in a beginning Japanese course during two separate stages in their learning experience. The correlational and regression analysis indicated that kanji recognition was the single significant factor in the first stage, and that recognition of both hiragana and kanji were significant in the second stage. This finding suggests that L2 readers of Japanese rely almost exclusively on kanji during the initial stages of their reading development. As learners improve, however, they tend to rely more on syllabary recognition skills to achieve comprehension. Koda hypothesized that the initial meaning retrieval process may be easier with kanji than with hiragana because of the kanji's meaning-based nature. Also, the visual characteristics of kanji seem to be more salient when placed among hiragana in the printed array.

In a different experiment, Koda (1990) administered similar test batteries to first-year Japanese students to differentiate between good and poor readers. While the regression analyses again revealed a significant effect for vocabulary knowledge, she found that particle knowledge was the most distinguishing factor separating the two groups. Koda hypothesized that grammatical particles are "essential to sentence comprehension and are language specific" (p. 413). They are obviously important cues in signaling the syntactic structure of the target language, cues that better learners are using to build comprehension. This is a significant finding in that it attests to the role of grammatical knowledge in accounting for individual differences among good and poor readers. Moreover, the good readers' more efficient symbol identification and the high correlations between verbal processing speed and comprehension point out the importance of efficient verbal processing skills, something that has been a general finding in L2 reading research (Bernhardt and James 1987).

Quantitative Analysis of Questionnaire Data

Researchers have used questionnaires to elicit data from subjects about their attitudes, motivations, and feelings about their language-learning experiences. Although this approach to inquiry could easily fall under the category of "survey research," it is common for researchers to collect attitudinal data from subjects and then look for relationships between these attitudes and the learners' proficiency in the language. Samimy and Tabuse (1992) used a combination of questionnaires and achievement test data to determine whether the difficulty of learning Japanese would trigger negative affective reactions that might affect both progress and performance. During the autumn and spring quarters of a beginning Japanese course, the researchers administered questionnaires to gather data on selected variables such as language-class risk-taking, sociability, and discomfort. The researchers also gathered background and attitudinal data from the students. The correlational and stepwise regression analysis indicated that initially, variables such as gender, undergraduate vs. graduate student status, and language-class risk-taking were significant factors in determining class achievement. At the end of three quarters, however, strength of motivation and use of opportunities to speak the target language out of class were the best determinants of the students' final grades. In both the autumn and the spring quarters, the analysis indicated that the students' risk taking ability was significantly influenced by language-class discomfort.

Investigators have also used regression analysis to assess the effectiveness of language programs. In an ongoing study designed to assess the contribution of study abroad in Russia to L2 gain, Brecht, Davidson, and Ginsberg (1991) began an extensive database consisting of aptitude, motivation, personality, and language-proficiency measures obtained from learners before and after their study-abroad experience. Among the preliminary findings are that students with knowledge of other non-Slavic languages gain more on average than students who have not studied another language. In addition, students who have previously been involved in a domestic or foreign immersion program also tend to gain more. There is also an indication that leadership potential is positively correlated with all measures of achievement.

A summary of the correlational studies reviewed in this section is provided in figure 8-5.

Figure 8-5. Predicting Success in Language Learning (J: Japanese; R: Russian)

Study	Language	Research Question	Sample	Dependent Measure	Design & Analysis
Koda (1989)	J	Transfer of skills from learners with orthographic backgrounds similar to Japanese	24 beginning L2 learners	Multiple proficiency measures	Correlations; discriminant analysis; multiple ANOVAs

Results: Orthographic background similar to Japanese seemed to transfer to learning of Japanese.

Study	Language	Research Question	Sample	Dependent Measure	Design & Analysis
Koda (1990)	J	What differentiates good and poor readers	39 beginning L2 learners	Multiple proficiency measures	Correlations; stepwise regression and discriminant analysis

Results: Particle knowledge and symbol identification speed were the most significant factors distinguishing good from poor readers.

Study	Language	Research Question	Sample	Dependent Measure	Design & Analysis
Koda (1992)	J	Relationship between lower-level processing skills and reading comprehension	58 beginning learners	Multiple proficiency measures	Correlation; multiple regression

Results: Efficiency in verbal processing significantly contributed to successful text comprehension.

Study	Language	Research Question	Sample	Dependent Measure	Design & Analysis
Samimy & Tabuse (1992)	J	What best predicts final course grades	70 beginning L2 learners	Questionnaires	Correlations; stepwise regression

Results: Risk-taking, motivation, and opportunities to speak Japanese outside of class were the best determinants of final grades.

Study	Language	Research Question	Sample	Dependent Measure	Design & Analysis
Brecht et al. (1991)	R	Contribution of study abroad on L2 gain	Database of L2 learners	Pre-, Post- measures	Multiple regression

Results: Students having previous experience with non-Slavic language or immersion experience tended to gain more.

Critique of Correlational Studies

With the advent of large mainframe and personal computers, researchers can now perform complex statistical analyses with ease. When performing correlational or regression-type analyses, however, it is important that researchers use instruments that reflect the construct they are attempting to evaluate. If the measuring instruments do not adequately reflect the construct under investigation, the researcher will be hard pressed to make any meaningful interpretation of the data. As with all research, common sense and a firm theoretical base will aid the researcher in developing precise measurement instruments. In addition, researchers need to be sensitive to the number of subjects or "cases" they have available for their studies. Stevens (1986) recommends the use of about 15 subjects per predictor when using multiple regression to ensure a reliable regression equation that is generalizable to another independent sample. Others (Tabachnick and Fidell 1983) believe a more ideal case-to-variable ratio is 20:1, and recommend an increase to 40:1 if the researcher is running a stepwise regression procedure because of its notorious capitalization on chance. Unless the LCT researcher is able to construct a large database over time that gives the desired case-to-variable ratio, multiple-regression procedures must be used with caution.

Survey Research

Survey research involves the collection and analysis of information about groups or institutions of interest to the language-learning profession. Are there, for example, agreed-upon standards used by high school teachers of Chinese? If high school learners of Japanese decide to continue their study of Japanese at the university, at what level can they be expected to begin their university study? Two very extensive surveys investigated these questions in the larger context of high school Chinese language programs and the general state of Japanese language learning in America.

Moore, Walton, and Lambert (1992) investigated a host of issues dealing with Chinese language teaching and learning in high schools. The study surveyed teachers, principals, and alumni of selected high schools that had been funded by the Dodge Foundation in an effort to encourage the study of Chinese in the secondary school setting. Jorden and Lambert (1991) used an even wider focus by surveying precollegiate and postsecondary institutions teaching Japanese. While these two studies collected data on a host of variables, two of the more problematic responses concern the areas of standards and articulation with university programs. As concerns course standards, Moore, Walton, and Lambert state that "there is a lack of consensus among teachers on what the ideal curriculum should be; on which skills should be emphasized; on the choice of phonetic transcription systems; on the type and number of characters that students should learn; on the selection and timing of specific linguistic patterns to be taught; and on the proper emphasis on and way of teaching Chinese culture" (p. 119). The precollegiate Japanese curricula seem to suffer the same symptoms and "do not, as yet, reflect a generally agreed-upon course of study, nor generally accepted standards" (Jorden and Lambert 1991: 180).

Another issue of concern is the lack of articulation between high school and university programs. "Data from a survey of Dodge program graduates who had gone on to college indicated that 65 percent of these students had taken additional Chinese language courses in college. Almost half of them (43 percent) were placed in the first term of college courses, and two-thirds (66 percent) were placed in the first year" (Moore, Walton, and Lambert 1992: 121–22). In Japanese "a significant percentage of those who had studied in high school, including 42 percent of those who had studied for all four years, began their Japanese study in college as first-year, first-semester beginners" (Jorden and Lambert 1992: 180). Clearly, creation and articulation of standards will be an ongoing challenge for administrators involved with the LCTs.

Critique of Survey Research

The National Foreign Language Center is to be commended for providing a broad-based profile of Japanese language instruction and high school Chinese language instruction in the United States. The authors went to great lengths to present the data as honestly as possible, stressing, for instance, the high standards and atypical nature of high schools originally selected to receive financial grants from the Dodge Foundation, schools that were eventually participants in this survey. Thus the survey represents "the most favorable case" (Moore, Walton, and Lambert 1992: 10) for depicting the instruction of these two languages.

Perhaps the greatest contribution of comprehensive survey research such as this is that it informs policymakers and administrators when our efforts under the most favorable conditions are not yielding acceptable results. The findings of these surveys that indicate shortcomings in such fundamentally important areas as teacher development, curriculum articulation and standards, and program evaluation are therefore very useful in highlighting areas for professional improvement.

The Future of Research in the LCTs

Framing a research agenda of the future can be facilitated by examining the ACTFL priorities for research. Bailey et al. (1991) suggest that three major areas should receive special focus: (1) acquisition in various classroom settings as compared with natural situations, (2) learner needs and characteristics, and (3) the role of the teacher and teacher preparation.

Before considering such an agenda for the LCTs, we must remember that the number of researchers actively investigating the LCTs is very small. Perhaps an ACTFL priority of the future should address the importance of training researchers as well as teachers so that inquiry into these languages can be undertaken in earnest. Certainly, the short-term answer to this problem is to form cooperative ventures so that teams of experts can bring their collective knowledge to bear in conceptualizing and carrying out research studies. In this way, research will become more interdisciplinary in nature and thus bring larger scope and richer conceptualization to the research process. With more diversified research expertise, we can begin to expand the focus of our research agenda to include not only the classroom setting but natural acquisition settings as well. One of our primary goals should be to produce research that is multidimensional in scope.

In the second research area—learner needs and characteristics—we can detect an obvious need for more qualitative research, research that more fully takes the learning environment into consideration. Much of the research cited in this chapter has been quantitative in nature, documenting performance that is largely based on theory generated by researchers in first-language acquisition or in the more commonly taught languages. Descriptive, ethnographic studies need to be conducted so as to articulate the *process* of learning the LCTs as much as the *product*. Much of the quantitative research carried out so far has been extremely helpful in generating baseline data with which to compare the performance of native and nonnative learners. Most of the studies reported in this chapter used research designs and statistical analysis more commonly employed with larger samples, a luxury that LCT research seldom enjoys. While statistical techniques such as power analysis and effect size can aid in the interpretation of small-group studies, descriptive research can yield rich data with which to form hypotheses for further testing. How, for instance, do learners study outside class? What are the strategies that successful learners use to learn and integrate new vocabulary in a non-Roman orthography? What are effective means of practice for students learning new orthographies, and what seem to be ineffective strategies? How do learners differ in cognitive style and strategy use? If it is indeed correct that the culture of the peoples who speak these languages "presents a complexity greater than the linguistic code" (Walker 1989: 125), will the data generated from discourse analysis studies help us construct the proper models with which to evaluate whether the culture and the code are being given effective classroom treatment? Finally, while research in reading seems to have received a great deal of attention, should we not be equally intrigued by questions related to listening, speaking, and writing proficiency? Have we constructed skill acquisition models that highlight the processing strategies that Western students need to develop? In other words, are we building theory along with databases? The research until now has provided snapshots of many of these processes, but only theory building and verification through testing will provide a strong framework from which to draw pedagogical conclusions.

Bailey et al. (1991) assert that "the teacher is, of course, a key variable in most language learning programs" (p. 89). Moreover, Moore, Walton, and Lambert's (1992) survey data dealing with secondary-level Chinese indicate that the principals, students, and teachers themselves believe "the success of a program depends most heavily on the skill and enthusiasm of the teacher" as well as "the degree of the teacher's professionalization" (p. 118). If this is indeed true, perhaps the time has come for prospective teachers of the LCTs to receive additional coursework in teaching methodology that is particular to the languages that they will teach. This strategy is currently being used to train LCT teachers in programs such as the Iowa Critical Languages Program, a collaborative effort involving the Ford Foundation, the University of Iowa, and Iowa school districts to train and place outstanding teachers of Chinese, Japanese, and Russian (Schrier 1993; Schrier and Everson 1993).

While these recommendations are clearly ones we may wish to follow, there are certain realities that may delay their implementation, at least on a large scale. Brecht (1991) puts things into perspective by commenting on the lack of collective action and a common voice in the debate over both foreign language and international studies. He also states that there "is no central source of information on programs or organizations" (p. 153). Indeed, the situation is similar for those seeking information on data-based research studies in the LCTs. When searching databases for such studies, one often discovers a certain degree of inconsistency in the storage and cataloging of the research. There are, however, indications that this situation may be changing. The National Foreign Language Center in Washington, D.C., has hosted several meetings of LCT representatives to help organize priorities for the future. The recent formation of the National Council of Organizations of Less Commonly Taught Languages is also a hopeful sign that the LCTs will have a central forum for voicing and publicizing their concerns. Perhaps this organization could serve as a clearinghouse for research studies that involve a larger variety of LCTs than has been cited here, as well as become a leader in encouraging LCT organizations to create their own language-specific research components within their organization to stimulate the research process. In this way, we can at least begin to answer some of the questions that can inform the process of teaching these challenging and interesting languages, languages that will be in the forefront of foreign language education as we begin the twenty-first century.

References

Research in the Less Commonly Taught Languages

Adams, Shirley J. 1982. "Scripts and the Recognition of Unfamiliar Vocabulary: Enhancing Second Language Reading Skills." *Modern Language Journal* 66,2: 155–59.

Alderson, J. Charles, and A. H. Urquhart, eds., 1984. *Reading in a Foreign Language.* London, Eng.: Longman.

Allen, Edward D. 1976. "Miscue Analysis: A New Tool for Diagnosing Reading Proficiency in Foreign Languages." *Foreign Language Annals* 9: 563–67.

Alosh, Mahdi. 1987. "The Perception and Acquisition of Pharyngealized Fricatives by American Learners of Arabic and Implications for Teaching Arabic Phonology." Unpublished Ph.D. diss., The Ohio State Univ., Columbus.

———. 1991. "Arabic Diglossia and Its Impact on Teaching Arabic as a Foreign Language," in Gerard L. Ervin, ed., *International Perspectives on Foreign Language Teaching.* Lincolnwood, IL: National Textbook.

Aweiss, Salem. 1993. "Reading Comprehension Assessment Measures: The Recall Protocol Revisited," in William N. Hatfield, ed., *Visions and Reality in Foreign Language Teaching: Where We Are, Where We Are Going.* Lincolnwood, IL: National Textbook.

Bailey, Kathleen M., Alice Omaggio Hadley, Sally Sieloff Magnan, and Janet Swaffar. 1991. "Research in the 1990s: Focus on Theory Building, Instructional Innovation, and Collaboration." *Foreign Language Annals* 24,2: 89–100.

Barnett, Marva A. 1989. *More Than Meets the Eye: Foreign Language Reading.* Englewood Cliffs, NJ: Prentice-Hall.

Berkemeyer, Victoria C. 1991. "The Effect of Anaphora on the Reading of German," in Jerry Zutell and Sandra McCormick, eds., *Learner Factors/Teacher Factors: Issues in Literacy Research and Instruction.* Fortieth Yearbook of the National Reading Conference. Chicago: The National Reading Conference.

Bernhardt, Elizabeth B. 1983. "Three Approaches to Reading Comprehension in Intermediate German." *Modern Language Journal* 67,2: 111–15.

———. 1985. "Cognitive Processes in L2: An Examination of Reading Behaviors," in John Lantolf and Angela Labarca, eds., *Delaware Symposium on Second Language Acquisition in the Classroom Setting.* Norwood, NJ: Ablex.

————. 1986a. "Reading in the Foreign Language," in Barbara H. Wing, ed., *Listening, Reading, Writing: Analysis and Application*. Middlebury, VT: Northeast Conference on the Teaching of Foreign Languages.

————. 1986b. "A Model of L2 Text Reconstruction: The Recall of Literary Text by Learners of German," in Angela Labarca, ed., *Issues in L2: Theory as Practice, Practice as Theory*. Norwood, NJ: Ablex.

————. 1991. *Reading Development in a Second Language: Theoretical, Empirical and Classroom Perspectives*. Norwood, NJ: Ablex.

————, and Charles J. James. 1987. "The Teaching and Testing of Comprehension in Foreign Language Learning," in Diane W. Birckbichler, ed., *Proficiency, Policy, and Professionalism in Foreign Language Education*. Lincolnwood, IL: National Textbook.

Brecht, Richard D. 1991. "Reaction." *Foreign Language Annals* 24,2: 151–53.

————, Dan E. Davidson, and Ralph B. Ginsberg. 1991. "The Empirical Study of Proficiency Gain among American Students of Russian," in Thomas J. Garza and Alexandr A. Barchenkov, eds., *Proceedings of the First Soviet-American Symposium on Theoretical Problems of Foreign Language Teaching and Learning*. Moscow, Russia: Rema.

Brod, Richard, and Bettina J. Huber. 1992. "Foreign Language Enrollments in United States Institutions of Higher Education, Fall 1990." *ADFL Bulletin* 23,3: 6–10.

Buswell, Guy T. 1922. "Fundamental Reading Habits: A Study of Their Development." *Supplementary Educational Monographs* 21. Chicago: Univ. of Chicago.

————. 1927. *A Laboratory Study of the Reading of Modern Foreign Languages*. New York: Macmillan.

Chu-chang, Mae, and Donald J. Loritz. 1977. "Even Chinese Ideographs Are Phonologically Encoded in Short-Term Memory." *Language Learning* 27: 75–84.

Dandonoli, Patricia. 1987. "Report on Foreign Language Enrollment in Public Secondary Schools, Fall 1985." *Foreign Language Annals* 20,5: 457–70.

DeFrancis, John. 1984. *The Chinese Language: Fact and Fantasy*. Honolulu: Univ. of Hawaii Press.

Draper, Jamie B. 1991. "Foreign Language Enrollments in Public Secondary Schools, Fall 1989 and Fall 1990." Yonkers, NY: American Council on the Teaching of Foreign Languages.

Everson, Michael E. 1986. "The Effect of Word-Unit Spacing upon the Reading Strategies of Native and L2 Readers of Chinese: An Eye-Tracking Study." Unpublished Ph.D. diss., The Ohio State Univ., Columbus.

————. 1988. "Speed and Comprehension in Reading Chinese: Romanization vs. Characters Revisited." *Journal of the Chinese Language Teachers Association* 23,2: 1–16.

Harada, Fumiko K. 1988. "The Effect of Three Different Orthographical Presentations of a Text upon the Reading Behaviors of Native and L2 Readers of Japanese: An Eye-Tracking Study." Unpublished Ph.D. diss., The Ohio State Univ., Columbus.

Hatasa, Kazumi. 1989. "A Study of Learning and Teaching of Kanji for L2 Learners of Japanese." Unpublished Ph.D. diss., Univ. of Illinois at Urbana-Champaign.

Hayes, Edmund B. 1987. "The Relationship between Chinese Character Complexity and Character Recognition." *Journal of the Chinese Language Teachers Association* 22,2: 45–57.

————. 1988. "Encoding Strategies Used by Native and L2 Readers of Chinese Mandarin." *Modern Language Journal* 72: 188–95.

————. 1990. "The Relationship between 'Word Length' and Memorability among L2 Readers of Chinese Mandarin." *Journal of the Chinese Language Teachers Association* 25,3: 31–41.

Henderson, Leslie. 1984. "Introduction," in Leslie Henderson, ed., *Orthographies and Reading: Perspectives from Cognitive Psychology, Neuropsychology, and Linguistics.* Hillsdale, NJ: Erlbaum.

Honeycutt, Charles A. 1982. "A Study of the Second-Language Reading Process Using a Cloze Procedure, Miscue Analysis, and Story Retelling with Third-Year High School French Students." Unpublished Ph.D. diss., The Ohio State Univ., Columbus.

Horiba, Yukie. 1990. "Narrative Comprehension Processes: A Study of Native and L2 Readers of Japanese." *Modern Language Journal* 74: 188–202.

Hosenfeld, Carol. 1977. "A Learning-Teaching View of Second Language Instruction: The Learning Strategies." Unpublished Ph.D. diss., The Ohio State Univ., Columbus.

Jorden, Eleanor H., with Richard D. Lambert. 1991. *Japanese Language Instruction in the United States: Resources, Practice, and Investment Strategy.* National Foreign Language Center Monograph Series. Washington, DC: National Foreign Language Center.

Just, Marcel, and Patricia Carpenter. 1980. "A Theory of Reading: From Eye Fixations to Comprehension." *Psychological Review* 87: 329–54.

Kamil, Michael L. 1984. "Current Traditions of Reading Research," in P. David Pearson, ed., *Handbook of Reading Research.* New York: Longman.

Kennedy, John Joseph. 1978. *An Introduction to the Design and Analysis of Experiments in Education and Psychology.* Lanham, MD: University Press of America.

Khaldieh, Salim A. 1990. "The Role of Phonological Encoding (Speech Recoding) and Visual Processes in Word Recognition of American Learners of Arabic as a Foreign Language." Unpublished Ph.D. diss., The Ohio State Univ., Columbus.

Koda, Keiko. 1989. "The Effects of Transferred Vocabulary Knowledge on the Development of L2 Reading Proficiency." *Foreign Language Annals* 22,6: 529–40.

———. 1990. "Factors Affecting Second Language Text Comprehension." *Literacy Theory and Research: Analyses from Multiple Paradigms.* Thirty-Ninth Yearbook of the National Reading Conference. Chicago: The National Reading Conference.

———. 1992. "The Effects of Lower-Level Processing Skills on Foreign Language Reading Performance: Implications for Instruction." *Modern Language Journal* 76: 502–12.

LaBerge, D., and S. Jay Samuels. 1974. "Toward a Theory of Automatic Information Processing in Reading." *Cognitive Psychology* 6: 293–323.

Leaver, Betty Lou. 1984. "Twenty Minutes to Mastery of the Cyrillic Alphabet." *Foreign Language Annals* 17,3: 215–20.

Levine, Martin G., and George J. Haus. 1985. "The Effect of Background Knowledge on the Reading Comprehension of Second Language Learners." *Foreign Language Annals* 18,5: 391–97.

Liu, Irene. 1983. "The Learning of Characters: A Conceptual Learning Approach." *Journal of the Chinese Language Teachers Association* 19,2: 65–76.

Mackay, Ronald, Bruce Barkman, and R. R. Jordan. 1979. *Reading in a Second Language.* Rowley, MA: Newbury House.

Mickel, Stanley L. III. 1980. "Teaching the Chinese Writing System." *Journal of the Chinese Language Teachers Association* 15,1: 94–98.

Miracle, W. Charles. 1989. "Tone Production of American Students of Chinese: A Preliminary Acoustic Study." *Journal of the Chinese Language Teachers Association* 25,3: 49–66.

Moore, Sarah Jane, A. Ronald Walton, and Richard D. Lambert. 1992. *Introducing Chinese into High Schools: The Dodge Initiative.* Washington, DC: National Foreign Language Center.

Oller, John W., Jr., and J. R. Tullius. 1973. "Reading Skills of L2 Speakers of English." *IRAL* 11: 69–80.

Omaggio, Alice C. 1979. "Pictures and Second Language Comprehension: Do They Help?" *Foreign Language Annals* 12,2: 107–16.

Packard, Jerome L. 1989. "High- versus Low-Pressure Methods of Chinese Language Teaching: A Comparison of Test Results." *Journal of the Chinese Language Teachers Association* 24,1: 1–18.

———. 1990. "Effects of Time Lag in the Introduction of Characters into the Chinese Language Curriculum." *Modern Language Journal* 74: 167–75.

Pederson, Kathleen Marshall. 1988. "Research on CALL," in William Flint Smith, ed., *Modern Media in Foreign Language Education: Theory and Implementation.* Lincolnwood, IL: National Textbook.

Rayner, Keith. 1983. *Eye Movements in Reading: Perceptual and Language Processes.* New York: Academic.

Reeves, Thomas C. 1986. "Research and Evaluation Models for the Study of Interactive Video." *Journal of Computer Based Instruction* 13,4: 102–6.

Robertson, Charles D. 1990. "The Effects of Orthographic Variation on Word Latency, Pronunciation, Speed and Comprehension of Nonnative Readers of Arabic." Unpublished Ph.D. diss., Univ. of Texas at Austin.

Rosengrant, Sandra F. 1987. "Error Patterns in Written Russian." *Modern Language Journal* 71: 138–46.

Saito, Yoshiko. 1992. "Effects of Relational Deletion in Japanese Texts," in Charles K. Kinzer and Donald J. Leu, eds., *Literacy Research, Theory, and Practice: Views From Many Perspectives.* Forty-First Yearbook of the National Reading Conference. Chicago: National Reading Conference.

Samimy, Keiko Komiya. 1989. "A Comparative Study of Teaching Japanese in the Audio-Lingual Method and the Counseling-Learning Approach." *Modern Language Journal* 73: 169–77.

———, and Motoko Tabuse. 1992. "Affective Variables and a Less Commonly Taught Language: A Study in Beginning Japanese Classes." *Language Learning* 42,3: 377–98.

Schrier, Leslie L. 1993. "Prospects for the Professionalization of Foreign Language Teaching," in Gail Guntermann, ed., *Developing Language Teachers for a Changing World.* Lincolnwood, IL: National Textbook.

———, and Michael E. Everson. 1993. "The Iowa Critical Languages Program: Developing Teachers of Critical Languages for Secondary Schools," in William N. Hatfield, ed., *Visions and Reality in Foreign Language Teaching: Where We Are, Where We Are Going.* Lincolnwood, IL: National Textbook.

Sergent, Wallace K. 1990. "A Study of the Oral Reading Strategies of Advanced and Highly Advanced Second Language Readers of Chinese." Unpublished Ph.D. diss., The Ohio State Univ., Columbus.

———, and Michael E. Everson. 1992. "The Effects of Frequency and Density on Character Recognition Speed and Accuracy by Elementary and Advanced L2 Readers of Chinese." *Journal of the Chinese Language Teachers Association* 27,1–2: 29–44.

Shen, Susan Xiaonan. 1989. "Toward a Register Approach in Teaching Mandarin Tones." *Journal of the Chinese Language Teachers Association* 25,3: 27–48.

Stevens, James. 1986. *Applied Multivariate Statistics for the Social Sciences.* Hillsdale, NJ: Erlbaum.

Swaffar, Janet K. 1988. "Readers, Texts, and Second Languages: The Interactive Processes." *Modern Language Journal* 72: 123–49.

————, Katherine M. Arens, and Heidi Byrnes. 1991. *Reading for Meaning: An Integrated Approach to Language Learning*. Englewood Cliffs, NJ: Prentice-Hall.

Tabachnick, Barbara G., and Linda S. Fidell. 1983. *Using Multivariate Statistics*. New York: Harper and Row.

Taylor, Insup, and M. Martin Taylor. 1983. *The Psychology of Reading*. New York: Academic.

Treiman, R. A., J. Baron, and K. Luk. 1981. "Speech Recoding in Silent Reading: A Comparison of Chinese and English." *Journal of Chinese Linguistics* 9: 116–25.

Tzeng, Ovid J. L., and Daisy L. Hung. 1981. "Linguistic Determinism: A Written Language Perspective," in Ovid J. L. Tzeng and Harry Singer, eds., *Perception of Print: Reading Research in Experimental Psychology*. Hillsdale, NJ: Erlbaum.

Walker, Galal. 1984. "'Literacy' and 'Reading' in a Chinese Language Program." *Journal of the Chinese Language Teachers Association* 19,1: 67–84.

————. 1989. "The Less Commonly Taught Languages in the Context of American Pedagogy," pp. 111–37 in Helen S. Lepke, ed., *Shaping the Future: Challenges and Opportunities*. Middlebury, VT: Northeast Conference on the Teaching of Foreign Languages.

————. 1991. "Gaining Place: The Less Commonly Taught Languages in American Schools." *Foreign Language Annals* 24: 131–50.

Walton, A. Ronald. 1989. "Chinese Language Instruction in the United States: Some Reflections on the State of the Art." *Journal of the Chinese Language Teachers Association* 24,2: 1–42.

————. 1992. *Expanding the Vision of Foreign Language Education: Enter the Less Commonly Taught Languages*. NFLC Occasional Papers. Washington, DC: National Foreign Language Center.

Zamojska-Hutchins, Danuta Barbara. 1986. "An Assessment of Reading Strategies and an Examination of Text-Related Background Information in Reading Comprehension among College Students of Russian." Unpublished Ph.D. diss., Univ. of Minnesota, Minneapolis.

9

Assessment Issues:
Prominent Paradigms

Grant Henning

The Pennsylvania State University

It has been suggested that the history of science can be understood as a progression of paradigm shifts (Kuhn 1962), with research foci successively organized around changing issues and the evolving methods and epistemologies for the investigation of those issues. The history of educational assessment in general and language assessment in particular is no exception. The fields of second and foreign language testing have witnessed an especially large number of paradigm shifts. Over the past several decades, a number of second/foreign language measurement issues have surfaced, often in response to practical testing problems. These issues, along with their attendant research methods and epistemologies, could be said to comprise paradigms—each paradigm adopted by cadres of interested contributing scholars. Although there has been a recognizable waxing and waning of interest in various issues, variation in the appeal and credibility of particular methods, and a continual changing of the guard with respect to those scholars participating, it is evident that a number of these research paradigms are still alive and well today. (For a thorough treatment of the early history of language assessment issues and methods, see Alderson and Hughes 1981, Skehan 1991, and Spolsky 1993).

The following treatment of current language testing paradigms and their associated issues, methods, and scholars is not at all exhaustive. Not every important theoretical or empirical contribution has been duly acknowledged. Further, it will be evident that there is considerable overlap among the various assessment issues, research paradigms, and contributing researchers and theorists discussed. For just as Kuhn fails to provide a clear definition of a research paradigm (Shapere 1964), so it is sometimes difficult here to differentiate precisely among the legitimate foci, methods, and terminologies

Grant Henning (Ph.D., U.C.L.A.) is Professor of Language Testing, Research Methods, and Cross-Cultural Communication in the Department of Speech Communication of The Pennsylvania State University. He has served as Senior Research Scientist coordinating research on the Test of English as a Foreign Language (TOEFL), the Test of Spoken English (TSE), and the Test of Written English (TWE) for Educational Testing Service in Princeton, New Jersey. In addition, he has taught English as a second/foreign language and trained ESL/EFL language teachers in several countries over a period of more than twenty years. His publications and conference presentations have been primarily concerned with issues in language assessment.

of the various paradigms considered. In this chapter, a *research paradigm* is defined as a unified research focus along with the collective methodology and epistemology employed for investigation and reporting.

Some of the paradigms discussed in the following pages have a long history (e.g., item and test format investigations). Others are comparatively recent (e.g., computerized assessment research). But most have developed concurrently. Some paradigms with a long history have passed through periods of comparative neglect and have recently experienced renewed interest (e.g., language aptitude testing). To minimize anachronisms, there has been some attempt here to organize these research interest centers by size of the coherent bodies of attendant literature in language assessment from largest to smallest, rather than to attempt chronological presentation. The nature of the topic is such that there can be no universal agreement on the relative importance of the various issues and methodologies. If past developments reflect future trends, many of the paradigms considered here will progressively be replaced and forgotten and the sequence of those remaining will change.

The twelve broad areas of research interest discussed in this chapter, along with the primary issues they address, are the following:

1. *Communicative-competence modeling:* What is the nature of proficiency?
2. *Item Response Theory:* How can classical measurement be refined?
3. *Item and test format investigations:* Which testing techniques are best?
4. *Item and test bias research:* How can bias be detected and eliminated?
5. *Computerized assessment:* How can technology enhance testing?
6. *Test dimensionality research:* How can test constructs be identified?
7. *Criterion-referenced assessment:* How can performance standards be set?
8. *Pragmatic assessment:* How should functional abilities be measured?
9. *Language aptitude testing:* How can learning ability be identified?
10. *Self-assessment research:* What is the proper role of self-evaluation?
11. *Affective considerations:* How do attitudes relate to test performance?
12. *Assessment contextualization:* What is the proper role of test context?

It will become obvious that most of these paradigms address additional important issues. For example, criterion-referenced assessment is not limited to a consideration of the issue of standards setting, but also includes concern for the content validity of tests. Also, pragmatic assessment has broader focus than just the measurement of functional language ability in the classroom or workplace; it is equally concerned, for example, with rationales and procedures for testing language for specific purposes in science and technology. Moreover, some of the issues listed above may also be considered under other paradigms. Thus, standards setting may be a secondary concern of item response theory and of pragmatic assessment, even as it is a primary concern of criterion-referenced assessment. The particular organization of terms and topics in this chapter has been chosen, therefore, to serve mainly as an aid to presentation and discussion of assessment and is not meant to represent an exhaustive or precise taxonomy.

1. Communicative-Competence Modeling: What Is the Nature of Proficiency?

Not surprisingly, the nature of language ability has long been a central concern of language-testing scholars and practitioners who are attempting to measure it. Over the past several decades, language theorists have argued in support of various theories or models of language proficiency or communicative language ability. Perhaps the earliest clearly articulated description of language proficiency was the skills/components model proposed by Lado (1961) and Carroll (1961). According to this model, language behavior could be divided into the four skill areas of listening, speaking, reading, and writing, and into several component categories extending across these skills (i.e., phonology/graphology, lexis, morphology, and syntax). The continuing influence of this model is evident in the organization of many modern standardized language-testing batteries (see Alderson, Krahnke, and Stansfield 1987). Subsequent language theorists have considered this model too restrictive and inadequate to represent explicitly the sociolinguistic, pragmatic, strategic, and discourse-level concerns of communicative language ability (Hymes 1972; Halliday 1973, 1976; Canale and Swain 1980; Carroll 1980; Hatch and Long 1980; Bachman and Palmer 1981; Spolsky 1989; Bachman 1990).

Hymes (1971) is credited with proposing the term "communicative competence" as distinct from the "linguistic competence" construct proposed earlier by Chomsky (1965). In Hymes's view, communicative competence reflected not only the knowledge of grammaticality of language as described by Chomsky, but also the knowledge of the appropriateness of language use. He maintained that, in addition to acquiring rules of grammar, a child "acquires competence as to when to speak, when not, and as to what to talk about with whom, when, where [and] becomes able to accomplish a repertoire of speech acts, to take part in speech events, and to evaluate their accomplishment by others" (Hymes 1972: 277–78). It is understandable that this conceptualization would lead to further developments in the study of language use, such as the development of speech-act theory that is concerned with the study of varieties of appropriate language use in particular contexts rather than just with structural accuracy of language use (Wolfson 1976, 1981; Cohen and Olshtain 1981; Blum-Kulka and Olshtain 1984; Olshtain, this volume).

In the realm of second-language assessment, Canale and Swain (1980) enlarged upon Hymes's view of communicative competence by proposing a model that contained three distinct but related competences with definable boundaries. These competences were (1) *grammatical competence,* knowledge of lexical items and of rules of morphology, syntax, sentence-grammar semantics, and phonology; (2) *sociolinguistic competence,* knowledge of sociocultural rules of use and rules of discourse; and (3) *strategic competence,* knowledge of verbal and nonverbal communication strategies that may be called into action to compensate for breakdown in communication due to performance variables or to insufficient competence. Duran et al. (1985) went on to propose a similar but more elaborate model of communicative competence for evaluating the content of the Test of English as a Foreign Language (TOEFL). Their model also consisted of three competence domains, as follows: (1) *grammatical competence,* in pronunciation, script, lexicon, morphology, and sentence formation; (2) *sociolinguistic competence,* factors defining rules of appropriateness for language usage in a given communicative event, language used to accomplish communicative purposes, formulaic expressions in routine usage for phatic communication such as the facilitative expression "you know" in casual conversation, indirect perspective toward a communicative event, and linguistic forms or speech modes not typical in broadcast or standard written English; and (3) *discourse competence,* that is, cohesion and coherence. Bachman and Clark (1987) subsequently advanced a still more complex model of communicative language proficiency, said to consist of domains of (1) *language competence,* grammatical, textual, illocutionary, and sociolinguistic abilities, (2) *strategic competence,* ability to recognize, assess, infer, and compensate for deficiencies, and (3) *psychophysical* skills, the visual, neuromuscular, auditory, and articulatory skills comprising the modes and channels underlying the ability to listen, speak, read, and write language. These recent models of communicative language ability tend to be generative rather than taxonomic, unlike the skills/components model. That is, they tend to be organized into interrelated hierarchies, rather than into discrete categories. There remains, however, very little empirical basis for any hierarchical ordering of the constituent components of these models. As Candlin (1986) aptly expressed it, "such elaborations . . . offer no explanation of which aspects are used in particular circumstances and how they are drawn upon in the process of making meanings" (p. 41).

As a chronologically parallel but theoretically contrasting development in the history of language proficiency modeling, Oller (1976, 1979) proposed that linguistic competence was the principal factor underlying all language skills, and that this competence was unitary in nature. Oller's *unitary competence hypothesis* (UCH) maintained, largely on the basis of limited factor analytic evidence (Oller and Hinofotis 1980), that all verbal tests tapped the same unitary linguistic construct. The further assertion was offered that, since language proficiency was considered to be an indivisible construct, the most effective way to measure proficiency was by use of integrative skills tests such as cloze and dictation rather than by means of batteries of discrete-point, separated-skills, or distinctive-features tests. Although the strong version of the unitary competence hypothesis and the primacy of integrative tests were later rejected on both theoretical and empirical grounds (Farhady 1979; Vollmer 1981; Sang et al. 1986) and the UCH was partially disclaimed by Oller himself, there were many positive outcomes from this debate. Perhaps foremost of these positive outcomes was a heightened expectation that language researchers would present evidence in the form of quantifiable data to support any language proficiency models or theories they wished to propose.

In addition to the work of Oller and Hinofotis (1980) and of Sang et al. (1986), other recent efforts to provide empirical evidence for competence models would include the attempts of Bachman and Palmer (1982) to validate some limited parts of their models using confirmatory factor analysis and multitrait-multimethod techniques. Also, Henning and Cascallar (1992) attempted an empirical synthesis of most of the earlier mentioned communicative competence models through repeated measures analyses and multiple regression analyses. They analyzed over 900 ratings of videotaped communicative language performance for 79 ESL learners on 36 variables across domains of grammatical, discoursal, sociolinguistic, pragmatic, and strategic competences in both oral and written language modalities. Henning and Cascallar found significant interaction effects between category of pragmatic function and level of social register for nearly all variables within competence domains. These results suggested that measurement of communicative performance was highly dependent on particulars of assessment context, communication purpose, and pragmatic function. Thus, it was concluded that attempts to test communicative performance as a valid construct would not likely be successful except within limited and well-defined situations involving necessary constraints on competence generalizations. This conclusion is not incompatible with a definition of communicative competence offered by Diez (1984) in the literature on native-speaker communication. She maintained that "communicative competence is situational, interactional, functional, and developmental" (p. 57). There appears to be growing consensus in some quarters that future language tests will need to be more communicatively oriented and more representative of authentic language usage. It also appears that future attempts to model and to test communicative competence will need to incorporate more systematically the situational, interactional, functional, and developmental concerns that Diez (1984) suggested.

Further recent developments in the modeling of language assessment constructs are represented by the work of Dunkel, Henning, and Chaudron (1993). They considered issues in the modeling of L2 listening comprehension.

The paradigm of communicative-competence modeling holds many challenges and opportunities for the future. Newer and more sophisticated statistical procedures will be needed to reflect the unique complexities of language acquisition and use. Efforts will be needed to standardize terminology, synthesize models where possible, evaluate models in terms of their utility and parsimony, provide empirical evidence of the interrelationships among model components, reject models where necessary, and recognize that a multiplicity of models may be needed to address particular modeling purposes.

2. Item Response Theory: How Can Classical Measurement Be Refined?

It has been accurately observed that item response theory (IRT), also termed latent trait theory, is not actually a theory but rather a collection of psychometric models serving a variety of practical measurement purposes (Goldstein 1980). Specifically, these models include the Perfect Scale (Guttman 1944), the One-, Two-, and Three-Parameter Normal Ogive Models (Lord 1952), the One-, Two-, and Three-Parameter Logistic Models (Birnbaum 1957, 1958, 1968; Rasch 1960; Lord and Novick 1968; Wright and Stone 1979), and the Four-Parameter Logistic Models (Barton and Lord 1981) for the analysis of dichotomous-item data. For the analysis of multicategory or continuous scoring data such as ratings of speaking or writing ability, models such as the Graded Response, Continuous Response (Samejima 1969, 1972), Nominal Response (Bock 1972), Rating Scale, and Partial Credit Models (Wright and Masters 1982) have been introduced. In language assessment applications, the One-, Two-, and Three-Parameter Logistic Models, along with the Rating Scale and Partial Credit Models, have been by far the most popular IRT models.

Much has been written about the appropriate selection of these models for specific purposes (Hambleton and Swaminathan 1985; Henning 1987). There remains some disagreement about which of the models are most appropriate for which testing applications. However, these collective models have offered such profound advantages over classical measurement theory that the advent of this new approach to assessment has been likened to the advent of nuclear physics to the world of classical Newtonian physics (Warm 1978). To appreciate this comparison fully, one would need to understand the limitations of classical test theory and the advantages offered by item response theory.

Classical test theory consists of a body of interrelated equations for test and item analysis based on posited relationships between true scores and errors of measurement; it also relies heavily on the correlation coefficient to estimate characteristics such as test reliability and validity and item discriminability and homogeneity. Perhaps the best explication of classical test theory is provided by Gulliksen (1987). In spite of the powerful contributions of classical test theory to language assessment since the early part of this century, a number of practical inadequacies have arisen. Henning (1984, 1987) has described some of these inadequacies, along with the potential advantages of item response theory in each regard. The following discussion is directed to these individual advantages of item response theory and some of the recent representative applications of IRT in language assessment.

Some item response theory models, unlike classical test theory, offer *test-free person measurement and sample-free item calibration.* Because classical estimates of person ability, test reliability, and item difficulty are test- and sample-dependent, it is not usually possible to generalize beyond the specific assessment situation. For example, individuals' scores on tests, and hence any direct judgment of their competence, will differ from test to test depending on the particular assembly of test items, even in the same content domain. Similarly, classical item difficulty and discriminability, and test difficulty and reliability estimates, depend on the particular sample of persons responding to the test at any given time. Therefore, precisely the same estimates cannot safely be expected for new samples, even when those persons are drawn from the same population and are responding to the same test. These limitations were overcome in the area of language assessment when, for example, the ESL placement examinations at UCLA and at Brigham Young University were calibrated by means of the One-Parameter Logistic (Rasch) Model, and scores on subsequent test forms involving different student samples could be interpreted with reference to their position on the same latent-trait proficiency continuum (Henning 1986; Madsen and Larson 1986). Still, there is room for greater capitalization on these advantages—especially in applications such as item banking, test equating, and computer-adaptive testing, as will be discussed later under computerized assessment.

Another advantage of item response theory lies in its capacity to offer *reconciliation of criterion-referenced and norm-referenced testing.* Classical theory has left a persistent and, at times, heated controversy over whether the proper focus of testing is on absolute behavioral standards of learning mastery, as in criterion-referenced assessment, or on relative standards of attainment reflected by standing among other learners, as in norm-referenced assessment (Glaser 1963; Ebel 1971, 1976; Popham 1978). However, in the area of second-language assessment, Henning (1984), using a 48-item, 8-passage reading comprehension test that had been calibrated by means of the One-Parameter Logistic (Rasch) Model, pointed out that the benefits of both criterion-referenced and norm-referenced assessment can be preserved within the same test application. Since both *persons* according to ability and *items* according to difficulty were positioned on the same equal-interval latent-trait continuum, test performance could easily be interpreted with respect both to mastery of graded behavioral tasks (i.e., calibrated reading items) and to standing among other examinees.

Because of its test-free person measurement and sample-free item calibration properties already noted, item response theory also offers a number of important advantages in technological applications of assessment, including *item banking, computer-adaptive testing, test equating, test tailoring,* and *automated test assembly.* By way of example, the Test of English as a Foreign Language (TOEFL) has for many years relied on the Three-Parameter Logistic Model for the equating of its many successive forms. Here the advantage lies in the fact that, unlike in the case of earlier classical test theory, test equating can proceed using a limited set of linking items. Thus, it is no longer necessary to administer all test forms to the same large sample of persons in order to determine the equated values of their respective test scores. Other examples of technological applications in the area of language assessment include a growing number of item banks and computer-adaptive language tests that rely on unidimensional or multidimensional IRT algorithms (Henning 1986, 1987; Jones 1991; Kaya-Carton, Carton, and Dandonoli 1991; Madsen 1991; Stevenson and Gross 1991).

As a further example of the capacity of item response theory to overcome sample-dependency constraints, it has been used for *providing multiple indicators of measurement error* instead of relying solely on a unitary global estimate of test reliability as does classical test theory (Henning 1984, 1987). Every test is susceptible to some error of measurement. It is known that this error tends to increase in relation to the distance above or below the mean score. Thus, very high scores and very low scores are more prone to error than are scores in the middle of the distribution, and measurement error is not the same for every person responding to the same test. Item response theory makes it possible to estimate the level of measurement error present for every possible score attainable on the test (Wright and Stone 1979).

Item response theory has stimulated research inquiry into the exact nature of the constraints of its *underlying assumptions.* This research has improved our understanding of the measurement process. Many of the same procedural assumptions were implicitly required in classical measurement theory (e.g., unidimensionality, local independence, sample invariance, and nonspeededness), but were not so well articulated or understood (Hambleton and Swaminathan 1985). In the future, there will likely be need for other measurement models with less restrictive assumptions. This will be especially true as we attempt to measure important language abilities such as fluency, which often requires use of speeded tests that few nonnative speakers of the target language can be expected to complete within the time allowed.

Several item response theory models offer probability estimates of the fit of person or item responses to the expectations of the models. *These fit statistics can provide additional evidence of response validity and item or person bias.* When bias is quantifiable for items and persons, it becomes possible not only to eliminate the source of bias but also to counterbalance bias in one direction with equivalent bias in the opposite direction (Wright, Mead, and Draba 1976). A growing number of language assessment studies have employed item response theory in the study of person or item differential functioning (Chen and Henning 1985; Henning 1990; Sasaki 1991). Test and item bias research is treated more fully later in this chapter as a separate research paradigm.

Numerous other advantages of the IRT paradigm exist that are only beginning to be studied in language assessment, such as the *quantification of guessing behavior* and the use of *constructed response scales* to measure speaking and writing ability (Wright and Masters 1982; Hambleton and Swaminathan 1985; Pollitt and Hutchinson 1987). Indeed, so much test development and research is currently in progress involving Rasch scalar analysis models that it is not unlikely that this area of language assessment may require separate identification as a distinct paradigm by itself (Davidson and Henning 1985; McNamara 1990; Hamp-Lyons and Henning 1991; Henning 1992a). As can be surmised from this limited discussion, item response theory continues to provide a fruitful paradigm for language testing theory and application.

3. Item and Test Format Investigations: What Are the Best Testing Techniques?

Much more has been written about traditional and innovative language testing techniques than can possibly be acknowledged in this brief chapter. Numerous possible integrative and discrete-point test-item formats have been described extensively, including formats that could be considered more or less communicative in form (Oller 1979; Heaton 1988; Hughes 1989). Perhaps hundreds of research studies have been conducted to examine the advantages and disadvantages of integrative tests (e.g., cloze tests, C-tests, dictation tests) by comparison with discrete-point tests (e.g., grammar-features tests, language-skills tests, vocabulary-recognition tests). See, for example, Porter (1978), Farhady (1979), and Klein-Braley (1985).

Numerous studies have analyzed a variety of formats for testing vocabulary (Meara and Buxton 1987; Perkins and Linnville 1987; Henning 1991b). Others have studied formats for testing language structure and other discrete-point abilities (Pike 1979). Still others have compared different ways of measuring listening and reading comprehension (Alderson 1986; Henning 1991a). Perhaps hundreds of other studies have investigated advantages and disadvantages of various techniques for the measurement of oral language proficiency. For example, Henning (1983) compared sentence imitation, sentence completion, and interview methods of oral language testing. Clark and Swinton (1979, 1980) conducted early research investigations that led to the development of the Test of English as a Spoken Language (TSE). A large number of other studies in the TOEFL Research Report Series published by Educational Testing Service contain useful comparisons of language-test and item formats in a variety of skill domains (Pike 1979; Duran et al. 1985; Henning 1991b).

Just as it is not possible here to cite all the fine work analyzing techniques of language assessment, so it is not possible either to indicate which techniques were found to be best for which purposes of language assessment. Obviously, such judgments depend ultimately on the particular purpose of testing, the nature of the examinee population, the time available for testing, and other operational constraints including the availability of technological aids for administering and scoring the tests. Indeed, the selection of particular testing formats and combinations of item types often becomes a principled balancing act where reliability, validity, and practicality combine as three (often competing) criteria of item and test design.

In spite of the massive contributions already available in the study of item formats, much more work is needed for the development of newer and more innovative testing techniques and for the classification of the techniques already available with regard to most appropriate applications. Innovative item types are needed that will harness the powers of new technologies. In view of the great need, it is encouraging that many persons are currently at work within this broad paradigm.

4. Item and Test Bias Research: How Can Bias Be Detected and Eliminated?

Along with the development of refined measurement methodologies and a growth of concern for social responsibility and fairness in assessment, there has been a steady increase in research into language-test and item bias (e.g., Chen and Henning 1985; Zeidner 1986, 1987; Sasaki 1991). Testing bias usually bears the negative connotation of systematic unfairness regarding any particular group of examinees, reflected in the underestimation or overestimation of their true ability levels through the use of flawed testing procedures. However, the test and item bias paradigm has recently become much broader than the original concern to detect unfair testing procedures. It now includes the study of systematic differences in estimates of group abilities, even when unfairness is not present. Thus, it has become popular to refer to this paradigm with expressions such as "differential item functioning" (DIF) or "differential person functioning" (DPF or DIP) rather than by using the pejorative term *bias*.

Unlike work in test and item bias outside the realm of language proficiency testing, where focus has been primarily on ethnic and gender bias (Angoff and Ford 1973; Scheuneman 1979; Berk 1982), second/foreign language assessment bias studies have been concerned primarily with potential bias stemming from the differing language and educational backgrounds of the examinees (Alderman and Holland 1981; Madsen and Larson 1986) and from the differing cultural and specialization content of the reading and listening passages of the test (Hale 1988; Angoff 1989; Henning 1990). Such studies to date have employed a variety of IRT, regression, ANOVA, and chi-square techniques to identify persons and items for which differential functioning has occurred.

In the case of item-bias and person-bias studies, as mentioned earlier, a distinction has usually been made between actual bias, with its negative connotations, and differential item and person functioning (DIF and DIP), which may not necessarily imply the presence of unfair bias. Interestingly, developments in IRT methodology have permitted the actual quantification of item bias in ways that can allow choice between elimination of biased items on the one hand, or counterbalancing their effects with items biased in the opposite direction on the other hand (Wright, Mead, and Draba 1976). Use of chi-square techniques such as the Mantel-Haenszel technique (Holland and Thayer 1986) has raised the possibility of identifying not only items biased for or against particular person groups, but also persons biased for or against particular item groups (Henning 1990). Thus, for example, just as it is possible to make inaccurate estimates of examinee ability by using biased items or tests, so it is also possible to make inaccurate estimates of item or test difficulty by using biased persons or groups of persons. To give a more concrete example, use of language teacher introspection may not always provide an unbiased estimate of the difficulty of language test items to be used with language students.

Additional research will continue to be needed to determine whether particular reading or listening texts are systematically biased for or against persons from specific academic, linguistic, or professional backgrounds. Research is needed to establish where specialization thresholds exist, beyond which testing biases may be expected to occur. Such thresholds may consist of durations and kinds of educational experiences of examinees or of measures of the extent of lexical specialization of oral and written comprehension texts used in testing. The impact of topic and prompt selection in tests of writing and speaking also continues to be a needed focus of bias research.

5. Computerized Assessment: How Can Technology Enhance Testing?

It is natural to expect that, with the emergence of newer and more powerful technologies, the characteristics of language assessment will undergo changes. A number of important contributions to this assessment paradigm are already available (Stansfield 1986; Alderson 1988; Jung 1988; Alderson and Windeatt 1991; Dunkel 1991). As some of these sources have noted, a broad array of computer-assisted curricula are already in use with varying degrees of effectiveness for the teaching of second/foreign languages. With regard to language assessment, extensive work has been done across the four major language skill areas. In particular, major developments have been in the areas of item banking (Henning 1986), innovative item formats (Alderson and Windeatt 1991; Manning 1986), computer-assisted testing (Hicks 1986), computer-adaptive testing (Tung 1986; Henning 1987, 1988a; Kaya-Carton et al. 1991; Madsen 1991), score scanning and reporting, score database maintenance, machine construction of tests, and computerized pronunciation and writing assessment (Molholt and Presler 1986; Reid 1986).

As described by Dunkel (1991) and Henning (1987), computer-adaptive testing has had particular appeal. Typically this approach has involved the selective presentation of test content by computer. Testing becomes more efficient when item difficulty is tailored to examinee ability in this way. Tests can provide more accurate estimates of ability using fewer items if items are neither too difficult nor too easy for the examinees. Also, test security becomes less worrisome when every examinee receives a different combination of test items tailored to unique examinee characteristics. Such testing is "adaptive" in the sense that the computer procedure searches for appropriate successive items to present to the examinee based on the patterns of examinee responses to previous items.

Still more recently, Henning et al. (1993) have developed and studied an IRT-dependent algorithm for use at the Defense Language Institute English Language Center for the automated assembly of pre-equated test forms from the same test-item bank. Those researchers demonstrated that multiple forms of language proficiency tests can be automatically constructed by computer to be equivalent in difficulty, reliability, content specifications, variance, and covariance, without the need for formal equating studies in advance. This development has important cost-saving implications for large-scale testing programs.

The application of technological innovations for the automation and enhancement of language assessment still presents many challenges for the future. How can we best take advantage of developments with interactive video and audio assessment? What new testing formats will be able to take us far beyond the era of multiple-choice testing? How can we best automate assessments so that score results and feedback on performance will be instantly available? How can we use technology to study the processes of test responding? How can we use satellite technology in ways that will facilitate efficient, secure, and inexpensive large-scale assessments around the world—even in places where computer technology is not widely available? Some of these innovative issues are beginning to be studied systematically by language testing researchers (e.g., some of the unpublished work of John Clark and his colleagues at the Defense Language Institute in Monterey, California).

6. Test Dimensionality Research: How Can Test Constructs Be Identified?

Sparked in part by the controversy surrounding the proposal of the Unitary Competence Hypothesis (Oller 1979) and fanned by heightened concern for understanding and satisfying the assumptions of classical and latent trait measurement theory (Hambleton and Swaminathan 1985; Henning 1987), there has been recent growing interest in the investigation of language test dimensionality (Henning, Hudson, and Turner 1985; Davidson 1988; Henning 1988b, 1992b; Boldt 1989; McNamara 1991). Test dimensionality is concerned with the ways in which items and persons interact to form homogeneous performance clusters or "dimensions" within particular tests or person groups. These clusters of items and persons working together in similar ways serve to define test dimensions or measurement constructs. Much impetus for this kind of study has come from the review of thirty potential methods of measuring test dimensionality described by Hattie (1985) as part of his doctoral dissertation.

Among the more interesting developments concerning this assessment paradigm are the establishment of improved methods for the investigation of dimensionality and construct validity of tests (Bejar 1980; Henning 1988b). Also, study has been made of the dimensionality both of language-item-response patterns and of examinee-person-response patterns (Lynch, Davidson, and Henning 1988). That is, items may be clustered together on the basis of how they function with persons, and persons may be clustered together on the basis of how they function with items. There is also a growing recognition of a distinction between "psychometric" (i.e., statistical) dimensionality and "psychological" dimensionality (i.e., the traits actually measured by the test). Psychometric dimensionality has been shown to be sample-dependent, so that the same test may be found to be unidimensional in structure with one group of examinees and multidimensional in structure with another group (Henning 1992b). By way of contrast, psychological dimensionality implies that the content of the test is associated with a psychologically real construct or constructs that do not depend for existence on the response patterns of any particular group of examinees.

Controversy has arisen around the notion that language behavior represents complex multidimensional "psychological" constructs that often need to be tested using tests that satisfy unidimensional "psychometric" assumptions. A concern has been whether unidimensional tests and testing models are adequate for application with most language behavior that is considered to be multidimensional and complex in nature. The potential problem is compounded by the recognition that tests that lack psychometric unidimensionality tend also to lack reliability, construct validity, and equatability (Henning 1992b). Fortunately, evidence is mounting that tests may be psychologically multidimensional at the same time that they are psychometrically unidimensional (Henning 1992b). This is a positive discovery from the perspective of those who desire to apply unidimensional tests and testing models in the study of language behavior and test performance.

A number of test-modeling studies have been conducted with an end not so much of confirming theories of communicative competence or language proficiency as of ascertaining the construct validity or factor structure of a given language test or test battery. Construct validity research has attained such central importance in language testing that it could even be viewed as constituting a distinct paradigm (Messick 1987); however, due in part to the overlap of modeling procedures involved, it is here considered together with test dimensionality research. Purcell (1983) employed a causal modeling procedure in the validation of models of pronunciation accuracy. Turner (1989) also employed a causal modeling procedure to test the factor structure of patterns of cloze test responses on the part of 182 Francophone subjects studying English as a second language. Her study confirmed a model with two language factors (L1 and L2) and a factor of nonlinguistic-specific knowledge as the best explanation of the data. Boldt (1989) employed a latent-structure analysis procedure to determine whether the assumption of a single latent proficiency variable was satisfied in TOEFL response data from two separate randomly assembled 5,000-person samples, in spite of the language background diversity of the examinees. Evidence for a single latent proficiency variable would support a conclusion of unidimensionality of the TOEFL response data, as would be required to use item response theory for equating test forms. He concluded that the assumption was satisfied, thus providing further support for the use of item response theory for the equating of TOEFL forms.

Oltman and Stricker (1990) employed multidimensional scaling with a sample of 53,169 TOEFL respondents to investigate patterns of item clustering. They found significant patterns of clustering, but there was not sufficient evidence that item clusters would provide diagnostic information beyond that already available in the section scores. These and a number of other modeling studies, including those employing confirmatory factor analyses and multiple regression analyses, serve to underscore the established importance of the dimensionality-modeling paradigm in language assessment (Perkins and Linnville 1987; Hale, Rock, and Jirele 1989).

As indicated earlier in conjunction with the studies cited, a great variety of statistical procedures have been used to identify dimensions, factors, or constructs within any given testing data set. Confirmatory and exploratory factor analyses, principal components analyses, multidimensional scaling techniques, causal (path) modeling, and many other techniques are represented above. In addition to those procedures, Generalizability Theory and Decision Theory have provided statistical tools for the better understanding of the components of measurement for several decades (Cronbach, Rajaratnam, and

Gleser 1963; Shavelson and Webb 1981). It is a more recent development that these powerful tools have been applied in the analysis of language-test-component variance. Generalizability Theory, for example, is particularly useful in specifying the content domain or "universe" of criterion-referenced tests.

In sum, the test-dimensionality paradigm holds many important implications for the further understanding of the nature of construct validity and the scalability of the language abilities we seek to measure.

7. Criterion-Referenced Assessment: How Can Performance Standards Be Set?

In many places and for many years, interest in language assessment has increasingly been moving away from a traditional focus primarily on relative standing among other learners (as in norm-referenced or standardized testing) and more toward concern for the attainment of content mastery, performance standards, and behavioral objectives by the individual learner (as in criterion-referenced or objectives-referenced testing). The distinctions between norm-referenced and criterion-referenced testing are thoroughly described by Glaser (1963) and Popham (1978), and comparative advantages and disadvantages of the two approaches are listed by Henning (1987). Interestingly, some of the very same item types are equally likely to appear on a criterion-referenced test as on a norm-referenced test, so that the distinction between the two approaches is often more in the kinds of inferences drawn from student performance on the test than in the different types of items used.

Criterion-referenced testing is particularly suited to the measurement of the degree of attainment of explicit objectives in a language instructional context. Because of the intentional use of instructional objectives to determine the content of criterion-referenced tests, such tests tend to provide strong content validity for the measurement of language-learning achievement. The exercise of formulating explicit learning objectives to focus instructional emphasis and delimit test content can have a particularly positive impact on the development of lesson plans and test specifications. One of the important challenges of this approach is to develop learning objectives that are at the same time meaningful to the learners, teachable, and measurable. Some educators have objected to the use of norm-referenced tests to measure achievement because such tests often lack relevance to the content and objectives of instruction (Popham 1978). Other educators have objected to the use of criterion-referenced tests on the grounds that concentration on measurable teaching and testing objectives may lead to neglect of important learning objectives that are not easily measurable.

"Proficiency" and "performance" testing approaches described below under the pragmatic assessment paradigm tend to be criterion-referenced in nature. For example, the Foreign Service Institute (FSI) Oral Proficiency Interview (OPI) and its reformulations in the American Council on the Teaching of Foreign Languages (ACTFL) Guidelines and the Interagency Language Roundtable (ILR) Oral Proficiency Interview (OPI) exhibit characteristics of criterion-referenced assessment (Lowe and Stansfield 1988). Particularly, such tests provide formal descriptors of behavior at each graded level of performance. Ratings of performance, then, are determined by reference to agreed behavioral standards or explicit performance criteria rather than by how examinees rank among other examinees in terms of normative language performance.

A number of language-testing researchers have been actively seeking to reap the advantages of criterion-referenced assessment in the context of second-language learning (Hudson and Lynch 1984; Brown 1990). These researchers in particular have provided the language-testing community with clearer definitions of what is intended by criterion-referenced assessment, what it means to reach criterion, and how reliability and validity of criterion-referenced tests may be established. They have also suggested useful techniques for judging item quality in a program-evaluation context. Such techniques represent the beginnings of systematic study of the relationships between instruction and assessment. The prospects are especially encouraging that simultaneous developments in item response theory may facilitate the realization of the benefits of both criterion-referencing and norm-referencing in the same identical measurement instruments (Henning 1987).

8. Pragmatic Assessment: How Should Functional Abilities Be Measured?

The term *pragmatic assessment* is intended here to represent several streams of activity aimed at targeting communicative functioning in more realistic ways. Included here are movements variously labeled "performance" assessment (Hauptman, LeBlanc, and Wesche 1985), "proficiency" assessment (Lowe and Stansfield 1988), and "authentic" assessment (Seliger 1985; Shohamy and Reves 1985; Spolsky 1985; Stevenson 1985). Such testing movements tend to reflect strong support for the face validity and the content validity of tests.

Performance assessment as described by Hauptman, LeBlanc, and Wesche (1985) has been concerned with the testing of language as it is used in particular communication contexts. Here focus has been directed to the measurement of the communicative functions the language user is able to or is required to perform, rather than to the testing of knowledge of the components of the language itself. This approach is consistent with legal expressions of language rights in the workplace. In the case of tests used for purposes of hiring or promotion, for example, it is incumbent on the test developer to demonstrate that test content and performance standards reflect bona fide occupational qualifications.

Related to performance assessment has been the concern of proponents of the "proficiency" movement championed by groups such as the American Council on the Teaching of Foreign Languages (ACTFL) and the Interagency Language Roundtable (ILR) (Lowe and Stansfield 1988). This movement has similarly advocated language assessment focused on the ability of the candidate to use language appropriately in authentic-language contexts. The ACTFL Guidelines represent an attempt to describe proficiency levels in terms of observable communicative language behavior. Some recent attempts have been made to provide partial validation of the ACTFL Guidelines in response to criticisms that insufficient empirical study had been made (Dandonoli and Henning 1990).

Parallel to the development of methods for the teaching of English and other languages for special purposes has been the development of methods of testing language in the specific purposes context. This approach advocates the teaching and testing of specialized language for engineers, business managers, hotel personnel, and so forth. These developments are reflective of a concern for the teaching and testing of "authentic" language. Many of the critical issues related to special-purposes assessment have been addressed by Alderson (1981) and Skehan (1984). At the most superficial level of consideration, it can be affirmed that, if specific purposes language instruction is required to accommodate the unique learning needs of any language student, then a need for appropriate tests to evaluate learning of the specialized content of instruction is axiomatic. In practice, however, there have been procedural difficulties.

The Munby (1978) model advocates that a language-needs analysis be performed as the basis for syllabus specification. Skehan notes that, except in unique circumstances, it has been difficult to gather a group of learners whose learning needs are identical. This implied need for individualizing of instruction, then, would logically require the individualization of assessment, with accompanying high costs. Such individualized tests are also difficult to develop in equated forms for use in large-scale language assessments. Thus, this area of testing represents a particularly ripe field for applications of the new technologies such as computer-assisted instruction and computer-adaptive assessment considered earlier. Computer-adaptive tests and interactive video technologies could be used, for example, to tailor test content to the needs of individual students. It will continue to be a challenge to ensure that individualized assessments are in some way comparable, so that fairness of standards can be guaranteed. Inasmuch as the degree of specialization, both of examinees and of test content, will vary from little or no specialization to high specialization, it will continue to be a challenge to grade the persons and materials to ensure appropriate levels of specialization in the assessment.

The pragmatic assessment paradigm presents many challenges to the field of second/foreign language testing. There remains a dynamic tension between the demands for authentic, individualized assessment of language functioning in specific communication contexts and the real-world constraints of large-scale assessment aimed at providing global-decision information in as fair and inexpensive a manner as possible.

9. Language Aptitude Testing: How Can Learning Ability Be Identified?

For many years there has been a practical need in some circles to identify candidates for formal language instruction who would be most likely to acquire a foreign/second language given highly limited time and resources available for training (Carroll 1965, 1981; Skehan 1989). This need has been particularly evident in military and diplomatic organizations. However, many of the test-development efforts in this paradigm have resulted in tests that show only low correlations with achievement (e.g., 0.4 to 0.5). Carroll identified four components of language aptitude that appeared to have promise for assessment: phonemic coding ability, grammatical sensitivity, inductive language-learning ability, and rote learning activity for foreign language materials.

Recent batteries for predicting language-learning success, such as the DLAB II Project of the Monterey Defense Language Institute, have attempted to build in measures of motivation, on the belief that cognitive abilities alone may be insufficient to account for language-learning success. As Skehan (1989) suggests, much additional work is needed to improve our understanding of the nature of language aptitude (e.g., Is it fixed and unchanging? Is it relevant in formal learning contexts only? What are its pure components?). At a very basic level there appears to be a lack of agreement about the meaning of the term *aptitude*. Is it synonymous with generalized verbal intelligence, or is the ability to learn a second/foreign language a more unique cognitive ability? Also, continuing language acquisition research is needed to identify those factors that contribute most to language-learning success and to establish how they interrelate in the prediction of that success. Multiple-regression techniques would seem to hold particular promise for this line of inquiry; however, it may be necessary to rely on curvilinear regression and other more sophisticated techniques when it is recognized that many predictor variables may have a nonlinear relation to achievement (e.g., age).

10. Self-Assessment Research: What Is the Proper Role of Self-Evaluation?

Due in part to the facility with which self-ratings can be obtained, the use and popularity of this approach to language proficiency assessment has grown in some quarters. While some researchers and language-testing programs have strongly advocated use of self-assessed and self-reported language-ability information (LeBlanc and Painchaud 1985; Oscarson 1989), others have criticized such approaches with equal fervor (Oller 1979). Although Oller found correlations of only 0.3 to 0.6 between self-ratings of language proficiency and objective tests, it is only fair to point out that some of the instruments cited for measuring self-reported proficiency tended to consist of a single test item. This would impose serious constraints on their reliability, with a consequent reduction in the magnitude of the correlation coefficients obtained. Better instrumentation could easily be designed. For example, the "can-do" scales developed by John Clark employed multiple items that were behaviorally oriented.

Error in self-assessment of language ability could come from any of a number of sources. Some error may result from the examinee's inability to make accurate self-appraisals about level of proficiency. Other error may result from unwillingness to report accurate judgments because of program consequences or personality idiosyncrasies. Development of more refined questionnaires and the provision of training in self-report may overcome the first type of error. Unwillingness to report levels of proficiency accurately may be overcome by minimizing the importance of the decisions to be based on outcomes or by accompanying self-report with other measures of language proficiency.

There are many reasons that the self-assessment paradigm deserves further research and development effort. Self-assessment done well is painless, inexpensive, and quick, and it may be motivating or empowering in that it involves the learner in the assessment process. In addition, there are pragmatic functions of language use that cannot easily be assessed in any way other than by self-report (e.g., How often do you speak English?

How well do you understand me when I talk with you on the telephone? How well do you understand television news commentators? Can you order food from a restaurant menu?). Self-assessment may have a complementary role in providing diagnostic information beyond that available from more traditional test scores.

11. Affective Considerations: How Do Attitudes Relate to Test Performance?

Ways in which test performance is influenced by motivation, anxiety, and other affective traits of the testee have long been the subject of research inquiry (Skehan 1989). Risk-taking behavior and introversion/extroversion are other affective concerns that have been suggested as possible correlates of successful test-taking. For persons with high test anxiety, there may be identifiable strategies for reducing anxiety and improving performance on tests. To some extent the anxiety produced in testing situations may accurately reflect the anxiety present for the language learner in an authentic second/foreign language-use situation.

Many of these affective factors may be even more negative in their effects when unfamiliar technology is involved in the assessment. It may be more difficult for some examinees to indicate their true speaking ability when they are speaking into a tape recorder than when they are talking face to face. Some examinees may have heightened anxiety when responding via a computer keyboard. Much further research is needed in this paradigm. For example, research needs to be directed to understanding the effects of various applications of technology on test-taking attitudes. Research is also needed to identify personality factors related to language-testing outcomes.

12. Assessment Contextualization: What Is the Proper Role of Test Context?

A growing number of language-assessment researchers have expressed concerns over the role of the assessment context in the appropriate judgment of language abilities (Douglas and Selinker 1985; Henning and Cascallar 1992). Douglas and Selinker have outlined a set of hypotheses related to the characteristics of a valid test of communicative competence. They note among other things that such a test must engage "prototypical discourse domains." Also, they call attention to the fact that examinees create a personal context even when a formal context is not specified by the test writer. Furthermore, if the supplied context is not one in which the test taker has "control," then interlanguage structures are not properly measured. They advocate that the examinee be engaged in the testing content domain in order to ensure appropriate contextualization in language testing.

Henning and Cascallar (1992) reached similar conclusions from a different route. Their research found significant interactions among social register, pragmatic function, and ratings of communicative language performance. They concluded that communicative-competence assessment was likely to be impossible except within well-defined contexts. For them, context had to do with the purpose of communication and the kinds of linguistic functions to be carried out, as well as with whom, where, and under what circumstances.

Related to the personal context that is created by the examinees in the process of test responding is a recognition of particular test-taking strategies and background schematic information brought to the examination by the examinees. Several language-testing researchers have investigated the nature and effects of test-taking strategies (Skehan 1989; Anderson, Bachman, Perkins, and Cohen 1991). Of concern has been whether use of a particular responding strategy or combination of strategies might lead to superior test performance or to more efficient learning. Anderson et al. looked at a variety of data sources on reading-comprehension test performance. Specifically, they gathered data for the same readers using retrospective think-aloud protocols, test-content evaluation, as well as traditional test-performance statistics. They looked at six main test-taking strategies over three main categories of item type. They found a significant chi-square dependency, suggesting that test-taking strategy was dependent on test-item type (i.e., main idea, inference, and direct statement). This line of inquiry has important potential to inform test developers of the validity of item formats; that is, which formats engage appropriate kinds of language activity as response strategies. Also, there is potential for study of the effects on test performance of training the most effective response strategies.

Much work remains to be done in the study of contextualization of assessment. Little systematic study has been made of the effects of different kinds of test instructions on test scores. Little work has been done to define prototypical contexts from a language-assessment perspective or to classify pragmatic functions and determine which are most appropriate for which language-testing purposes.

As was indicated earlier, the language-assessment paradigms considered here are by no means exhaustive, and the diversity of the vast literature on language testing would certainly lend itself to other approaches to organization and presentation in a chapter of this kind. Had space permitted, it is certain that additional issues and paradigms would have been considered, such as "social responsibility in testing" and "issues in the scaling of ability." It is hoped, however, that the issues and paradigms reported here do provide a broad overview of many of the current interests in language-testing theory and practice.

References

Assessment Issues: Prominent Paradigms

Alderman, Don, and Paul Holland. 1981. *Item Performance across Native Language Groups on the Test of English as a Foreign Language.* TOEFL Research Report 9. Princeton, NJ: Educational Testing Service.

Alderson, J. Charles. 1981. "Report on the Discussion on the Testing of English for Special Purposes," in J. Charles Alderson and Arthur Hughes, eds., *Issues in Language Testing.* ELT Documents No. 111. London, Eng.: British Council.

———. 1986. "Processing Hierarchies for Reading Comprehension Items." Paper presented at the annual TESOL Convention, Anaheim, CA, March.

———. 1988. "Innovation in Language Testing: Can the Micro-Computer Help?" *Language Testing Update: Special Report No. 1.* Lancaster, Eng.: Lancaster Univ.

————, and Arthur Hughes, eds. 1981. *Issues in Language Testing.* ELT Documents No. 111. London, Eng.: British Council.

————, Karl J. Krahnke, and Charles W. Stansfield, eds. 1987. *Reviews of English Language Proficiency Tests.* Washington, DC: Teachers of English to Speakers of Other Languages.

————, and Scott Windeatt. 1991. "Computers and Innovation in Language Testing," in J. Charles Alderson and Brian North, eds., *Language Testing in the 1990s: The Communicative Legacy.* London, Eng.: Macmillan.

Anderson, Neil J., Lyle Bachman, Kyle Perkins, and Andrew Cohen. 1991. "An Exploratory Study into the Construct Validity of a Reading Comprehension Test: Triangulation of Data Sources." *Language Testing* 8,1: 41–66.

Angoff, William H. 1989. *Context Bias in the Test of English as a Foreign Language.* TOEFL Research Report 29. Princeton, NJ: Educational Testing Service.

————, and S. F. Ford. 1973. "Item-Race Interaction on a Test of Scholastic Aptitude." *Journal of Educational Measurement* 10: 95–106.

Bachman, Lyle F. 1990. *Fundamental Considerations in Language Testing.* Oxford, Eng.: Oxford Univ. Press.

————, and John L. D. Clark. 1987. "The Measurement of Foreign/Second Language Proficiency." *Annals of the American Academy of Political and Social Science* 490: 20–33.

————, and Adrian Palmer. 1981. "The Construct Validation of the FSI Oral Interview." *Language Learning* 31,1: 67–86.

————, and Adrian Palmer. 1982. "The Construct Validation of Some Components of Communicative Proficiency." *TESOL Quarterly* 16,4: 449–65.

Barton, M. A., and Fredrick M. Lord. 1981. "An Upper Asymptote for the Three-Parameter Logistic Item-Response Model." *Research Bulletin 81-20.* Princeton, NJ: Educational Testing Service.

Bejar, Isaac. 1980. "A Procedure for Investigating the Unidimensionality of Achievement Tests Based on Item Parameter Estimates." *Journal of Educational Measurement* 12: 283–96.

Berk, R. A. 1982. *Handbook of Methods for Detecting Test Bias.* Baltimore: Johns Hopkins Univ. Press.

Birnbaum, Alan. 1957. *Efficient Design and Use of Tests of a Mental Ability for Various Decision-Making Problems.* Series Report No. 58-16. Project No. 7755-23, USAF School of Aviation Medicine, Randolph Air Force Base, TX.

————. 1958. *On the Estimation of Mental Ability.* Series Report 15. Project No. 7755-23, USAF School of Aviation Medicine, Randolph Air Force Base, TX.

————. 1968. "Some Latent Trait Models and Their Use in Inferring an Examinee's Ability," in F. M. Lord and M. R. Novick, *Statistical Theories of Mental Test Scores.* Reading, MA: Addison-Wesley.

Blum-Kulka, Shoshana, and Elite Olshtain. 1984. "Requests and Apologies: A Cross-Cultural Study of Speech Act Realization Patterns." *Applied Linguistics* 5,3: 196–213.

Bock, R. D. 1972. "Estimating Item Parameters and Latent Ability When Responses Are Scored in Two or More Nominal Categories." *Psychometrika* 37: 29–51.

Boldt, Robert F. 1989. "Latent Structure Analysis of the Test of English as a Foreign Language." *Language Testing* 6,2: 123–42.

Brown, James Dean. 1990. "Short-Cut Estimators of Criterion-Referenced Test Consistency." *Language Testing* 7,1: 77–97.

Canale, Michael, and Merrill Swain. 1980. "Theoretical Bases of Communicative Approaches to Second Language Teaching and Testing." *Applied Linguistics* 1: 1–47.

Candlin, Christopher N. 1986. *Toward Communicative Competence Testing: Proceedings of the Second TOEFL Invitational Conference.* TOEFL Research Report 21. Princeton, NJ: Educational Testing Service.

Carroll, Brendan J. 1980. *Testing Communicative Performance.* London, Eng.: Pergamon Institute of English.

Carroll, John B. 1961. "Fundamental Considerations in Testing English Proficiency of Foreign Students," in *Testing the English Proficiency of Foreign Students.* Washington, DC: Center for Applied Linguistics.

———. 1965. "The Prediction of Success in Foreign Language Training," in R. Glaser, ed., *Training, Research and Education.* New York: Wiley.

———. 1981. "Twenty-five Years of Research on Foreign Language Aptitude," in K. C. Diller, ed., *Individual Differences and Universals in Language Learning Aptitude.* Rowley, MA: Newbury House.

Chen, Zheng, and Grant Henning. 1985. "Linguistic and Cultural Bias in Language Proficiency Tests." *Language Testing* 2,2: 155–63.

Chomsky, Noam. 1965. *Aspects of the Theory of Syntax.* Cambridge, MA: MIT Press.

Clark, John L. D., and Spencer Swinton. 1979. *An Exploration of Speaking Proficiency Measures in the TOEFL Context.* TOEFL Research Report 4. Princeton, NJ: Educational Testing Service.

———. 1980. *The Test of Spoken English as a Measure of Communicative Ability in English-Medium Instructional Settings.* TOEFL Research Report 7. Princeton, NJ: Educational Testing Service.

Cohen, Andrew, and Elite Olshtain. 1981. "Developing a Measure of Sociocultural Competence: The Case of Apology." *Language Learning* 31,1: 113–34.

Cronbach, L. J., N. Rajaratnam, and G. C. Gleser. 1963. "Theory of Generalizability: A Liberalization of Reliability Theory." *British Journal of Statistical Psychology* 16: 137–63.

Dandonoli, Patricia, and Grant Henning. 1990. "An Investigation of the ACTFL Proficiency Guidelines and the Oral Interview Procedure." *Foreign Language Annals* 23,1: 11–22.

Davidson, Fred. 1988. "An Exploratory Modeling of the Trait Structures of Some Existing Language Test Datasets." Unpublished Ph.D. diss., Univ. of California–Los Angeles.

———, and Grant Henning. 1985. "A Self-Rating Scale of English Difficulty: Rasch Scalar Analysis of Items and Rating Categories." *Language Testing* 2,2: 164–79.

Diez, M. E. 1984. "Communicative Competence: An Interactive Approach," pp. 56–79 in R. N. Bostrom, ed., *Communication Yearbook 8.* Beverly Hills, CA: Sage.

Douglas, Dan, and Larry Selinker. 1985. "Principles for Language Tests within the 'Discourse Domains' Theory of Interlanguage Research: Research, Test Construction, and Interpretation." *Language Testing* 2,2: 205–26.

Dunkel, Patricia, ed. 1991. *Computer-Assisted Language Learning and Testing: Research Issues and Practice.* New York: Newbury House/Harper Collins.

———, Grant Henning, and Craig Chaudron. 1993. "The Assessment of an L2 Listening Comprehension Construct: A Tentative Model for Test Specification and Development." *Modern Language Journal* 77,2: 180–91.

Duran, Richard P., Michael Canale, Joyce Penfield, Charles W. Stansfield, and Judith E. Liskin-Gasparro. 1985. *TOEFL from a Communicative Viewpoint: A Working Paper.* TOEFL Research Report 17. Princeton, NJ: Educational Testing Service.

Ebel, Robert L. 1971. "Criterion-Referenced Measurement: Limitations." *School Review* 79: 282–88.

———. 1976. "The Paradox of Educational Testing," in *Measurement in Education.* Washington, DC: National Council on Measurement in Education.

Farhady, Hossein. 1979. "The Disjunctive Fallacy between Discrete-Point and Integrative Tests." *TESOL Quarterly* 13: 347–57.

Glaser, R. 1963. "Instructional Technology and the Measurement of Learning Outcomes." *American Psychologist* 18: 519–21.

Goldstein, H. 1980. "Dimensionality, Bias, Independence and Measurement Scale Problems in Latent Trait Test Score Models." *British Journal of Mathematical and Statistical Psychology* 33: 234–46.

Gulliksen, Harold. 1987. *Theory of Mental Tests.* Hillsdale, NJ: Erlbaum.

Guttman, Louis A. 1944. "A Basis for Scaling Qualitative Data." *American Sociological Review* 9: 139–50.

Hale, Gordon. 1988. *The Interaction of Student Major-Field Group and Text Content in TOEFL Reading Comprehension.* TOEFL Research report No. 25. Princeton, NJ: Educational Testing Service.

———, Donald Rock, and Thomas Jirele. 1989. *Confirmatory Factor Analysis of the Test of English as a Foreign Language.* TOEFL Research Report 32. Princeton, NJ: Educational Testing Service.

Halliday, M. A. K. 1973. "Relevant Models of Language," in M. A. K. Halliday, ed., *Explorations in the Functions of Language.* New York: Elsevier North-Holland.

———. 1976. "The Form of Functional Grammar," in G. Kress, ed., *Halliday: System and Function in Language.* Oxford, Eng.: Oxford Univ. Press.

Hambleton, Ronald K., and Hariharan Swaminathan. 1985. *Item Response Theory: Principles and Applications.* Boston: Kluwer-Nijhoff.

Hamp-Lyons, Liz, and Grant Henning. 1991. "Communicative Writing Profiles: An Investigation of the Transferability of a Multiple-Trait Scoring Instrument across ESL Writing Assessment Contexts." *Language Learning* 41,3: 337–73.

Hatch, Evelyn, and Michael Long. 1980. "Discourse Analysis, What's That?" in Diane Larsen-Freeman, ed., *Discourse Analysis in Second Language Research.* Rowley, MA: Newbury House.

Hattie, John. 1985. "Methodology Review: Assessing Unidimensionality of Tests and Items." *Applied Psychological Measurement* 9: 139–64.

Hauptman, Philip C., Raymond LeBlanc, and Marjorie Bingham Wesche, eds. 1985. *Second Language Performance Testing.* Ottawa: Univ. of Ottawa Press.

Heaton, J. B. 1988. *Writing English Language Tests.* London, Eng.: Longman.

Henning, Grant. 1983. "Oral Proficiency Testing: Comparative Validities of Interview, Imitation, and Completion Methods." *Language Learning* 33,3: 315–32.

———. 1984. "Advantages of Latent Trait Theory in Language Testing." *Language Testing* 1,2: 123–33.

———. 1986. "Item Banking via DBASE II: The UCLA ESL Proficiency Exam Experience," in Charles W. Stansfield, ed., *Technology and Language Testing.* Washington, DC: Teachers of English to Speakers of Other Languages.

———. 1987. *A Guide to Language Testing: Development, Evaluation, Research.* New York: Newbury House/Harper and Row.

———. 1988a. "Computer Adaptive Language Testing: An Algorithm for Item Selection," in Udo O. H. Jung, ed., *Computers in Applied Linguistics and Language Teaching.* Frankfurt, Ger.: Peter Lang.

———. 1988b. "The Influence of Test and Sample Dimensionality on Latent Trait Person Ability and Item Difficulty Calibrations." *Language Testing* 5,2: 83–99.

———. 1990. "National Issues in Individual Assessment: The Consideration of Specialization Bias in University Language Screening Tests," in John H. A. L. de Jong and D. K. Stevenson, eds., *Individualizing the Assessment of Language Abilities.* Clevedon, Eng.: Multilingual Matters.

————. 1991a. *A Study of the Effects of Variations of Short-Term Memory Load, Reading Response Length, and Processing Hierarchy on TOEFL Listening Comprehension Item Performance*. TOEFL Research Report 33. Princeton, NJ: Educational Testing Service.

————. 1991b. *A Study of the Effects of Contextualization and Familiarization on Responses to TOEFL Vocabulary Test Items*. TOEFL Research Report 35. Princeton, NJ: Educational Testing Service.

————. 1992a. *Scalar Analysis of the Test of Written English*. TOEFL Research Report 38. Princeton, NJ: Educational Testing Service.

————. 1992b. "Dimensionality and Construct Validity of Language Tests." *Language Testing* 9,1: 1–11.

————, and Eduardo Cascallar. 1992. *A Preliminary Study of the Nature of Communicative Competence*. TOEFL Research Report 36. Princeton, NJ: Educational Testing Service.

————, Thom Hudson, and Jean Turner. 1985. "Item Response Theory and the Assumption of Unidimensionality for Language Tests." *Language Testing* 2,2: 141–54.

————, Pansy J. Johnson, Albert J. Boutin, and H. Ruth Rice. 1993. "Automated Assembly of Pre-Equated Language Proficiency Tests." *Language Testing*. [in press]

Hicks, Marilyn M. 1986. "Computerized Multilevel ESL Testing, a Rapid Screening Methodology," in Charles W. Stansfield, ed., *Technology and Language Testing*. Washington, DC: TESOL.

Holland, Paul W., and D. T. Thayer. 1986. "Differential Item Performance and the Mantel-Haenszel Procedure." Paper presented at the American Educational Research Association Annual Meeting, San Francisco.

Hudson, Thom, and Brian Lynch. 1984. "A Criterion-Referenced Measurement Approach to ESL Achievement Testing." *Language Testing* 1,2: 171–201.

Hughes, Arthur. 1989. *Testing for Language Teachers*. Cambridge, Eng.: Cambridge Univ. Press.

Hymes, Dell H. 1971. "Competence and Performance in Linguistic Theory," in R. Huxley and E. Ingram, eds., *Language Acquisition: Models and Methods*. London, Eng.: Academic.

————. 1972. "On Communicative Competence," pp. 269–93 in B. J. Pride and J. Holmes, eds., *Sociolinguistics*. Harmondsworth, Eng.: Penguin.

Jones, Neil. 1991. "Test Item Banker: An Item Bank for a Very Small Micro," in Charles Alderson and Brian North, eds., *Language Testing in the 1990s*. London, Eng.: Macmillan.

Jung, Udo O. H., ed. 1988. *Computers in Applied Linguistics and Language Teaching: A CALL Handbook*. Frankfurt, Ger.: Peter Lang.

Kaya-Carton, Esin, Aaron S. Carton, and Patricia Dandonoli. 1991. "Developing a Computer-Adaptive Test of French Reading Proficiency," in Patricia Dunkel, ed., *Computer-Assisted Language Learning and Testing*. New York: Newbury House/ Harper Collins.

Klein-Braley, Christine. 1985. "A Cloz-up on the C-Test: A Study in the Construct Validation of Authentic Tests." *Language Testing* 2,1: 76–104.

Kuhn, Thomas. 1962. *The Structure of Scientific Revolutions*. Chicago: Univ. of Chicago Press.

Lado, Robert. 1961. *Language Testing*. New York: McGraw-Hill.

LeBlanc, Raymond, and Gisele Painchaud. 1985. "Self-Assessment as a Second Language Placement Instrument." *TESOL Quarterly* 19,4: 673–87.

Lord, Fredrick M. 1952. *A Theory of Test Scores*. Psychometric Monograph No. 7.

————, and Melvin R. Novick. 1968. *Statistical Theories of Mental Test Scores*. Reading, MA: Addison-Wesley.

Lowe, Pardee, Jr. and Charles W. Stansfield, eds. 1988. *Second Language Proficiency Assessment: Current Issues.* Englewood Cliffs, NJ: Prentice-Hall Regents.

Lynch, Brian, Fred Davidson, and Grant Henning. 1988. "Person Dimensionality in Language Test Validation." *Language Testing* 5,2: 206–19.

Madsen, Harold S. 1991. "Computer-Adaptive Testing of Listening and Reading Comprehension: The Brigham Young University Approach," in Patricia Dunkel, ed., *Computer-Assisted Language Learning and Testing.* New York: Newbury House/ Harper Collins.

———, and J. W. Larson. 1986. "Computerized Rasch Analysis of Item Bias in ESL Tests," in Charles W. Stansfield, ed., *Technology and Language Testing.* Washington, DC: Teachers of English to Speakers of Other Languages.

Manning, Winton. 1986. "Using Technology to Assess Second Language Proficiency through Cloze-Elide Tests," in Charles W. Stansfield, ed., *Technology and Language Testing.* Washington, DC: Teachers of English to Speakers of Other Languages.

McNamara, Timothy F. 1990. "Item Response Theory and the Validation of an ESP Test for Health Professionals." *Language Testing* 7,1: 52–75.

———. 1991. "Test Dimensionality: IRT Analysis of an ESP Listening Test." *Language Testing* 8,2: 139–59.

Meara, Paul, and Barbara Buxton. 1987. "An Alternative to Multiple Choice Vocabulary Tests." *Language Testing* 4,2: 142–54.

Messick, Samuel. 1987. *Validity.* Research Report 87-40. Princeton, NJ: Educational Testing Service.

Molholt, Garry, and Ari M. Presler. 1986. "Correlation between Human and Machine Ratings of Test of Spoken English Reading Passages," in Charles W. Stansfield, ed., *Technology and Language Testing.* Washington, DC: Teachers of English to Speakers of Other Languages.

Munby, John. 1978. *Communicative Syllabus Design.* Cambridge, Eng.: Cambridge Univ. Press.

Oller, John W., Jr. 1976. "Evidence for a General Language Proficiency Factor: An Expectancy Grammar." *Die Neueren Sprachen* 75: 165–74.

———. 1979. *Language Tests at School.* London, Eng.: Longman.

———, and Frances Hinofotis. 1980. "Indivisible or Partially Divisible Competence," in John W. Oller, Jr. and Kyle Perkins, eds., *Research in Language Testing.* Rowley, MA: Newbury House.

Oltman, Philip K., and Lawrence J. Stricker. 1990. "Developing Homogeneous TOEFL Scales by Multidimensional Scaling." *Language Testing* 7,1: 1–12.

Oscarson, Mats. 1989. "Self-Assessment of Language Proficiency: Rationale and Applications." *Language Testing* 6,1: 1–13.

Perkins, Kyle, and Steven E. Linnville. 1987. "A Construct Definition Study of a Standardized ESL Vocabulary Test." *Language Testing* 4,2: 125–41.

Pike, L. W. 1979. *An Evaluation of Alternative Item Formats for Testing English as a Foreign Language.* TOEFL Research Report 2. ETS Research Report 79-6. Princeton, NJ: Educational Testing Service.

Pollitt, Alastair, and Carolyn Hutchinson. 1987. "Calibrated Graded Assessments: Rasch Partial Credit Analysis of Performance in Writing." *Language Testing* 4,1: 72–92.

Popham, W. James. 1978. *Criterion-Referenced Measurement.* Englewood Cliffs, NJ: Prentice-Hall.

Porter, Donald. 1978. "Cloze Procedure and Equivalence." *Language Learning,* 28: 333–40.

Purcell, Edward T. 1983. "Models of Pronunciation Accuracy," in J. W. Oller, Jr., ed., *Issues in Language Testing Research.* Rowley, MA: Newbury House.

Rasch, Georg. 1960. *Probabilistic Models for Some Intelligence and Attainment Tests.* Copenhagen, Den.: Danish Institute for Educational Research. [Reprinted Chicago: Univ. of Chicago Press, 1980.]

Reid, Joy. 1986. "Using the Writer's Workbench in Composition Teaching and Scoring," in Charles W. Stansfield, ed., *Technology and Language Testing.* Washington, DC: Teachers of English to Speakers of Other Languages.

Samejima, F. 1969. *Estimation of Latent Ability Using a Response Pattern of Graded Scores.* Psychometric Monograph No. 17.

————. 1972. *A General Model for Free-Response Data.* Psychometric Monograph No. 18.

Sang, F., B. Schmitz, Helmut J. Vollmer, J. Baumert, and P. M. Roeder. 1986. "Models of Second Language Competence: A Structural Equation Approach." *Language Testing* 3,1: 54–79.

Sasaki, Miyuki. 1991. "A Comparison of Two Methods for Detecting Differential Item Functioning in an ESL Placement Test." *Language Testing* 8,2: 95–111.

Scheuneman, Janice. 1979. "A Method of Assessing Bias in Test Items." *Journal of Educational Measurement* 16: 143–52.

Seliger, Herbert W. 1985. "Testing Authentic Language: The Problem of Meaning." *Language Testing* 2,1: 1–15.

Shapere, Dudley. 1964. "The Structure of Scientific Revolutions." *Philosophical Review* 73: 383–94.

Shavelson, Richard, and Noreen Webb. 1981. "Generalizability Theory: 1973–1980." *British Journal of Mathematical and Statistical Psychology* 34: 133–66.

Shohamy, Elana, and Thea Reves. 1985. "Authentic Language Tests: Where from and Where To?" *Language Testing* 2,1: 48–59.

Skehan, Peter. 1984. "Issues in the Testing of English for Specific Purposes." *Language Testing* 1,2: 202–20.

————. 1989. *Individual Differences in Second-Language Learning.* London, Eng.: Edward Arnold.

————. 1991. "Language Testing: State of the Art Review," *Language Teaching Abstracts.* Cambridge, Eng.: Cambridge Univ. Press.

Spolsky, Bernard, 1985. "The Limits of Authenticity in Language Testing." *Language Testing* 2,1: 31–40.

————. 1989. *Conditions for Second Language Learning.* Oxford, Eng.: Oxford Univ. Press.

————. 1993. *Measured Words: A History of Modern Language Testing up to 1965.* [in press]

Stansfield, Charles W., ed. 1986. *Technology and Language Testing.* Washington, DC: Teachers of English to Speakers of Other Languages.

Stevenson, Douglas K. 1985. "Authenticity, Validity, and a Tea Party." *Language Testing* 2,1: 41–47.

Stevenson, Jose, and Susan Gross. 1991. "Use of a Computerized Adaptive Testing Model for ESOL/Bilingual Entry/Exit Decision Making," in Patricia Dunkel, ed., *Computer-Assisted Language Learning and Testing.* New York: Newbury House/Harper Collins.

Tung, Peter. 1986. "Computerized Adaptive Testing: Implications for Language Test Developers," in Charles W. Stansfield, ed., *Technology and Language Testing.* Washington, DC: Teachers of English to Speakers of Other Languages.

Turner, Carolyn E. 1989. "The Underlying Factor Structure of L2 Cloze Test Performance in Francophone, University-Level Students: Causal Modelling as an Approach to Construct Validation." *Language Testing* 6,2: 172–97.

Vollmer, Helmut J. 1981. "Issue or Non-Issue: General Language Proficiency Revisited," in J. Charles Alderson and Arthur Hughes, eds., *ELT Documents III: Issues in Language Testing.* London, Eng.: The British Council.

Warm, Thomas A. 1978. *A Primer of Item Response Theory.* Oklahoma City, OK: U.S. Coast Guard Institute.

Wolfson, Nessa. 1976. "Speech Event and Natural Speech: Some Implications for Sociolinguistic Methodology." *Language in Society* 5: 189–209.

————. 1981. "Invitations, Compliments and the Competence of the Native Speaker." *International Journal of Psycholinguistics* 24.

Wright, Benjamin D., and G. N. Masters. 1982. *Rating Scale Analysis.* Chicago: MESA.

Wright, Benjamin D., R. Mead, and R. Draba. 1976. *Detecting and Correcting Item Bias with a Logistic Model.* Research Memorandum 22. Chicago: Univ. of Chicago, Statistical Laboratory, Department of Education.

Wright, Benjamin D., and Mark H. Stone. 1979. *Best Test Design.* Chicago: MESA.

Zeidner, Moshe. 1986. "Are English Language Aptitude Tests Biased Towards Culturally Different Minority Groups? Some Israeli Findings." *Language Testing* 3,1: 80–98.

————. 1987. "A Comparison of Ethnic, Sex, and Age Bias in the Predictive Validity of English Language Aptitude Tests: Some Israeli Data." *Language Testing* 4,1: 55–71.

10

Language-Learning Research: *Cottage Industry or Consolidated Enterprise?*

John L. D. Clark

Defense Language Institute Foreign Language Center

Fred Davidson

University of Illinois

Introduction

Research on language learning—defined as the principled investigation of phenomena associated with the acquisition of skills or abilities in an other-than-native language through formalized learning activities and/or naturalistic exposure—is at a watershed point within the United States and internationally. Through the consistent and, in large part, highly successful efforts of a number of individual investigators, and with the support of organizations such as ACTFL, TESOL, and others, the language-teaching profession can point with justifiable pride to a large body of research-based information available both to the research community and to practitioners in the field. On the whole, pride can also be taken in the quality of the studies reported. These studies may be considered to have made noteworthy advances in research design and procedural rigor, with the net result of appreciably increasing the validity and informational utility of the obtained results.

The primary purpose of this chapter is to suggest that, largely as a result of these prior efforts, it is now entirely feasible—and highly desirable—for the language-research field to move away from what might be characterized as the individualized approach

John L. D. Clark (Ed.D., Harvard University) is Dean of Program Evaluation, Research, and Testing at the Defense Language Institute Foreign Language Center, Presidio of Monterey, California, where he directs a fifty-member staff involved in foreign language test development, applied research, and evaluation of classroom-based and "distance" instruction. His current interests include improvement in the theory and practice of speaking proficiency assessment and the increased application of technology in language teaching and testing.

Fred Davidson (Ph.D., University of California–Los Angeles) is Assistant Professor in the Division of English as an International Language, University of Illinois at Urbana–Champaign, where he teaches in the M.A. TESL program. His major research interests include criterion-referenced language test development and the statistical investigation of the trait structure of language tests. In addition, he works in the area of refinement of data structures for applied linguistics research.

to research activities toward a much more explicitly collaborative and consolidated effort. In such an effort, individual researchers would not carry out their work in isolation but as part and parcel of a larger, formally established and operated endeavor. The goal of such an undertaking would be to obtain and disseminate empirically sound and pragmatically useful information on important language-learning issues. This would be accomplished through a series of individual research activities that would be planned, conducted, and reported within the context of this larger collaborative framework. For purposes of discussion, a completely voluntary, highly networked undertaking of this type will be referred to as a Research Consolidation Project (RCP).

It should be mentioned at the outset that a consolidated research initiative along the lines described in this chapter could be viewed by some readers as a top-down effort to impose a particular theoretical perspective upon independent researchers. It is the authors' belief that such a concern, although certainly appropriately raised, would not be borne out in the context of the proposed undertaking for a variety of reasons. First, the RCP, or any similar collaborative effort, would be, *de facto,* a strictly voluntary undertaking on the part of the individual participants. In the event that, following a reasonable period of familiarization with the RCP process and with its conceptual and operational characteristics, particular researchers or groups of researchers were to find that they could not in good conscience support the research directions or activities taking place under RCP auspices, they would certainly not hesitate to "vote with their feet" or (more desirably) provide their own substantive input and suggestions on specific changes that they feel should be made. Indeed, by virtue of the networking capabilities inherent in the RCP structure, dedicated researchers with a differing orientation toward a particular research issue might obtain, through this means, broader dissemination and consideration of their position within the profession than would otherwise be the case.

Second, except for a small advisory board and an even smaller technical/administrative staff, there would be, under the proposed RCP system, no "top" that could or would impose perspectives not generally shared by the RCP constituency. Electronic communication from RCP members to the project office would be a major mechanism for information exchange and policy development and would include frequent opportunities for all RCP members to comment and "ballot" on substantive issues with respect to the scope, nature, and direction of RCP activities.

Third, it would be anticipated that actively participating RCP members would have considerably more freedom and available time to explore research areas of particular interest to them by taking advantage of the variety of services available through the RCP. These would include contact opportunities with other individual researchers or interest groups in particular topical domains and the use as desired of a variety of types of electronically stored information available through the RCP in these areas. Of particular significance would be the opportunity to avoid or minimize the laborious planning and development of data-collection instruments, interview protocols, and other operational components of the research process by being able to access and directly utilize (or appropriately modify) potentially useful materials already carefully elaborated by colleague researchers.

The concept of and need for complete academic freedom in the research process is unequivocally endorsed by the authors, who also believe that the fuller discussion to follow of the RCP concept and its proposed manner of operation will substantially and properly respond to any reader concerns with respect to this issue.

The specific organizational structure of the suggested RCP is described more extensively later in the chapter. For purposes of this overview, its basic components include

- A small project staff, working under the auspices of a representative advisory board, with a solid foreign/second-language research background as well as a high level of technical capability in database design and computer-based information processing and retrieval
- An electronic networking system with full capabilities for individual and group electronic mail; uploading and downloading of textual, statistical, and other types of data, including audio and video material; on-line "browsing" and retrieval of computer-stored material; and on-line conferencing by individual interest groups
- Physical facilities for occasional on-site meetings of project participants to carry out project-related activities not adequately handled through electronic communication means
- Self-generated and/or externally provided income adequate to maintain the core staff and physical facilities, including the electronic network system, as well as to provide modest honoraria to project members for specified activities on behalf of the project

It is the authors' opinion that successful implementation of a joint, entirely voluntary project along these general lines would provide a meaningful conceptual framework, as well as a practical operational vehicle, through which the language-learning field could take advantage of the considerable expertise, insights, and resources currently available to and being applied by individual researchers. An undertaking of this sort would permit a much higher level of common effort, synergy of results, and overall usefulness to the field than is presently the case. In this regard, it is anticipated that the suggested approach would have considerable positive impact on each of the major components of the research process, including (1) initial selection of particular areas and topics to receive research attention; (2) study design; (3) instrumentation and data-gathering activities; (4) data analysis; and (5) data storage and dissemination.

In the remainder of this chapter, each of the five component areas of the research process identified above is described and discussed in some detail from the perspective of the conceptual and operational benefits that could be obtained through an organized, intentionally collaborative approach to the activities at issue in that area. This discussion is followed by a more detailed description of the suggested organizational structure for the proposed RCP, including an indication of several developmental steps that might be undertaken during the initial stage of project operation.

Selection of Research Areas and Topics

As previously indicated, foreign/second-language researchers—including the present authors—guard with considerable diligence and vigor the concept of academic freedom. This concept includes, among other things, the important provision that the individual researcher must have the ultimate authority and responsibility for the selection of research areas or topics of inquiry that he or she chooses to address in any given study. Particularly to be avoided are any intellectual, political, institutional, financial, or other types of coercion that would hamper or inappropriately influence the choice of research topic or study procedure. Although this bedrock principle is of crucial importance not only to the individual researcher but also to the overall integrity of the research process, it is also undeniably the case that numerous other factors may bear, to at least some extent, on the final identification of a research topic. For example, for research conducted by graduate students, a major influence is often the recommendation of the thesis or dissertation adviser, frequently coincident with the adviser's own primary research area or current topical interests. At the department or institutional level, a tradition of specialization or research emphasis in a particular area often influences both senior and more junior researchers in topic selection. Across the board, relatively "comfortable" lines of inquiry, in which a sizable body of literature or straightforward data-gathering and analysis procedures have already been established, may play an appreciable role in the topic-selection process.

On the other hand, there are two major considerations in topic selection that do not appear to be regularly taken into account on an adequately widespread or systematic basis. The first is the degree of pragmatic value that the development of additional reliable information in a particular area would be expected to have for either the overall improvement of formalized language instruction or the provision of increased knowledge about the nature of informal language acquisition. It is believed that RCP-based mechanisms for ongoing practitioner involvement in the identification of potential "high yield" studies in this regard will provide very useful input for participating researchers to consider when deciding on research topics to be addressed.

A second issue in topic selection is the nature and degree of "fit" of a given study within a larger conceptual framework that attempts to characterize language learning and acquisition phenomena at a more holistic level. Such a framework can serve to demonstrate or suggest interrelationships among phenomena that could provide a more generalized and more powerful view of the language-learning/acquisition process than could be discerned through the examination of individual studies and their particular discrete findings.

With respect to this second consideration, a potentially very productive approach to the establishment of an overall research framework within which individual studies could be situated—and from the perspective of which their outcomes could be usefully characterized and reported—has been proposed by Bernard Spolsky in his recently published *Conditions for Second Language Learning* (Spolsky 1989). Notwithstanding one reviewer's criticism of this framework as being overly general and insufficiently operationalized (DeKeyser 1991), the Spolsky volume has been well received within the field and was awarded the 1989 Kenneth W. Mildenberger Prize as the outstanding research publication in foreign language teaching and literature for that year.

The Spolsky Model

The foreign/second-language field is not without numerous and often conflicting theoretical descriptions of the language-acquisition process, as evidenced by the some forty separate models identified by Larsen-Freeman and Long (1991: 227). The analytical framework proposed by Spolsky, however, is of considerably greater scope than other current models and may have greater utility by virtue of the fact that it attempts to take into account all possible processes and influences that operate to determine the nature and extent of language learning. These include, in Spolsky's formulation, the broad subcategories of (1) variables associated with the language being learned (for example, its degree of linguistic similarity or distance from the learner's native language); (2) the social context in which the language learning takes place, including the relative emphasis or status accorded the language within the political, religious, educational, and other social systems; (3) personal and background characteristics that the individual language learner brings to the learning process, including such variables as general intelligence, language-learning aptitude, attitudes toward and motivation for learning, prior study of or informal exposure to the same or a similar language, and so forth; and (4) the specific opportunities for learning to which the learner is exposed, either in a formal academic setting or in a more naturalistic acquisition environment. Across these four major categories, Spolsky identifies a total of 74 individual variables or "conditions for learning" that he posits as responsible, in varying degrees and combinations depending on the learning context, for the actual linguistic outcome, that is, for the nature and extent of language performance ability attained by the learner.

The power of the Spolsky model and, by the same token, its considerable research appeal lie precisely in its synoptic nature, which seeks to embrace all areas and traditions of principled investigation in the language-learning field. These include comparative linguistic analysis, description and quantification of learner variables associated with language-learning success, sociological and sociometric issues, curriculum and instructional design, and, of major consequence to the entire undertaking, the design and use of appropriate data-gathering instruments. This latter category includes not only the criterial measures of linguistic outcomes against which the nature and degree of influence of the independent-variable learning conditions are assessed, but also any and all types of instrumentation used to categorize or quantify the learning conditions themselves. Potential instrumentation types include such diverse measures as background questionnaires, attitude/motivation scales, learning preference and learning styles inventories, language aptitude tests, and standardized descriptions of instructional processes, used to characterize the particular learning opportunities provided the student in a given instructional setting. By the same token, the Spolsky model may be considered sufficiently broad to mitigate the frequent criticism that bottom-up data collection and analysis are inherently prone to inappropriately narrow theorizing (see McLaughlin 1987: 80).

As we have seen, the broad scope of the Spolsky model brings within the conceptual purview of a single descriptive scheme a large panoply of topical domains and investigative approaches at issue in the language-learning/acquisition research field. In view of this fact, the present authors would suggest, as the first step in the development of a consolidated, cooperative research program, that the Spolsky model receive serious consideration for adoption as the initial, prototype descriptive framework within which individual research topics and their associated studies could be situated. Such an approach would certainly not rule out the possibility that accumulated practical experience with the Spolsky model and the results of relevant empirical studies could lead to its progressive fine tuning, substantial revision, or perhaps even outright rejection. However, given the obvious necessity to start from at least some agreed-upon taxonomic perspective in initiating an integrated, systematically designed research effort, the Spolsky model has much to recommend it in this regard.

If, for purposes of discussion, the provisional initial adoption of the Spolsky framework can be assumed, three further steps would be required to make this framework maximally useful as an aid for identifying and selecting research topics First, an RCP-convened working group of interested researchers, ideally encompassing all major subject-matter areas and investigatory disciplines within the purview of the model, would need to review carefully each of the Spolsky condition statements and produce associated scope notes further operationalizing the meaning and intended coverage of the statement. For example, a scope note to accompany Condition 70—entitled "Simplified Language" and defined by Spolsky as "The language is simplified and controlled"—would attempt to clarify how this condition might be operationalized in an instructional context. Such a scope note might indicate that "simplified and controlled language" includes any printed target-language texts that are not completely authentic (that is, not taken directly from a real-life, nonpedagogically oriented source), as well as any listening-comprehension situations in which the speaker is addressing an interlocutor known to be nonnative in the target language. The main goals of this activity would be to (1) make it as clear as possible where a particular study or proposed study "fits" within the Spolsky framework with respect to the learning condition(s) at issue, and (2) suggest specific approaches to quantifying and measuring these conditions within an empirical research context.

As a second undertaking, it would be necessary to determine, at least on an approximate basis, what amount of prior research has been conducted within the areas encompassed by a given learning condition. This determination could give researchers a rough initial idea of where within the Spolsky model there may indeed be an abundance (or even over-abundance) of research information available, and where major lacunae may still exist. Other things being equal, proposed topics in the lesser-explored areas would be expected to take research precedence over those for which ample and solid empirical information is already available. Although the rough estimates of research specialists would probably have to suffice in the near term, it should be possible, in the longer term, for the RCP to conduct or commission targeted literature reviews that would have as objectives both quantifying the general amount of research available in a given topical area and developing a substantial database of such studies. Entries within this database would be indexed and retrievable with respect to specified elements of the Spolsky framework (or an appropriate later adaptation) and would provide an extensive, well-developed, and extremely useful point of entry to the available studies for use by future investigators in the same or similar areas.

Third, it would appear very important to take into account already available or obtainable data about the most critical information needs of second-language teachers, school administrators, or other non-researcher practitioners that could be addressed through targeted research undertakings. While an appreciable overlap certainly already exists between current research efforts and what teachers and front-line administrators would like to know, it is also likely that there are numerous disconnects, the nature and magnitude of which could be determined through a structured, ongoing process for practitioner involvement in identifying research needs. Such a process could involve regular meetings and/or electronic networking, facilitated by the RCP effort, in which knowledgeable representatives of the practitioner community would identify significant knowledge gaps that, in their collective opinion, pose major impediments to efficient and effective language learning. Such impediments might be identified with respect to issues in curriculum design, instructional procedures, or other practical facets of the learning process.

Study Design

The accuracy and adequacy of the study design for any given research undertaking are critically dependent on the expertise of the investigator(s) and, by the same token, on the care taken to ensure that all consequential aspects of the research process are properly accounted for in the study design. Crucial considerations in this regard include the initial selection of subjects (with the associated sampling and generalizability-of-results concerns); validity and reliability of the data-collection instruments; proper operational or statistical control of extraneous variables; and appropriateness and proper application of the statistical analyses or other data-reduction procedures employed. Although study design per se is not usually a problematic issue in studies conducted by recognized experts in a given research area, other researchers active or potentially active in the field might benefit substantially from an initial design-review service that could be provided under the auspices of a consolidated research program. This would be especially appropriate for "part-time researchers" wishing to carry out a properly conceived and executed study in a particular area of interest as an adjunct to their primary teaching or administrative duties. However, even more experienced researchers might find it advantageous to be able readily to contact, via the RCP system, one or more recognized specialists in a given research area for expert consultation on an as-needed basis.

In addition to providing such a design-review and consultation service, the RCP could serve as a focal point for the collection and dissemination of authoritative "how-to" materials and procedural aids to interested requesters. Such aids could cover not only study design but also other major components of the research process, including data reduction and statistical analysis. These materials could include both existing guides—such as the ITEMS (*Instructional Topics in Educational Measurement*) series published by the National Council on Measurement in Education in its *Educational Measurement* newsletter—as well as other instructional materials expressly prepared for inclusion in the RCP database.

Instrumentation and Data Gathering

By "instrumentation" is meant any stimulus materials or standardized procedures used to obtain subjects' responses in the course of the research study. This includes background or self-rating questionnaires, paper-and-pencil tests, and performance tests such as oral proficiency interviews. Although the foreign/second-language field has recently made substantial progress toward increased standardization of data-gathering instruments and processes, it is still quite far from typical practice in other fields of inquiry, particularly in the natural sciences, which routinely use uniform, agreed-upon data-gathering vehicles across a large number of individual studies in a given research area. Notwithstanding the inherently "softer" nature of empirical inquiry in the language-learning field, there are numerous areas in which greater commonality could readily be achieved through RCP-coordinated efforts to identify or develop and jointly utilize standardized instruments or other codified data-gathering procedures on an across-studies basis.

One immediate example of the potential power and utility of standardized instrumentation can be given in relation to the collection of data on subjects' age. A substantial increase in the comparability and inter-interpretability of any of the large number of studies for which subjects' age is a variable of interest could be provided by the uniform collection of this datum in the form of the actual month, day, and year of birth, as opposed to more eclectic and less commensurate choices such as "How old are you?" or "When were you born?"—both often resulting in year-only responses. Availability of exact date-of-birth information, coupled with appropriate computer subroutines, would make it possible to use the fine-grained "total days of age" in any statistical analyses. In turn, this could result in the identification of between-groups differences that would not be apparent in a less precise "age in years" classification, particularly in studies involving nearly contemporaneous groups (for example, 4th grade vs. 5th-grade FLES students). The essential point to be made is that there is potentially much to be gained in providing an opportunity and an organizational mechanism for language-learning researchers to collaborate in the selection or, when necessary, the design and development of standardized data-gathering instruments and procedures. Such instruments and procedures would properly serve individual research purposes while providing a standardized and common framework within which to better report and interpret the results of a larger corpus of studies within a given area of inquiry. The proposed RCP approach would provide a very practical mechanism for both the initial design and subsequent use of specified standardized instruments and their efficient distribution to participating researchers in the field.

For purposes of further discussion, "instrumentation" will be divided into three major categories: (1) language proficiency tests or other criterial *outcome measures* used to determine each subject's ability or standing with respect to the linguistic performances being investigated; (2) interview protocols, questionnaires, tests, or other instruments used to measure such *learner-related variables* as interest in language study or aptitude for successful language learning; and (3) observation protocols, self-report questionnaires, or other instruments or procedures intended to classify or quantify the *process variables* at issue in the study. Process variables are defined as those instructional activities and/or naturalistic learning events taking place during the study that would be expected to exert a material influence on the criterial performance outcomes.

Outcome Measures

With respect to criterion outcome measures, the specific measure(s) to be used in a study should reflect, as closely as possible, the specific type and degree of subjects' language performance at issue. Depending on the scope and purpose of the study, appropriate criterion measures could range from highly focused tests of a discrete aspect of performance to more general tests of overall functional proficiency. For example, in a study investigating subjects' ability, following some specified instructional intervention, to pair certain spoken target-language words with their pictorial representations, the appropriate outcome measure would probably consist of a direct work-sample test of this particular ability. Such a test might provide a numerical score corresponding to the number of word-picture pairs successfully identified. On the other hand, studies aimed at assessing students' overall language performance at the end of a relatively lengthy instructional program might be expected to make use of considerably more generalized testing procedures. The results of these procedures might be expressed in such broad descriptive terms as "Can handle with confidence but not with facility most social situations including introductions and casual conversations about current events."

To consider first the broader "general proficiency" measures, the language field is at present in the rather fortunate position of having access to a number of well-conceived, rigorously developed and standardized tests of listening and reading comprehension, based on the Interagency Language Roundtable/American Council on the Teaching of Foreign Languages (ILR/ACTFL) verbal descriptions of functional performance in these two skill areas. General proficiency measures for speaking, although necessarily less standardized than the analogous listening/reading measures because of their human-rater requirements, have been administered in the government sector for over thirty years. Within about the past ten years, they have also become reasonably widespread throughout the secondary and postsecondary academic community, largely as a result of ACTFL's dissemination efforts and corresponding tester training and certification program.

It must be acknowledged, however, that a lively debate exists within the profession over the validity of the ILR/ACTFL descriptive scales and associated testing approach. Questions have been raised, for example, about whether it is possible to develop a measure of general proficiency that is completely independent of instructional processes or the sequencing of instructional events. (For discussion of this and other issues, see Lado 1978; Lantolf and Frawley 1985; Bachman and Savignon 1986; Lowe 1986; Clark and Clifford 1987; and Clark and Lett 1988.) Nonetheless, pending the progressive elaboration and refinement of proficiency testing concepts and instruments in general, taking into account as appropriate the criticisms and developmental suggestions of knowledgeable individuals, the language-learning research community could take a major practical step forward in increasing the degree of standardization and interinterpretability of research efforts involving general proficiency measurement if it were to make the fullest possible use of ILR/ACTFL-based instruments and approaches as a common metric in these studies.

With regard to studies addressing discrete elements of linguistic behavior, such as vocabulary development via computer-based tutorials or phonetic-accuracy gain following specified pronunciation exercises, the criterion behaviors at issue are inherently more discrete and more highly study-specific than is the case in studies of general proficiency development. Nonetheless, even here, it is possible to envision at least some acrossstudy use of similar measurement instruments. Such standardization could be appreciably advanced through the establishment of an RCP-supported database of criterion test instruments previously administered by participating researchers, appropriately indexed and available for use by other researchers in a given topical area. Of course, the unmodified use of a particular instrument might not be possible in all instances. For example, a test of Russian lexicon could obviously not be used "as is" in a subsequent study involving learners of Spanish. However, the specific test instructions, item-presentation formats, and several other operational features of the initial test could be directly incorporated in a Spanish version. Use of this closely comparable instrument in the Spanish study would considerably increase the measurement comparability and mutual interpretability of the two studies.

Learner-Related Variables

Considerable strides have been made over the past several years in the objectification and quantification of several major independent variables typically at issue in language-learning research—in particular, the intellectual, attitudinal, motivational, and other personal characteristics of the learners themselves. Reliable and thoroughly validated measures of general cognitive ability (IQ) have been available for years, as have tests of specialized aptitude for language learning, most notably the *Modern Language Aptitude Test* (Carroll and Sapon 1959) and the Pimsleur *Language Aptitude Battery* (Pimsleur 1966). More recently (see Parry and Stansfield 1990), research efforts have been undertaken to develop improved measures of potential language-learning success. These new instruments may provide the ability to predict differentially the particular language skills (for example, reading vs. speaking) and the particular type of language (for example, tonal languages vs. highly inflected languages) at which the learner may prove more adept. With respect to motivation and attitudinal variables, a number of relevant instruments have been developed over the past twenty years (Gardner and Lambert 1972; Gardner 1990). Although these are not readily available through commercial sources (as are the Carroll-Sapon and Pimsleur batteries), it may prove possible to include these and other similar noncommercial tests in a comprehensive database of measurement instruments available for direct use (or principled modification) by RCP participants.

Other candidates for inclusion, in a readily retrievable form, in a research-instrument database would be measures of student learning styles and preferences—in particular the ambitious 121-item *Strategy Inventory for Language Learning* (SILL) questionnaire developed by Rebecca Oxford and her associates (Oxford and Nyikos 1989; Oxford 1990). This inventory is designed to determine the particular types of language-learning procedures (for example, memorization of word lists vs. active interaction with native speakers of the language) favored by the respondent. In addition to its use as a practical pedagogical aid, the SILL would be expected to provide very valuable data in the context of language-learning studies, as a measure of student behavioral characteristics associated with language-learning success or lack of success in particular instructional settings.

Process Variables

In addition to the criterion measures used to evaluate the output of a given language-learning/acquisition activity and the learner-specific variables that characterize important aspects of the human input to the system, the instrumentation and data-gathering procedures for a given study must include some means to typify the learning or acquisition process. This process has been defined by Clark and O'Mara (1991) as "any and all external situations, stimuli, or other influences encountered by the learner that are known, or reasonably expected, to influence the course, nature, or extent of acquisition of some type of language 'ability' on the learner's part" (p. 87). Objective characterization of the learning/acquisition process, in some usefully quantified (or at a minimum, categorized) form, is perhaps the most challenging measurement task facing the foreign/second-language researcher. At one extreme, the learning process to which the learner is exposed in the course of a small-scale, highly defined learning task (for example, the aural comprehension of spoken lexical items) can be very explicitly described, as well as readily replicated in follow-up or cross-validation studies. At the other extreme, in a research effort to determine the effects on general speaking proficiency of a junior-year abroad program, the process at issue would consist of all the myriad of formal language-learning and informal language-exposure contingencies operating on each of the program participants throughout the lengthy time period involved. In such a complex environment, adequate process-data gathering would require the simultaneous use of a variety of procedures. These would be expected to include not only the diligent collection of available "hard" data (for example, the number of classroom hours of formal instruction) but also the use of a variety of self-report techniques or other less direct approaches to information gathering in less immediately quantifiable areas. One example would be a questionnaire eliciting subjects' estimates of the amount and nature of their exposure to the target language outside of the classroom, both in a receptive mode (newspaper/magazine reading, television watching, and so forth) and as an active interlocutor in conversational situations with native speakers.

Regardless of the degree of specificity or generality of the learning/acquisition process being investigated, a consolidated approach would be expected to provide, in total, considerably more comprehensive, valid, and useful information about the phenomena being evaluated than would a series of studies with little or no commonality of instrumentation or of data-gathering procedures. At the "discrete learning task" level of inquiry (for example, two or more separate investigations of vocabulary learning with or without the use of contextual aids), prior coordination and agreement to use the same or highly similar procedures and data gathering instruments across each of the studies would result in what would essentially be replicated, cross-validating experiments. In this regard, the networking capabilities potentially available under the aegis of the proposed RCP would greatly facilitate both the identification of candidate studies for replication using other languages or learner populations and the direct sharing of instruments and protocols for joint use in these efforts. By the same token, at the more holistic, "junior-year-abroad" level of inquiry, such networking would offer the possibility of incorporating identical or highly similar student-background and self-report questionnaires or other more generalized data-gathering protocols in multiple studies within this same topical area. An RCP-based interest-group approach to the identification or development—and subsequent across-study use—of operationally comparable criterion- and/or independent-variable measures would permit the synergistic combining of the insights and experience of several different researchers, both in the process of initial instrument selection or development and in the analysis and interpretation of results obtained through the common use of these instruments.

Data Analysis

As previously suggested with respect to initial research design, the quality and appropriateness of the data-analysis procedures used in a given study are highly dependent on the technical background and experience of the researchers. In this regard, it would probably not be expected that the level of assistance available to a "junior" researcher through the previously mentioned RCP-coordinated review service would be of the extent and depth needed to produce an autonomously competent statistical analyst. However, it would be quite reasonable to envision that a detailed prior review, by more expert participants, of the data-analysis plan for a given study would provide a number of highly useful recommendations for enhancing or strengthening the plan, including the identification of appropriate bibliographic references, procedural aids, and so forth.

A considerably greater contribution of the RCP with regard to the data-analysis component of the research process would be the encouragement and facilitation of *meta-analytic studies*. The meta-analytic process may be viewed as the statistical analog of the verbal "literature review." The literature review in a given area of inquiry attempts to point out differences and similarities in the research approaches and observed results across a number of studies and to arrive at a synthesized verbal description of what the totality of studies appear to indicate about the phenomena under investigation. In a comparable manner, the meta-analysis attempts to combine and simultaneously analyze the statistical results of two or more individually conducted studies to produce a "meta" result that is more robust from a statistical perspective and of broader practical applicability than any of the constituent studies considered separately. (For further information on the meta-analytic process, see Cochran 1954; Light and Smith 1971; Glass 1976.)

The conduct of meta-analytic studies within a given area of inquiry would be significantly facilitated in the context of a consolidated research effort. First, assuming that studies conducted under such auspices would be situated and indexed within the topical framework of the Spolsky learning-conditions model (or an appropriate modification of or substitution for this model), it would be readily possible to identify common-topic groupings of studies to be considered for meta-analytic attention. Second, to the extent that several of these studies were to make use of the same criterion output measures (and, to the extent possible, the same or similar input and process measures), the interpretive power and extent of applicability of the meta-analytic results would be correspondingly increased. Third, the initial identification of topical areas to be considered for meta-analytic attention could be informed by the recommendations of RCP-convened "practitioner" representatives, who would be asked to assist in the identification of the most critical information needs from instructional, administrative, or other user perspectives.

Data Storage and Dissemination

As will be discussed in detail in this section, recent conceptual and technical advances in the field of electronic database design and information processing have raised the very real prospect of a paradigmatic shift both in the way that "data" are conceptualized and in the way that "reports" based on these data are produced and disseminated. In this regard, it will be useful to characterize two fundamentally different orientations to data storage and dissemination; these will be referred to, respectively, as *individual/ nonelectronic* and *collective/electronic.*

It is doubtful that any reader of this volume would be unfamiliar with the individual/ nonelectronic approach to data storage and dissemination. This approach, which reflects a long and respected tradition in the research field, is perhaps best exemplified by the typical dissertation project, in which, following arduous effort on the part of the researcher, the painstakingly obtained data find their designated final storage in a dusty (and perhaps even unlabeled) cardboard box in the attic, with the information derived from the data having been reported in a carefully typed, bound, and shelved dissertation copy. Similar procedures are also usually followed in subsequent research studies, such as those supported by the researcher's own institution, in which the analogous storage device may well be an archival file kept in the basement or other marginally accessible location, with the project report characteristically in the form of a hard-copy document, printed in relatively low volume and provided on request to other interested researchers.

Under the individual/nonelectronic mode, little attention is typically paid to storing the data in a manner that would facilitate their subsequent use or distribution. Indeed, individually held data are often highly idiosyncratic in format and are poorly documented with regard to content description, coding procedures employed, and other basic characteristics. With respect to results reporting or other types of dissemination in a nonelectronic mode, virtually the only way in which an optimum "packet" of information—suitably tailored in its overall length, content, and other important features—can be provided to a particular reader or category of reader is by laboriously drafting and reproducing a separate hard-copy report.

The collective/electronic orientation to data storage and dissemination provides a sharp contrast to the individual/nonelectronic mode. First, with respect to data storage, the current availability of both mainframe- and microcomputer-based hard-disk drives and other electronic media with storage capacities measured in gigabytes (each gigabyte representing a billion digits or characters) makes it readily possible to store and maintain— in electronic form and at a single location—primary response data, analyzed data sets, the full text of project reports, ancillary documents (for example, summaries of major findings), and even digitized audio and video components for a large number of individual studies. Second, as a direct consequence of the electronically coded form in which the data are represented in the database (and assuming that they have been appropriately indexed at the point of entry into the system), all or selected subsets of this information can be easily retrieved and provided to the user on an immediate (real-time) basis. This capability, in turn, makes operationally feasible the concept of a virtually infinite number of different, individually tailored "reports" that could be generated and made available on the basis of the data contained in the system. Such tailored assemblages of information could and would include not only the traditional narrative descriptions of project activities and findings, but also a large variety of other types of data of significant interest and importance to colleague researchers and others in the language-learning/acquisition field. Under the individual/nonelectronic mode of operation, such data have characteristically been highly difficult and unwieldy to collect and disseminate to potential users.

In order to discuss more fully the conceptual characteristics and technical attributes of a comprehensive data storage and dissemination system along the lines mentioned above, it will be useful to define and briefly characterize seven types or categories of data. Collectively, these definitions include, but also stretch appreciably beyond, the kinds of records and documents usually thought of as data. However, this more synoptic characterization is necessary to fully cover each of the currently feasible constituents of a consolidated, electronically mediated research database.

Primary data are defined as the observable responses made by subjects in the course of the activity under investigation. For example, in tests of oral proficiency, the primary data are the actual examinee speech performances that the investigator hears and observes in real time. In studies of listening comprehension or other internalized processes that cannot be directly observed, primary data are those overt real-time responses made by the subject in response to the particular data-gathering contingencies arranged by the researcher. For example, primary data related to the investigation of listening comprehension ability might consist of written-out or multiple-choice answers to printed questions on the content or meaning of heard material. With respect to the capture and storage of primary data as defined above, it should be noted that, insofar as overt speech or other "production" responses on the part of the subject are concerned, the truly primary data are observable only once, on a real-time basis, and are immediately lost to any subsequent observations. In all such instances, data storage and reexamination are possible only with respect to mechanically produced recordings of the original behaviors (for example, audio or video recordings of tests of oral proficiency). For purposes of the present discussion, primary data will be defined to include recordings of real-time performances, although it should also be mentioned that the overall fidelity of the recording, in the sense of adequately reproducing all features of the original behavior that would be considered of any operational relevance to the judgments at issue in the study, is a significant research design and instrumentation question in its own right.

Quantified data are defined as those individual records, expressed in categorical or numerical terms, that result from human or mechanical determination of the amount or quality of performance exhibited by subjects in response to a given stimulus situation. These evaluative records may be produced on a real-time basis immediately following the subjects' production of the primary data (for example, judges' scoring at a diving competition), or at a later time on the basis of (recorded) primary data (for example, audio or video recordings of tests of oral proficiency, forwarded to a central rating facility). With respect to multiple-choice testing, quantified data are the right-wrong (or other categorical) records of the subjects' responses to individual test items.

Analyzed data are the recorded results of additional numerical or categorical processing of the quantified data that has been carried out with the goal of making the outcomes of the study more readily apparent to the researcher and, ultimately, to other reviewers or users of the research information. The scope and complexity of analyzed data range from the simplest types of verbal or statistical summaries (for example, a subject's overall rating of "good" across three separate performances, or a given total score on a multiple-choice test) up to the most highly sophisticated multivariate analyses, which attempt to take into statistical account a large amount of additional quantified data about the subjects and/or the research environment that are known or presumed to have exerted some effect on the study results in addition to that attributable to the main variable(s) at issue.

Reported data consist of the formal written account of the study and its results, typically including relevant descriptions of study procedures, analysis of subjects' performance, and conclusions concerning the results of the study. The supporting argumentation for these conclusions is also typically given. In most instances, the main narrative section of the final study report would constitute the "reported data" as defined here.

Instrumental data include any printed or otherwise presented (for example, audio/ video) materials that have played an operational role in the study by having been either (1) administered to or in some other way formally encountered by the subject in the course of the study or (2) used by the researcher or other study personnel (for example, essay test graders) as procedural or evaluative guides during the study. Examples of instrumental data in the first category include any and all learning materials or exercises, tests or other instruments (either criterion- or independent variable-related), and questionnaires or survey materials of all types. Instrumental data in the second category include interview protocols, rating guides, test scoring aids, and so forth. Typically, a variety of types of (paper-based) instrumental data are provided as appendices to the study final report, either in their full form or as exemplary excerpts (for example, sample items from a longer operational test). Instrumental data are also considered to include, somewhat arbitrarily, references to the particular researcher(s) involved in a given research study, or to other recognized experts or resource persons in the topical area in question.

Derivative data consist of any stand-alone summaries, synopses, reformulations for different audiences, and so forth, of information contained in the original reported data. The typical journal article, describing study procedures and results in a relatively summary fashion and for a somewhat broader audience than that of the official study report, would be a common example of derivative data, as would a two-page "this is what we found out" report of study findings intended for presentation to a district school board.

Citation data are brief descriptions used to identify and denote the existence/availability of discrete sets of data within any and all of the other six data types. For both reported and derivative data, the corresponding citation data would consist of an appropriate bibliographic reference to the study or other document at issue. Analogous citation data for primary data sets might include a brief description of the contents of the data set, the number of subjects involved, researcher name and affiliation, date of entry into the data storage system, and so forth. Citations for instrumental data would be expected to include the nature of the instrument (for example, multiple-choice test, interview protocol), subject content (for example, verb recognition drill, student opinions about language study), instrument length and total administration time, author(s), availability information, and so forth. The distinguishing characteristic—and primary function—of all citation data is to serve as a brief description of, and pointer to, sets of other types of data. In order to serve their intended function properly, all individual items of citation data would need to include a number of searchable indexing terms or be amenable to free-text search by users interested in retrieving particular citations (and potentially, the corresponding reported, instrumental, or other data themselves) within a given area of inquiry.

As a result of recent significant conceptual and technical advances in the field of electronically mediated data storage and on-demand retrieval, it is at present possible to accomplish the centralized and cross-referenced electronic storage of any and all of the seven types of data defined above. This can be done in a highly practical and cost-effective manner that would permit the immediate retrieval and transmission of readily usable paper or other-medium (audio/video) copies of these data to other researchers or qualified recipients for use in a large variety of subsequent applications. Due to the constantly improving performance/cost ratio of microcomputer equipment in general, the necessary computer and related peripheral equipment to provide full query and retrieve capability for all data types, in the relevant medium, may already be affordable to many individual academic researchers, and it is certainly well within the budgetary capabilities of most university departments or similar organizational entities.

Most of the equipment needed for an individual RCP "user station" having the operational capabilities described above is readily available in the form of what is generally referred to as a multimedia personal computer (MPC). The typical MPC consists of a fairly fast central processing unit (CPU), together with a high-resolution color monitor; good-sized hard disk; dual floppy-disk drives; a compact-disc (CD-ROM) player with stereo audio output and small auxiliary loudspeakers; and a quality dot-matrix or (preferably) laser printer. As of mid-1993, typical consumer prices for a complete MPC unit as described are in the range of $2,500 to $3,000.

MPCs involved in research consolidation activities would of course need to be connected to existing computer networks. At major universities or other organizations of similar scope, faculty and staff members typically have access to a local area network, or LAN. Under the LAN system, all the computers on campus (as well as, in some instances, in individual residences) are connected to a mainframe computer. This mainframe is, in turn, interconnected with other similar mainframes and, by the same token, with their corresponding LAN-connected microcomputers throughout the United States and internationally. The result is the capability for an individual researcher to communicate electronically with researchers throughout the world. In addition to facilitating traditional types of correspondence between researchers (although now at the speed of light rather than at that of the post office), these networks permit the real-time transmission of a variety of other types of information, including primary data, texts of research reports, data-gathering instruments, bibliographic records, and so forth. Depending on the needs or intentions of the network users, data transmission can take place directly between two collaborating researchers; among several researchers participating in an electronic forum on a specified topic; or between an individual researcher and a larger data-storage facility, the latter serving both as an information source from which the researcher "downloads" particular types of data and as a repository of information "uploaded" to it by the participating researcher.

In complement to the technical components of the data-storage and dissemination approach described above, recent advances in computer-science theory, in particular the work on so-called "intelligent" databases (Parsaye et al. 1989), show promise for making all these types of data readily available to foreign/second-language researchers, teachers, administrators, and other interested individuals in a highly personalized and directly usable form. This is accomplished by means of an "expert system" process, in which the computer applies previously codified human decision rules to engage the user in a progressive dialogue about the user's interests and the material available in the database, in an effort to clarify, refine, and optimally satisfy the user's information needs.

In addition to the expert system capability, the following features are crucial to the operation of the intelligent database as elaborated by Parsaye et al. (1989): (1) management and retrieval of contiguous written (including transcribed) text—a computer function already widely used in second-language acquisition research; (2) handling of traditional row-by-column database structures—characteristically involving individual subjects on one axis and their obtained values on tests or other measured variables on the other axis; (3) capability of handling relational database, in which specified data retrieval and reporting relationships are set up between two or more row-by-column data sets (as when a student database is linked to a school database); (4) ability to store and retrieve both text and audio or video data in a hypermedia environment—one in which the user is able to interact with the computer in a nonlinear way to follow particular informational "branches" of greatest personal interest; and (5) the ability to carry out all of the preceding functions within the context of an "object-oriented" system. An object-oriented system is a recently developed conceptual and operational approach that makes it possible to search for, retrieve, or otherwise manipulate various types of data (for example, continuous-text excerpts, row-by-column statistical data, audio passages) within a single coordinated database structure.

Although space does not permit a more detailed discussion of the technical aspects of object-oriented intelligent database systems, the following example of a hypothetical information search within such a database provides some indication of the general nature and power of the system. Let us assume that a user queries the system with respect to available information about "learning strategies." The database might respond by indicating that it has at its disposal:

1. A total of 15 row-by-column data sets containing learner responses to three different learning-strategy questionnaires administered at five language-teaching institutions

2. Copies of the actual text of two of these questionnaires, immediately available for downloading and further use as desired

3. Transcripts of 32 interviews with high school language students about their language-learning experiences, each analyzed (tagged) for the student's mention of the use of particular learning strategies

4. The videotape of an instructional program developed to help students learn to initiate and sustain conversations with native speakers (other than instructors) in order to increase their exposure to authentic target-language speech samples

5. A total of 47 bibliographic references to research reports or other printed documents dealing exclusively or primarily with the issue of learning strategies in second-language acquisition

6. A list of 11 individuals actively conducting learning-strategy research or otherwise closely involved with learning-strategy issues, together with contact information including electronic-mail addresses

Depending on the background and interests of the user, further inquiries following up on this initial information could be made on a real-time, interactive basis. For example, users could make requests to (1) see on screen the full text of the two learning-strategy questionnaires; (2) download, in conventional database format, all the row-by-column learner data for one of these questionnaires for further statistical analysis and "data snooping"; (3) obtain the vendor name and address and cost of the videotape program; (4) determine whether any of the bibliographic references involve derivative data reports of interest to classroom teachers or others not specialized in the "learning strategy" area; or (5) download the full text of one or more of the derivative reports to a home or office printer for local reproduction and distribution.

The above example reflects a search scenario making relatively little use of the "intelligence" potential of the database system. A more sophisticated scenario would be possible following a reasonable period of use of the operational database and the corresponding opportunity for the database developers to program into the system a high level of branching capability, based on documented background characteristics and use patterns exhibited by the various clients of the system. For example, under an "intelligent" operating mode, the computer might ask a series of on-screen questions to determine the user's background and experience level with respect to the particular area being searched, whether the person making the request is a researcher or a practitioner, and other relevant characteristics. The result of this query process would be a more efficient and more informationally useful match-up between the computer and the user with respect to the initial data-selection choices presented and the subsequent branching options provided.

It must readily be acknowledged that a number of rather complex technical, administrative, and organizational matters would have to be addressed and resolved in order to bring the intelligent database concept to operational fruition. For example, the issue of which individuals or groups would be responsible for initially specifying (and subsequently fine-tuning) the algorithms used by the expert system would need to be addressed. Other issues would include determining what steps were needed to resolve questions of copyright, data-use permissions and privacy of subjects, disability access, and other legal and social responsibility matters. Also at issue are technical and organizational (including financial) considerations in linking existing electronic networks, individual users, and centralized computer facilities within a single integrated system. However, it is the authors' sincere belief and contention that none of these issues is presently insurmountable and that their resolution can best be viewed as part and parcel of the crucial developmental efforts that could be cooperatively planned, undertaken, and successfully accomplished within the general framework of the proposed RCP.

Implementation

The preceding sections have sought to illustrate the considerable value to the profession that could be realized through undertaking a comprehensive Research Consolidation Project along the general lines described. It is obviously the case that such an effort could not succeed in the absence of an established administrative structure that would be both endorsed in concept and actively supported by the language-teaching and research community. Although the present authors make no claim to particular insight or expertise in organizational design, the following represents one example of a possible structure for such an undertaking. It is offered simply as a point of departure for more detailed review, discussion, and modification by any individuals or organizations interested in further refining and developing the RCP concept.

Advisory Board

It is suggested that the development and guidance of RCP activities be the responsibility of a 12- to 15-member advisory board consisting of

- Organizational representatives of the foreign language and English as a second-language communities and of major government and academic language-teaching institutions
- Representatives of the three current Title VI Foreign Language Resource Centers (at the University of Hawaii-Manoa, San Diego State University, and the Center for Applied Linguistics-Georgetown University), as well as of the OERI-funded Center for Research on Cultural Diversity and Second Language Learning at the University of California–Santa Cruz; and possibly other research/research-dissemination centers of the same general scope and orientation
- Two to three senior project advisers, together with other qualified researchers drawn from ESL, FL, applied linguistics, and related areas, and representing both U.S. and international backgrounds and perspectives
- Highly reputed classroom practitioners in ESL and FL, covering all levels of language instruction from elementary school through college/university courses
- Major educational policymakers and administrators familiar with and involved in addressing foreign/second-language competence needs and their associated instructional requirements at the state or federal level

The primary responsibilities of the advisory board would include

- General advocacy for the RCP concept with respect to other components of the foreign/second-language field and the public at large, including data gathering as necessary to align RCP activities with perceived informational needs in each of these areas
- Oversight and guidance of a small central project staff and its activities
- The making of policy decisions concerning major aspects of RCP operation, with these decisions taking fully into account the results of electronic surveys and other contacts with active RCP members concerning the matters at issue
- Fiscal oversight of the RCP, including decisions on the nature and amount of charges to users of RCP services (for example, fees for database access time and document downloading); the establishment of a reasonable yearly membership fee for RCP members; and the seeking of foundation grants or other types of external funding to support ongoing RCP operations and developmental activities

Project Office

It is suggested that a small permanent project office be established at a major research institution having mainframe computer capabilities. Such a center should also have the technical capability to establish and maintain computer networks with other research sites participating in the RCP and with the potentially large number of individual researchers who would be interested in becoming active RCP members.

A small central office staff consisting of a full-time technical director and two to three support staff would be envisioned. Specific duties would include

- Administrative implementation of the overall operational guidance for the project as provided by the RCP advisory board
- Assistance in establishing electronic networking capabilities for the exchange of RCP-related text materials and other types of data among the central computer, participating computer nodes, and individual researchers and practitioner users
- Establishment and maintenance of an intelligent database system for the acquisition, storage, and real-time electronic dissemination to RCP participants of each of the various types of instruments, reports, data sets, and other categories of data previously discussed; this would include categorizing and indexing these according to the element(s) of the Spolsky framework (or appropriate modification) to which they are considered to apply, as well as on the basis of other classifications relevant to the proper implementation of the intelligent database concept
- Maintenance of an up-to-date "coverage chart" outlining the various components of the theoretical model and providing a quantified indication of the extent to which each of the various components of the model is represented with respect to the number of studies known to be conducted or under way relevant to that component
- Conduct of, or contracting for, meta-analytic studies in research areas of perceived greatest interest and benefit to researcher/practitioner audiences, based on advisory board discussion and recommendations, and as informed by periodic electronic surveys of individual RCP members
- The convening, physically or via electronic conferencing, of interest groups within each of a number of specified research or research-related areas (for example, learner-strategy research, classroom-observation procedures, proficiency test development and validation), with the goals of sharing information and, in particular, encouraging the selection or development of testing instruments or other standardized data-gathering procedures for joint, across-studies use

RCP Membership

Any foreign/second-language researcher, teacher, administrator, or other interested individual, both in the United States and abroad, would be eligible to become an active member of the RCP through payment of a modest annual fee. Membership privileges and responsibilities would include the following:

- Maintenance of an electronic communication link with the RCP central office and, on an interest-group basis, with other RCP members

- The ability to access and search the RCP database and to download selected reports, data files, and other materials or documents as desired (possibly at a reasonable additional charge for this service)
- The ability (and responsibility) to upload suggestions for the improvement or expansion of RCP operations and, wherever relevant, to "vote" electronically on issues presented by the advisory board
- Access to a continually updated organizational chart summarizing research activities by RCP members within each of the major functional areas of the Spolsky model or other established descriptive framework

In addition to the above general items pertinent to all RCP members, the following would apply to individuals joining the RCP membership in a "researcher" capacity:

- For "junior" researchers, the opportunity to obtain electronic access to any of a list of qualified experts in research design, sampling procedures, and statistical analysis for consultative assistance in these areas and detailed review of proposed research plans (possibly at a modest pass-through fee)
- For senior researchers willing to participate in this undertaking, expert review and commentary on research design, conduct, and analysis plans and questions submitted by "junior" colleagues
- Regardless of research seniority, agreement in principle to use, wherever possible and appropriate in the conduct of their own studies, standardized elicitation protocols, questionnaires, tests, and other instruments available on-line through the RCP database or referenced as separately available through other sources
- The ability to search for, download, and use without fee any standardized data-gathering instruments contained in the RCP database
- The opportunity to submit for review, abstracting, and inclusion in the RCP database formal reports of any research conducted while a member of the RCP, as well as any derivative reports subsequently produced

Although it is not possible to project very far into the future the detailed activities of the proposed RCP, it would be envisioned that the following major areas would receive emphasis in the first year or so of operation and would be continued thereafter as appropriate:

1. Establishment of a comprehensive and efficient electronic network of project staff, advisory board, and "charter members" of the RCP, including both researchers and other interested participants
2. The holding of face-to-face meetings of relevant individuals, supplemented by electronic conferencing, as needed, to further analyze, fine-tune, and operationalize the individual learning conditions included in the Spolsky model. (Forums such as the ACTFL and TESOL annual meetings would serve as natural venues for the targeted discussion of these and other RCP-related issues, both in prearranged working meetings and in other more general contexts.)

3. Conceptual development and functional specification of a database structure based on the Spolsky learning-conditions framework with regard to the operational labels assigned to various database items, and including a number of additional descriptors and indexing terms needed for the implementation of an expert-system approach to item selection (for example, type of medium involved, intended audience). Although it would probably be possible to have a rudimentary database on-line by the end of the first year of project operation, technical implementation of the full-blown "intelligent" system would be a longer-term prospect.

4. Compilation of tests, questionnaires, interview protocols, and other data-gathering instruments to be proposed as standardized instruments for use as appropriate by participating RCP researchers. These instruments would be referenced in the RCP database and, to the extent possible, would also be available on-line for immediate downloading and use.

5. With the lead taken by the RCP advisory board, and taking into account both feedback provided by other RCP members and the current contents of the database with respect to available studies, identification of one or more foreign/second-language acquisition topics most appropriate for meta-analysis and initiation of at least one such analysis under the coordination of the RCP central staff

6. By the end of the first year of operation, the making of at least one general "state of the project" presentation at a major professional conference, with the intent both of informing the language community about RCP activities to date and of developing expanded membership in the RCP and increased use of RCP-based information and networking capabilities

The second and following years of operation would be expected to involve expansion of the electronic networking system, progressive augmentation of the RCP database, and the introduction of enhanced search and retrieval capabilities utilizing expert-system processes. To the extent that solid results of project operation were evident at that point, the RCP staff and advisory board would be in an effective position to seek additional funding support for maintenance and expansion of the RCP program.

Conclusion

In this chapter, the authors have attempted to make and support three basic points with respect to the effective conduct of empirical research on foreign/second-language learning and acquisition in the United States and beyond:

1. A collaborative, joint-effort approach to research planning, conduct, and results reporting may be expected to exert a synergistic and highly beneficial effect on the amount, quality, robustness, and interpretive power of the accomplished research, by comparison to similar outcomes under the "individual-researcher" paradigm and its associated processes.

2. The Spolsky "conditions for learning" model is viewed as a strong candidate to provide a conceptual and descriptive scaffolding within which cooperative research

activities could effectively be undertaken, classified, and reported. Although no single theoretical description of language learning/acquisition can ever be expected to fully reflect all and only the "truth" about this extremely complex process, the broad scope of the Spolsky formulation—which simultaneously embraces language, learner, and instructional/environmental variables along with sociological and sociolinguistic considerations—makes it possible to bring within a single descriptive framework a larger number and variety of research areas (and their associated investigatory disciplines) than has previously been the case. At the same time, however, it is readily acknowledged that further experience with the Spolsky model and, in particular, the results of studies conducted to test various hypotheses explicit in or implied by it would probably result in progressive modification of the model or even more extensive reformulation.

3. Recent major advances in electronic database design, information-processing theory, and associated technical breakthroughs have made it possible not only to envision but also to implement a highly networked, computer-based information system on both a national and international basis. Using such a system, a given researcher would be able to communicate instantaneously with other individual researchers, research groups having common investigatory interests, and central facilities for purposes of data transmission and retrieval. "Data" in this regard would encompass a wide spectrum of electronically mediated print, audio, and video material, including primary and analyzed data; study reports and related documents; and precise facsimiles of the tests, questionnaires, or other data-gathering instruments used in the reported studies. The same system would also be readily accessible to language teachers and other non-researcher practitioners, who would use it to obtain study reports or other derivative information pertinent to their own daily activities, as well as to provide feedback to the system concerning areas of needed research or suggest other ways in which the system could be of greater value to the practitioner community.

It would appear that all three of the above elements—the potential for strengthened and improved research on foreign/second language through an explicitly collaborative approach to study design, instrumentation, and conduct; the availability of a descriptive framework for language learning/acquisition of sufficient scope to serve as a reasonable point of departure for characterizing and "situating" individual research efforts within a broader interpretive context; and the ready availability of electronic systems and media fully equipped to handle the operational tasks involved in the networking, database development, and information dissemination activities discussed in this chapter—could be auspiciously conjoined as of the present time.

Cottage industry or consolidated enterprise? We now have the clear opportunity and, indeed, the responsibility—both as individual researchers/practitioners and as members of the broader language-teaching/learning community—forthrightly to respond to this question. In so doing, we would do well to heed the somewhat paraphrased but nonetheless telling observation of the great philosopher, Pogo:

"We have met the future, and it is us."

References

Language-Learning Research: Cottage Industry or Consolidated Enterprise?

Bachman, Lyle F., and Sandra J. Savignon. 1986. "The Evaluation of Communicative Language Proficiency: A Critique of the ACTFL Oral Interview." *Modern Language Journal.* 70: 380–90.

Carroll, John B., and Stanley M. Sapon. 1959. *Modern Language Aptitude Test.* New York: Psychological Corporation.

Clark, John L. D., and Ray T. Clifford. 1987. "The FSI/ILR/ACTFL Proficiency Scales and Testing Techniques: Development, Current Status, and Needed Research," pp. 1–18 in Albert Valdman, ed., *Proceedings of the Symposium on the Evaluation of Foreign Language Proficiency.* Bloomington: Indiana Univ.

Clark, John L. D., and John A. Lett, Jr. 1988. "A Research Agenda," pp. 53–82 in Pardee Lowe, Jr., and Charles W. Stansfield, eds., *Second Language Proficiency Assessment: Current Issues.* Englewood Cliffs, NJ: Prentice-Hall Regents.

Clark, John L. D., and Francis E. O'Mara. 1991. "Measurement and Research Implications of Spolsky's Conditions for Second Language Learning." *Applied Language Learning* 2: 71–113.

Cochran, William G. 1954. "The Combination of Estimates from Different Experiments." *Biometrica* 10: 101–29.

DeKeyser, Robert. 1991. "Conditions for Second Language Learning" [review]. *Language* 67,3: 641–44.

Gardner, Robert C. 1990. "Attitudes, Motivation, and Personality as Predictors of Success in Foreign Language Learning," pp. 179–221 in Thomas S. Parry and Charles W. Stansfield, eds., *Language Aptitude Reconsidered.* Englewood Cliffs, NJ: Prentice-Hall Regents.

————, and Wallace E. Lambert. 1972. *Attitudes and Motivation in Second Language Learning.* Rowley, MA: Newbury House.

Glass, Gene V. 1976. "Primary, Secondary, and Meta-Analysis of Research." *Educational Researcher* 5,10: 3–8.

Lado, Robert. 1978. "Scope and Limitations of Interview-Based Language Testing: Are We Asking Too Much of the Interview?" pp. 113–28 in John L. D. Clark, ed., *Direct Testing of Speaking Proficiency: Theory and Application.* Princeton, NJ: Educational Testing Service.

Lantolf, James P., and William Frawley. 1985. "Oral Proficiency Testing: A Critical Analysis." *Modern Language Journal* 69: 337–45.

Larsen-Freeman, Diane, and Michael Long. 1991. *An Introduction to Second Language Acquisition Research.* London, Eng.: Longman.

Light, R. J., and P. V. Smith. 1971. "Accumulating Evidence: Procedures for Resolving Contradictions among Different Research Studies." *Harvard Educational Review* 41: 429–71.

Lowe, Pardee L., Jr. 1986. "Proficiency: Panacea, Framework, Process? A Reply to Kramsch, Schulz, and, Particularly, to Bachman and Savignon." *Modern Language Journal* 70: 391–97.

McLaughlin, Barry. 1987. *Theories of Second Language Learning.* London, Eng.: Edward Arnold.

Oxford, Rebecca L. 1990. "Styles, Strategies, and Aptitude: Connections for Language Learning," pp. 67–125 in Thomas S. Parry, and Charles W. Stansfield, eds., *Language Aptitude Reconsidered.* Englewood Cliffs, NJ: Prentice-Hall Regents.

————, and Martha Nyikos. 1989. "Variables Affecting Choice of Language Learning Strategies by University Students." *Modern Language Journal* 73: 291–300.

Parry, Thomas S., and Charles W. Stansfield, eds. 1990. *Language Aptitude Reconsidered.* Englewood Cliffs, NJ: Prentice-Hall Regents.

Parsaye, K., M. Chignell, S. Khoshafian, and H. Wong. 1989. *Intelligent Databases: Object-Oriented, Deductive, Hypermedia Technologies.* New York: Wiley.

Pimsleur, Paul. 1966. *Language Aptitude Battery.* New York: Harcourt Brace.

Spolsky, Bernard. 1989. *Conditions for Second Language Learning.* Oxford, Eng.: Oxford Univ. Press.

Glossary

acceptability judgment tasks: experimental tasks that require subjects to judge whether particular sentences are possible or impossible. Sometimes also called *grammaticality judgment tasks.*

achievement test: * an achievement test measures the extent of learning of the material presented in a particular course, textbook, or program of instruction.

acquisition order research: research that examines the order in which certain functional morphemes (e.g., past-tense and subject-agreement markers) are mastered by learners.

affect: (1) an individual's emotional or subjective reaction to situations, tasks, and people; (2) in neurobiology, a construct for the positive to negative evaluation placed on a stimulus.

affective scalar schema: in psychological measurement, a group of positive and negative terms for evaluation (e.g., *good, nice, terrible*) arranged along a scale.

alternate (equivalent) forms: * testing instruments whose items are different but whose scoring distributions must exhibit equal means, variances, and covariances (i.e., equal correlations with an external criterion) in order for them to be classified as equivalent.

amygdala: an area of the brain that psychologists posit to be involved in directing "selective attention" to stimuli and attaching affect to the stimuli.

analysis of covariance (ANCOVA): * a variation of analysis of variance that permits the removal of effects associated with concomitant variables that might otherwise contaminate the results and lead to faulty conclusions.

analysis of variance: * a family of statistical procedures used to test the strength of main effects and interaction effects by determining the partition of overall variance attributable to each effect and relating that to associated error variance.

analyzed/nonanalyzed language: chunks of the language may be learned without analysis of their components. These chunks may break down and become part of the analyzed system as memory consolidation takes place.

ANOVA (Analysis of Variance): a family of statistical techniques used to determine whether the difference between two or more means is a function of chance. *See also* MANOVA.

aptitude test: * a test designed to measure capability or potential, whether it is capability to succeed in an academic program, to learn a foreign language, to pursue a specific vocation, or some other capability.

aspect: a nondeictic notion in language that refers to the different ways of viewing the internal temporal constituency of a situation. For example, the morpheme *-ed* in English marks past tense, whereas *-ing* marks progressive aspect. *Compare* Tense.

---

*Asterisked items are adapted from *A Guide to Language Testing,* by Grant Henning, Copyright © 1987 by Newbury House Publishers, a division of Harper & Row, Publishers, Inc., with the permission of the publisher.

ATRANS: in script theory, transfer of ownership of an object (e.g., teacher hands papers back to the students). *See also* PTRANS.

audiolingualism: a language teaching methodology, based on a structural approach to language, that emphasizes oral language proficiency. Language is learned by hearing and repeating correct forms of the second language. The basis of this methodology is dialogues and drills.

augmented transition networks: systems that interpret a grammar as a program to transform a syntactic string into semantic structures. An example of such system is James A. Anderson's (1983) conceptual theory of script representation.

automatic/nonautomatic access: the nature of an individual's access to learned behavior or information. While connections are weak, access to knowledge in the connections requires time. Once connections are strengthened, consolidated, and interconnected, access is rapid and effortless.

automaticity: the shift from conscious and controlled processing to fluent processing requiring little attentional effort.

autonomy thesis: the claim that the human linguistic capacity (Universal Grammar) is independent of all other cognitive capacities. The thesis is a fundamental postulate of generative research. *See also* Generative acquisition research, Universal Grammar.

behaviorism: a psychological theory that views learning as a result of habits attained through stimulus-response sequences.

between-subjects variable: in experimental design, a variable in which each subject may experience only one level of treatment. For example, let us say that a researcher is interested in determining the best of three teaching methods. The independent variable could be named "teaching methods," and be divided into three levels termed Method A, Method B, and Method C. If each subject were subjected to *only one* method of instruction, "teaching methods" would be a between-subjects variable. *Compare* Within-subjects variable.

*bias:** the nonrandom distribution of measurement error. It usually results in an unfair advantage for one or more groups or categories of individuals over other groups taking the same test.

bilingual aphasia: language impairment of bilingual speakers.

bottom-up processing: comprehension of text through decoding of letters and words.

branching: the preprogrammed capability, within a computer program, for the user to choose, at given points, where next to go in the program. For example, in a computer library search, the computer might show an on-screen menu from which the user could ask the computer to next search either journal catalogs or (instead) book catalogs.

CALL: abbreviation for Computer-Assisted Language Learning.

canonical order: the order of linguistic items that is considered standard within a linguistic system. For example, the canonical word order in English is S(ubject)-V(erb)-O(bject), whereas the canonical word order in Japanese is SOV.

CHILDES: abbreviation for CHIld Language Data Exchange System, the database maintained at Carnegie Mellon University that includes primarily longitudinal data on first-language acquisition, language disorders, and, to a limited extent, second-language acquisition.

cloze test: a test that asks subjects to recreate a passage from which there have been systematic or random deletions. Usually every fifth or seventh word has been removed, beginning at a randomized starting point.

code switching: the switching back and forth between two linguistic systems, such as between two languages or dialects.

cognitive phase models: descriptions of possible internal mental processes that might account for the linguistic behavior of learners.

cognitive style: preferred or habitual patterns of mental functioning or information processing.

coherence: relationships that link the meanings of utterances in discourse, contributing to the organizational quality of the text.

cohesion: overt grammatical and discourse features of a written or spoken text that create unity.

comprehensible input: in Monitor theory, language that a learner hears or reads that the learner can understand.

*computer-adaptive testing:** This is a procedure using computer hardware and software to present content to examinees in ways that allow for iterative considerations of ability demonstrated in the ongoing testing process. Items are chosen to match individual testee ability.

conceptual dependency theory: a conceptual theory of script representation developed by Roger Schank (1984). It is based on the notion of *dependencies,* referring to relations between conceptual categories (such as ACT for "action").

To say that a concept is dependent on another means that it cannot be understood without the other.

conceptual metaphor: everyday rather than literary metaphor. For example, we talk about teaching as though it were a journey: *we've covered a lot of ground today.* We talk about learning as if it were osmosis: *It just won't sink in! They didn't absorb anything I said!* We use weaving metaphors to talk about writing: *the fabric of the text that is being woven; weaving of old and new information.* For further discussion, see Lakoff (1987) and Lakoff and Turner (1989).

*concurrent validity:** shown by the magnitude of correlation between scores for a given test and some recognized criterion measure. The test is said to have concurrent validity if it correlates highly with the established criterion.

connectionism: the view that learning takes place as neural connections of the brain are formed, elaborated, and consolidated. These connections form interlinked networks that act in parallel as (language) knowledge is accessed for comprehension and production.

construct: an essential aspect of a theory on which certain tests and/or observations are based. A construct is the actual characteristic or ability in a human being, which can be tested or observed only through certain instances, or *variables.*

construct validation, statistical: in cognitive measurement, quantitative testing of the degree to which like items (believed to be linked to some construct) in a test group vary together. Since constructs can be observed only indirectly, it is essential to demonstrate experimentally that a given set of items is really measuring a certain construct. Construct validity may be established by confirmatory factor analysis or by comparing measurement of the same construct by other methods, as in multitrait-multimethod validation.

*construct validity:** the validity of the constructs measured by a test. This may be established by confirmatory factor analysis or by comparing the same constructs measured via a variety of methods, as in multitrait-multimethod validation.

*content validity:** the usually nonempirical expert judgment of the extent to which the content of a test is comprehensive and representative of the content domain purported to be measured by the test. *See also* Face validity.

*correlation:** a family of computational procedures used to determine the extent to which variables may be said to covary. The most common parametric version is known as Pearson product-moment correlation and is the mean cross-product of z-scores.

*criterion-referenced test:** a test that assesses achievement or performance against a cut-off score considered to reflect mastery or attainment of specified objectives. Focus is on ability to perform tasks rather than group ranking.

cross-talk model: a connectionist model developed by Giovanni Flores d'Arcais and R. Schreuder (1983) that assumes that processing works in a parallel fashion across all levels of connections and that all levels communicate with each other directly.

data snooping: exploratory informal analysis of data.

declarative knowledge: factual representations or "what" we know in long-term memory that can be stated or "declared."

deictic reference terms: elements in a language, such as personal pronouns (e.g., I, you, she) and adverbials of place and time (e.g., here, now) whose meaning or reference can only be stated relative to the particular place and time of utterance.

dependent variable: a measure used to determine the effect of manipulation of the independent variable(s). To determine which of three teaching methods was superior, the dependent variable might be performance on an achievement test. *Compare* Independent variable.

descriptive statistics: the statistics used to summarize data that allows the description of sample data. In comparison, the statistics used to expand the findings of the sample to predictions about a more general population are called *inferential statistics.*

developmental sequences: plateaulike stages that occur in interlanguage word-order development. *See* Interlanguage hypothesis.

diacritical markings or diacritics: in writing systems, symbols used to indicate sound characteristics particular to the language.

*diagnostic test:** a test designed to provide information about the specific strengths and weaknesses of the test taker. It is usually designed to guide remedial instruction.

*difficulty index:** in classical measurement theory, the proportion p of respondents who scored correctly on an item. Thus, the higher the proportion, the easier the item is said to be.

*direct test:** a test that measures ability directly in an authentic context and format, as opposed to an indirect test that requires performance of a contrived task from which inference is drawn about the presence of the ability concerned.

discourse analysis: the branch of linguistics that studies language beyond the sentence.

*discrete-point test:** a test that employs items measuring performance over a unitary set of linguistic structures or features. An example would be a multiple-choice test of article usage.

*discriminability:** the capacity of a test item to differentiate between those who have the knowledge or skill measured and those who do not. This capacity is measured in several ways, including item-total point biserial correlation.

EFL: abbreviation for English as a Foreign Language.

episodic memory: in reading theory, the reader's recall of particular people or ideas in a particular situation or context in the text. Memory research suggests readers are more likely to recall distinct, uniquely framed events than descriptions that blur distinctions of time and place or texts that fail to structure information in terms of such segments. Titles and subtitles are often used to highlight individual idea episodes within longer narratives to aid the reader's recall.

*equated forms:** tests or forms of a test having scoring distributions adjusted or interpreted to coincide with the same scale. Methods of equating such as equipercentile or regression are used to permit performance comparisons across tests.

equivalent forms. See Alternate forms.

error correction (direct and indirect): In *direct* error-correction techniques, the instructor supplies the correction, as compared with *indirect* correction techniques, where the instructor gives a clue to help the student correct his or her own errors.

ESL: abbreviation for English as a Second Language

ethnography: an in-depth description of a cultural scene, group, or event; normally requires extensive observation and interviewing and involves cultural interpretation.

face-threatening speech act: a speech act that is inherently offensive or threatening to the hearer's freedom of action.

*face validity:** a subjective impression, usually on the part of examinees, of the extent to which the test and its format fulfills the intended purpose of measurement. Some authors do not distinguish between face and content validity (q.v.).

*factor analysis:** a variety of multivariate, correlational statistical procedures used to aggregate data into nonoverlapping or minimally overlapping categories or factors.

field dependence vs. field independence: a dimension of learning style defined by inability or ability to perceive simple geometric figures in complex designs. Field-independent learners distinguish details from background with relative ease; field-dependent learners do not easily perceive details, but tend to perceive the field in a global or holistic manner.

finite auxiliary verbs: in descriptive grammar, finite refers to a conjugated (inflected) form of a verb; e.g., *went* (finite) versus *to go* (infinite). A finite auxiliary is a conjugated form of the verb *to be* or *to have.*

FLES: abbreviation for Foreign Languages in the Elementary School.

*formative evaluation:** evaluation that is ongoing and iterative (repeated) during an instructional sequence. This kind of evaluation permits midstream adaptation and improvement of a program.

generative acquisition research: examines the way in which Universal Grammar interacts with positive data to yield interim as well as adultlike (implicit) structural knowledge. Some in this discipline examine first-language acquisition, others second-language acquisition, others still language disorders. See also Universal Grammar, implicit structural knowledge.

generative-transformational grammar: the particular theory of Universal Grammar common in the 1960s and 1970s. As a theory of language acquisition, generative-transformational grammar has been replaced by Principles and Parameters Theory. *See also* Generative acquisition research, Principles and Parameters Theory, Universal Grammar.

Government and Binding (GB) Theory: the particular theory of Universal Grammar generally associated with Chomsky's (1981) *Lectures on Government and Binding.* GB rejects the rule-based format of traditional generative-transformational grammar in favor of abstract principles and parameters. *See* Universal Grammar, Generative-Transformational Grammar, Principles and Parameters Theory, Principles of Universal Grammar.

grammar-translation: a teaching methodology in which the emphasis is on memorizing formal rules of grammar and on translating sentences to and from the language studied.

grammaticality judgment tasks: See Acceptability judgment tasks.

hierarchical treeing: a prewriting teaching technique that provides a visual way of organizing and generating data, often in the shape of a tree trunk with branches. The goal of such "trees" is to encourage analytical, hierarchical thinking.

holistic assessment of writing: evaluation based on the quality of a piece of writing as a whole (for example, considering content, fluency of expression, and accuracy together), as opposed to evaluation that assesses different pieces or aspects of the essay separately.

hypermedia: text, audio, and/or video material that is available to the user in both linear form and nonlinear form. For example, in working with the on-screen text of a book or other document in hypermedia format, the user could read the entire document either sentence-by-sentence (linear processing) or in a nonlinear fashion (by, for example, having the computer sequentially display all the sentences in the document containing a specified word).

hypertext: text in a hypermedia form. The term *hypertext* predates *hypermedia,* the latter term including audio and video material as well as text.

i + 1: in Krashen's model of language learning, *i* refers to a particular stage of a learner's knowledge, and *i + 1* is the subsequent stage.

illocutionary intent: the goal of any particular speech-act realization.

ILR: abbreviation for Interagency Language Roundtable, a consortium of language-teaching agencies within the U.S. government that meets periodically to discuss topics of mutual interest.

implicit structural knowledge: the subconscious knowledge of grammatical structure that is shared by all speakers of a given language, regardless of educational preparation.

independent variable: a variable of interest manipulated in some respect by the researchers so as to assess its effect upon experimental subjects. If, for example, a researcher wanted to assess the effectiveness of three different methods of instruction, "methods of instruction" would be the independent variable and each of the particular methods would be levels of that variable.

indirect data: refer to a learner's realization that particular structural configurations do not occur in native-speaker speech. In generative acquisition research, such data are assumed to play no necessary role in the acquisition of implicit structural knowledge. *See also* Generative acquisition research, Negative data, Positive data, Implicit structural knowledge.

indirect test: * a test that fosters inference about one kind of behavior or performance through measurement of another related kind of performance. An example would be the measurement of vocabulary use through a test of vocabulary recognition.

innateness: the concept that human knowledge develops from structures, processes, and ideas that are in the mind at birth (i.e., innate) rather than from the environment.

integrative test: * a test that measures knowledge of a variety of language features, modes, or skills simultaneously. An example would be dictation, which could be used to measure listening comprehension, spelling, or general language proficiency.

interactional sociolinguistics: the study of interactional exchanges focusing on the interplay of linguistic, contextual, and social presuppositions and negotiation. For discussion, see Gumperz (1986).

interactive processes: in reading theory, the parallel or back-and-forth way readers register multiple textual features, both bottom-up (such as letters and words) and global or top-down textual concepts (such as main ideas and arrangement of those ideas—their sequence, weighting, etc.).

interlanguage: in second-language learning, a term coined by Larry Selinker (1972) to refer to the systematic knowledge of an L2 that is independent both of the learner's L1 and of the target language. An interlanguage is the (transitional) system that is observed at a single stage of L2 development.

interlanguage hypothesis: the hypothesis that second-language learners possess transitional grammars that may be different from the grammar of the native language and different from the grammar of the second language.

Internet: the massive global computer network. The term *internet* refers to the fact that it is a collection of preexisting networks. Estimates put its growth at 10 percent per month in number of connected computers, with well over one million computers now connected. The Internet provides three main functions: e-mail (electronic messages); remote log-in (use of a computer from a distance); and file transfer or "ftp" (transfer of computer files from point to point). *See also* Network.

interrater reliability: * the degree of correlation between different raters' ratings of the same objects or performances, adjusted by the Spearman-Brown Prophecy Formula, used as a measure of score consistency across raters.

intertextuality: in discourse analysis, relationships between texts.

introspection: a common research method that involves talking about an activity as it is taking place (i.e., *think-aloud*). *See also* Retrospection; Retrospective survey.

*item bank:** a collection of test items administered and analyzed for use with an intended population. The bank also contains information about the items and links them to a common difficulty scale using latent trait measurement procedures.

*item response theory (IRT):** also called *latent trait theory:* a family of probabilistic models for positioning person and item response parameters of ability, difficulty, discriminability, and guessing on hypothesized characteristic curves on a latent trait continuum.

JOSEF: abbreviation for Japan Overseas Students Education Foundation. An organization in Japan that offers foreign language maintenance programs for returnee students.

L1: abbreviation for the first language.

L2: abbreviation for a language learned after the first language has been learned.

language acquisition device (LAD): the special mental mechanism held responsible for the acquisition of implicit structural knowledge. The term is generally associated with traditional generative-transformational grammar; it is not often employed in more recent generative acquisition research, where Universal Grammar (q.v.) is the more common term. *See also* Implicit structural knowledge, Generative-transformational grammar, Generative acquisition research.

language attrition: the loss of language as a result of destroyed or weakened neural connections. In more general terms, it refers to the deterioration of the ability to use a language mostly due to lack of contact with and/or use of the language.

language distance hypothesis: Eric Kellerman's (1977) hypothesis that perceived differences between L2 and L1, described as "distance," as an influence on the amount and type of transfer. For example, it has been found that there is generally less "interference" in learning an L2 when the L2 is similar in word order to that of L1.

latent trait theory. See Item response theory.

learnability: the claim that certain speech-processing strategies available to language learners at any given time during language acquisition constrain what the learner can process or comprehend and thus restrict what is learnable to the learner in the course of development. *See also* Teachability.

learning modalities: the different sensory processes needed to learn, e.g., listening, listening and reading, tactile reading (as Braille).

learning strategy: thoughts or behaviors that individuals use to comprehend, learn, or retain new information.

learning style: the way in which individuals prefer to learn or to process information.

Likert scale: a categorical scale of measurement that describes various points along a continuum; evaluators select the category that best describes their point of view.

Example: I am nervous when speaking in front of a class.

never / not often / sometimes / often / always

linguistic repertoire: the range of possibilities of linguistic forms in any particular language.

links (ISA, HASA): connections between concepts and instances of concepts represented in a script model. ISA link shows that a certain lexical item (e.g., teacher) is an instance of a concept (e.g., TEACHER) and inherits all the characteristics of that role. HASA link represents certain properties required for or assigned to a role (e.g., NURSE HASA UNIFORM).

literacy continuum: the continuum between oral/context-imbedded language use and written/context-reduced language use.

local and global error distinction: Marina K. Burt and Carol Kiparsky (1972) propose that the position of an error in a sentence is a key factor underlying comprehensibility. Errors that concern relations among major sentence constituents (global errors) are more detrimental to comprehension than errors that occur within a particular constituent or clause or complex sentence (local errors).

logography: a writing system in which each symbol corresponds to a morpheme or word. Logographies are considered meaning-based systems. Chinese employs a logographic system of writing.

longitudinal research: research in which phenomena are studied over a significant period of time.

MANOVA: abbreviation for Multivariate Analysis of Variance, a statistical procedure to determine differences in mean group performance on more than one dependent variable across one or more independent variables. *See also* ANOVA.

marked and unmarked forms: linguistic elements that are considered more basic, natural, and frequent are *unmarked forms,* whereas those which are less basic, natural, and infrequent are *marked forms.*

memory consolidation: a change in the quality of memory over time as previously unintegrated connections consolidate into one assembly which,

then, forms the basic unit for further reorganization and integration of information. Each restructuring allows more and more complex learning to take place.

memory organization packets (MOPS): in the script model of cognition, the higher-level organization of scripts.

metacognition, metacognitive strategies: in reading theory, the readers' mental plans that motivate and determine what they do when they read. When L2 readers decide on their goals (e.g., write a term paper or decide which computer to buy), they apparently assign themselves individual cognitive strategies such as scanning for specific information, reading some segments more than once, looking up some words in the dictionary, etc., in an effort to create their own concept of the text as a tool to accomplish that goal.

metacognitive knowledge: in learning theory, awareness of the task, prior experience with similar tasks, and task-appropriate strategies for learning.

metalinguistic knowledge: an individual's knowledge about language as opposed to one's use of language.

mixed design: an experimental design that uses a combination of between-subject and within-subject variables.

modified input: a form of language addressed to learners. This is also known as "foreigner talk."

MTRANS: in the script model of cognition, the concept for mental transfer of information (e.g., exchange ideas). *See also* PTRANS.

multidimensional scaling analysis (MDS): analysis of distancelike data that indicate the degree of similarity or dissimilarity between two things. It displays the structures of these data as a geometrical picture. Having its origins in psychometrics, MDS traditionally looked at subjective data obtained by asking people to judge the dissimilarity of pairs of things, MDS is now used in a wide variety of fields to analyze objective data, such as frequencies of interaction between pairs of students in class.

multiple regression analysis: a statistical technique used to assess the relationship between one dependent variable and several independent variables.

*multitrait-multimethod validation:** a technique used for testing construct validity through the examination of a correlation matrix of specified traits and methods.

negative data: data that inform the learner directly (e.g., through parental correction) of structural ill-formedness. Negative data are widely assumed in generative acquisition research to play no necessary role in the acquisition of implicit structural knowledge. *See also* Generative acquisition research, Implicit structural knowledge, Positive data, Indirect data.

negotiated interaction: conversations in which there is some negotiation in order to arrive at mutual understanding.

neocortex: cortex on the external surface of the brain.

network (or net): a connection between two or more computers allowing communication, program sharing, and file sharing. *See also* Internet.

neural probe research: research technique carried out by neurosurgeons where they stimulate various parts of the brain to discover whether such disruption at any pressure point affects language. The technique has been used successfully to map out some areas important for language, thereby increasing our knowledge of brain anatomy and language function.

NNS: abbreviation for NonNative Speaker of a language.

nonauxiliary finite verb: any conjugated verb form other than an auxiliary.

nonresponse bias: research, bias introduced into a study, usually a survey, when an inadequate number of subjects respond.

*norm-referenced test:** a test that evaluates ability against a standard of mean or normative performance of a group. It usually implies standardization through prior administration to a large sample of examinees.

NRT: abbreviation for Nucleus Reticularis Thalami. A neural structure located in the medial temporal lobe (inner-side part of the brain) that is thought to be involved in selective attention.

NS: abbreviation for Native Speaker of a language.

*objective test:** a test that can be scored with reference to a scoring key and, therefore, does not require expert judgment in the scoring process. This is unlike a subjective test that depends on impression and opinion at the time of scoring.

*one-parameter model:** a variety of latent trait measurement models, such as the Rasch model, that operate with a single ability/difficulty scale for the calibration of persons and items and the estimation of fit to model predictions of response patterns.

one-to-one mapping: the situation in which only one linguistic form corresponds to one single meaning.

on-line comprehension: comprehension in real time.

operationalize: to define a construct so that it can be tested. For example, one cannot test whether forms have been fossilized since one does not know whether learning has actually ceased. However, fossilization can be operationalized as "no change in a two-year period of time," thereby allowing one to test whether fossilization has occurred.

orthography: how a writing system is structured with regard to its graphic nature and rules for representing meaning and sound.

parallel distributed processes (PDP): in contrast to serial, linear models, PDP assumes that processing of all types of information proceeds simultaneously across multiple networks that interlink or "talk to each other."

perceptual saliency: the ease with which a linguistic item is perceived. For example, a stressed syllable is perceptually more salient than an unstressed syllable.

permastore: permanent, long-term memory. The term was originally coined by Harry P. Bahrick (1984a, 1984b) to refer to linguistic knowledge that is immune to loss regardless of minimal use of the language.

phases: in information processing, changes in types of processing used to solve a problem.

phonemic analysis: analysis of units of pronunciation and their correspondence to units of meaning.

phylogenetic: in taxonomy, pertaining to evolutionary development of a species of animal or plant.

*point biserial correlation:** the correlation between a binary and a continuous variable, such as between item scores and test scores. It is a variation of the Pearson product-moment correlation.

positive data: utterances (phrases, clauses) in context to which learners are exposed. Positive data are assumed in generative acquisition

research to comprise the only data that are necessary for the acquisition of implicit structural knowledge (q.v.). *Compare* Negative data, Indirect data.

pragmalinguistics: the study of relationships between linguistic and pragmatic factors.

pragmatics: the branch of linguistics that studies language in use.

précis: a nonlinear scheme (hence not an outline) for representing how the reader reconstructs and connects the information and ideas in texts. The précis has four hierarchical levels, each of which represents a different processing style (global, organizational, detail, implicative). It should be read vertically as well as horizontally.

prelinguistic endowment: a near-synonym of Universal Grammar (q.v.).

principles and parameters theory: broadly, modern theory of Universal Grammar (q.v.) without implicating the particular theory proposed in Noam Chomsky's (1981) work. *See also* Government and Binding Theory.

principles of Universal Grammar: denote the individual abstract structural conditions of Universal Grammar. Some principles are assumed to have associated options or parameters among which learners choose on the basis of exposure and that account for cross-linguistic variation. *See also* Universal Grammar, Generative acquisition research.

procedural knowledge: representation in long-term memory of what we know "how" to do or of what can be enacted.

production system: condition-action sequences that specify what mental action will be taken when a given condition occurs; used to represent procedural knowledge.

*proficiency tests:** a test measuring general ability or skill, as opposed to an achievement test that measures the extent of learning of specific material presented in a particular course, textbook, or program of instruction.

propositional language: two definitions seem to coexist at present. (1) For many researchers, a division of the verbatim language of the text into idea units—the "who, what, when, where, how, and why" within individual sentences. In the sentence "the boy caught the ball quickly," the idea units might be tagged as "the boy" (who), "caught the ball" (what state of being or action and linked element), "quickly" (how). (2) For researchers such as Walter Kintsch, propositions refer to the concepts that, for a particular reader, *represent* the verbatim language of the text and generally consist of an abbreviated internal representation of complex language or factual information that retains essential meanings of sentences or concepts.

protocols (think-aloud/verbal; recall): a set of research procedures used to gain insights into how subjects accomplish a linguistic task. In writing research, think-aloud protocols ask subjects to verbalize what they are thinking about as they write. In other areas, often listening, for example, subjects do recall protocols, in which they say or write down what they remember after doing the research task.

PTRANS: in the script model of cognition, actions that involve physical transfer of objects (e.g., teacher moves books to a table). The actual movements within PTRANS are further specified in the script model. *See also* ATRANS and MTRANS.

qualitative research: research in which data are collected, analyzed, and reported primarily in narrative and other nonquantitative ways.

quantitative research: research in which data are collected, analyzed, and reported in primarily quantitative (numerical) ways.

Rasch model: * a family of one-parameter logistic latent trait measurement models used to calibrate item difficulty and person ability and give probabilistic estimates of performance fit to model predictions of person-to-item response behavior.

recall protocols: a reading comprehension measure in which readers write down, from memory, what they recall after reading a text. Then, most commonly, researchers divide the verbatim text into idea units (*See* Propositional language), check between two or more raters to establish whether they agree on most units (interrater reliability), and count the number of propositions in each summary. Recall protocols need not be verbatim. For practical purposes, recall protocols focus research attention on texts of fewer than one thousand words.

reliability. See Interrater reliability, Test-retest reliability.

research: disciplined inquiry into a question or hypothesis.

retrospection: a common research method that involves talking about an activity after it has taken place. *See also* Introspection.

retrospective survey: a questionnaire that asks subjects to reflect on past experiences and offer a description or evaluation of them, often in terms of what the subject did or how the subject felt. It is often questioned how accurately subjects can recall and represent behaviors and feelings after some time has passed.

rhetorical structure modeling: a description of the organization of components in particular types of text (e.g., narrative, description, argumentation, news report, obituary).

row-by-column database: a set of information on a number of variables arranged in rows and columns: for example, a test score roster where each row corresponds to a person and each column or set of columns corresponds to the scores obtained by that person on the different parts of the test.

RST (Rhetorical Structure Theory): a theory developed by William Mann and Sandra Thompson (1988) that shows how the relations between portions of text reflect the intentions and goals of the speaker or writer.

scaffolding: assistance provided to learners in a context of social interaction. Instructional supports are gradually reduced over time as concepts or skills are acquired.

schema modeling: to model the encoding of experiential information in terms of formal structure representation.

schemata: representation in long-term memory of a concept, object, or event while retaining its essential features.

script: a basic descriptive representation (template) of an event.

semantic field taxonomy: the arrangement of groups of terms as they relate to semantic categories (e.g., kinship terms, terms for types of clothing, terms for types of motion).

semantic schemata: plans about the overall structure of events and the relationships between them that are stored as knowledge in long-term memory.

semiotics: the relationships and relative importance attributed to signs and symbols within any system or code such as languages, mathematics, cinematic media, etc. Semiotics typically includes the branches of pragmatics, semantics, and syntactics.

sensorimotor: the neural functions related to sensing and motion.

SLA: abbreviation for Second-Language Acquisition.

social capital: public opinions and attitudes toward people, places, events, and ideas resulting in their (often transitory) commercial value and social-psychological importance. Public opinion polls are one currently favored way of measuring (and manipulating!) social capital in the late-twentieth-century United States.

social distance: the level of social familiarity between speaker and hearer.

sociometric issues: issues related to the measurement of traits within a society or of individuals within a society. The U.S. census reports are prime examples of sociometric data.

sociopragmatics: the interface of social and pragmatic factors.

speech act: the deliberate choice of utterances that have illocutionary force of action.

speech-act set: the major linguistic and pragmatic realizations of a particular speech act.

*speed test:** a test that limits time allowed for completion so that the majority of examinees will not be expected to finish it. The material contained in the test is usually so easy that, given enough time, most persons would respond correctly.

stage models: models that show the changes in production of language forms over time and attempt to account for those changes with acquisition principles.

*standardized test:** a test that has been administered to a large group of examinees from a target population, often more than 1,000 persons, and has been analyzed and normed for use with other samples from that population.

stepwise regression: a regression analysis procedure that is often used to determine how well a set of variables can predict a dependent variable. The procedure enters at each step in the analysis the variable that adds most to the prediction equation in order to determine each one's relative contribution to an effect on a dependent variable. For discussion, see Tabachnick and Fidell (1983).

structural ill-formedness: denotes that a particular structure is in violation of Universal Grammar. *See also* Universal Grammar, Structural well-formedness.

structural well-formedness: the extent to which particular grammatical structures conform to the constraints of Universal Grammar. In acquisition, the notion must be understood relative to the learner's developing grammar rather than relative to the adult-state grammar. *See also* Universal Grammar, Structural ill-formedness.

*summative evaluation:** evaluation that comes at the conclusion of an educational program or instructional sequence.

syllabary: a phonetic system of writing in which each symbol represents a syllable. Examples are the Japanese writing systems of hiragana and katakana.

symbolic models: theoretical models that show language as rule-governed behavior where systems are made up of units (symbols) and processes that operate on the units. Rules are hierarchically arranged in linear order.

teachability: the claim that what is *teachable* is restricted by what is *learnable* by the learner. The implication is that attempts to teach structures that involve processing beyond the learner's current level is futile. *See also* Learnability.

temporal lobe: the side (i.e., close to the ears) area of the brain that includes structures whose function, presumably, is to work with information represented in connections that are still being reorganized (i.e., "intermediate memory" processing).

tense: a deictic notion in language that relates the time of the situation referred to (i.e., event time) to some other time, most often the time of utterance (i.e., speech time). *Compare* Aspect.

TESOL: abbreviation for Teachers of English to Speakers of Other Languages.

*test-retest reliability:** an estimate of the consistency of scores with a given test. It is obtained by testing the same persons with the same test at two different times within a reasonable time interval and correlating the scores from the two administrations.

think-aloud: a research method in which a subject talks about an activity while it takes place (i.e., *introspection*).

*three-parameter model:** a latent trait measurement model that usually incorporates estimates of ability/difficulty, discriminability, and guessing.

TL: abbreviation for Target Language, or the language being learned.

top-down processing: comprehension of text through analysis of the text meaning as represented in main ideas, subordinate ideas, and related details.

*T-test:** a statistical test used to determine whether the difference between two means is statistically significant or a function of chance. It is also used to test the difference between correlation coefficients and to measure goodness of fit to the Rasch model.

T-unit analysis: a means of measuring syntactic complexity or maturity that serves as an index of language development. A T-unit (minimal terminable unit) is commonly defined as a main clause and all subordinate clauses and nonclausal structures that are attached to or embedded in it. Longer T-units are associated with greater language development.

*two-parameter model:** a latent trait measurement model that includes an additional measurement parameter beyond the ability/difficulty parameter of one-parameter models. Usually the second parameter is an item discriminability parameter.

U-shaped curve: a learning curve on a graph of learning by a learner, *S,* where *S*'s beginning and final scores are high but drop during a medial period.

underdetermined knowledge: knowledge that cannot be traced to environmental sources. In generative work, underdetermination is held to be a primary rationale for the existence of Universal Grammar. *See also* Universal Grammar, Generative acquisition research.

Universal Grammar: the innate linguistic endowment that underlies (acquisition of) implicit structural knowledge. *See also* Principles and Parameters Theory, Government and Binding Theory, Generative acquisition research, Autonomy thesis.

*validity:** the extent to which a test measures the ability or knowledge that it is purported to measure. *See also* Concurrent validity, Construct validity, Content validity, Face validity.

*variance:** a measure of dispersion around the mean. It is equal to the square of the standard deviation and is obtained as the mean squared difference between observed scores and the mean.

verbatim or surface language: in reading theory, the actual order and linguistic form of words as they appear in the text, which may or may not be equal to the reader's psychological concept of the text.

within-subjects variable: in experimental design, a variable in which each subject must experience all treatment levels. For example, a researcher interested in determining the best of three teaching methods could name the independent variable of interest "teaching methods" and divide it into three levels termed Method A, Method B, and Method C. If each subject were subjected to *all three* methods of instruction, "teaching methods" would be a within-subjects variable. *Compare* Between-subjects variable.

ZISA: abbreviation for Zweitspracherwerb Italienischer und Spanischer Arbeiter. A project on the acquisition of German as an L2 by Italian and Spanish workers in Germany conducted in Germany by researchers such as Manfred Pienemann, Jürgen Meisel, and Harald Clahsen.

References, Glossary

Anderson, James A. 1983. *The Architecture of Cognition.* Cambridge, MA: Harvard Univ. Press.

Bahrick, Harry P. 1984a. "Semantic Memory Content in Permastore: 50 years of Memory for Spanish Learned in School." *Journal of Experimental Psychology: General* 113,1: 1–31.

———. 1984b. "Fifty Years of Second Language Attrition: Implications for Programmatic Research." *Modern Language Journal* 68: 105–18.

Burt, Marina K., and Carol Kiparsky. 1972. *The Gooficon: A Repair Manual for English.* Rowley, MA: Newbury House.

————. 1981. *Lectures on Government and Binding*. Dordrecht, Neth.: Foris.

Flores D'Arcais, Giovanni, and R. Schreuder. 1983. "The Process of Language Understanding: A Few Issues in Contemporary Psycholinguistics," in Giovanni Flores D'Arcais and Robert Jarvella, eds., *The Process of Language Understanding*. New York: Wiley.

Gumperz, John J. 1986. "Interactional Sociolinguistics in the Study of Schooling," pp. 45–68 in Jenny Cook-Gumperz, ed., *The Social Construction of Literacy*. Cambridge, Eng.: Cambridge Univ. Press.

Kellerman, Eric. 1977. "Toward a Characterization of the Strategy of Transfer." *Interlanguage Studies Bulletin* 2: 59–92.

Lakoff, George. 1987. *Women, Fire, and Dangerous Things: What Categories Reveal about the Mind*. Chicago: Univ. of Chicago Press.

————, and Mark Turner. 1989. *More than Cool Reason*. Chicago: Univ. of Chicago Press.

Mann, William, and Sandra Thompson. 1988. "Rhetorical Structure Theory: Towards a Functional Theory of Text Organization." *TEXT* 8,3: 243–81.

Schank, Roger. 1984. *Conceptual Information Processing*. Amsterdam, Neth.: North Holland.

Selinker, Larry. 1972. "Interlanguage." *International Review of Applied Linguistics* 10: 209–31.

Tabachnick, Barbara G., and Linda S. Fidell. 1983. *Using Multivariate Statistics*. New York: Harper and Row.

Index of Authors

Index of Topics and Institutions